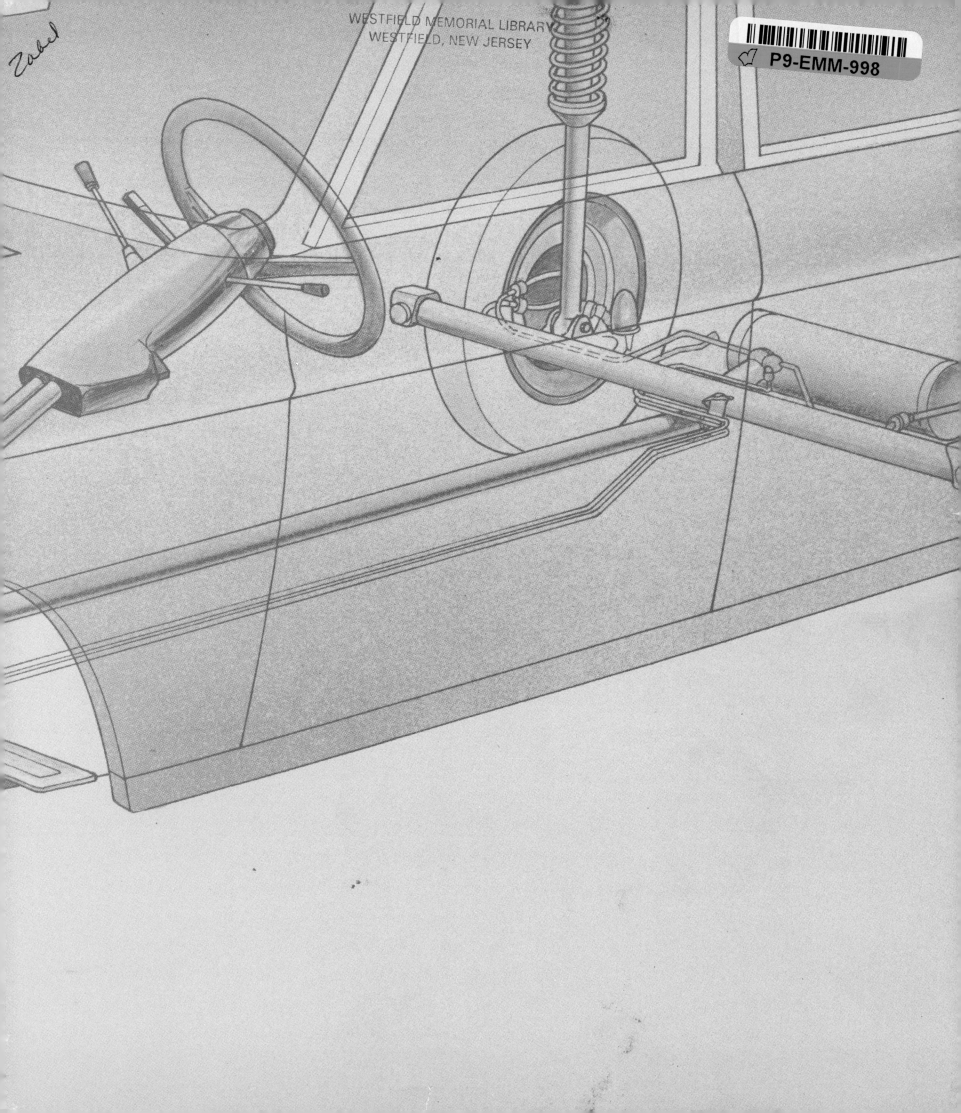

CARS OF THE 50s AND 60s

CARS

OF THE FIFTIES AND SIXTIES

MICHAEL SEDGWICK

CRESCENT BOOKS

CARS OF THE 50s AND 60s

This 1990 edition published by Crescent Books,
distributed by Outlet Book Company, Inc.,
a Random House Company,
225 Park Avenue South,
New York, New York 10003

Printed and bound in Italy

ISBN 0-517-37557-5

CARS OF THE 50s AND 60s has been originated, designed, and produced by AB Nordbok, Gothenburg, Sweden, in close collaboration with the author and photographers.

Artwork: Syed Mumtaz Ahmad, Gerry Browne, Bob Freeman, Kevin Jones, Lars Jödahl, Steve Leverington, Hans Linder, Lennart Molin, David Penney, Regina Richter, Ed Stuart, Ulf Söderqvist.

Nordbok would like to express its sincere thanks to Björn-Eric Lindh for advice. The following have also been of great assistance in providing illustration reference material from which new artwork has been produced by the Nordbok studios.
The Autocar: pages 53 top left, 64, 82, 84 top left, 93, 96, 97, 224, 225 bottom.
The Motor: pages 20, 25 bottom, 28 top, 32, 34, 35, 41, 57 top, 68 bottom right, 73, 76, 77, 120, 124, 174, 208, 209, 212, 225 top.

Colour photography

Elly Arnstein/John McGovren: Pages 46 top, 47, 50, 55, 59, 87, 111 top, 179 bottom, 199 top.

Elly Arnstein/Andrew Morland. Pages 15 bottom, 27 top, 91 top, 219 top.

Elly Arnstein/National Motor Museum: Pages 123, 194 top.

Neill Bruce: Page 175 centre right.

Peter Haventon: Pages 10, 11, 14, 15 top, 22, 23 top, 38, 39 top and centre, 46 bottom, 62, 63, 67 bottom, 91 bottom, 94, 95 bottom, 102, 103, 114, 115 top, 122 top, 170, 175 centre left, 179 top, 182, 194 bottom, 199 bottom, 202, 206 top, 207 bottom, 210 top, 211 centre, 214, 215, 218, 219 bottom, 222 bottom, 223, 226, 227.

Holden: Page 234.

Halwart Schrader: Page 39 bottom.

Nicky Wright: Pages 18, 19, 23 bottom, 26, 27 bottom, 30, 31, 51, 54, 58, 66, 67 top, 70, 71, 74, 75, 78, 79, 82, 83, 90, 95 top, 106, 107, 110, 111 bottom, 115 bottom, 118, 119, 122 bottom, 126, 127, 171, 174, 175 top, 178, 183, 186, 187, 190, 191, 195, 198, 203, 206 centre and bottom, 207 top, 210 centre and bottom, 211 top and bottom, 222 top, 235.

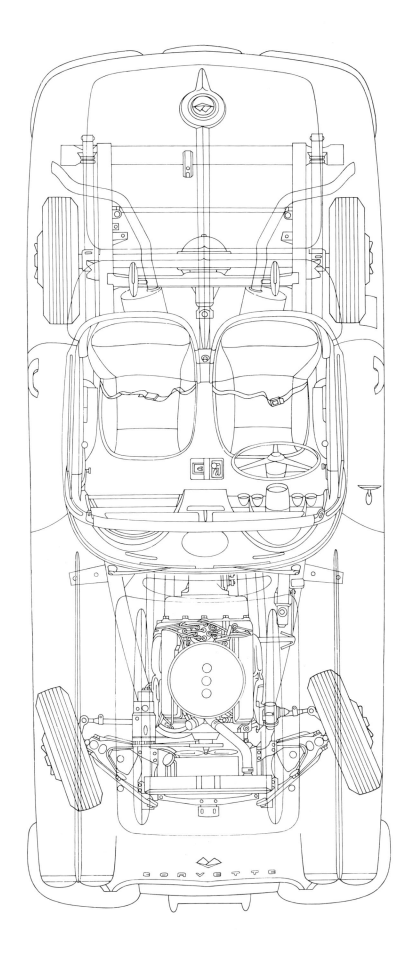

Nordbok expresses gratitude to all the owners who allowed their cars to be photographed for this book. Among them are: Bengt Abrahamsson, A-C-D Museum (Auburn, Indiana), Peter Agg, Bill Arnold, Bud Bassett, Ingemar Berndtsson, D.E. Boyd, Keith Boyer, R.H. Brock, Charles W. Coleman, P. Colles, Ed and Joan Dagen, Ludde de Geer, Kevin E. Dooley, W.E. Dowsing, N. Durban, Bob Edson, Harald Eriksson, T. Fleckney, Fredrik Gadler, G.K. Harris, Mike Hayes, Claes Hermansson, Åke Hultberg, L.G. Hunter-Cox, Sture Idner, Hans Josefsson, Robert Kirkpatrick, Lars Lindström, Mr. and Mrs. Lumley, Larry Lunz, G.R. Mason, R. Mellor, Mark Meyer, Von Milliner, Tom Olson, Dr. J.E.R. Palmer, T.J. Plummer, Robin Richmond-Jones, Larry K. Riesen, Terry Robinson, J. Schreiber, Peter Shinwell, Britt Sjöberg, Burnis G. Sparkman, Lars Sporrong, John A. Stevens, David Stride, P.J. Stuart, A. Treagus, Sten Wigrell, Bud Wilson, Denis Winebrenner, Ivan Wrandahl, R.L. Zigher, Johan Ålander, Jan Älfvåg, Lars Öhman.

CONTENTS

PREFACE

In 1951 the transportation of five people at 100 mph (160 km/h) called for five litres of engine in America: Jaguar managed it on 3.4 litres and Mercedes-Benz on only three. Outside the United States, such speeds were permitted, though as yet there were few highways that could accommodate them. And nowhere was there adequate tyre or brake technology to assure any degree of safety.

By 1969, the magic "ton" was within the compass of 2-litre sedans—French Peugeots, British Vauxhalls, Japanese Toyotas—all capable of returning 25 mpg (11 litres/100 km) in normal usage, thanks to improved engine design and higher-octane fuels. (It would have been a light-footed owner who habitually extracted better than 17 mpg (16.5 litres/100 km) from the old Jaguar or Mercedes.) Disc brakes and radial-ply tyres eliminated most of the hazards but, on the debit side, the vast motorway network was all too often reduced to a hooting, six-lane crawl around rush hours. Legislators were imposing more and more "blanket" speed limits, even if we were still a long way from the stringent days of the 1974 energy crisis.

One cannot summarize the fifties and sixties as easily as one can the thirties, that era of automobiles created for mass transportation under the eagle eye of cost accountants, and also the era when painless, foolproof operation became a major goal. Not that the Old World's masses were motoring in 1939: Adolf Hitler's concept of a Volkswagen in every German garage was still a dream. But thirty years later, the U.S.A.'s one car per 2.4 inhabitants was close-run elsewhere—one to 3.4 in Australia, 4.8 in Switzerland, and 5.0 in Federal Germany. Even Japan, who made more cars than she used, had a rapidly increasing 1:19 ratio, indicative of over five million vehicles.

The motor car's influence had spread relentlessly. Neither the Korean War nor the Suez Crisis of 1956 did more than interrupt the even tenor of progress, although the latter prolonged the butterfly-like existence of the bubble-car by maybe three years. True, the Arabs had turned off the taps: but there were other sources. Oklahoma and southern California floated on oil, did they not? More people could afford cars, and they wanted them faster, more comfortable, and painless to operate.

The performance landmarks were not, effectively, great roadgoing sports models like the 300SL Mercedes-Benz (1955), the E-type Jaguar (1961), and the Daytona Ferrari (1968). The mood was more closely typified by the American horsepower race, at its zenith throughout the 1950s. The actual year-by-year gains were irrelevant, since they could only legally be demonstrated in the downtown traffic-light "Grand Prix". But give the public a gaudy, subtly different package and it

would buy. The stylistic side-effects rubbed off on Europe, which didn't want 300-horsepower V-8s, but was still susceptible to Detroit rather than, as later, to Milan and Turin. Sweden's Volvo 120 looked horribly like a 1955 Chrysler, the 1100-103 Fiat from Italy aped Ford, and the British Hillman Minx sprouted meaningless tail fins. Chromium-plated decoration, conceived to protect slab-sided bodies from damage, became first a cheap means of updating a shape, and ended our era as a model-identification feature to which the safety lobby could not object.

Better roads, fuel, brakes, and suspension bred safer speed—but not always, since driver training did not keep pace. In fact, when the crusading fervour of Ralph Nader burst upon a startled world in 1965, it seemed that only an Armageddon could halt the march of the automobile.

The more cars you produce, the less the cost per copy, hence painlessness can be built in. Better still, the exchange-unit philosophy established in the 1930s meant that one no longer repaired a complicated component—one threw it away and replaced it. In 1934, last-minute panic had deterred André Citroën from offering his *traction* with automatic transmission. Not so in the 1950s. To servo brakes, familiar on more expensive machinery way back in the twenties, were added automatic and power steering, both general practice in the U.S.A. by 1955, and widely used elsewhere by 1964. All these were valuable adjuncts, especially the last-mentioned: the alternative on a large car was winding the wheel through six turns, lock to lock. Heaters, radios, and screenwashers were already accepted in 1950, as were power dividers on limousines, and power tops on convertibles. But now the aids would include power windows, seat adjustment, radio antennae, trunk lids, and even the tail-gates on station wagons. Only one old favourite from the twenties was ignored, the gearbox-driven tyre pump. Modern tubeless tyres did not puncture, or so they said.

Even in 1969, the safety and emission lobbies had yet to bite. There was but one fly in the ointment: growing traffic congestion. Its consequences had already been visible at the shows of the 1959–60 season—the American compacts and the British Motor Corporation's Mini. As in the case of the old French Cyclecar Laws, the former breed led to an unintentional result, the pony-cars such as Ford's Mustang and Chevrolet's Camaro. These were compact, but totally divorced from utilitarian concepts, and they would enjoy a short and merry life before the axe of new legislation descended in the 1970s.

The Mini was something different. It did not pioneer mass-produced front-wheel drive, or even the use of a transverse engine—DKW of Germany had achieved both targets in 1931, with ensuing worldwide sales of over 200,000 units. It did not pioneer the ultra-compact four-seater, either: Dante Giacosa's rear-engined 600 Fiat (1955) was only a little longer, and significantly narrower, than the Mini. What it did was to point the way to a new compact *package* with all the works up the more suitable end, and give the world a front-wheel-drive car which needed no skill to conduct. And if few rivals actually mounted their transmission in the sump, the basic idiom had caught on with a vengeance by 1969. If nobody ever matched the sophistication of Citroën's D family (with us since 1955), BMC had mounted an in-line six athwart the structure, and General Motors had applied the system to vast, fully automated Cadillacs and Oldsmobiles.

The old order was, however, by no means dead. Ford, General Motors (on lesser models), and Mercedes-Benz and Volvo were among those who decided that the known way was economically safer. As a result, Ford's orthodox British Cortina habitually outsold the Austin/Morris 1100 family. Fiat hedged their bets with models using all three rival layouts.

More cars were now made in more different countries, though with a lack of rationalization which seems hard to comprehend in this era of Ford Fiestas and J-cars by General Motors. It was only in 1968 that Ford began to standardize their European product, after a period in which Cologne had run a programme of front-wheel drive and vee-engines, while Dagenham developed variations on the *système* Panhard with in-line power. In Australia the mainstay of their wares was the obsolescent Falcon compact from Detroit, while in Brazil a fusion with local Willys and Renault interests led to some astonishing hybrids.

Of car-making nations already known in 1950, Sweden and the U.S.S.R. became major exporters. Spanish industry, while it offered nothing significant of indigenous design, successfully put the country back on wheels. Even in 1960, her roads resembled a scruffy, perambulating motor museum. Nine years later, the interest had gone, but SEAT's output of obsolescent Fiat models was sufficient for a useful export trade. In Australia, GM's Holden was joined by Ford, Chrysler, and BMC derivatives—these last including, incredibly, a short-block six not made anywhere else. For purely domestic consumption, Israel had her Sabra, Turkey her Anadol, India her Morris-based Hindusthan (and a local strain of Fiat as well), and Taiwan the YLN of Datsun origin. In Argentina and Brazil, production took off with a vengeance.. The 1959 statistics show about 15,000 private cars made in the former land, and practically none in the latter. Comparable figures for 1969 were 153,665 and 254,910 respectively. All were, of course, variations on familiar American and European themes, but local content was often as much as 100%.

Finally, there was Japan. In 1950, Japanese automobiles (there were only 1,594 delivered) were antiquated, handbuilt variations upon a pre-war theme by Austin, and only Nissan-Datsun built in appreciable numbers. Eight years later, ten makers were turning out cars, still rather old-fashioned, but closer to the European norm. Yet 1969's performance (3,200,000 cars made, half a million exported) not only presented a line-up comparable to that of West Germany or Britain, but also came from fewer companies. Daihatsu and Hino were under Toyota's control, and Prince and Aichi had been swallowed whole by Nissan.

We were still a long way from the late 1970s, though. Even without the four-wheel-drive brigade (there was nothing as yet to compare with the Audi Quattro), the kit-cars, the van-based mobile homes on the borderland of our theme, and the nostalgia-cars creeping into the picture as the true Classics attracted inflationary prices, variety was infinite.

When writing of the cars of the 1930s, I had to confess that few of them were fun to drive—indeed, outside the sports-exotic sector, I can only remember two I really enjoyed. But the sixties were a memorable era: a first taste of the Mini's road-clinging qualities, 7000 rpm coming up in third on an early NSU-Wankel Spyder without a touch of vibration, and first acquaintance with a 356 Porsche in San Francisco where even an unfamiliar rule of the road could not stop me cornering 15% faster than I'd ever done before. Or the Alfa Romeo Giulia with its sensitive steering and beautifully spaced five-speed transmission—what a pity it was a rust-trap. Or, for that matter, of the 850 Fiat coupé I was driving in 1969. The rev counter often had to be pushed into the red sector to get the best results, but on one memorable run up from Wales I achieved the remarkable average of 45 mph (72 km/h) and 45 mpg (6.3 litres/100 km). None of these cars came in the plutocrats-only class, either.

There were the miseries, too, like a 1960 Chevrolet Impala with full-house V-8 engine, two-speed Powerglide, and drum brakes with minimal cooling, almost literally a case of coming home on a wing and a prayer. But—and let us never forget—for most of the era we were able to enjoy or endure these cars without fastening seat belts, without a weather eye open for smoky exhausts, and without anxious glances at a dropping fuel-gauge needle.

Chapter 1

SELLER'S MARKET, ADIEU

The important new cars of the 1950–51 season were the Chrysler V-8 in America, the Mk.VII Jaguar and the Ford Consul and Zephyr in Great Britain, the Simca Aronde in France and, from Germany, the first fresh models of Mercedes-Benz since the 1936 Berlin Show. These two years combined would see 2,648,673 Chevrolets, 2,087,892 Fords, and 1,193,129 Plymouths pouring off Detroit's assembly lines—big business beside the 229,800 Fiats, 186,851 Renaults, and 175,974 Volkswagens contributed by western Europe's three leading producers. By contrast, the entire Japanese passenger-car output accounted for 5,205 units, of which precisely six were exported.

Outside America, waiting lists remained the order of the day. On a cheap British family saloon, three years were quoted: for Jaguars, or anything else sporting that appealed to customers in the United States, there was no guarantee of home-market deliveries at all. Germany still had her war losses to make up, and few examples of the sub-utility 2CV Citroën trickled onto France's *routes nationales* although it had been visible since 1948. If petrol rationing belonged to the past, the mania for mobility did not. One tended to set one's sights on any car, however old, rather than dreaming of the latest models on their turntables at Earls Court, the Grand Palais, or the exhibition halls of Turin and Geneva. Even in 1952, the Family Ten class with a capacity around 1.2 litres, for which a Briton had paid £175 ($875) new in 1939, was likely to cost double that sum at the local used-car lot. True, the current dollar equation of $900 sounded less inflationary, but sterling had been devalued twice since the outbreak of war.

Further, one took what one's domestic industry offered. Before the war, and despite the savage protectionism of France, Italy, and Czechoslovakia, a foreign car could be bought in most countries. Yet now, only the creditor nations—and those without any automobile industry—purchased from abroad. The foreigners were shut out of Britain until 1954, and not until the end of our first decade was a French, German, or Italian motorist able to choose among the world's products. The 1965 West German buyers' guide listed nine American, seven British, six Italian, four French, and two Swedish makes, plus one each from Austria, Holland, and Czechoslovakia, whereas in 1951 a citizen of the *Bundesrepublik* faced an effective range of just thirteen models, all German, from nine factories.

Better things were on the way. The 1960s would mark the zenith of the motor car as personal transportation. It advanced technically as well as in sheer numbers, and its progress was unbridled. It grew bigger (especially in America), faster, and more efficient. While the 180 horsepower of a Chrysler V-8, and the 160 hp of a six-cylinder Jaguar, were

exceptional in 1951, they became the expected norm for almost any engine size over 3 litres at the beginning of the 1970s. In addition, there were few rules about safety and pollution. Even in the 1960s, Ralph Nader was a voice crying in the wilderness, and most car-lovers hoped he would stay that way. As late as 1969, one could drive legally without a seat-belt all over the world. Overall speed limits were largely confined to the United States, and so was a vocal anti-motorists' lobby against cars. On the contrary, advertising agencies churned out copy to promote the liberating influences of the automobile. Thus a vicious circle arose—more cars led to more railway closures, so the need for personal transportation increased.

The big problems involved congestion. It bred traffic jams of prodigious length, particularly in countries like Britain, as yet barely launched into the motorway age. The classic urban bottlenecks—Sydney Harbour Bridge, the Golden Gate Bridge in San Francisco, the freeway link between Los Angeles and the San Fernando Valley—became nightmares at every rush-hour. A snarl-up 35 miles (56 km) long was recorded in Devonshire during a British bank-holiday weekend in 1964. Another evil, overdependence on the automobile, took more time to be exposed in full, notably after the energy crisis of 1973. Nobody had anticipated a dearth of cheap oil, although a warning note had already been struck in 1956 when the Egyptians closed the Suez Canal and Arab protests answered Western meddling. Europe then suddenly returned to a 1940s situation and, while the shortage lasted only seven months without any punitive restrictions, it was surprising to find how little one could do on an allocation of sixty litres (fifteen gallons) per month.

With the spread of car ownership—Italy's registrations, a mere 342,000 in 1950, had passed the million mark in the year of Suez—came a more critical attitude toward the car itself. This had not only been stultified by the shortages of the 1940s. A German who bought a new Opel in 1930 was probably disposed to favour the same make twenty-five years later, without too close a look at rival Borgwards, DKWs, Fords, or Volkswagens, all to a certain extent competitive. An Italian's choice still lay between Fiat and abstinence, but France's big three (Citroën, Peugeot, Renault) and Britain's big six (Austin, Nuffield, Rootes, Standard, Ford, Vauxhall) all had their devoted adherents. In America, matters were even worse, with a totally uneducated public overwhelmed by propaganda and advertising jargon, while press road tests in the European sense did not exist before 1950. British and French tests, although rather naive, at least told the customer what kind of car he was buying, on the basis of some performance statistics.

State of the art in America at the end of the forties.

(*Above*) On the 1948 Cadillac, the curved windscreen, wide rear window, and vestigial tail fins (inspired by the wartime Lockheed P-38 twin-engined fighter aircraft) indicate the shape of things to come, and most of that season's cars were equipped with the Hydra-matic automatic transmission first seen on 1940 Oldsmobiles. The engine is still, how-ever, the good old iron-head side-valve V-8 of 1936, now in its last season, and giving 150 horsepower from 5.7 litres, or enough to propel this heavy sedan at 95 mph (152 km/h). By 1970s standards, of course, the car was incredibly cheap, at $2,833 (about £1,000), but then earnings were lower, too.

(*Opposite*) Stylewise, the 1950 Oldsmobile Rocket 88 fastback coupé belongs to an older generation, that of 1941, when this body style (first tried out by General Motors' Austra-lian subsidiary, Holden, in 1935) became fashionable in Detroit. Technology at Oldsmobile, however, shared with Cadillac the pioneering of the modern short-stroke overhead-valve V-8 engine, so this car has a nominal 135 horsepower from 5 litres, and a genuine 100 mph (160 km/h) on tap. Again on this one, automatics were very much in the majority.

Now, however, the public started to read such appraisals and even comprehend them. Confronted with a mushrooming choice—Dutch cars for Germans, Australian cars for Britons, and Japanese cars everywhere—they bought selectively. By the end of our period, "oversteer" and "understeer" had become accepted girl-talk, especially as the fair sex grew familiar with such opposites as Renault's Dauphine and the two-stroke Saab.

Economic conditions moderated the boom. In 1951, cars were still something of a luxury outside the U.S.A., along with the raw materials to build them. Steel shortages prevented France and Italy from regaining their full stride until 1953, and the German phoenix was still a long way from its zenith. Indeed, 1951 was the first year in which the *Bundesrepublik* caught up with the Third Reich's best pre-war production, and the million mark in cars would not be passed until the late 1950s. Britain's industry pursued a strong upward path, but could not turn out enough vehicles to feed both the domestic customers and flourishing export markets. Here the "covenant" restrictions, under which new-car buyers agreed not to resell for two years without official permission, were not finally repealed until 1953. Nevertheless, recessions as such did not occur: individual sectors of the business might be hit, even mortally, yet the overall picture was of constant improvement. The Korean War, with its fresh wave of material shortages, was a minor hiccough in the inexorable progress of Detroit. Her top ten makers turned out a paltry 3,750,000 cars in 1952, while the battle was at its height, but a year later the figure had levelled off again at a respectable five-and-a-half million.

The early 1950s constituted a kind of plateau in automotive engineering. True post-war designs had evolved, and were consolidating themselves. The *système* Panhard—engine at the front, gearbox amidships, and drive to the rear wheels—was still firmly in the ascendancy, although renounced by that company in 1946. The other major advocates of front-wheel drive were Citroën in France, and the assorted disciples of the German DKW: its compatriots the Goliath and the Lloyd, and such foreign derivatives as the Russian-sponsored IFAs from Saxony and Sweden's new Saab. Of the rear-engine adherents, both the Volkswagen and Czechoslovakia's Tatra were pre-war designs, leaving only Renault as a fresh recruit. Every full-sized American, British, Italian, and Russian car in series production retained the traditional layout.

Within these parameters, however, the wind of change blew steadily. A transition to mass-produced engines with pushrod-operated overhead valves was almost complete. The vast majority of European makers did favour in-line power units, the principal deviationists being Lancia with a narrow-angle vee, as well as Jowett and the new small Citroën with opposed cylinders. True, in America the old flathead sixes and straight-eights retained some popularity, not to mention Ford's famous V-8, a 1932 debutante. But there were no all-new side-valve models in view, unless we count Ford of Britain's 100E series with 1,172 cc from 1953, which kept the cylinder dimensions and architecture of its forebears in refined form. Weeding out the flatheads took time, yet even in ultra-conservative Britain the bastions were to fall: Hillman in 1957, and Ford in 1961. As to ancillaries, downdraught carburettors and coil ignition had long been established, as had mechanical fuel pumps. Unfortunately, the new high-compression engines designed to run on high-octane fuels would have to await the end of the petrol shortage.

11

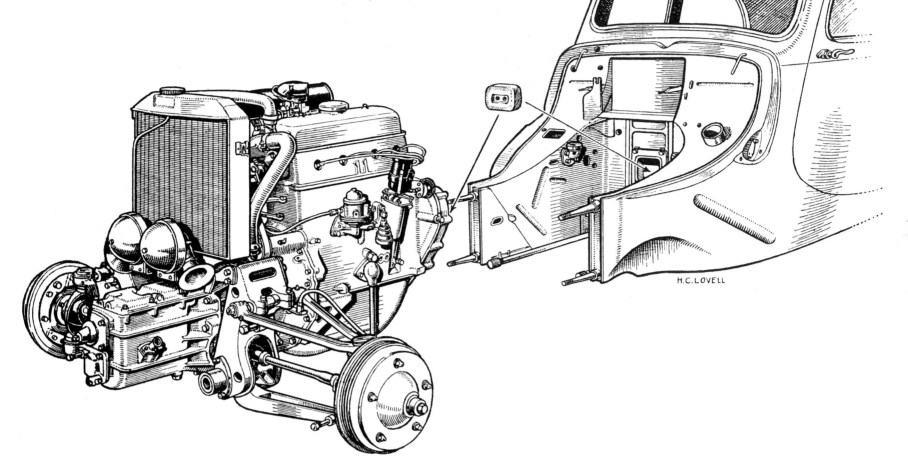

Front-wheel drive in 1934—and also indicative of the state of Citroën's art in 1955, since the famed *traction* had a run of over twenty years and nearly three quarters of a million cars. This picture shows how the power pack was attached to the front horns of the unitary structure. Alas, mounting the gearbox in front of the engine meant vulnerability, excessive length, a wide turning circle, and heavy steering at parking speeds. The classical long-stroke 2-litre four-cylinder engine would outlive its "chassis" by a decade.

H.C.LOVELL

Europe offered no immediate parallel to the class of short-stroke over-head-valve V-8s burgeoning in the U.S.A., where the 1949 lead of Cadillac and Oldsmobile was soon followed by the entire industry, the dying Kaiser empire apart.

The vexed question of the actual number of cylinders stayed unresolved. In the early 1930s, smoothness and flexibility had called for a swing toward multi-cylinderism. This bred not only Britain's pint-sized sixes, but also the Depression-era twelves and sixteens of America. Better sound-damping, painless shifting, and sophisticated suspensions ironed out some of the faults that had encouraged such designs, and by the late 1930s the big four was back in vogue, with 2.4-litre units produced by firms like Riley in Britain, Renault in France, and Stoewer in Germany. Wartime shortages and an urge for simplicity accentuated the trend outside the U.S.A., and cars were generally smaller—apart from that strange phenomenon of the 1940s known as "Vanguarditis", which produced hefty compacts such as the Standard Vanguard, the Russian Pobeda, the Fiat 1400/1900 family, and the Renault Frégate, lasting for much of our period.

These models are often adduced as evidence for the decline of the multi-cylinder engine. Given the continuing spectre of petrol rationing, only just on its way out in 1950, a four is more economical as well as cheaper to make. Thus, a manufacturer rationalizing in the category of 2–2.5 litres will choose a four rather than a six. But it should be remembered that the foreign branches of General Motors (Opel, Vauxhall,

and Holden) all built small-capacity sixes: Holden, in fact, made nothing else until the later 1960s. Ford's 1951 British range included a new six, even if their German factory would be content with fours until 1964. Other all-new sixes of the period were the Rover P4 and the Mercedes-Benz 220, although these were up-market items, indicative of a new trend associated with an increasingly affluent society and, of course, with the switch from a seller's to a buyer's market. The customer with £1,100–1,500 ($3,100–4,200) wanted something smoother than a large-capacity four, as several British makers discovered to their cost. They were, after all, up against Mercedes-Benz, Rover, and Jaguar, not to mention a new small V-8 from BMW.

As for America, the swing to the V-8 will be discussed along with technical developments in our era. While fuel remained cheap and plentiful, and automatic transmissions continued to make headway, an American wanted nothing to do with four cylinders in the family sedan, although he might be quite happy with them in his wife's foreign import or his weekend fun-car. Chevrolet's inspired bet on a 2.5-litre overhead-valve four in 1962 came a decade too soon. During the six years of compacts available with this engine—totalling one and a quarter million—around one per cent were actually ordered with it. General Motors, luckily, could afford such a miscalculation, and this "153" unit found a good life in Brazilian Chevrolets. The only other American makers to explore the same type in our period were Willys, who already had a use for it in the Jeep, and Kaiser who bought it from Willys but

A new recruit to rear-engined principles. In 1946 Renault followed Volkswagen and Tatra by mounting the engine at the back on their new 760-cc 4CV minicar. So small a power unit could be mounted longitudinally without excessive overhang or loss of space; thus the gearbox lived behind. To be seen here are (*1*) the hydraulic foot-brake and (*2*) mechanical handbrake systems, and (*3*) the coil-spring independent rear suspension. An unusual reversion to older practices was shown by (*4*) the use of fixed wheels with demountable rims—but Renault used steel instead of wood, and the object of the exercise was weight-saving and not, as on American cars of the 1920s, making life easier for the ladies in the event of a puncture.

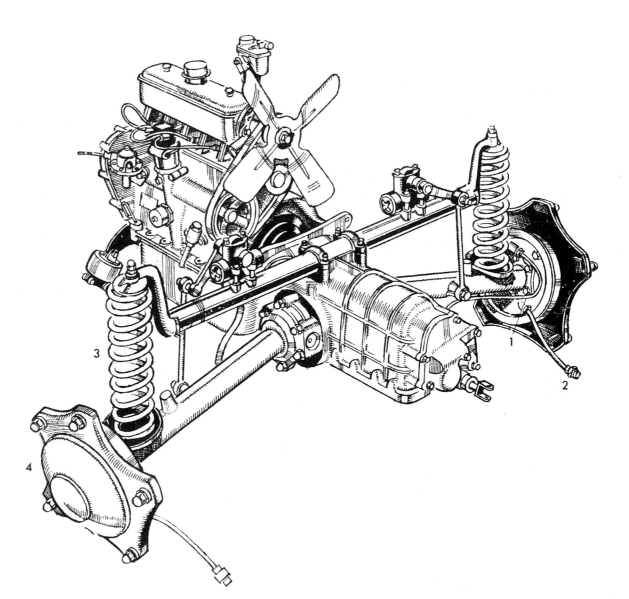

restricted its application to their "Waterloo", the Henry J compact of 1950–54.

Just as fuel technology held back the spread of the new V-8s, it also delayed adoption of the overhead-camshaft engine. The twin-cam units of Salmson and Alfa Romeo had been joined in 1949 by the XK Jaguar, but there were fewer cheap single overhead-cam units in 1950 than in the 1920s and 1930s—the era of the Fiat 509 and British Rhodes, Wolseleys, and Singers. Only Singer remained faithful to the type, until absorbed by Rootes in 1956. What survived was the two-stroke: effectively limited in 1950 to the DKW and its countless progeny (in East Germany, Sweden, Czechoslovakia, and briefly Denmark), this ageless design theme had another twenty years ahead of it, but tougher emission standards would eventually prove fatal. On the whole, though, the two-stroke's appeal was always limited, and its increasing incidence from 1955 onward can be related directly to the spate of bubble-cars and minicars. While we shall encounter them later in the story, they never represented mainstream thinking, and none of them could be compared in impact with the VW, the Mini, or the Toyota Corona family.

More interesting was a pronounced swing toward the short-stroke, high-revving unit. Some of the factors behind this change were already present in the 1930s and 1940s, and can be traced back to Italy's *autostrade* and the German *autobahnen*. High sustained speeds on such roads encouraged not only superior aerodynamic shapes, but also en-

gines and gearing capable of equating maximum and cruising speeds. To see the results in practice, one may compare Continental and British cars of the late 1940s. In the 1,100-cc class, we find the VW (with an oversquare ratio of bore to stroke, at 77×64 mm) and the Fiat 1100 (nearly square, at 68×75 mm), both current in 1939 although the Beetle's engine was slightly smaller. Peugeot, with an eye on Europe as a whole, were moving toward the new idiom with their 202 engine (at 68×78 mm). But more typical of the old guard was Renault's Juvaquatre, an Opel copy with the most un-Opel-like dimensions of 58×95 mm. In Britain, the popular Hillman Minx had a bore of 63 mm and a stroke of 95 mm. The abolition of the archaic British taxation formula, based on the number and bore of the cylinders alone, was taking effect. After 1946, the Minx no longer had to be a "10 hp", so its bore was opened out to 65 mm in 1950—yet it remained a statement of the old way of thinking until 1954, when the unit was redesigned from scratch with a square ratio at 76×76 mm.

Fiscal restrictions on engine size were becoming fewer. In France and Italy, they were still punitive but, as taxation was based upon overall capacity, the short-stroke unit suffered no special penalty. Only in Japan was industry stifled right through our first decade. Misfortunes there, indeed, were supremely irrelevant to the rest of the motoring world, even in 1959 when a row developed between Renault and Hino because the latter failed to pay royalties on licence-built 4CV cars. The French government's view is a sobering commentary on Western indif-

ference: how cruel "to pick on this poor little country which has such a task to feed hundreds and millions of inhabitants"!

In regard to transmissions, single-plate clutches and synchromesh were generally used. Few makers, however, offered a synchronized bottom gear in 1950, one of the rare exceptions being Standard. Even the Americans would not bother with this until the mid-1960s, since the lowest ratio was seldom employed, and more and more customers were specifying automatic shift. The main legacy of the 1940s was column shift, an American innovation from 1938, and bearable only where three forward speeds sufficed. Its sole advantage was an unobstructed front-compartment floor, which made sense in an era when the American-type family sedan still appealed as a "world car". Alas, what Americans term "four on the tree" led to cumbersome shift patterns, the principal dishonours falling to Austin, Mercedes-Benz, and Peugeot.

Nor did synchromesh have things all its own way. Preselectors were declining, and the star of automatic transmission was in the ascendant. Already in 1951 it was difficult, if not impossible, to buy an American luxury model with conventional stick shift. In the middle-class sector, 80 % of all new Packards, 78 % of all Buicks, and 70 % of all Hudsons were self-shifters. Buick turned out two million automatic gearboxes between 1948 and 1954, while Chevrolet, who adopted the system in 1950, were fitting Powerglide to 20 % of their production within a year, raising the proportion to about 60 % by 1957.

Automatics had yet to reach Europe: tooling costs were undoubtedly the chief obstacle, and the inherent power losses of self-shifting would have been disastrous at a time when 45–50 horsepower were the norm

(*Opposite, top*) DKW revival in Czechoslovakia, 1946, though the Aero Minor name is misleading. The car was based on Jawa's licence-built DKW, and not on the pre-war Aero, also a two-stroke twin with front-wheel drive! Beneath the teardrop shape in the Hanomag/Volvo idiom is the usual 615-cc transverse-twin engine. But the four-speed transmission with its overdrive top, the forked backbone frame, all-independent springing, and the radiator behind the power unit differentiated it from the old F8 theme still being manufactured in East Germany. The Aero Minor was current until 1952.

(*Opposite, bottom*) Being up-to-date in 1939 meant that one could pursue themes unchanged into the mid-1950s, as in the case of General Motors' German offering, the Opel Olympia, here seen in 1951 guise with the same oversquare 1.5-litre overhead-valve four-cylinder engine, unitary structure, and three-speed transmission which it had used pre-war. Styling changes, likewise, are limited to a frontal facelift, even the old and ugly headlamp nacelles in the hood sides being retained. European buyers could have their small GM car in British or German form. Neither Opel's coil-spring front end nor Vauxhall's torsion bars made for good handling, and whether you bought British or German depended on whether you preferred four doors to two on a sedan (Opel didn't offer the former configuration) or if you wanted a station wagon, in which case Vauxhall had nothing for you. A re-emergent Germany was already coming out on top: that year's deliveries of Opel Olympias alone ran to 40,154 cars, more than Vauxhall's total production of fours and sixes. The British Bedford truck range, however, sold better than Opel's Blitz family.

(*Top right*) Soldiering on (with time out for a war) from 1934 to 1957 was the front-wheel-drive 11CV Citroën. The definitive 1,911-cc overhead-valve four-cylinder engine had arrived within eight months of the car's introduction. But apart from rack-and-pinion steering (1936) and an extended rear boot (1952), very little was changed otherwise. The short-wheelbase 11 Légère was the classic model. Here, for variety, is the 11 Normale, a full six-seater on a longer wheelbase of 122 in (3.1 m). This car dates from 1951 and is one of the last small-boot types. The light grey finish does not indicate a British model: although French-made cars were invariably black in the early post-war years, the Swedish importers also applied a little colour.

(*Bottom right*) Most modern-looking of the Vanguard-era sedans, here is Renault's 2-litre four-cylinder Frégate in 1954–56 guise. The ideas are scaled-down American, while the thick windscreen pillars and limited rear vision reflect Detroit's thinking of the 1940s. The independent rear springing and four-speed transmission are, however, strictly European, though nobody much cared for the Frégate's all-indirect ratios (this from the pioneer of direct drives!) or their sound effects. In any case, the Régie Renault had strong domestic competition in the big-car class: if Simca's Ford-derived Vedette never amounted to much, Citroën's *traction* was eighteen years old when the Renault made its *début*, and from 1956 there was the *avant-garde* Déesse as well.

for a 1.5-litre engine. This penalty remained formidable for many years, as anyone will testify who has driven a Hillman or Singer with Borg-Warner transmission from the early 1960s. It is, therefore, hardly surprising to find that the only European automatics on offer in 1950 were the truly gearless Invicta—whose makers were in the process of going bankrupt—and the Borgward, which was made in very small numbers and was soon discarded on grounds of fragility.

For transmitting power to the rear, one might expect an open propeller shaft, although torque tubes still had their adherents. A spiral-bevel back axle was the type in general use, and had been since the early 1920s. The underslung hypoid type, however, became more and more popular as it lowered the driveline and, thus, the centre of gravity. The worm drives of Peugeot and Daimler were notable exceptions, the latter company remaining loyal to this configuration on all conventional designs until 1968.

Suspensions at the front of the car were invariably independent, apart from odd archaisms such as the small British and German Fords—and these, too, were in the process of making the change, Dagenham's Consul and Zephyr appearing at the 1950 shows, and Cologne's Taunus a year later. The sports cars followed suit: the MG Midget had acquired coils on the TD series early in 1950. While coil layouts of the short-and-long-arm configuration predominated, Morris, Volkswagen, and Citroën were among those who preferred torsion bars, and a transverse-leaf arrangement was favoured by the Rootes Group on some of their older designs. Ford of France were as yet the sole adherents of the McPherson strut system, which became popular only in the 1970s.

Independent rear ends were scarcer, being considered too complex and expensive to build by the majority of makers, although many a German factory had espoused them before the war and, on subsequent models, the system was retained by Borgward, VW, and Mercedes-Benz, as well as by Skoda and Tatra in Czechoslovakia. So far, the most important new recruit had been Renault, on the little rear-engined 4CV. But Fiat would leave the idea alone until 1952, and Britain, for all her important early contributions (Alvis, Atalanta, and the latest 2.6-litre Lagonda), would not apply it to a popular car until 1959. In America, of course, the safe way was the known way, and independent rear springing was not obviously associated with painless motoring.

In the braking department, a hydraulic system working in drums on all four wheels was almost mandatory, as was an emergency hand-operated system working only on the rear wheels. The main exception to the first rule was the British hydromechanical layout, a compromise favoured by Rolls-Royce for safety, and by others on grounds of economy. Nothing better was really needed: roads had suffered from the ravages of war, tyre technology was at a fairly primitive stage, and cruising speeds of 60–65 mph (100–110 km/h) were normal for "fast" cars. Your small family sedan could reach 70 mph (112 km/h) but cruised around 50 mph (85 km/h). Handbrake variations were more limited, and the same principle applied to foot-operated emergency brakes preferred in America by Buick and Oldsmobile. The only major heresy was the obstinate adherence of Fiat and Chrysler—who made quite a lot of cars—to the transmission brake, a device of undoubted efficiency, but hard on drivelines unless used strictly for parking.

On its way up, of course, was unitary construction. From having just a few pre-war advocates, it now became the general practice for mass-produced European sedans, the chief exceptions being Standard's Vanguard and the tubular backbone frame of the VW. The method's economics were, in fact, to govern the development of the motor car for

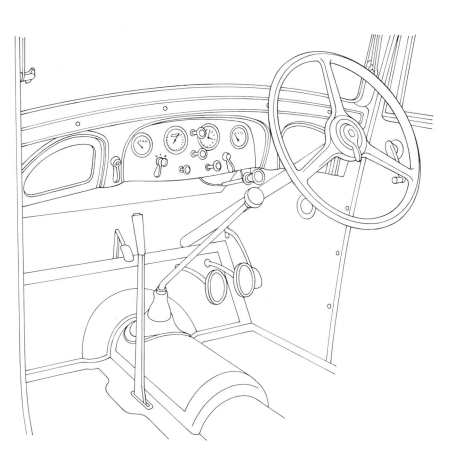

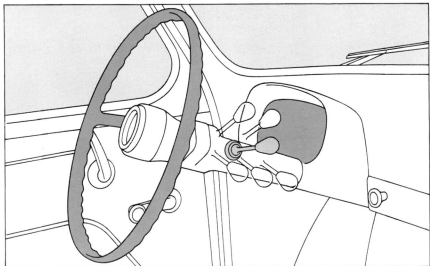

The changing face of gear-shifting: Fiats of 1934 (*left*) and 1956 (*above*). The older car's central lever with its neighbouring, loco-motive-sized handbrake obstructed the front compartment, while the former's long and willowy configuration did not make for quick, positive shifts, whatever the sentimentalists said. By contrast, the later 1100-103's column selector took up less room, but the nature of this diagram from a contemporary instruction manual suggests that the general public did not find it easy to regard the new layout as "just an ordinary shift laid on its side". As the linkage had to travel all the way down to the column and then under the floor to the gearbox, actual shifts were even woollier, though the Fiat's was one of the better specimens of a depressing period.

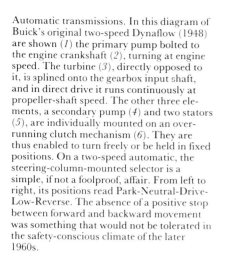

Automatic transmissions. In this diagram of Buick's original two-speed Dynaflow (1948) are shown (1) the primary pump bolted to the engine crankshaft (2), turning at engine speed. The turbine (3), directly opposed to it, is splined onto the gearbox input shaft, and in direct drive it runs continuously at propeller-shaft speed. The other three elements, a secondary pump (4) and two stators (5), are individually mounted on an over-running clutch mechanism (6). They are thus enabled to turn freely or be held in fixed positions. On a two-speed automatic, the steering-column-mounted selector is a simple, if not a foolproof, affair. From left to right, its positions read Park-Neutral-Drive-Low-Reverse. The absence of a positive stop between forward and backward movement was something that would not be tolerated in the safety-conscious climate of the later 1960s.

the next twenty years, since it was cost-effective only in relation to long production runs, and was susceptible neither to a wide range of bodies nor to great changes in style. As it caught on, new designs with a separate chassis grew rare: hence the "Look, It's Got a Chassis" publicity campaign behind the Triumph Herald in 1959.

As yet, inherent corrosion problems of unitaries had barely emerged. Anyone shopping for a pre-war Opel or Citroën *traction* model was well advised to investigate closely—but if it was not actually sagging in the middle, it at least represented transportation. In any case, the only countries with annual inspection laws in 1951 were the U.S.A. and New Zealand. Unitary construction made little headway in America, where the annual production run could be relied upon to pay the tooling bill for a separate chassis. With the latter, too, the effects of falling sales were less catastrophic. Hudson had a bad time trying to sell their unitary Stepdown, a 1948 debutante, once the shape went out of fashion. The sales graph was eloquent enough: a peak of 140,000 cars for the first three seasons, falling to 93,000 in 1951 and to a dismal 32,287 in 1954, the company's last year of financial independence. Nash, admittedly, fared rather better, and unitaries would reach the big battalions in due course, but it was a hazardous policy.

Concerning bodies, we were still in the era of the seller's market, when customers could not afford to argue about style, colour, or equipment. Early post-war VWs came out in a nondescript grey, and most British family sedans were black, Ford offering no home-market alternative in 1946. Even in 1951, Citroën *tractions* from the Quai de Javel factory were all black: if you wanted maroon or green, you opted for right-hand drive from the British assembly plant at Slough. Moreover, sedans were the only style available in 1950 for Peugeots, Opel Olympias, and Fiat 1100s, while the spread of unitary construction tended to

(*Opposite*) Traditional but still modern. It looks Italian, its ancestry is German, and it bears the hallowed British name of Frazer Nash. This is the actual Targa Florio Gran Sport roadster exhibited at the London Show in October, 1952, and a direct descendant of the 328 BMW (1936), probably the best all-round sports car of its decade. The triple-carburettor pushrod 2-litre six-cylinder engine develops 125 horsepower, and the suspension—by an independent transverse-leaf arrangement at the front and by torsion bars at the rear—is pure BMW. The name has a meaning, too: a Frazer Nash was the only British car ever to win the Targa Florio Race in Sicily, in 1951. Top speed is about 120 mph (192 km/h), but production was very limited—probably less than 20 cars built to this specification between 1952 and 1955.

(*Below*) The first modern GT, a Lancia Aurelia coupé in 1953 form. The racing numbers and lack of trim indicate a competition version and, like all Lancias of those days, it's still right-hand-drive. But the formula is the classic one: compact, narrow-angle 2.5-litre V-6 engine, four-speed synchromesh transaxle, and inboard rear brakes. Even in standard tune, 105 mph (168 km/h) present no problems, and one can settle down on one's favourite *autostrada* at 90–95 mph (145–155 km/h). But despite an eight-year run and countless rally successes, barely 5,000 of these cars found buyers.

(*Below*) British chassis of 1946, not quite classical. The Triumph 1800 uses an overhead-valve 1.8-litre four-cylinder engine. It looks old-fashioned mainly thanks to its traditionally shaped radiator, but observe (*1*) the transverse-leaf independent front suspension, (*2*) hydraulic brakes, (*3*) column-mounted gear lever, and (*4*) tubular chassis frame, this being adopted because steel tube was freely available in the austere economic climate of early post-war Britain. Technical progress does not always stem from truly technical motives. One might have contrasted a classical chassis of the same date as on the Lea-Francis Fourteen, which retained semi-elliptic springs at each end and mechanical brakes, as well as a centrally mounted selector for its four-speed synchromesh gearbox: the only feature that stamped it as post- rather than pre-war was the use of disc instead of wire wheels, the latter being normal then for a luxury sedan of mildly sporting character with the same engine capacity.

1

(*Above*) Chassis, American style. This is a 1949 Cadillac with the latest in 160-horse-power short-stroke overhead-valve V-8 engines and an automatic transmission, but the construction is a direct legacy of the 1930s, with coil-spring independent front suspension, and the hypoid rear axle which became fashionable from 1936 to lower the car. Even more typical is the rigid central cruciform bracing, destined to survive into the 1950s in the U.S.A.—and even later on some American cars with convertible body-work which called for the maximum of reinforcement.

(*Top*) Some legacies of the 1940s—and of the 1930s as well, though in the case of the 1950 American Ford (*left*) only the side-valve V-8 engine, and its alternative in-line six, were common to the pre-war species. For 1949, Ford's chief engineer Harold Youngren had not only given the car a new skin: he had dispensed with the old beam axles and transverse leaf springs, in favour of independent coils at the front and longitudinal semi-elliptics at the back. The hypoid rear axle spelt an overdue farewell to that "high on its legs" look that had characterized all previous Fords, wherever made, and all seats were well within the wheelbase. The car looked very long, but it had only put on one inch (2.5 cm) over the superseded 1941–48 shape. It was also 240 lb (90 kg) lighter and had a lot more internal width for passengers.
The 1954 R-type Bentley Standard Steel sedan (*right*), by contrast, looked a true late-thirties motorcar, but was also largely post-

war beneath the skin, though its independent front suspension had first been applied to a Rolls-Royce product in 1935, and the factory-built body (itself a post-war idea) followed closely upon the shape created by Park Ward for the stillborn Mk.V of 1940–41. The six-cylinder engine's combination of overhead inlet and side exhaust valves was common to all Rolls-Royce units in the 1946–59 period, and brakes were of the traditional Hispano-Suiza servo type as used since 1924, although now with hydromechanical actuation. By 1954, too, a Hydramatic gearbox designed by General Motors had replaced the well-loved synchromesh transmission with right-hand floor shift. The German Veritas Scorpion cabriolet of 1950 (*opposite, left*) had started life in the dark years of 1946–47 as a competition "special" using pre-war Type 328 BMW mechanics, including the twin-tube chassis. Since most of the bits were secondhand, even the Occupation

authorities could not really object to such a "factory", but by the beginning of our period the Veritas had acquired a five-speed gearbox and a new, seven-bearing overhead-camshaft engine by former aircraft manufacturer Ernst Heinkel. Specifications varied from car to car, but as much as 140 horsepower was available—and even with the "standard" 100-horsepower tune, top speed was around 105 mph (165–170 km/h). Reputedly Veritas lost about £1,000 ($2,800) per car, and the rapid renaissance of West German industry had put the little firm out of business by 1952. As for the Tatraplan from Czechoslovakia (*opposite, right*), with its *avant-garde* looks and a 2-litre rear engine, it was wholly pre-war in concept. The whale-like silhouette with central backbone frame, all-independent suspension, and air-cooled power unit (quick-detachable for servicing) had taken its bow at the 1934 Berlin Show, and this latest, more economical flat-four version had

been visible by 1938. Post-war cars had more power (52 against 40 hp), torsion-bar rear suspension (which helped the handling), and an unpleasing steering-column gearshift. The car would be the last Tatra sold abroad in any numbers. There was a lapse in private-car production between 1952 and 1955: when manufacture resumed, Tatra were back with rear-engined V-8s, badges of rank in their own country, not mass-produced. A development of this theme, the T613, was still being made in small numbers in 1983.

(*Opposite, bottom*) Yes, this car was actually made in 1954 and five years later you could have bought its twin from your friendly British Ford dealer for the £444 it was probably still worth as a curiosity in 1982. The recipe is simple: the 1932 Model-Y chassis updated in 1938, the body of its 1940 replacement (the Anglia), and the bigger 1,172-cc side-valve four-cylinder engine first seen in the Anglo-German Model-C Ten in 1935. Synchromesh, true, but not hydraulic brakes, while the transverse leaf springs at either end are the same medium which supported Model-T way back in 1908. Creature comforts were minimal, but anything is better than a bubble-car . . .

(*Above*) On the market in October, 1948, and still with us in 1970, to the tune of over 1,600,000 units—Alec Issigonis' Morris Minor. The Traveller Estate introduced in 1953 accounted for 204,000 cars. By 1966 it was beginning to look old-fashioned and cramped: it had had only one major restyle, in 1956, when it got a new grille and a single-panel curved windscreen. It had, however, gone through four engines, from a 27-horse-power 918-cc side-valve to the present 1,098-cc pushrod unit giving 48 horsepower, and top speed was up from 62 mph (100 km/h) to nearly 80 mph (128 km/h). The wood on these cars was both authentic and structural, a hazard to restorers of a model that would become highly collectable in the 1980s.

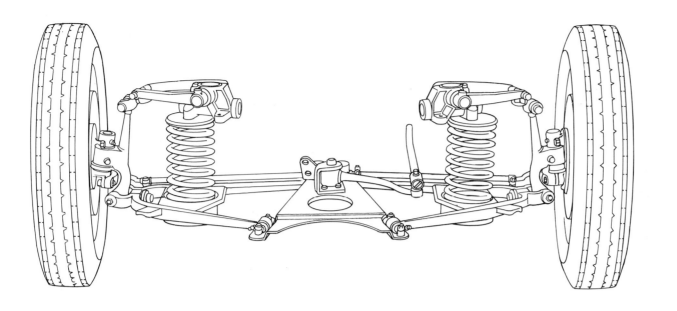

eliminate varieties of style. Whereas 1934 had seen five body styles for the Austin Ten, and four for Morris, their 1950 counterparts—the A40 and the Oxford—allowed far less choice. Morris made only a unitary sedan, and Austin's catalogue included just a van-type station wagon although, for 1951, the separate chassis enabled them to add a sports four-seater cabriolet built for them by Jensen.

A strong legacy of the 1940s was the station wagon. Such a body had first been catalogued by Ford of America as long ago as 1929, and examples were offered by nine more U.S. makers by 1940, when Ford delivered 13,000 new wagons, and Chevrolet 2,904. These vehicles were, of course, the traditional "woodies", which shared nothing with other standard body styles and had to be built up like vans from chassis/cowl units. As yet, only Ford were prepared to work in wood— General Motors drew on three independent coachbuilders. In Europe, among those who listed wagons were Peugeot, Hillman, and Austin. Having been a specialist low-volume style before the war, it was no longer despised as a dual-purpose vehicle for tradesmen or, as in Britain, an estate hack for transporting guns to the butts, guests to the station, and servants to the village "hop". What really put the wagon into favour was the gradual elimination of timber, first for structural members and then for the whole vehicle. The pioneer all-metal estate car was the 1949 Plymouth, and henceforward timber became purely decorative, so that wagons could be processed through the factory's main body shops. We were still a long way from estate cars sharing most of their panels with sedans, let alone such dual-purpose sedans as the Renault 16 of 1965 and the Austin Maxi of 1969. But the trend had been set in motion.

Another novelty, the hardtop coupé, was barely visible at the end of the 1940s. Chrysler claim to have invented it on the strength of a few prototypes made in 1946, while the same year's Armstrong Siddeley Typhoon is a valid claimant, but what is generally accepted as the first hardtop—the Riviera—came from Buick in 1949. The recipe was quite simple: take a two-door convertible body shell and fit it with a permanent steel top. Thus, several birds are killed with one stone, providing a convertible's sporty lines without the endemic draughts, the short-lived canvas top, the relays needed for power operation, and a space-wasting well (often as much as 30 cm wide) which the top occupies in the down position. Hardtops also lent themselves admirably to two-tone colour schemes that broke up the large slab-sided masses favoured by contem-

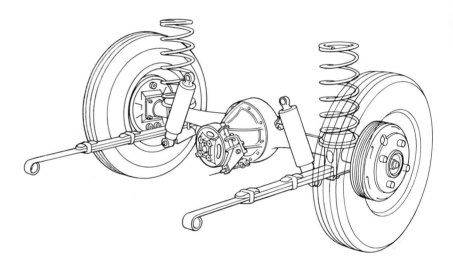

(*Above, centre*) Emergency brake, old style— albeit favoured by two big manufacturers, Fiat and Chrysler, throughout the 1950s. This rear end of a 1950 Fiat 1400 shows the handbrake drum on the rear axle. The use of a live axle and vertical coils is also noteworthy. Transmission brakes were exceedingly efficient, but the resultant "sudden death" stop could do terrible things to the back axle, and normally one used the device strictly for parking.

(*Opposite, centre*) Already known in 1949 was the disc brake, here seen as applied to Chrysler's Crown Imperial. This exploded view shows the double discs inside their finned two-piece housing. Braking action was achieved by forcing the discs apart, and the system was said to give 35 % more friction

surface than a twelve-inch drum, the biggest size of conventional brake viable with the 15-in wheel which was then standard equipment in America. Full enclosure meant protection from road dirt, but this early type of disc was expensive to make—so it was confined to the top of the Chrysler range, produced at the rate of a few hundred per year. Contrast the simplicity of Dunlop's 1956 disc brake (*opposite, bottom*), showing two pistons moving in a caliper attached to the back plate, and exerting pressure on circular pads in contact with the disc. The friction pads respond to hydraulic pressure, and high working temperatures require that the hydraulic fluid should be thermally insulated from the pads. Deep pads were said to ensure a working life of 50,000 km (30,000 miles), though about two-thirds of this was as much as the average motorist expected.

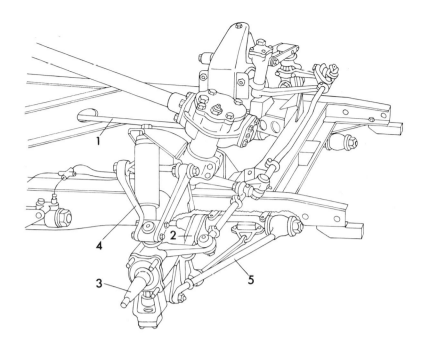

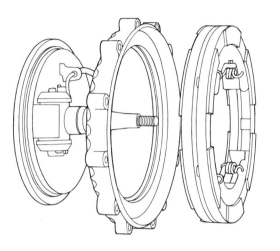

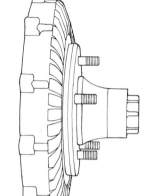

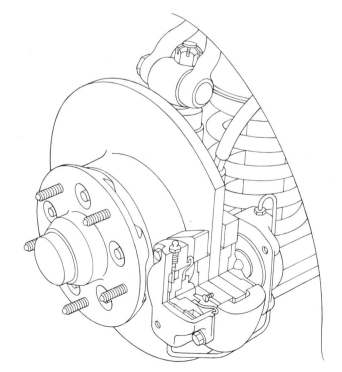

porary stylists. Better still, if the maker's range embraced a two-door unitary sedan, or even a four-door sedan, this could easily be transformed into a hardtop coupé with no loss of structural strength. Thus, by 1951, every U.S. firm offered such a style. It took longer to catch on in Europe, where convertibles were rarer as well, but outstanding early examples came from Hillman in Britain and Simca in France, although Fiat's Gran Luce 1900 was less felicitous.

Given all these advances, it may seem that by 1950 the only thing needed would be sufficient economic stability to keep the demand going. So what was required in order to bring the state of the automotive art up to the standard of the late 1960s, beyond breaking the stranglehold of the *système* Panhard? What did a car of 1950 signally lack from the viewpoint of a motorist nurtured on later machinery? Let us answer by looking at three typical models of that year—the Austin A40, the Peugeot 203, and the Chevrolet Styleline.

While all three seem hopelessly outmoded in appearance today, nothing archaic can be observed immediately under their bonnets, and one would notice their unsophisticated suspensions only after a drive. Synchromesh has not changed much, despite the difficulty of shifting with either the Austin's long and willowy floor-mounted lever or the Peugeot's column linkage. The Chevrolet is easier with "three on the tree", and its unsynchronized bottom gear would never normally be engaged. Brake fade, or trouble with the systems as such (hydromechanical on the Austin and hydraulic on the others), are unlikely. But the bother would begin with the handbrakes mounted under the dash, and the poor all-round vision due to thick screen pillars and small rear windows: wrap-rounds lie a year or so in the future. Only the Chevrolet offers a luggage boot of truly family proportions; accessory roofracks are desirable adjuncts on the other two models.

Once at the wheel, you would find it necessary to turn a key as well as pressing a starter button, since no key-starting exists outside America and even there it is not general practice. The European cars have electric wipers, but not of the modern two-speed type, and screenwashers do not always feature in the approved accessory list of this time. Radios and heaters are also extras (even if the latter are added for local sale in cold climates), looking and feeling like the bolt-on goodies that they amounted to—a fast downshift could land your foot in the heater fan, while the radio might bark the front passenger's knees. All automobile electrics were then based on the dynamo, and nobody had even thought about transistors in this context. Internal power assistance for seats or windows sounded as science-fictional as power steering: although this amenity in fact lay just round the corner, it was available only on American luxury cars. Automatic transmission was available for the Chevrolet, but disc brakes were virtually unknown. The Chevrolet is unlikely to have been riding on tubeless tyres, and these certainly would not be forthcoming for either of the European cars. Seat belts? One wore them in airliners when taking off and landing . . .

As for performance, the Chevrolet's 85 mph (138 km/h) from 3.8 litres may seem entirely adequate in our age of fuel conservation and overall speed limits. Even in 1967, a comparable cheap American six, the Plymouth Valiant, found 95 mph (152 km/h) hard work. But when accelerating, one notices the differences, as the Chevrolet takes 15 seconds to reach 50 mph (80 km/h) and the Plymouth only 9.2 seconds. With an average brake-pedal pressure, 86 ft (26 m) are needed in which to stop the Chevrolet from 30 mph (50 km/h), whereas the Plymouth managed it in just over 32 ft (10 m) even as a pre-disc model. The Austin and Peugeot have very similar general performance, albeit delivered in a quite different fashion, the Peugeot being taut to handle and the Austin wallowy. The latter's figures are, however, a true indication of the state of the art in those days. With a 1.2-litre engine giving 40

(*Opposite*) No, not a press shot from the 1939 Berlin Show: Adolf Hitler had been eight years dead when this first-series Mercedes-Benz 220 sedan was built. A new model for 1951, it was distinguishable from the last pre-war series only by its recessed headlamps and alligator hood. The all-independent suspension, hydraulic brakes, backbone frame, synchromesh gearbox, and 6-volt electrics were all legacies from 1939. But in place of the old, sedate side-valve six, there was a new four-bearing overhead-camshaft unit which offered 90 mph (145 km/h), easy cruising at 75 mph (120 km/h), and excellent flexibility. The column shift was, however, a particularly nasty one.

(*Top right*) The Daimler Conquest Century sedan of 1954–58 retained the classic fluted radiator and alligator hood dating back to 1904, and styling was authentic 1940s. Also present were a separate chassis and those good old British hydromechanical brakes, while until 1957 the preselective fluid fly-wheel transmission (regular equipment on Daimlers since 1931) was standardized, though supplanted on the last Centurys by an automatic gearbox. Handling was sure-footed, and the twin-carburettor Century was good for 90 mph (145 km/h). The basic Conquest was slower and cheaper. The name, incidentally, was an historical pun, dreamed up when the original price was costed out to exactly £1,066 (the year of the Norman Conquest of Britain).

(*Bottom right*) A familiar sight on British roads throughout our period was "Auntie Rover", alias the P4 sedan, over 135,000 being made between 1950 and 1964. Subtle and progressive stylistic changes passed almost without comment, although in detailed analysis this 1961 car of the 100 series looks very different from the original 75 with its central, Cyclops'-eye spotlamp. What started with four speeds, column shift, and a freewheel ended with four-on-the-floor plus overdrive, and engines fitted at various times ranged from a 2-litre four to the 2.6-litre overhead-inlet-valve six with outputs of up to 123 horsepower (in this car it gives only 104). Later examples, too, had front disc brakes and a servo, a far cry from the hydro-mechanical layout used on the original series.

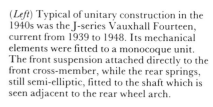

(*Left*) Typical of unitary construction in the 1940s was the J-series Vauxhall Fourteen, current from 1939 to 1948. Its mechanical elements were fitted to a monocoque unit. The front suspension attached directly to the front cross-member, while the rear springs, still semi-elliptic, fitted to the shaft which is seen adjacent to the rear wheel arch.

(*Right*) Anatomy of a popular European sedan, 1949. The Peugeot 203 was new at the 1948 Paris Salon and was marketed until 1960. There was, of course, no chassis—and the skeleton, consisting of engine, transmission, suspensions, propeller shaft, and reinforcing tube, was not drivable: nor could it be used as a base for special bodies. This

exploded view has been "elongated" by the press department to suggest Cadillac-like proportions, whereas its cylinder capacity was a mere 1,290 cc and its overall length 4.35 m (171 in). Clearly visible are the all-coil suspension (*1, 2*), rack-and-pinion steering gear (*3*), steering-column gear-change (*4*), and radiator (*5*) tucked well away behind a heavy grille, although Peugeot had mercifully abandoned their pre-war practice of mounting the headlamps between grille and radiator. By this time, too, the worm-drive rear axle (*6*) was a rarity on private cars, Daimler being almost the only other user in 1949. Just visible (*7*) is an unusual refinement, the sliding roof, normally regarded as a British preserve, and one that was reluctantly sacrificed by Britons in the cause of dust-sealing for export sales. It would remain a Peugeot option throughout our period and beyond.

(*Bottom*) Advanced body construction. On the Bristol 401 (1949) the base design was the work of Touring of Milan (they had built very similar coachwork on pre-war Fiat and Alfa Romeo chassis), and featured aluminium panels laid over robust tubular-steel framework. Mechanically, this 1,971-cc overhead-valve sporting six-cylinder sedan was descended from the pre-war German Type 327 BMW, but aimed at a far wealthier market. In 1951 one paid £2,460 ($6,890), an interesting comparison with the £700 ($1,960) asked for a mass-produced British 2-litre like the Standard Vanguard.

horsepower at 4,300 rpm, it is flat out at 68 mph (110 km/h), attains 46 mph (74 km/h) in third gear, and takes 12.3 seconds to reach 40 mph (64 km/h), 20.5 seconds to 50 mph (80 km/h), and a laboured 34.8 seconds to 60 mph (100 km/h). The fuel consumption is reasonable at 32 miles per gallon (9 litres per 100 kilometres), but a leaden foot quickly brings thirst up to a less acceptable 25 mpg (11.5 litres/100 km). The car is light enough at 2,240 pounds (1,015 kg) and fairly compact, measuring 153 in (3.9 m) from stem to stern.

Now let us contemplate a new design from 1969, the Fiat 128. For all its front-wheel drive and transverse engine, it is barely an inch longer than the Austin, and there is far less wasted space. At 70 mph (112 km/h), it is faster in third gear than the British car is in top, and under favourable conditions it can be pushed to nearly 90 mph (145 km/h). A comfortable cruising speed is 75 mph (120 km/h), and even 80 mph (129 km/h) can be held although with a bit too much noise. While overall consumption differs little, the Fiat's 38 mpg (7.4 litres/100 km) on a long run could not be matched by the Austin, if only because such averages—say 65 mph (104 km/h) with a good proportion of motorway travel—would be excessive for the older car's engine, not to mention its chassis engineering. In acceleration, with the two sedans starting level, the Fiat would be doing over 40 mph (65 km/h) by the time the Austin had attained 30 mph (50 km/h) and, with the British car levelled off at 50 mph (80 km/h), the modern Italian would be running at 65–70 mph (104–112 km/h). Both cars could stop from 30 mph (50 km/h) in 30 ft (9 m), but the pedal pressures are interesting, the Austin's at 140 pounds (64 kg) being almost twice the Fiat's. Inflation, alas, renders accurate price comparisons impossible: the Austin's original owner would have paid £442 sterling, or half of what a Fiat cost in 1970, but against this must be set British import duty on the Italian car, whose

home-market figure would have been at least 20 per cent lower.

The foregoing are only individual cases, however typical. We were still a long way from "world cars" such as Ford's 1976 Fiesta and its sequels. Model T had died in 1927 with no real successor. The Standard Vanguard and its contemporaries, mere restatements of conventional American compacts like the Willys Whippet and the Model A Ford at their zenith in 1928–30, represented a type that continued to engage the attention of designers, but it was doomed: too much car. The Volkswagen, although very much with us in 1950, had barely penetrated outside Europe. If relatively few nations were as yet producing cars, this was simply because industry needed time to get into full post-war swing.

National cars were being planned. In Sweden, Volvo had not become an international firm, while not a single Australian Holden had reached a customer outside the Commonwealth. The Dutch DAF and Spain's Fiat-based SEAT lay in the future. The supra-national J-cars, T-cars, and Fiestas would not descend upon us until thinking had swung firmly in the other direction, toward production of an integrated design wherever it was convenient and viable. That new industries were backed by the existing giants—America's big three in Australia, the British Motor Corporation in India, Datsun in Taiwan, and Fiat almost everywhere—did not in any way preclude the creation of local derivatives bearing only incidental affinities with the mainstream product.

Nonetheless, the structure of manufacturing had changed. In the 1920s there had still been good prospects for the "assembled" car, built up from standardized proprietary components: engines from CIME (France), Meadows (England), or Continental in the U.S.A., with Moss and Warner gearboxes, and Salisbury back axles. Identical elements were often shared by a diversity of makes and models, only the

(*Top*) Made in 1953, but essentially a car of the 1940s, is this Chrysler Windsor convertible. Unlike its more exciting stablemates, it still uses the familiar 4.1-litre side-valve six found (in essence) under the bonnets of its pre-war forebears, while chassis, suspension, and brakes are likewise little changed. The styling is warmed-over 1949 (hardly a banner year for Chrysler in this department) with the now-mandatory one-piece curved windscreen. Power steering is already an option, but only those who ordered after June could have anything better than a semi-automatic trasmission.

(*Opposite*) A shape in search of an engine. The Kaiser empire's "Last Onslaught On Detroit" (to quote Richard M. Langworth) did not fail through lack of good ideas. This Kaiser Manhattan sedan was built in 1953, but it had first been seen in the spring of 1950 as a 1951 model, and it certainly could not be confused with anything from General Motors' studios. You had built-in safety and an infinite diversity of colour treatments, within and without. Hydramatic, and—by 1953—power steering were available to order, but there was no V-8 to go under a hood that could easily have housed it: only a 3.7-litre side-valve six developing 118 horsepower. Hence the model-year's deliveries were a mere 27,000 units.

(*Bottom*) Common-sense five-passenger sedan, or—in this case—taxicab. Checker of Kalamazoo, Michigan, built this basic design from 1959 to 1982, with a happy disregard for all Detroit's stylists. This one dates from the late 1970s, but the only outward and visible sign of recognition lies in the heavy energy-absorbing bumpers. The engine, of course, is an overhead-valve Chevrolet V-8 instead of the side-valve in-line Continental six of early days, while the front disc brakes (offered by not a single American maker in 1959) are now standard. So are power steering and automatic transmission, though one pays extra for air conditioning. Further, in nineteen years the basic price (around $2,500 in early days) has all but tripled.

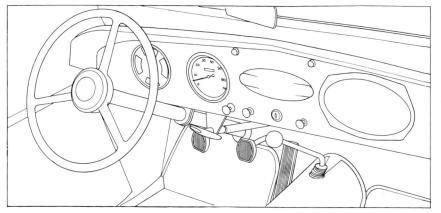

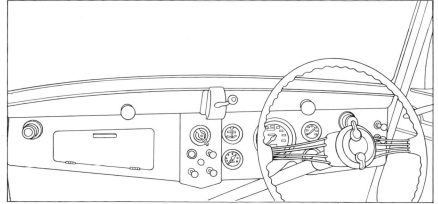

(*Above left*) An unloved feature of many cars from the late 1930s onwards—it was at its zenith in the fifties—was the under-dash-mounted handbrake lever with its plastic "umbrella handle". An awkward action outweighed all its alleged advantages. This one is seen on the 1949 Crosley, among the few American baby-cars to sell in any quantity.

Unfortunately a 722-cc engine, an overall length of 3.46 m (136 in), and a thirst of 7.4 litres/100 km (38 mpg) were not what the U.S. public wanted in an era of cheap and plentiful fuel.

Facias old and new. The 1946 Lea-Francis (*above right*) depicts the British way as it would be on the more expensive cars well into the 1950s—a polished wood dash, well-calibrated circular black-faced dials, and a rather unergonomic set of switches and knobs in the centre. If you wanted a radio, it went under the dash where it barked the pas-

senger's knees. Very much in the late-1940s idiom (*below*) is the plastic facia of the Polish Warszawa, actually 1962, but with roots going back sixteen years. At least the main dials are circular, but small rectangles suffice for lesser instruments. The radio, however, fits neatly into the centre, in the best Detroit style.

manner of combination and the odd stylistic touch furnishing a degree of individuality. But the Great Depression had forced the assemblers out of the popular market, where they were no longer competitive. Indeed, except perhaps in Britain, they had a limited future even in the specialist sector, and they did not reappear until after World War II. True, Continental's immortal side-valve six crops up again in our period with two American makes, Kaiser and Checker: yet the former's units were produced in a Kaiser-owned factory, and the Checker was made only in modest numbers as well as being Chevrolet-powered by the later 1960s.

In spite of that, the cars of the fifties and sixties were assembled cars, even if their sponsors did not hunt through the catalogues of component suppliers to select a bit here and a bit there. Specialists flourished so far that many a supposedly self-contained "factory" was nothing more

than an assembly plant for such products. Only General Motors could truly be said to make their own carburettors, those of Cadillac and Opel being ascribed to the chassis maker. In fact, it was common for a big company to control a captive supplier—SU in the case of Nuffield, Ball and Ball with Chrysler, Weber with Fiat. Briggs bodies were tied to Chrysler in the U.S.A. and to Ford in Britain, while Nash obtained bodies mainly from the Seaman firm acquired as long ago as 1919. Even the new science of automatic transmission was in the hands of a few by 1960: General Motors not only built their own, but offered a variety of types and could actually afford selling gearboxes (to Lincoln in 1950, for instance) and manufacturing licences (to Rolls-Royce) among outside companies. With few exceptions, the standard automatic on British cars was the American Borg-Warner, built in a branch factory at Letchworth. In due course, the Jatco would assume the same role in Japan, although Toyota and Honda made their own.

Why? It seldom paid to do one's own manufacturing when one could buy from a specialist and thus cut down tooling costs. If the run was long enough, a car maker might even finance some feature not shared by any model outside his range. Attempts to compete against the established firms were catastrophically expensive, and often yielded worse quality than the standardized product. Two evident disasters of the period were Studebaker's mechanical power steering (1953) and Rover's complex Roverdrive automatic (1957). The former never reached the paying customers, while the latter had a two-year run and a lukewarm press reception before being scrapped in favour of the familiar Borg-Warner with its well-understood driving technique and exchange-unit service.

To show how the system worked, one need only study any major new-car announcement of the period and notice who took credit in terms of paid advertisements. The XJ sedan of 1968 was every inch a Jaguar, and in no way mistakable for the product of some other design team or factory. But its integrated design hardly proved that most of the car emanated from the Jaguar plant at Allesley. One excepted Triplex glass and Dunlop tyres, just as a Borg-Warner automatic gearbox was predictable. Less obvious, however, were the steering connections and suspension units from Alford and Alder, the Mazak die-cast grilles, Delaney-Gallay heaters and air conditioners, Hepolite pistons, Hertfordshire rubber sealing, Marston radiators, Adwest power steering, Huntfield exhaust fittings, GKN transmission lines, and English Steel Company forgings for the engine and gearbox.

The system naturally had its drawbacks. Already in 1946, a series of suppliers' strikes in the U.S.A. had nearly brought Detroit to a standstill, with production losses of up to 50,000 cars per month, and these would only be the first of many. To gain security by duplicating suppliers could put quality at risk. There was also the appalling prospect of what might happen if a major supplier should fall into the hands of one's rival. In Britain, Jowett received a *coup de grâce* when Ford acquired Briggs Motor Bodies, who built the Javelin's body/chassis structure since that small Bradford firm had never budgeted to cope with it. A lesser tragedy befell Alvis in 1954 when both of their body sources were taken over, Mulliners of Birmingham going to Standard-Triumph, and Tickford of Newport Pagnell to Aston Martin Lagonda, so that the little Coventry company needed four years to find a regular supplier again. Further, even if component suppliers were captive numbers of a big organization, a rationalization drive could leave a car model without an essential element. In 1979, the Jaguar XJ-S sports coupé was to become an automatic-only item, because British Leyland considered it uneconomic to tool for a manual gearbox exclusive to this model. Lesser Jaguars were able to use Rover's five-speeder, but the XJ-S could not, so customers who preferred to shift for themselves had to shop elsewhere.

Not that the small specialist car maker was finished. We shall find him cashing in on the desire to be different: with Italy's way-out Fiat derivatives (Abarth, Siata, Moretti), with Britain's kit-cars and, towards the end of our period, in the first wave of replicars, those mixtures of modern proprietary elements masquerading as Classics of the twenties and thirties. But such operations, although very much a part of our story, lay beyond the mainstream of automobile manufacture. Britain, home of the specialist, turned out 1,805,846 cars in 1969—yet a bare 3,500 of them were made up of the "odds and ends". Incidentally, the smallest producer for whom an individual statistic appeared desirable was Jensen, with 400 cars using Chrysler engines and transmissions.

Contraction of the industry proceeded at a mounting pace throughout our period. Minor independent makers struggled ever harder to stay alive, and the football-league atmosphere of the sales race became

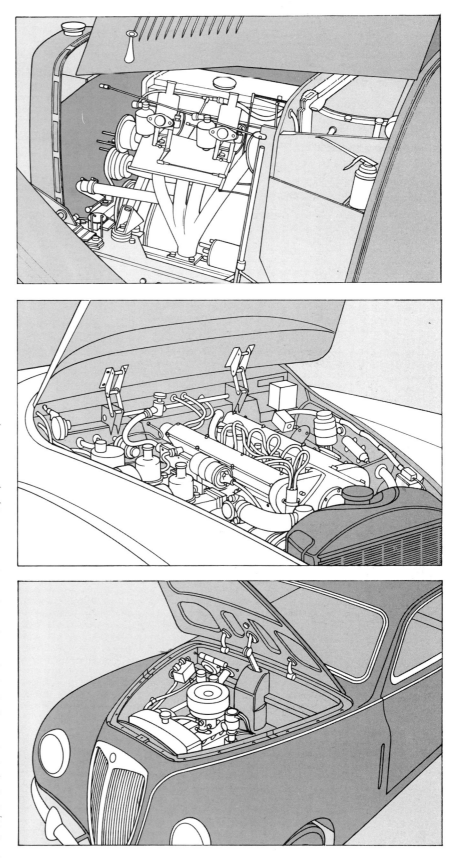

Diminishing access—or the miseries of the alligator bonnet. Incredibly, the limited-production HRG 1500 sports car from Britain (*top*) qualifies for our period, having been available from 1936 right through to 1955. It typifies the maximum of access available with a side-opening hood and unstreamlined wings. What happened in the 1950s was less felicitous, especially when a large and complicated engine was combined with a low line, as on the 1952 Jaguar XK120 (*centre*). Things were not much better on the 1950 Lancia Aurelia (*bottom*), for all its narrow-angle V-6 engine. High sides and an air-cleaner mounted atop the engine saw to that.

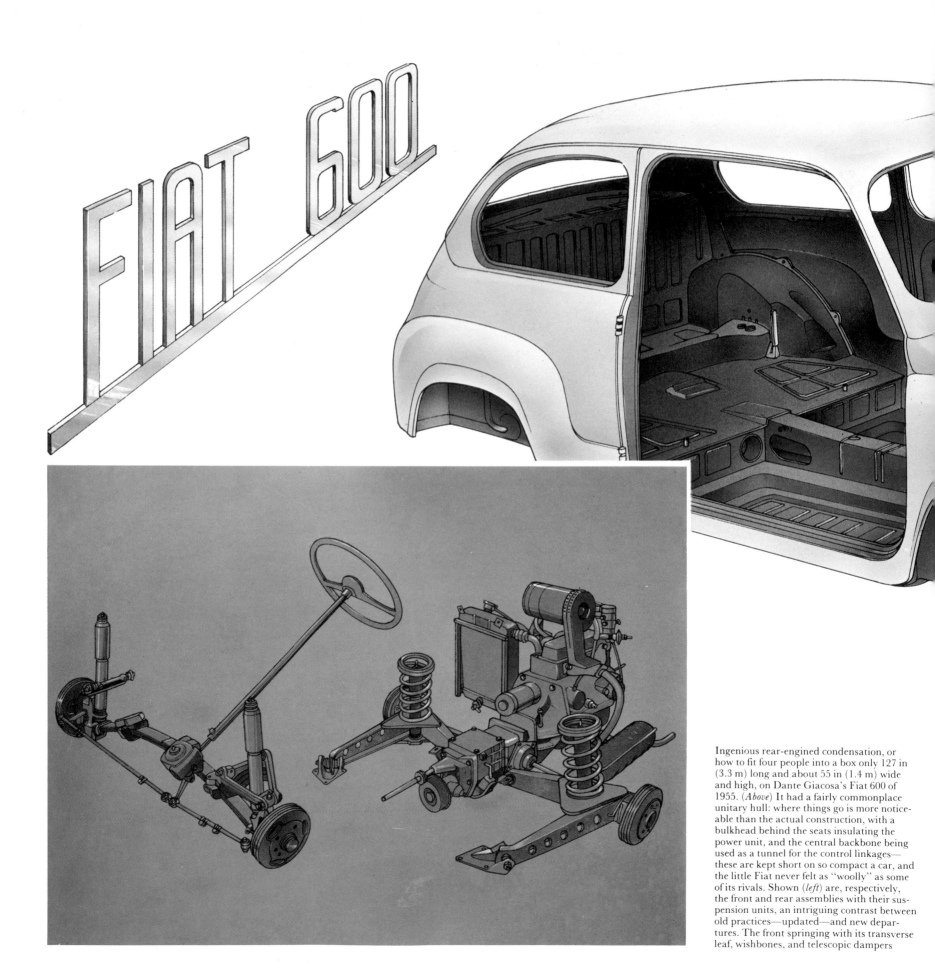

FIAT 600

Ingenious rear-engined condensation, or how to fit four people into a box only 127 in (3.3 m) long and about 55 in (1.4 m) wide and high, on Dante Giacosa's Fiat 600 of 1955. (*Above*) It had a fairly commonplace unitary hull: where things go is more noticeable than the actual construction, with a bulkhead behind the seats insulating the power unit, and the central backbone being used as a tunnel for the control linkages—these are kept short on so compact a car, and the little Fiat never felt as "woolly" as some of its rivals. Shown (*left*) are, respectively, the front and rear assemblies with their suspension units, an intriguing contrast between old practices—updated—and new departures. The front springing with its transverse leaf, wishbones, and telescopic dampers a heater! (*Top right*) Observe the two suspension units at work: the Fiat, with its minimal overhang, handled better than most small rear-engined cars, although it is fair to say that there was little room for real "vice" on the original version, with its modest 21.5 horsepower and a top speed of less than 60 mph (96 km/h). Finally (*bottom right*) we see the complete, though non-running, floorpan as supplied to specialists coachbuilders. The rear panel shown here was not an integral part of the package, although it is fair to say that had it been, Abarth could never have transformed the 600 into a tiny coupé, barely 48 in (1.2 m) high, on which—even with a slightly over-bored 747-

cc pushrod engine (the original ran to 633 cc)—speeds of 95 mph (153 km/h) were possible, not to mention a *mean* fuel consumption of 42.6 mpg (6.6 litres/100 km). Careful driving could yield 70 mpg (4 litres/100 km), not that anyone but a masochist would try on those delightful little Zagato two-seaters. The 600 was made in Turin for over fifteen years to the tune of more than two and a half million examples. It was also produced in West Germany as a Neckar, in Spain as a SEAT, in Yugoslavia as a Zastava, and in Argentina as a Fiat-Concord. International buyers' guides listed the two latter variants as still current in 1982.

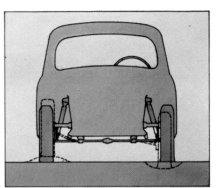

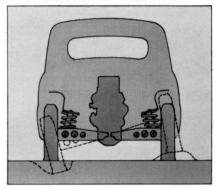

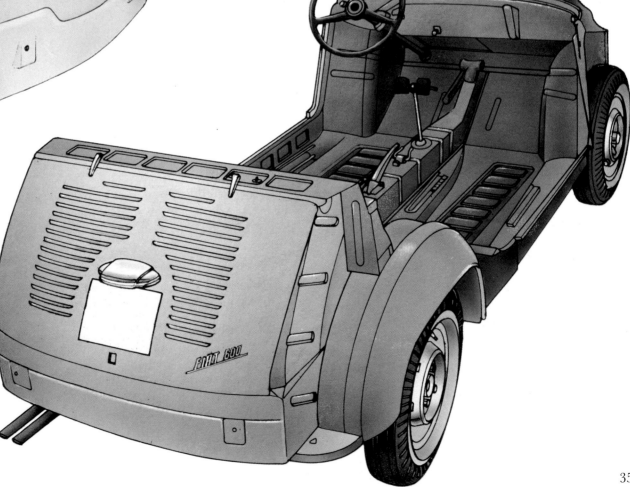

derives directly from the old front-engined *topolino*, just supplanted after a run of nearly nineteen years. But at the rear, the driving wheels are independently sprung by a combination of vertical coils, wishbones, and trailing links. (The company had already tested all-independent springing on its 8V sports coupé of 1952, made in very small numbers.)

By mounting the engine behind its four-speed gearbox, one not only saves space but improves servicing techniques, since everything withdraws easily rearwards for a major overhaul or the fitting of exchange units. More space still is saved by mounting the radiator on the side of the engine: on the *topolino*, it had sat safely behind, out of harm's way and dispensing with the need for nightmarish. The minimum point for survival rose steadily from 5,000 cars in 1923, and 35,000 in 1939, to around 80,000 at the beginning of the fifties. Towards their end, a consistent failure to dispose of 250,000 cars per year was enough to render any of America's big three companies hesitant over that division's future. Hence the short, tragic run of Ford's Edsel (1958–59), and the demise of Chrysler's De Soto in 1960 after a patchy post-war record which exceeded 100,000 for the last time in 1957.

Independents, whether in the U.S.A. or elsewhere, had fewer dealers, fewer regional assembly plants in the large countries, and a higher unit advertising cost. Such firms in America needed to present a challenge in virtually every sector of the market in order to remain competitive. It proved too much for them to take on Buick, Mercury, and Chrysler as well as Chevrolet, Ford, and Plymouth. The Kaiser-Willys merger of 1954 possessed all the aura of a deathbed wedding. By 1966, the last remnants of Studebaker-Packard, another union from 1954, had gone to the grave after a short spell as a "foreign import" made in Canada. This, in effect, left only American Motors with the Nash and Hudson to rival the big three.

A similar picture is encountered elsewhere. Britain entered the period with her big six producers, backed by an equal number of "major-minors" (Armstrong Siddeley, Daimler, Jaguar, Jowett, Rover, Singer) outside the true specialist league (typified at different levels by Rolls-Royce, Lea-Francis, and HRG). By 1960, the Austin and Nuffield interests had merged, Rootes had absorbed Singer, Daimler had fallen to Jaguar, and Standard-Triumph had become part of the Leyland truck empire. Armstrong Siddeley were out of car-making, and Jowett out of business altogether except as a small concern supplying parts for extant vehicles. Nine years later, the huge Leyland conglomerate had gathered unto itself Austin/Morris, Jaguar/Daimler, and Rover—picking up Alvis with the latter, and terminating this firm's line of specialist cars after forty-seven distinguished years. Rootes were now just a cog in the American works of Chrysler. Further, subordinate makes of now merely sentimental interest (Riley, Singer) had been discontinued.

The trend was repeated in other countries. Fiat, at their zenith in 1969, controlled Autobianchi, Lancia, and Ferrari, while a tie-up with Citroën in France gave them a stake, although a short-lived one, in

Maserati as well. In France, Chrysler owned Simca, and the hallowed name of Panhard—long a Citroën subsidiary—was reserved for specialist military vehicles since its cars and trucks had disappeared in 1967. In Germany, the struggles of the great independent, Carl Borgward, came to a bankrupt end in 1961. The closely linked Mercedes-Benz and VW empires now owned not only Auto Union (Audi) but NSU as well. Japanese mergers ran through the 1960s with the frantic aura of a speeded-up movie: thirteen separate firms were building cars in 1959, yet there were just eight in 1969 despite the successful intrusion of Soichiro Honda, a motorcycle magnate who achieved what the Kaiser millions had failed to do in America during our first decade.

Even where survival was permitted, the badge-engineer took his pound of flesh. This pernicious craft had its origins in a desire for greater coverage of dealers, as well as in cutting costs. Canadian Plymouths with Dodge or De Soto badges were a phenomenon from the 1930s, joined immediately after the war by Ford's Meteor (a Mercury for Ford dealers) and Monarch (a Ford for Lincoln-Mercury dealers). In New Zealand, Rootes invented the Humber Ten, a deluxe Hillman Minx, to gain a second import quota. At the level of sentiment, there were the incomprehensible permutations of Daimlers, Lanchesters, and BSAs in the middle thirties. Once again, a difference in name did not always mean a different product.

The disease was, perhaps, less prevalent at the beginning of our period. Engine and body rationalizations by General Motors and Chrysler in the U.S.A. were still aimed at preserving a fair degree of brand-identity, and GM's divisions still had their independent design offices even in 1969. Individual makes within the British Motor Corporation remained easily recognizable, although several of these shared the same engine by Austin, whose own interests were firmly in control of the old Nuffield Organisation by 1955. But the 1960s proved that uniformity had taken over. In England alone, Alec Issigonis' front-wheel-drive 1100 came with five different badges, the compact Jaguar sedan was also a Daimler, and the latest four-door sedan by Rootes—a lineal descendant of the Hillman Minx—could be bought as a Hillman, Humber, or Singer. To top it off, the little rear-engined Imp, while beneath the dignity of a Humber label, was considered sporting enough to be a Sunbeam on occasion.

Chapter 2

POWER ASSISTANCE FOR

EVERYTHING

The twenty years from 1951 to 1969 witnessed a vast explosion in the automobile business. World production rose from a mere 6,858,000 in 1951 to nearly thirteen million in 1960, and to a staggering 22,752,363 in 1969. Of these, over ninety per cent came from the factories of the top twenty companies, headed by General Motors and Ford in America, and by Volkswagen in Germany. Eleven manufacturers or groups reached the half-million mark, and another thirteen turned out at least 200,000 cars each. The simultaneous contraction in the number of makers and their offerings is almost as impressive. An absence of measurable falls in the U.S.A. and Britain is explained by the advent of the smaller specialists during the 1960s, which actually left Italy with thirteen firms rather than the nine she had in 1951. But in Germany and France, where the economic climate did not favour such operations, the field of producers shrank respectively from 17 to 7, and from 16 to 9.

Range structures also altered. With second-division competitors either falling out or being taken over, a major manufacturer had to widen the scope of his offerings. General Motors, leading America and the world throughout our period, listed seven makes and thirteen basic models in 1951, yet doubled the latter figure by 1960 and again by 1969. In 1951, there was one basic model of Chevrolet—and also of Vauxhall, though this came with an engine choice of four or six cylinders—whereas 1969 saw eight Chevrolets with nine alternative power units of four possible configurations: in-line four, in-line or flat six, and V-8. Capacities varied from 2.5 up to 7 litres.

To be sure, this trend was not consistent or universal. In Britain, the 1951 merger of Austin and Nuffield sparked off a great process of rationalization, a word in neither partner's vocabulary until then. At the time of fusion, their ranges ran to eighteen models, fourteen "chassis" including some unitary types, and fourteen engine variations, with badge-engineering confined to Morris and Wolseley sixes. Admittedly, there were three more models in 1960, but the new front-wheel-drive Mini had been badge-engineered into identical twins from Morris and Austin. The entire 1.5-litre sedan range had received similar, indeed more complex, treatment—further confused by the use of two separate chassis/body structures, one originating from Austin and the other from Nuffield. While engines differed in capacity, these consisted essentially of straightforward pushrod types, two with four cylinders and two with six. By the end of the 1960s, the process was brought to a successful conclusion. Its total of twenty-six models is less puzzling when we note that four were Minis, six belonged to the 1100/1300 family, three were

the bigger front-drive 1800s, and even the cheap Austin-Healey Sprite sports two-seater had an *alter ego* with the octagonal MG emblem.

Others were content to make what they could sell, forgetting the general-provider role. Renault of France, ranking sixth among the world's producers in 1966 and eighth in 1969, went through both our decades with just seven models, none of which ran for less than eight years, and all but two becoming million-sellers. Volkswagen built only air-cooled, rear-engine, flat-four cars from start to finish, although such a narrow policy was arguably hazardous: partly because the VW 1600, that "better Beetle" of 1961, did not represent the improvement it should have been, and partly because overall design concepts were already swinging away from rear engines. VW were also very late with the adoption of disc brakes—hence 1967 would see a 7.5% fall in their turnover, and a more alarming 16% drop in their export figures.

The VW situation highlights the grave dilemma confronting the car maker. Should he create a classic design and run it for twenty years for the sake of amortization, even at the risk of losing customers? Or should he swing into line with fashion, maybe too late, and then be stuck with the wrong design? Occasionally a latecomer succeeded: Chevrolet's Camaro pony-car arrived nearly three years after the Ford Mustang but soon caught up. By contrast, a promising contender from Rootes, the Hillman Imp, took an unconscionable time to develop, and was unveiled in 1963 only to find that BMC's Mini had cornered the market as well as setting the pattern for what would follow. That Minis outsold Imps by ten to one was not the real catastrophe, since Rootes lacked the production capacity of BMC even before the big Leyland merger. What did matter was that the whole Imp concept had become obsolescent by 1963, and totally obsolete by the time the countless teething troubles had been ironed out. Yet to have postponed the introduction still further in the cause of reliability would have guaranteed a failure. One cannot say categorically that the Imp killed Rootes, but it did drive them into the arms of the Chrysler Corporation, landing this empire with a headache instead of a healthy British outlet.

Here we also approach the vital technical issue of our second decade—where to put the works. This had never been a vexed question before World War II. Rear-engined cars were in the minority ever since the Panhard layout overwhelmed Karl Benz's philosophies back in 1899, while front-wheel drive had few adherents even in 1951. Of these, the British Bond was a cyclecar and not to be taken seriously, although the Citroën *traction* had found enough time since 1934 to eliminate bugs and train garage mechanics to cope with its idiosyncrasies. Panhard's

"We dig the Beetle", though in fact only 114,348 citizens worldwide did so in 1952, when this sedan (*left*) was made. Still, the next best-selling German car was Opel's Olympia, with less than 44,000 customers. Seen through modern eyes, the 1952 car appears austere and claustrophobic: on 1,131 cc and 25 horsepower, neither maximum nor cruising speeds were much in excess of 62 mph (100 km/h). Hydraulic brakes were listed on the "export" model from May, 1950, but this car won't have synchromesh unless it was made after September, 1952. By 1968, the 1600 TL (*top right*) retained the Beetle's basic and by now outmoded engineering, but capacity and output are up, respectively, to 1,584 cc and 54 horsepower, all four gears are synchronized, the front brakes are discs, and options include a three-speed semi-automatic transmission and fuel injection. This "better Beetle", stemming from 1961's model 1500, never really took the old car's place. Sales in 1968 were nearly 1,200,000 of the traditional series, but only 237, 617 of the 1500/1600 family.

(*Centre right*) The ageless shape—this Porsche dates from 1958, but it could easily be any year from the early fifties to 1965: the 356 series changed so little outwardly. Here was a car that took some learning, yet cornered 10 % faster than any of its rivals, could survive alarming accidents, and used less fuel than most of the opposition. Your 1958 car retained drum brakes, of course, but could be had with its VW-inspired 1.6-litre flat-four engine in two stages of tune: respective top speeds were 100 mph (160 km/h) and 109 mph (175 km/h). Nor were Porsches impossibly expensive—DM 12,700 in Germany, £1,996 in Britain, and 15,950 francs in Switzerland.

(*Bottom right*) By 1965, one would not think of launching an all-new 1,500-cc family car without front disc brakes, though one might offer a cut-price edition without them. Auto Union, however, fitted them to each and every Audi, all cars having pushrod four-cylinder engines driving the front wheels, and torsion-bar rear suspension. Maybe the choice of name was unfortunate (the original front-drive Audi Six of 1933–38 had been an expensive flop) but the new car caught on well, to the tune of 63,000 sales in its first full calendar year—and it was a timely replacement for the traditional two-stroke DKW, increasingly a victim of tougher exhaust emission standards. And if the first 1.5-litre Audis were a trifle lacking in power, this was rectified when the 1,696-cc version became available late in 1966. Note the *Vier Ringe* badge commemorating the four component companies of the original Auto Union combine—Audi, DKW, Horch, and Wanderer. Only the two former makes would survive World War II, though the Horch name was used briefly on cars (and trucks) in East Germany.

The original DKW-Front light car of 1931 had an east-west engine driving the front wheels, and so did its countless post-war descendants in several countries. Typical was the Bremen-built Lloyd minicar (*photo page 218*): seen here, in 400-cc form of 1953, is the power pack complete with transverse-leaf independent front suspension (*right*). With only two cylinders, of course, one could mount the transmission alongside the motor. Unfortunately, when makers of such cars (DKW in West Germany, IFA in East Germany, Saab in Sweden) wanted more power, they added an extra cylinder, and were forced to adopt a longitudinal mounting. The 1-litre engine from the 1966 East German Wartburg (*below*) was set well over the wheel centres with its four-speed gearbox behind (*see ill. page 141*).

(*Opposite*) Saving space with front-wheel drive. (**A**) The four-cylinder Volvo 122, a conventional rear-drive 1.8-litre family sedan of 1962, is 4.45 m (175 in) long, with plenty of legroom thanks to the hypoid rear axle,

but the propeller shaft still has to go under the passenger compartment. On the 1.9-litre 11CV Citroën *traction* in its 1934–52 form (**B**), the main advantages of front-wheel drive are a low centre of gravity and good handling. It is only fractionally shorter than the Volvo, is barely a five-seater, and has about half the Swedish car's luggage accommodation. The forward-mounted transmission is a splendid space-consumer. Renault's 16 of 1965 (**C**) still wears its gearbox in front of the 1.5-litre in-line engine, but the power pack is much further aft than on the Citroën, and the new hatchback body turns it into a useful load-carrier. A British contemporary of the Renault, the Triumph 1300 (**D**), is an altogether smaller four-seater with 1,296 cc, 3.95 m (156 in) long—but while a longitudinal engine is retained, the gearbox is mounted in the sump, Mini-fashion. Finally the classic BMC/Issigonis formula in 1962 guise as the Morris 1100 (**E**): east-west engine, gearbox in the sump, and the majority of its 3.68 m (145 in) length devoted to passengers and their baggage.

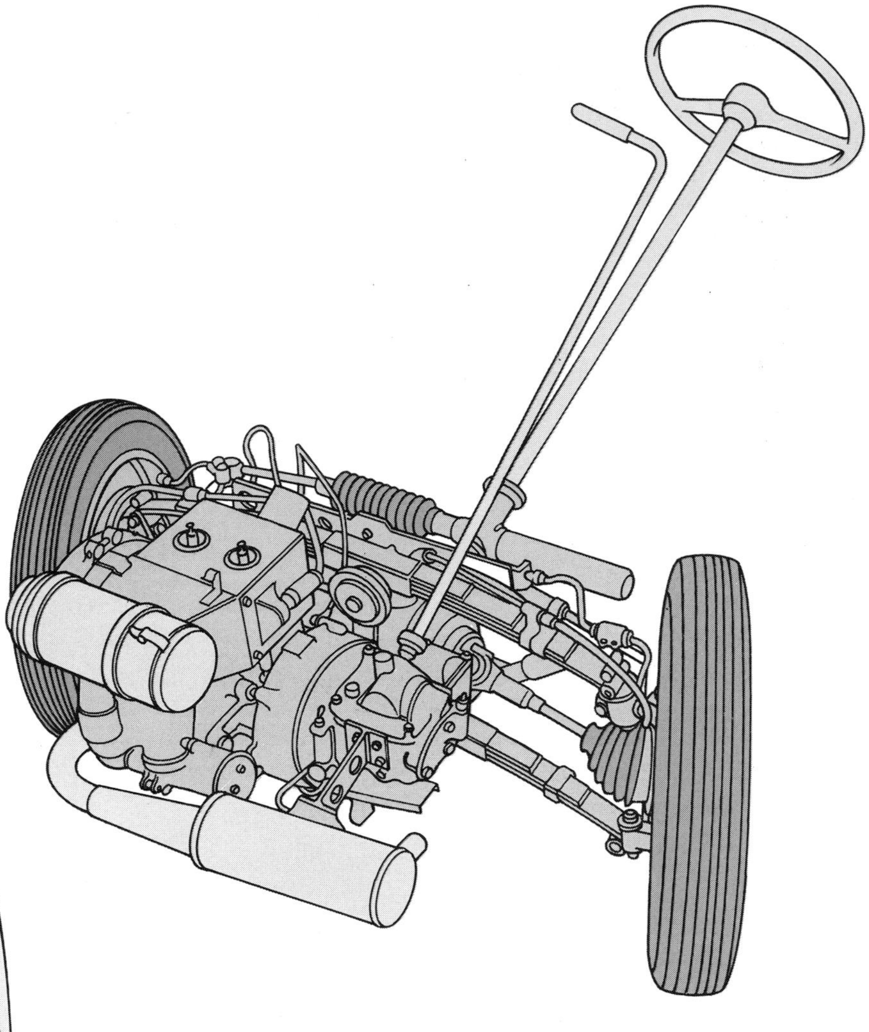

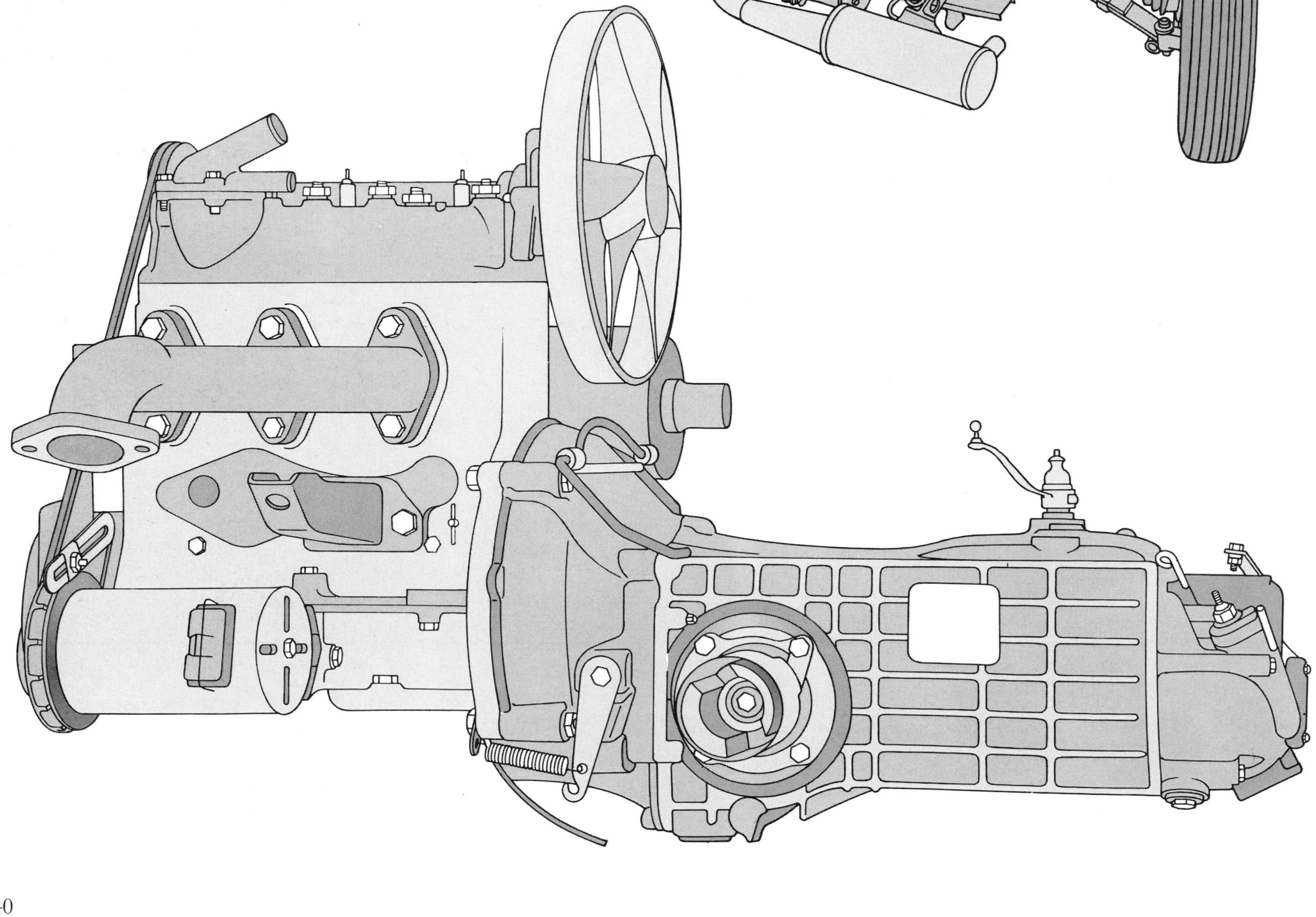

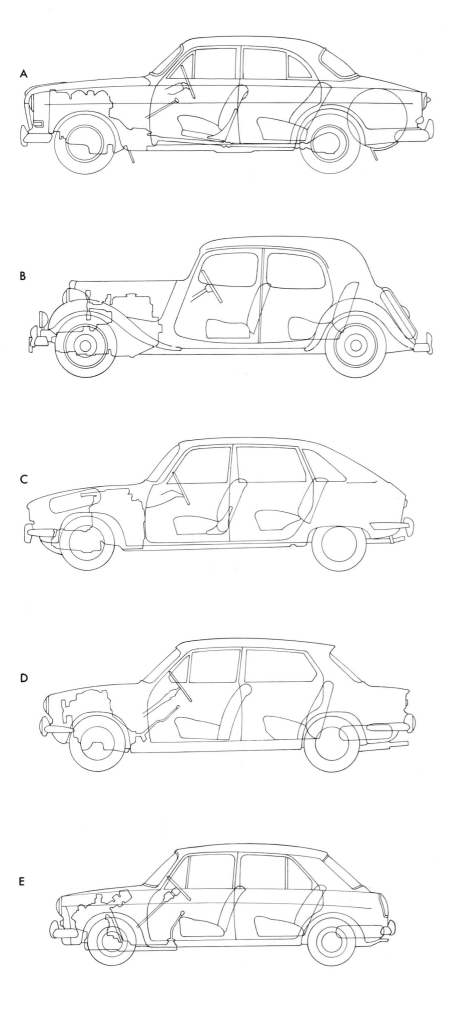

flat-twins, inspired by Grégoire, were newcomers and reached full production status during 1948. The Grégoire had already seen a somewhat chequered and obscure history as a proposed "people's car", with which other French, Belgian, British, and Australian sponsors had toyed.

As for the rest—the DKWs, Goliaths, and Lloyds of West Germany, the IFAs from the Democratic Republic, the Swedish Saab, the Aero Minor from Czechoslovakia, and the obsolescent Eucort from Spain—all were direct descendants of the transverse-engined DKW-Front theme first seen at the 1931 Berlin Show. Such advocates of front-wheel drive were old hands at the game, apart from Panhard whose model had a less than rapturous reception. Fast it certainly was, streets ahead in performance when compared to other miniatures. It handled well, and could win rallies: but it was rough, noisy, fragile, and cursed with a reputation for selecting two gears at once. To the end of its days, it would remain an enthusiast's car rather than a hack for the masses. Rear-engine supporters were even fewer, although two of their number, Renault's 4CV and the Volkswagen, were best-sellers. The only other serious contender, the Czechoslovak 2-litre flat-four Tatraplan, was produced chiefly for that country's Communist bureaucracy, some being sold in the West too.

The argument against the *système* Panhard, with its front-mounted engine driving the rear wheels, was that it wasted space. In addition to the assortment of mechanical elements at both ends, a propeller shaft ran down the centreline of the vehicle and intruded into the passenger compartment. Transaxles, on which the gearbox was combined with the differential, got rid of the gearbox hump but not the drive-shaft. The shaft might, of course, be made to earn its prominence by forming part of a backbone frame, as on some Mercedes-Benz and Lotus models. From the servicing standpoint, a complete overhaul meant a total stripdown, whereas with alternative arrangements the power unit could be removed and the remainder left undisturbed. Thus, by unbolting the front "horns" on a Citroën, the engine, transmission, and front end could be wheeled away. Yet this looked too simple in contemporary technical illustrations: the trouble was that, if you didn't want to take the whole lot off, the Citroën was not an easy car to work on. Nor, for that matter, was the rear-engined VW, with a flat-four engine set low and two sparking plugs awkward to reach.

Front-wheel drive as comprehended in the early 1950s did not economize particularly on space, either. The original DKW with transversely mounted engine was an exception, but more than two cylinders could not be set athwart the frame. When DKW and their disciples began the change to threes in 1950, a longitudinal arrangement had to be adopted, reviving the old problem. If you put the gearbox in front of the engine, it gives you plenty of legroom at the price of an extremely vulnerable power unit (a head-on collision means scrapping the car) and also of excessive length. The conventional 2-litre Standard Vanguard, a full six-seater, was 164 in (4.65 m) long, whereas Citroën's 11 Légère—admittedly a much older design—came out 9 in (23 cm) longer and sat five at a pinch, even if it looked every bit a car and its lower centre of gravity gave it the handling which the Vanguard signally lacked. The 2CV Citroën, with abbreviated flat-twin motor, measured 149 in (3.79 m) from stem to stern, taking up more parking space than did 800-cc conventionals like the Austin A30.

Equally endemic to such layouts were a wide turning radius and complex gear-shift linkages. The dashboard changes of both DKW and Citroën were confusing, although neither breed had as yet essayed a four-speed box. Memories of early front-wheel drives, such as the 1929 Cord, reappeared with headaches of weight transference and the big car's reluctance to re-start on hills. Further, outside Germany and

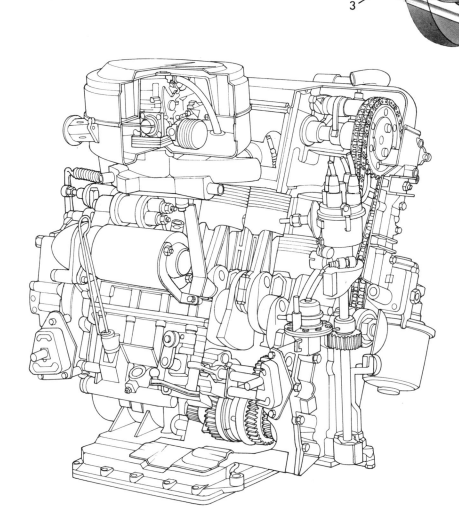

The Mini theme enlarged and developed on the French Peugeot 204, introduced in the summer of 1965 and destined to sell over 1,600,000 units in petrol- (and subsequent diesel-) powered versions. There were a coupé, a convertible, a station wagon, and a panel van, as well as the sedan shown in cutaway form (*above*). It was a bigger car than either Mini or 1100, with a 102-in (2.6-m) wheelbase, a length of 157 in (4 m), and a dry weight of 1,775 lb (805 kg). Seen here are the east-west engine of die-cast aluminium (*1*), the rack-and-pinion steering gear (*2*), front suspension (*3*) by McPherson struts and coils, and rear suspension (*4*) by coils and trailing arms, the latter pivoting on a tubular cross member. (*Left*) The 1,130-cc

overhead-camshaft engine is mounted at a 20-degree slant. The carburettor (at top) is enclosed within its air-cleaner to keep hood height down (a problem when the transmission is mounted underneath), and the robust five-bearing camshaft typifies 1960s practice even if it is still chain-driven. (*Top right*) A simplified diagram of the drive line, very much in the Mini idiom, shows the clutch output shaft running coaxially with the crankshaft, and in direct mesh with the gears on the primary drive of the four-speed all-synchromesh transmission. In the final drive unit (*bottom right*), there are double joints (*1*) at the outer ends to give a good steering lock, and constant-velocity inner joints (*2*).

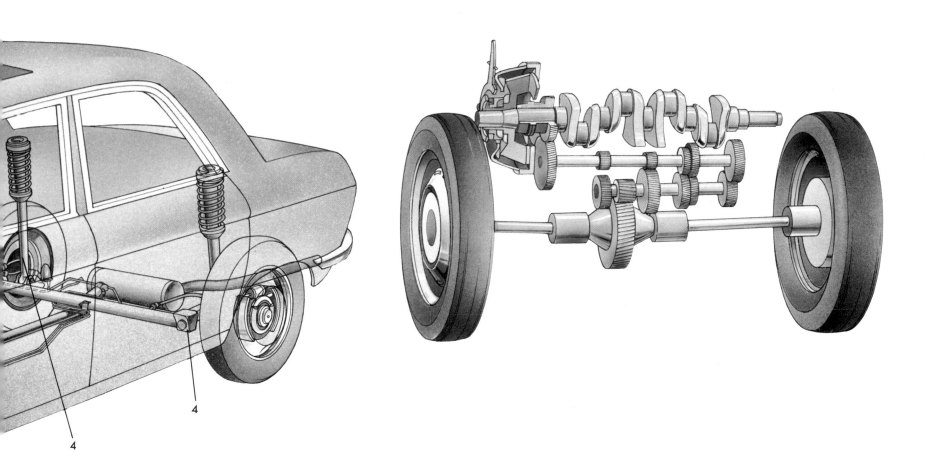

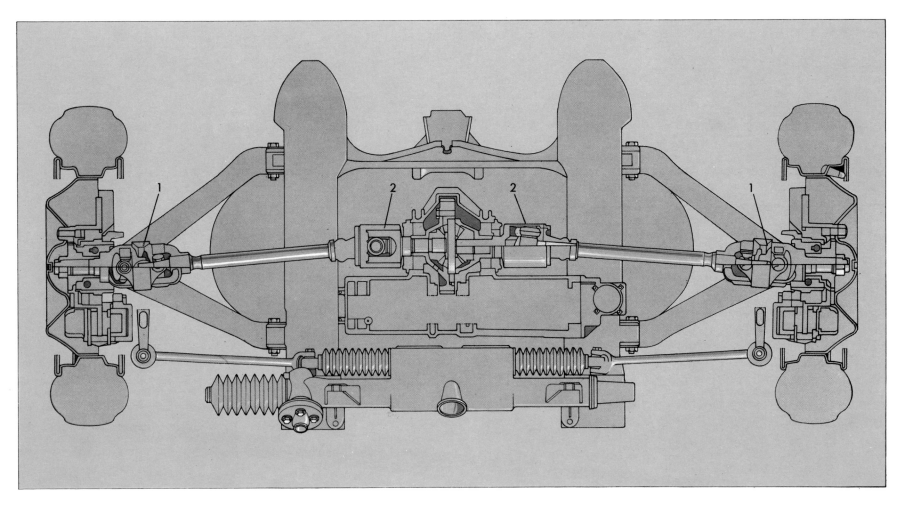

France, and their most consistent export markets, the public was not educated in techniques of driving with front-wheel drive. Another difficulty, associated specifically with the combination of two-stroke engines and driven front wheels, was that type of motor's tendency to "snatch": DKW and Saab incorporated free wheels into their transmissions as a palliative, which also gave the engine adequate lubrication on long downhill stretches. Understandably, then, front-wheel drive attracted few important recruits to its cause during most of the 1950s. No matter how revolutionary was Citroën's brilliant Déesse of 1955—it will crop up frequently in our story—it added nothing to this branch of the art, while Britain's Berkeley, a miniature sports car launched in 1956, was primarily an exercise in glass-fibre unitary construction.

The real breakthrough came in 1959 with Alec Issigonis' BMC Mini, which licked nearly all the bogeys of front-wheel drive at one fell swoop. It was more than just the original DKW theme brought up to date. By combining a transverse engine mounting with a gearbox built into the sump—and with a proper floor change as well—two extra cylinders could be added with no increase in length. The transmission was now farther away from the accident-prone front end than it had been on Citroëns, and the result was a full four-seater, 120 in (3.05 m) long, 55 in (1.40 m) wide, and 52 in (1.32 m) high. There was still room for some luggage, while such compact dimensions made the Mini ideal transportation in congested cities. A simple springing system with rubber in torsion as the medium gave a good ride, and the vexed question of steering lock was resolved by using wheels of a mere 10 in (25 cm) diameter. One certainly paid for this in terms of tyre scrub and heavier wear, but these factors were peculiar to tight-turning vehicles regardless of their drive arrangements: the conventionally-engineered Triumph Herald's famed "U-turn", appealing to housewives in virtually every English-speaking country, was no party-trick to be indulged by those who could not afford new tyres! Above all, the Mini was among the most forgiving cars to drive. One could even lift one's foot with impunity on the apex of a corner, something not recommended on any Saab or Citroën, and unwise even on the later 128 Fiat which incorporated many of the Mini's principles.

Others were quick to follow, notably Fiat with the Autobianchi Primula (1965) and Peugeot with the 204. Honda updated the old DKW transverse-twin theme in 1968, although using a four-stroke overhead-camshaft engine. Lancia's 1961 Flavia, a revival of the abortive 1948 Cemsa-Caproni, saved space with a conventionally located flat-four, while Ford of Germany produced a longitudinal V-4, this engine being adopted by Saab as well for 1967. BMC themselves progressively widened their range, continuing the Mini theme: the four-door 1100 came in 1962, and the roomy 1800 sedans in 1964. In 1969, their Australian branch managed to squeeze an in-line six across the front, although this did not reach Europe until 1972 and was never an unqualified success.

Longitudinal in-line engines still had some following, as being less complicated to service. The Renault 4, small and austere, appeared in 1961: like the later 16 (1965) and 12 (1969), it housed the gearbox ahead of the engine and managed to avoid extra length. But not until the end of our second decade did that firm combine front-wheel drive with a reasonably positive floor shift. Triumph on the 1300 (1965), and Saab on the 99 announced two years later, circumvented the gearbox problem by choosing a location below the clutch/flywheel assembly—the drive was taken forward beneath the block, with an integral output shaft in the final drive assembly. This cut down excessive length, but gave a more positive gear change than on other longitudinal layouts. On the 1.7-litre Audi (1965), Auto Union hung the engine well over the front axle centreline, with the gearbox behind.

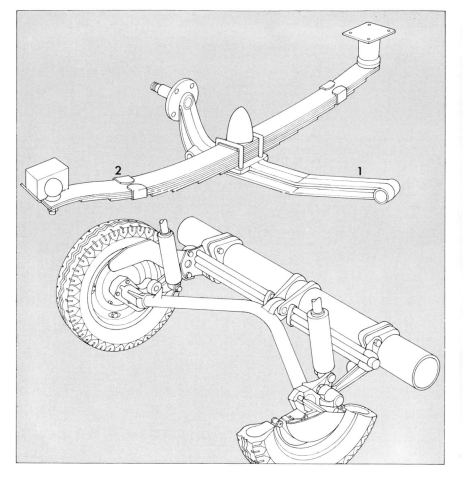

Really big cars with front-wheel drive had never quite succeeded. The 2-litre Citroën Déesse family as yet seemed to represent the limit of size. A predecessor, the 2.9-litre 15 with six cylinders (1939–55), had been too long in relation to its carrying capacity. It also suffered from punitively heavy steering at parking speeds, and a turning circle that would not have shamed a bus. Thus, in its later years, it tended to be the choice of vintage enthusiasts rather than family men. America, however, tackled front-wheel drive with a vengeance. Power steering and automatic transmissions were used to circumvent the problem of heavy controls. Further, there was a novel space-saving device on Oldsmobile's 1966 Toronado coupé, first of the new breed. A chain primary drive linked the V-8 engine with an automatic gearbox, mounted alongside the crankcase. The rest of the driveline was orthodox enough, but such a layout was viable only where overall dimensions were of secondary importance. In the Toronado's case, "short" was a relative term. Styling considerations alone dictated a formidable overhang at either end. Still, at a length of 211 in (5.36 m), it was 12 in (30 cm) shorter than a comparable rear-drive four-door sedan.

By 1969, designs with front-wheel drive had spread across the world. Major adherents included Audi, Ford, and NSU in Germany; Austin, Morris, and Triumph in Britain; Autobianchi, Fiat, Innocenti, and Lancia in Italy; Saab in Sweden; Peugeot, Renault, Simca in France; Cadillac and Oldsmobile in the U.S.A.; Honda and Subaru in Japan; and a few central European DKW-hangovers such as the Polish Syrena and the East German Wartburg and Trabant. NSU's marriage of the compact Wankel rotary-piston engine, front-wheel drive, and a semi-automatic transmission seemed to be an augury for the future. Two of these manufacturers, NSU and Renault, were recent converts from rear engines, while Fiat and Simca kept a foot in both camps. It was not lost

(*Opposite*) On front-wheel-drive cars, the rear end presents little problem, and some smaller and cheaper cars were simple in the extreme. Here are two from the late 1950s. On the German Lloyd Alexander (*top*), we see a combination of swinging half axles (*1*) and longitudinal semi-elliptic springs (*2*), the latter on rubber mounts. By contrast, the French Dyna-Panhard (*bottom*) prefers Citroën-type torsion bars as the springing medium, the wheels being supported on a curved dead axle. Both cars were powered by air-cooled twin-cylinder engines, the Panhard's—at 850 cc—being appreciably bigger than the Lloyd's 600-cc unit. The German designer, however, preferred a vertical layout with chain-driven overhead camshaft, whereas the Panhard's cylinders were horizontally opposed with pushrod-operated overhead valves.

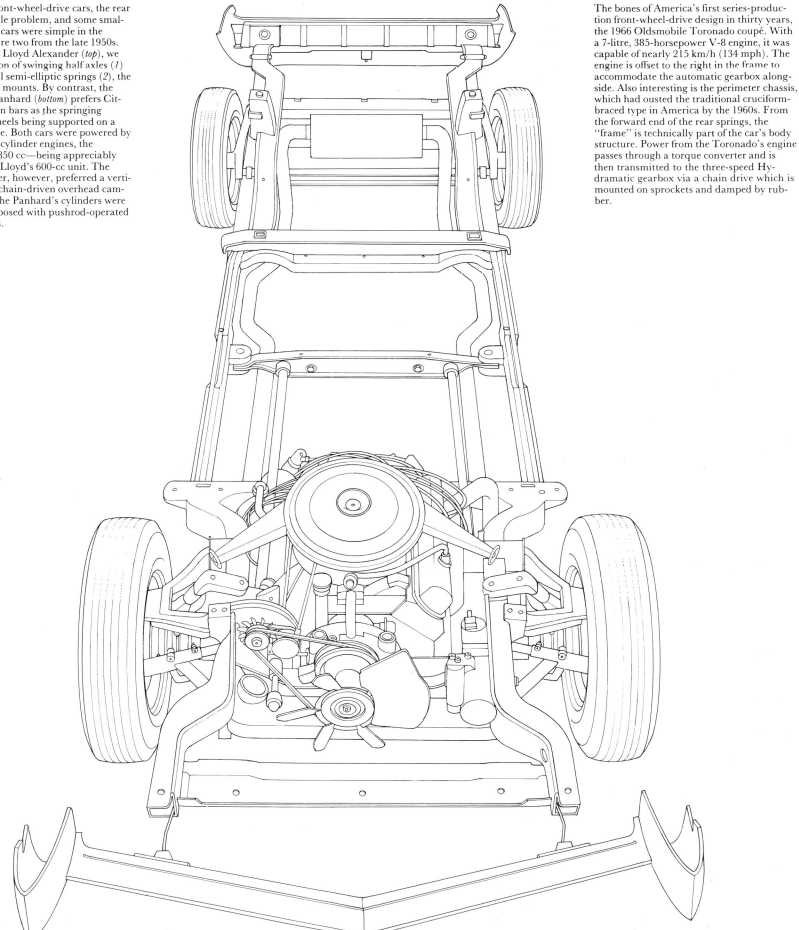

The bones of America's first series-production front-wheel-drive design in thirty years, the 1966 Oldsmobile Toronado coupé. With a 7-litre, 385-horsepower V-8 engine, it was capable of nearly 215 km/h (134 mph). The engine is offset to the right in the frame to accommodate the automatic gearbox alongside. Also interesting is the perimeter chassis, which had ousted the traditional cruciform-braced type in America by the 1960s. From the forward end of the rear springs, the "frame" is technically part of the car's body structure. Power from the Toronado's engine passes through a torque converter and is then transmitted to the three-speed Hydramatic gearbox via a chain drive which is mounted on sprockets and damped by rubber.

(*Left*) Ideally a Mini should be photographed squeezing its way into a narrow slot between two Mercedes-Benz or Cadillacs. The grille pattern identifies this 1964 car as Morris rather than Austin, though this does not necessarily guarantee manufacture at the Oxford factory. The price paid for compact design was, of course, austere furnishings, sliding windows, door pulls resembling cheap clothes-line, and poor luggage accommodation, not to mention "dentist-drill" vibration when the engine was working hard in the indirect gears. But the result was safe, stable, and very forgiving.

(*Right*) There's no denying the compact functional appearance of the British Motor Corporation's ADO (for Austin Design Office) 16 theme, better known as the BMC 1100, with its interlinked Hydrolastic suspension and east-west engine driving the front wheels. Front disc brakes, too, were advanced on a small, cheap family sedan in 1962. In an eleven-year run, the firm sold a lot of cars, which included some 143,000 MGs that never knew Abingdon. MG customers got an extra carburettor (though not with the later 1300 engine), more speed, acceleration, and noise, a walnut facia, and usually (though not in this case) two-tone paintwork. Permutations were complex: on a left-hand-drive export 1100 (this one dates from 1966) you could have two doors or four, but Britons had to wait till 1967 and the bigger engine if they wanted the former layout!

Two cases of designs too late from Chrysler in Europe, though in fact the empire inherited ready-created designs from Rootes (*top*) and Simca (*bottom*). The Hillman Imp, here seen in 1965 form, was the cleverer of the two, with ingenious rear hatch and slanted 875-cc overhead-camshaft four-cylinder engine to Coventry-Climax design. But the original pneumatic throttle linkage gave much trouble, and a long teething period encouraged people to forget the better-than-usual handling and the superb, unbeatable synchromesh. Chrysler gave it up after thirteen years, during which sales failed to achieve the half-million level, even with the addition of badge-engineered Singer and Sunbeam variants. In France, however, they persevered with the Simca 1000 family (this is a 1970), unloading over one and a half million cars between 1962 and 1978. Like the Hillman, it had all-drum brakes in early days: unlike the Hillman, it had acquired front discs by the end of our period. Nobody liked its handling characteristics, but its fuel economy matched the Imp's, and the four doors helped sales along. Simca's technical links with Fiat are reflected in the fact that during the 1960s they tried the *système* Panhard, rear engines, and (from 1968) front-wheel drive as well.

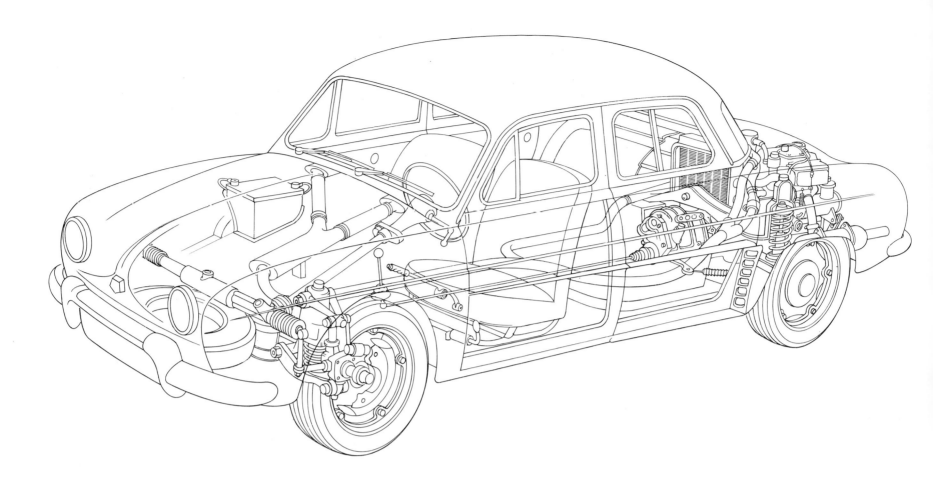

on anyone that few all-new rear-engined designs were making their appearance. There were still some best-sellers in their ranks—the evergreen VW Beetle, the Renault 8/10 family, and Fiat's 600 and 850—but the Beetle itself was old hat. Improved water-cooling systems diminished the attractions of its own frost-proof engine. On other models, maximum speed (and a higher one at that) was also cruising speed, and low drag no longer called for a teardrop shape with poor headroom and all-round visibility.

Rear-engined cars were space-savers only to the extent that they occupied less room. Further, like the swing-axle suspension system, the layout's inferiority was highlighted when made to transmit more power. One might dismiss oversteer and rear-end breakaway as mere quirks of the 1946 Renault 4CV with 19 horsepower, or of the early VW with a 25-horsepower engine. But the hotter editions of Renault's later Dauphine could be hair-raising in such circumstances, and not averse to becoming airborne in a cross-wind. As power increased, Volkswagen were finally forced to redesign their suspension in 1970, while Porsche's admirable 356 sports car, current until 1965, was a tricky beast to drive. In the right hands, it sailed through corners a good 10 mph (16 km/h) faster than the opposition. The unskilled did not always live to tell the tale. Rear-end breakaway, said to be terrifying on the big Tatra, plus extreme sensitivity to cross-winds and tyre pressures: this was a disconcerting picture, to be expected with front/rear weight distributions as unequal as 38/62%. The Hillman Imp, generally a stabler car than either Beetle or Dauphine, could do alarming things on a wet road if the tyre pressures were raised (obeying the instruction manual) for fast driving.

Gear linkages were as remote, if not remoter, than on cars with front-wheel drive, and some were horribly inexact although the Porsche and Hillman provided honourable exceptions. The problem of rearward

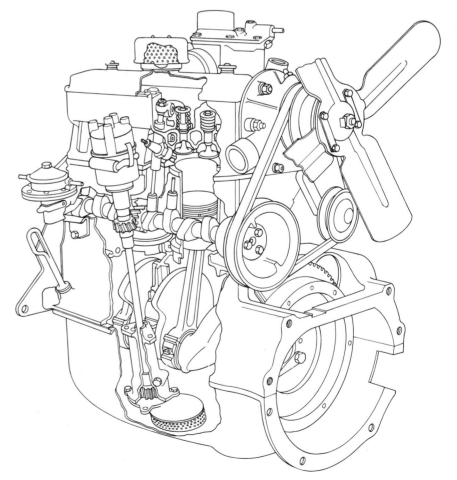

vision, an early bugbear, was averted in the Hillman only by a slanted engine mounting. There were other warring elements. Among the rear-engined car's great theoretical advantages was that, with no mechanical elements up front, it was possible to have a short slanting nose and, consequently, maximum forward vision. But the public wanted a car to look like a car, and the short nose offered room for little more than a spare wheel. On Fiat's delightful 850 coupé (1965), if the rear seats were occupied, one put the baggage items on the rear window ledge—which blocked rearward vision—or squeezed them under the shallow "bonnet". It was thus understandable that, once the Mini had shown the way, others would fall into line.

Perhaps significantly, apart from the Tatra and Chevrolet Corvair, all the major rear-engined contenders were in the up-to-1,300-cc class, although VW finally worked their design to the 2-litre level and the specialist Porsche, in its ultimate form beyond our period, ran to over 3 litres. The minicars may typify the ideal application of rear-engine design, since few of these were meant to carry more than two people, and even fewer had sustained cruising speeds of above 50 mph (80 km/h). Renault would persevere with the layout right through to the early 1970s, achieving Europe's first two-million seller with the Dauphine (1956–68). Next into the game was Fiat's Dante Giacosa, who chose a rear engine as the only means of shoehorning four people into a car smaller than the legendary *topolino* of 1936, while still holding capacity down to 633 cc. This target was achieved by the suppression of water passages between the two rear cylinders and a lateral radiator. A lack of overhang ensured good handling, but there was never much room for luggage. The Fiat range was later extended to include the six-seater

Multipla (so beloved of Italian cabbies), the yet smaller air-cooled twin-cylinder 500, and the sports 850s of the later 1960s.

The German BMW and NSU belong properly to the ranks of the minicars, even if the latter firm worked up to 1.2 litres and four air-cooled cylinders in their later efforts. This left only three major recruits to the theme during the sixties—Hillman with the Imp, Simca with the four-door 1000 in 1961, and Skoda's 1000 series starting, like the Hillman, in 1963. This last wore its four-cylinder engine longitudinally over a swing axle, a recipe for very peculiar handling. Cheap and tough it might be, but its overall dimensions alone were a strong argument for front-wheel drive. Compared with the contemporary BMC 1100, the Skoda was 17 in (40 cm) longer, 4 in (10 cm) wider, and 1 in (2.5 cm) higher, while offering no more interior space.

What really killed rear-engined cars, however, was Ralph Nader's one-man campaign in America against the "sporty Corvair", which he termed "unsafe at any speed". Chevrolet's 1960 contender in the compact-car stakes can best be described as an overgrown Volkswagen with a fully unitary hull, and six opposed cylinders instead of four. It had all the rear-engine characteristics, but was not as unsafe as its detractors insisted, especially since its maximum speed was a modest 85 mph (136 km/h), illegal anywhere in the United States. The Corvair's fault was that it possessed handling features unfamiliar to a generation of motorists nurtured on the American stereotype—the *système* Panhard with an orthodox weight distribution. Given the indifferent brakes of the period, and the fashionable automatic option of two-speed Powerglide on which low gear could only be engaged at 50 mph (80 km/h) or less, the car was too easy for the inexperienced to "lose".

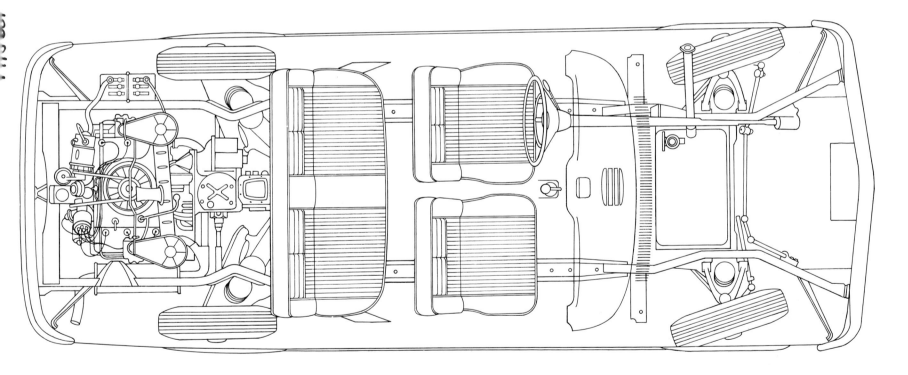

Studies in rear-engined cars. (*Opposite, top*) The Renault Dauphine was current from 1956 to 1968 and was France's first two-million seller. Its engineering was based on the earlier 4CV of 1946, with an 845-cc overhead-valve four-cylinder engine transmitting its power via a three- (later four-) speed gearbox, all-independent springing, and rack-

and-pinion steering. Latter-day Dauphines had all-disc brakes, too, though this early car has drums. The engine (*below*) typifies small-car practice in the 1950s and early 1960s: pushrod-operated overhead valves, two valves per cylinder, and three main bearings where one would expect five in ensuing decades.

(*Above*) A plan view of the controversial 1960 Chevrolet Corvair shows all-independent suspension and a 2.3-litre flat-six engine driving forward to a transaxle (three- or four-speed manual, or two-speed automatic). "Rear engine design," said the catalogue, "puts more of Corvair's weight over the rear wheels, offers superior traction on all sur-

faces". The first half of the quote was true, to the tune of some 63 %, but this was the car against which crusading attorney Ralph Nader directed most of his invective.

Essentially a 1970s phenomenon was the mid-engine layout. This had become general practice on Formula I racing cars by 1961, and had been applied to a roadgoing sports car, the Italian ATS coupé, as early as 1962. By placing the engine well forward of the rear axle centreline, and inside the body, designers could not only reduce drag but also improve front/rear weight distribution. One may simply compare the 41/59% of a 1960s Beetle with the more balanced 46/54% of the 1967 Lotus Europa, among the few such cars to appear during our period. Others were the De Tomaso Mangusta, the Lamborghini Miura, Ferrari's first "small" car, the Dino (1968), and the French Matra M530 with V-4 Ford engine. For obvious reasons, mid-engine machinery was confined to sports models. There was room for at most two people, luggage space was limited and of awkward shape, and—with the engine just behind the cockpit—noise levels were likely to be high. This last factor was compounded by the final switch from open to closed sports-car bodywork, which coincided with the advent of the new configuration.

Nonetheless, the *système* Panhard was still firmly entrenched in 1969. Although General Motors continued to turn out their last Corvairs and offered a couple of "specialty cars" with front-wheel drive, they and the majority of their rivals were not yet ready for change. Nor, in principle, were the Japanese, the overseas branches of GM and Ford (the front-wheel-drive Taunus from Germany was on its way out), and such up-market makers as Alfa Romeo, Mercedes-Benz, Rover, and Volvo. If Renault were totally committed to "works" at one end or the other, Fiat demurred. So, for that matter, did Leyland in Britain, whose big 3-litre married the latest in sophisticated suspensions to conventional rear-wheel drive. Further, Leyland were about to make amends for their frenetic badge-engineering by separating their advanced designs with front-wheel drive (henceforth to be Austins) from a more orthodox generation of Morrises. They had little option: in England, the most consistent best-seller of recent years had been not the Mini or the 1100, but the straightforward Ford Cortina, without an original thought in its conception, yet reliable and cheap to service.

(*Opposite*) NSU's return to car manufacture in 1958 was based on a range of fast but somewhat noisy sedans with rear-mounted, overhead-camshaft, air-cooled engines. From 1964, the original twins were joined by a line of aluminium-alloy fours, all with synchromesh gearboxes incorporating an overdrive top. This is the standard 1200, with 1,177-cc 60-horsepower engine as current from 1968 to 1973. But as much as 70 horsepower were extracted from the smaller-capacity TTS series, capable of 100 mph (160 km/h). Nor was safety neglected. High-performance NSUs came with front disc brakes as standard, and all the fours sold in Britain with right-hand drive had these.

(*Above*) Mid-engined weakness revealed, on the Lotus Europa coupé introduced in 1966. The hatch on the rear deck, admittedly, lifts off, and routine items such as carburettors, battery, and oil filler are quite easy to reach. The original version with pushrod Renault 16 engine did 115 mph (184 km/h), and accelerated to 60 mph (100 km/h) in around 10.4 seconds. The cutaway upper body sides, spider-type wheels, and twin fuel fillers, however, identify this car as a later (1971) example with the 1,558-cc twin overhead-camshaft Lotus-Ford unit. 9,230 Europas of all types were built, the last of them in 1975.

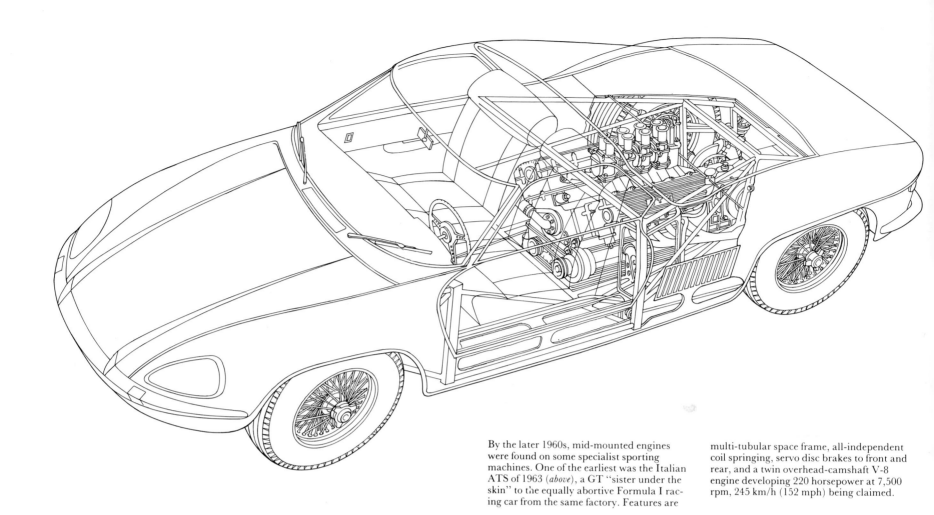

By the later 1960s, mid-mounted engines were found on some specialist sporting machines. One of the earliest was the Italian ATS of 1963 (*above*), a GT "sister under the skin" to the equally abortive Formula I racing car from the same factory. Features are multi-tubular space frame, all-independent coil springing, servo disc brakes to front and rear, and a twin overhead-camshaft V-8 engine developing 220 horsepower at 7,500 rpm, 245 km/h (152 mph) being claimed.

In 1951, to be sure, neither front-wheel drive nor rear engines represented mainstream thinking. We have already encountered specimens of that year's automobile: the stereotype remains to be examined. An average European model in the popular category of 1,100–1,600 cc would have a four-cylinder overhead-valve engine giving 40–48 horsepower at 4,000 rpm. It tended to have unitary construction, although some 25 % of the more important models retained a separate chassis—not so surprising when one reflects that less than half our sample was of truly post-war conception. Four forward speeds and column shift were in the majority, while a good 90 % featured synchromesh gearboxes even if none of them extended this refinement to bottom gear. Independent front suspension likewise commanded 90 % of the field (the Fords made up the balance), coils (59 %) taking precedence over torsion bars (23 %) and transverse-leaf arrangements (18 %). Beam rear axles were the rule, as were hydraulic brakes, the only exceptions being a few ancients with mechanical actuation and a couple of British models with the hydromechanical compromise, a dying legacy of the forties.

Few dramatic changes appear by 1960, but beam front axles have gone forever. The percentage of engines with oversquare dimensions has increased from 21 to 52, and their outputs are up, predictably, to a mean of 58 horsepower at 4,500 rpm. The in-line, pushrod engine predominates even in 1969, yet output rises again to an impressive 70 horsepower at 5,350 rpm. As for gearboxes, 65 % of the cars are back with floor change, 88 % have synchromesh on all four ratios, and no less than 47 % are available with automatic. Coil springing at the front is still a firm favourite (74 %) but the percentage of cars with independent rear suspension has grown in nine years from 12 to 41. Most

important of all, 71 % feature disc brakes on the front wheels, and 15 % have discs all round.

The American car continued to pursue its own isolationist course. The form for 1950–51 was essentially that of 1939, except for automatic transmission and the opening bars of that V-8 orchestra which was to reach its crescendo with 400 or more units of horsepower advertised under the bonnets of 1968's muscle-cars. Where V-8s were not yet available, engines were in-line sixes and eights with side valves. However, Buick, Chevrolet, and Nash wore their valves upstairs—and all but the cheapest models of Ford had a flathead V-8, as did Lincoln and Mercury. Six-volt electrics, obsolescent elsewhere, were still customary, and would remain so for another three years, Cadillac and Oldsmobile leading the changeover in 1953. Americans, like Europeans in general, preferred the simple mechanical fuel pump to the electric type. Manual gearboxes, where offered, were invariably three-speeders, and the gearshift was on the steering column. Suspension arrangements were, almost without exception, a combination of independent coils at the front and semi-elliptics at the rear, although Buick and Oldsmobile headed the list of those favouring coils—if not independence—all round. Nearly everyone used a separate chassis, brakes were hydraulic, and steering was as yet unassisted, with a predilection for worm-and-roller or recirculating-ball systems. Cruciform braced frames, still widely employed, would soon give way to the simpler perimeter type, except on convertibles.

How many cylinders? Singles and twins were the preserve of the minicar, but Citroën and Panhard offered full four-door sedans with air-cooled flat-twin engines. In Europe, the four continued to stay

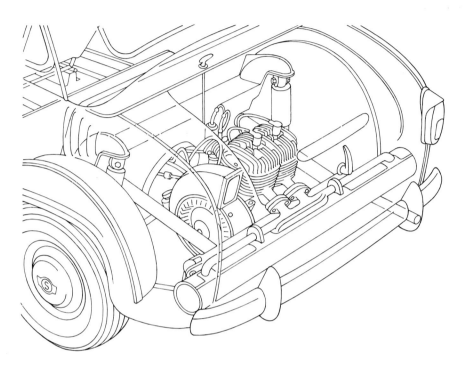

Horizontally opposed engines caused accessibility problems, especially with water-cooling, though on the Jowett Javelin of 1947–53 (*left*) the radiator was mounted behind. On this car, the side portions of the radiator grille were detachable, which helped. There was also a tendency for such engines to "drown" in freak weather conditions. Small transverse twins would fit just as well at the rear as they would at the front: the German Glas Goggomobil of 1955 (*below*) kept its engine in the "boot". Unusually for a two-stroke miniature, it offered full four-seater accommodation (*see photo page 215*), and in 400-cc form (250-cc and 300-cc versions were also listed) it attained 100 km/h (62 mph). Over 280,000 were sold, the last of them in 1969.

ahead of the six, powering some 42 % of the world's production types throughout the 1950s, with some small variations. By 1964, this share had gone up to 53 %, which remained about the norm for the rest of our period. By far the majority of these were water-cooled in-lines, exceptions being the air-cooled flat-fours of Volkswagen, Porsche, and their relatives, and water-cooled opposed types such as the Jowett (1947–54), Lancia (1961 onward), and Subaru (1968). The only new V-4s were the German and British Fords of the 1960s, although Lancia—who had pioneered this configuration in 1922—continued to build it right up to the end of their independent existence.

Poor accessibility was the Achilles' Heel of the flat-four. For the same reason, nearly all sixes were of in-line type. Porsche and Chevrolet, however, built opposed air-cooled types in the 1960s, while the V-6s of Lancia and of Ford in Europe were joined by General Motors, who began to take a fresh interest in compactness. Buick's first effort, also supported briefly by Oldsmobile, was launched in 1962. The day of the V-6 was to come. Sixes, however, came back slightly into vogue during our period, even though France, with her fiscal problems, offered no such engine after the demise of the 15CV Citroën in 1955. The watershed between fours and sixes was now just over two litres in capacity, with a tendency—especially in Britain and Germany—to use the extra pair of cylinders on prestige models. Classic examples were the 220s and 250s paralleling Mercedes-Benz' cheaper four-cylinder line, the 2.6-litre and 2.9-litre Austins with the C-type engine, the Kapitäns and Commodores of Opel, and the more expensive Borgwards. Apart from a short break in 1957–58, there was always a six-cylinder Super Snipe to complement the stolid Hawk in Humber's catalogue.

Sixes generally were moving up into the prestige bracket. Big fours were still viable in family sedans, but not in luxury models with a sporting flavour—as Armstrong Siddeley discovered to their cost in 1956, when they challenged the new compact Jaguar with their Sapphire 234. True, the Siddeley's styling was a catastrophe, but it handled better than the Jaguar and was nearly as fast. The lumpy feeling of that four-cylinder engine was the last straw. The pattern of four-versus-six, though, remained uneven. Rover, who concentrated most of their efforts on sixes, went back to an overhead-camshaft four in 1964 for their very successful 2-litre 2000, while Fiat tended to withdraw from the six-cylinder market in the later 1960s. The Humber Super Snipe ended a run of over a quarter century in 1967, while Alfa Romeo's 2600 and Lancia's Flaminia were neither of them impressive sellers. On the other hand, Triumph reintroduced a 2-litre six for 1964 and did very well with it, while BMW's overhead-camshaft family (1968) were to become one of the great commercial successes of the 1970s. A year later came a new 2.6-litre from Volvo. One that did not stage a comeback was the pint-sized six: the sole bid in this sector came from Triumph, who revived their 1931 formula of a small six-cylinder engine in a slightly lengthened four-cylinder chassis. The resultant 1.6-litre Vitesse (1962) was smooth and fast, but handled rather oddly. Nobody followed suit and the Vitesse soon acquired the 2000's 2-litre engine. The British fiscal system no longer called for such improvisations.

While the six moved up-market, the straight-eight quietly expired during the first four seasons of our period. Fashions in styling ceased to favour this impressively lengthy unit: the V-8 did the job better, thanks to superior sound insulation which eliminated its irritating "wuffle".

(*Opposite*) The European family sedan of the 1950s at its best—although both of these Borgward Isabellas, the sedan (*top*) and the station wagon (*bottom*), date from 1960. The overhead-valve engine and all-independent suspension were inherited from the car's 1934 ancestor, the Hansa 1100, but coils now replaced a transverse-leaf arrangement at the rear. The hydraulic brakes are to be expected, yet more sophisticated (even for 1954) are the hydraulically actuated clutch, the synchronized bottom gear, and the full-width styling. What, however, would have had four doors in other countries made do with two in Germany, which meant two doors on the station wagon as well. The steering-column change, unremarkable in the mid-fifties, was becoming a trifle old-hat by 1960, and the Borgward was a big car, 172 in (4.37 m) long and 66 in (1.7 m) wide. Isabella was also a bit heavy, at 2,253 lb (1,022 kg) dry, but in high-performance TS form she could cruise in the low 80-mph range (128–130 km/h). Still, for a small firm, full unitary construction was a risky venture and, though Borgward managed to dispose of over 200,000 assorted Isabellas in eight seasons, the money ran out for good in 1961.

(*Top right*) Lancia's Fulvia Berlina, made to the tune of over 190,000 units between 1963 and 1973. The firm had first adopted front-wheel drive in 1961 on the bigger Flavia, but this time they reverted to the traditional narrow-angle V-4 engine after the Flavia's Fessia-designed flat-four. The Fulvia's transverse-leaf front suspension, likewise, is a far cry from the famous "sliding pillars" first seen on the 1922 Lambda and retained well into the 1960s on older types. By this time, though, right-hand steering is reserved for British and Commonwealth markets. All-disc brakes are standard, and on this late (1971) example you will find a 1.3-litre 85-horsepower motor, five forward speeds, and quad headlamps.

(*Bottom right*) The V-8 remained the principal V-type of engine in use, though a successful V-4 was predictably the Lancia, still produced under independent management. This is the 1,091-cc power pack used to drive the front wheels of the Fulvia model introduced in 1963. It had twin overhead camshafts and was mounted in unit with a four-speed all-synchromesh gearbox.

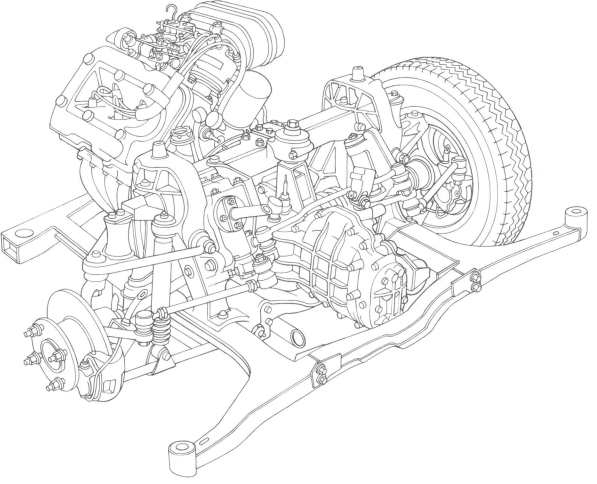

America's last two eights-in-line, Pontiac and Packard, were discontinued after 1954, leaving the Russian ZIS (a Packard derivative) to soldier on into 1958 before it, too, gave way to the ZIL with a V-8 unit. Our period also spans the golden years of the V-8 in America, during which the 90-degree short-stroke overhead-valve type swept the country. Cadillac and Oldsmobile were first in 1949, followed by Chrysler and Studebaker two years later. The other manufacturers had no option but to fall into line. Ford had an overhead-valve engine on sale by 1954, and 1955 saw V-8 Chevrolets and Plymouths.

The type possessed many advantages. Unit cost had been held to reasonable levels ever since Ford devised a means of monobloc casting, way back in 1932. The V-8 fitted conveniently into the space between two independently sprung front wheels, and width was not a factor which worried Americans. Better still, a short power unit meant that the same chassis and body could be applied to economical in-line sixes: in straight-eight days, one had to think in terms of two wheelbase lengths even if the two models shared a common range of bodies. As high-octane fuels came into use, the call was for rigid engines, and V-8s were rigid. Finally, four-throw crankshafts with five main bearings meant excellent balance. Early carburation problems were solved by using a single four-jet instrument instead of the twin-choke type with one half feeding an individual bank of cylinders. As for the V-8's thirst, this would be no hindrance until 1973's safety and emission drives.

The ensuing horsepower race merits a book in itself and, in any case, the remarkable outputs quoted were for engines running "bare" on a test bench, with no allowance made for power losses between flywheel and rear axle. But whether or not the figures were genuine, the progress was formidable. At the beginning of our period, 160 horsepower from 5.4 litres represented the norm. Then came Chrysler's "hemi" with 180 horsepower, and the race was on. By 1955, the hairiest Chrysler was good for 300 hp, and even the cheaper cars were available with "power packs" boosting output to around 200 hp as well as adding some 3 mph (5 km/h) to maximum speed, and lopping a vital 2 seconds off the 0–60 mph (0–100 km/h) acceleration time, the latter being very important in a country where overall speed limits were already in force. Chrysler were on top again in 1958 with 390 hp—one horsepower per cubic inch (16 cc)—and the ultimate was achieved in 1967 by Chevrolet, who were extracting 435 hp from their most powerful unit. Also offering over 400 hp were Ford, Plymouth, and Dodge. Even if these fantastic performances owed much to the advertising agencies, let us remember that the 1955 Chrysler 300 was a heavy car weighing 4,000 lb (1,800 kg), yet would top 135 mph (215 km/h).

There was little scope for V-8s in Europe, since the big-car market was modest and long runs were less than viable. Firms as well established as Rolls-Royce and Mercedes-Benz could afford them for prestige lines. But BMW's admirable 2.6-litre and 3.2-litre units were an unacceptable extravagance when related to sales of less than 15,000 units in a decade, and brought their sponsors to the verge of bankruptcy. The Turner-designed Daimler likewise had a ten-year run, but was dropped by a Leyland management already wedded to the Buick-based Rover and a design from Triumph which did not appear until 1970. One may dismiss the 2.3-litre Simca Vedette (1955–61) as a hangover from the past: it was merely an updated edition of the unloved "60" engine produced by Ford in 1936. Similarly, V-12s were reserved exclusively for Italian super-cars, their sole protagonists being Ferrari and Lamborghini. The Lincoln had disappeared in 1948, and the twin overhead-camshaft Jaguar would not reach the public until 1971. Whatever the motives behind the twelves of the 1930s, one may doubt whether Enzo Ferrari was in any way influenced by the ability of his early "street" engines to pull down to 7 mph (11 km/h) in top gear.

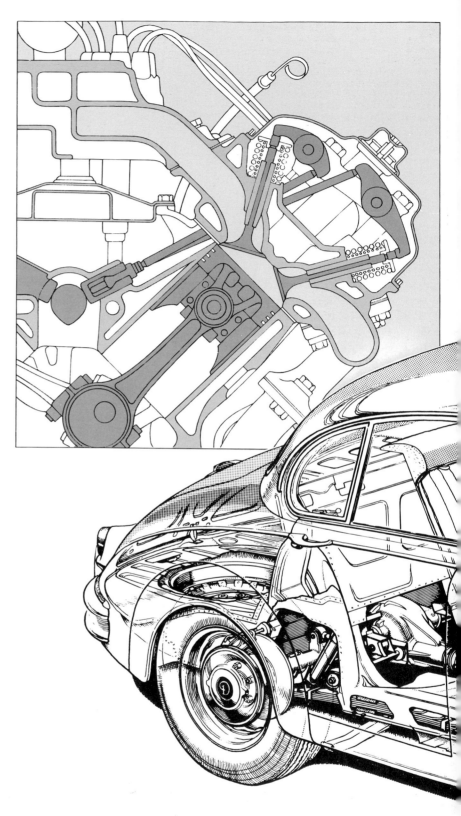

V-8s various. (*Top left*) The 1951 Chrysler Firepower unit (5.4 litres, 180 horsepower) was the one that sparked off the American performance race in the fifties, and was worked up to give double its advertised output, even if—as in the case of most U.S. motors—by no means all the advertised horses reached the back wheels. It had big inlet valves and excellent breathing, though the type was always expensive to make, and Chrysler Corporation's cheaper power units used a simpler top-end design. One of

Europe's few successful V-8s was the Edward Turner-designed Daimler, originally planned for the glass-fibre bodied SP250 sports car of 1959, but seen here (*centre*) in its most familiar application, beneath the bonnet of the 2.5-litre sedan (17,620 sold between 1962 and 1969). This was brought out after Jaguar had bought Daimler, hence everything save the engine was authentic Mk. II "compact" Jaguar. Initially, however, the Daimler version was offered only with automatic transmission. Far more com-

plex was the 1951 Pegaso Z102 (*top right*), a
2.8-litre unit fitted to Spain's most exotic
sports car, "a jewel for the rich" as its makers called it. Castings were of light alloy and
there were twin overhead camshafts per
block. In standard form it gave around 170
horsepower, although an alleged 285 were
available with the aid of twin superchargers.
The absence of a gearbox is easily explained:
the Pegaso used a five-speed transaxle.

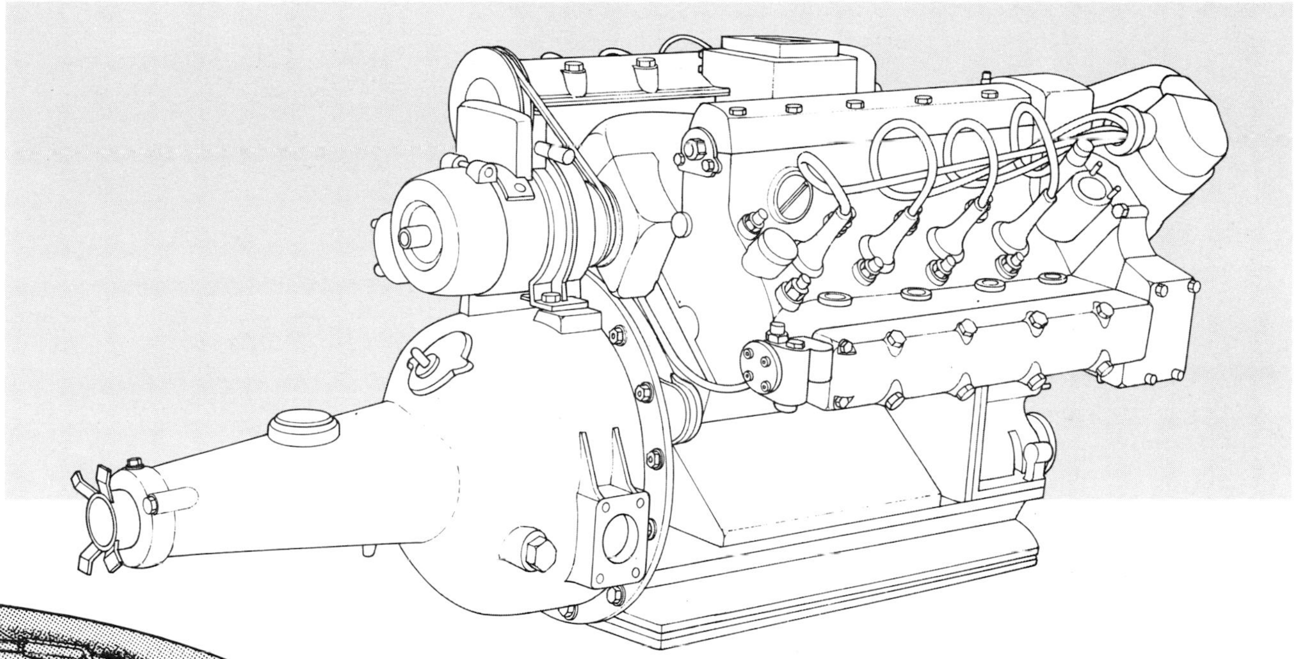

Autocar
copyright

57

Alternative power remained only a talking point in both our decades. No attempt was made to commercialize an electric car. Diesels, however, had a modest appeal on various grounds. The fuel they used was untaxed in several countries, their fuel consumption was frugal in the extreme, and they would run immense distances between overhauls. Such virtues commended themselves to commercial travellers and cabbies. Less attractive was a high manufacturing cost, reflected in list prices, although by the early 1960s Mercedes-Benz had brought the differential down to a mere 7–8%. Problems were the high-capacity batteries required to turn a high-compression engine over from cold, the unacceptable noise level, and the offensive exhaust fumes. The increased weight of a diesel could play havoc with handling if installed in a chassis designed for a petrol unit—the Fiat 1400D being a classic instance—while performance was lethargic. The limit for any diesel-powered sedan in 1969 was about 80 mph (130 km/h). Finally maintenance, when needed, was very expensive. Thus the market was limited, and the only major builder of such engines for private-car use was Mercedes-Benz, who had turned out over 600,000 diesel sedans by 1968. Others to try their hand in this field were BMC, Borgward, Fiat, Peugeot, and Standard, while diesel-powered 4×4 Landrovers were available from 1958 and, in certain Western countries, the Russian Volga and Moskvitch were marketed with conversions. Perkins, Rover, or Indénor engines were fitted in such cases.

An intriguing development of the late 1950s was Felix Wankel's rotary piston engine. It consisted of a triangular piston with rotational and orbital movements within a figure-eight casing, pursuing an epitrochoid path. The rotor or piston had three points of contact at the rotor top seals, which rubbed against the side of the casing. Thus, the spaces between the sides of the rotor increased and decreased in volume twice with every revolution. Such an engine, of course, dispenses with the crankshaft, connecting rods, and valves. It was also compact and light: the original production-type NSU unit, regarded by German tax authorities as a 1.5-litre, weighed only 275 lb (125 kg) complete with all ancillaries. Except at low speeds, it was vibrationless, and one could run it up to an unrecommended 7,000 rpm without being aware of this. But alas, high machining standards rendered Wankels expensive to make, and their tolerance of low-octane fuels was not matched by other virtues. Fuel and oil consumption alike were high, and rotor seals were such a constant headache that, in later years, many Ro80 sedans from NSU were fitted with Ford engines. Only NSU and Mazda of Japan actually marketed the type, although Citroën, among others, indulged in long-term testing programmes before jettisoning the idea. By 1982, Mazda alone were still selling cars with rotary piston engines. The emission-conscious 1970s had taken their toll.

The gas turbine stalked through our decades as a chimera, never anything more. Tantalizingly simple, it had an air compressor, a combustion chamber to heat the air, and a vaned wheel in which high-velocity gases blasted continuously to produce the power output. Among its other attractions, an unfussy palate would burn such improbable fuels as tequila and peanut oil. It needed no warming-up period or regular oil changes, was lighter than an internal-combustion unit, and had 80% fewer parts. Successful experiments were conducted in Britain by Rover from 1950 onward, as well as by Renault and Fiat. As early as 1956, Chrysler Corporation's experimental Plymouth turbocar was driven from New York to Los Angeles, the trip being repeated in 1962 on a later version. Chrysler went so far as to release 55 hardtop coupés in "turbine bronze" for assessment by selected private individuals under daily-use conditions. The idol, however, had feet of clay: building a gas turbine called for costly technology and metallurgy, while the best fuel consumption one could hope for was 13 mpg (21 lit/100 km). The irritating power lag of several seconds could be a problem, tailpipe temperatures were high enough to imperil curious pe-

(*Opposite*) Classically British, if with some post-war touches. The twin-camshaft high-pushrod four-cylinder engine of this 1953 2.5-litre RMF-series Riley sedan dated back to 1937, and its base design to 1926. Styling is essentially late-thirties, but there is independent torsion-bar suspension at the front, and later examples—from a run which ended in this particular year—had full hydraulic brakes (earlier cars had that great British compromise, hydromech) and hypoid rear axles. On 100 horsepower, 100 mph (160 km/h) were very nearly there, but the Riley suffered from the no-longer-acceptable beat of a big four-cylinder engine, and the steering was extremely heavy in town traffic. Sales of 8,960 units in eight seasons were nonetheless creditable.

(*Right*) Only those neatly slanted quad headlights told the British motorist that the car on his tail was a Mk. I Triumph Vitesse (Sports Six to Americans) of 1962, capable of nearly 90 mph (145 km/h), and not the humble four-cylinder Herald. Planting a 1.6-litre six in the nose, allied to swing-axle rear suspension, resulted in handling problems, and there was as much (or as little) room as there was in the identically-bodied Herald. Unless the optional overdrive was specified, fuel consumption ran to a daunting 25 mpg (11 litres/100 km). In the early 1930s, Triumph's slogan had been "The Car That Is Different", and this was perhaps the kindest thing one could say of the original Vitesse, though of course front disc brakes were standard.

destrians, and the unit had a propensity for sucking in foreign bodies, with expensive consequences. In Britain, the development money ran out. In America, Chrysler's 1964 trials coincided almost with the first wave of Naderism, and the insurance companies panicked. Since 1973's energy crisis, nothing further has been heard of gas turbines for passenger-car use.

In conventional engines, pushrod-operated overhead valves were found on 65–70% of all units throughout our period. The side-valve configuration, on its way out in 1946, was allowed to die with the old pre-war hangovers. Few new flatheads made their appearance, the most notable ones being the huge 5.1-litre six-cylinder Hudson Hornet (1951) and a redesigned version of the traditional 1,172-cc British Ford (1953), the latter lingering on into 1961. Other ancients destined to reach the end of the first decade were the Simca-Ford V-8 and the Austin-inspired Datsun, still around in 1959 as was the Austin 7, now made by Reliant of Tamworth for installation in three-wheelers. Chrysler Corporation of America were still making side-valve sixes in 1959, and continued these into the mid-1960s for light truck use, while the little 3-litre Studebaker Champion—a 1939 debutante—would not acquire upstairs valves until 1961.

Hemispherical combustion-chamber design improved the performance of overhead-valve engines. This was the secret of the famous 1951 Chrysler, and it also appeared on the successful 2.4-litre Riley of 1938–56, as well as on numerous overhead-camshaft models. Maintenance problems, plus the spectre of noise, discouraged the widespread use of the overhead camshaft itself on touring engines during the 1950s. Camshafts were still usually chain-driven and, in the early period, there were more defectors than new adherents to the overhead scheme. The 2.2-litre Morris/Wolseley family of sixes were never best-sellers and fell by the wayside after only 38,000 had been sold. Singer switched to Rootes pushrod designs in 1958 and Lancia, a long-standing user, also made the change to pushrods at the beginning of our story, in 1950. Probably the most persistent supporter was Mercedes-Benz, who brought out their successful 220 and 300 six-cylinder series in 1951, and spent the next few years phasing out the old side-valve hangovers from pre-war days. Coventry-Climax's small fours turned up in a number of specialist cars, notably Lotus and TVR, before being adapted to the Hillman Imp in 1963. Other notable users of the 1960s included Rover in Britain, BMW in Germany, and Willys and Pontiac in the U.S.A.

Curiously, the complicated twin overhead-camshaft engine had more initial impact. Salmson of France and Alfa Romeo of Italy had used nothing else since the 1930s, and kept this faith—the former until their demise in 1957, the latter right through to 1969 and beyond. Jaguar, whose 3.4-litre XK six with 160 horsepower had been among the sensations of the 1948 Shows, phased out the last of their pushrod designs in mid-1951 to concentrate on the newer type. Although their production figures (250,000 units by the end of 1966) could not match those of Alfa Romeo, the astonishing Jaguar soon proved its reliability with 250,000 miles (400,000 km) between major overhauls, besides its development potential of up to 265 horsepower on touring engines and more for racing, not to mention its versatility. Apart from Jaguar's own range, the big sixes went into Daimler limousines, racing cars and motorboats, armoured cars, and ambulances.

Twin overhead camshafts per block, on vee and horizontally opposed engines, were reserved for the super-sports cars, notably Porsche's Carrera series (1955 onward) and the fastest Ferraris of the later 1960s. Perhaps the most extreme case was the Spanish Pegaso of 1951, a V-8 with an incredibly noisy camshaft-drive by a train of gears, and with dry sump lubrication. With one of the very few supercharger installations catalogued in the 1950s, Pegaso claimed 225 hp at 6,800 rpm from

(*Opposite, top*) The four-stroke Wankel engine consists of an equilateral piston (*1*) mounted on a drive shaft (*2*), which it turns by rotating inside a casing with a cooling duct (*3*). The rotor points form gas-tight seals for three chambers (*4, 5, 6*). The working cycle begins (**A**) with a fuel-and-air mixture sucked through a duct (*7*) into chamber *4*, whose volume increases as the rotor turns. (**B**) The mixture in chamber *5* is being compressed at the same time, until ignited by a spark-plug (*8*). The combustion gases expand and force the rotor round. (**C**) The gases in chamber *6* have begun to leave through the uncovered exhaust duct (*9*) and are now almost gone. This chamber will soon move round to start the working cycle anew. (**D**) Two rotors are often used together for greater efficiency, mounted oppositely so that the engine will run smoothly. The combustion chambers (*10*) are partly sunk into the rotors.

(*Bottom*) In 1967, Mazda of Japan marketed their first Wankel-powered car, the Cosmo Sport coupé, using a twin-rotor engine of a nominal 1-litre capacity. Unlike the NSUs, it had a conventional layout, with a conventional synchromesh transmission in place of the NSU Ro80's semi-automatic. Front disc brakes were fitted, and a top speed of 185 km/h (115 mph) was quoted, but only about 1,200 were built.

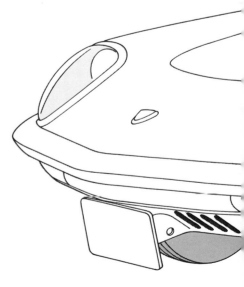

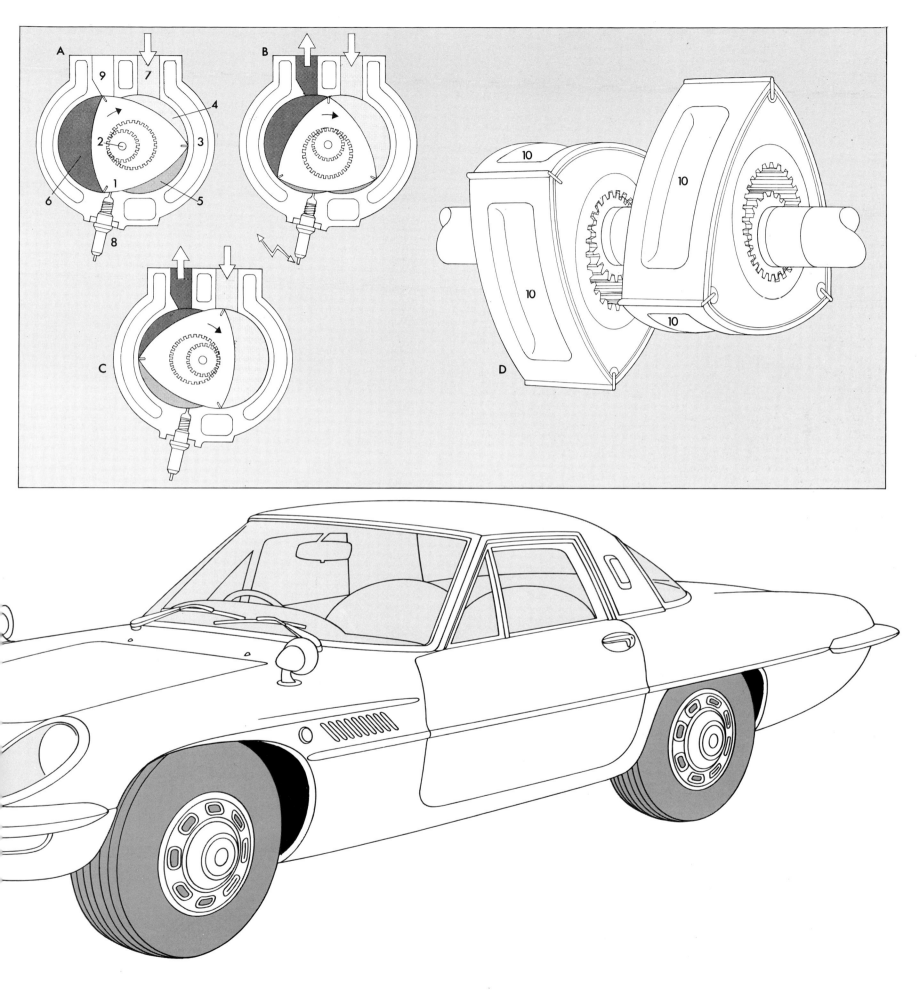

(*Opposite*) Solid Teutonic engineering: the 220S Mercedes-Benz sedan, 1957. This unitary version replaced the original separate-chassis type during 1954, and continued into 1959 without styling changes, though a lot of improvements crept in under the skin—servo brakes in 1955, an automatic-clutch option in 1957, and the SE series with fuel injection for 1958. The swing-axle rear suspension, as always, had its limitations, but output of the 2.2-litre four-bearing overhead-camshaft engine climbed steadily from 95 to 115 horsepower. For quiet cruising in the mid-80 mph range (130–135 km/h) the car had few rivals. Annual sales, likewise, were rising to around the 30,000 level by the late 1950s.

(*Below*) BMW "marked" Mercedes-Benz like an opposing footballer in the later 1950s, pitting a line of sophisticated V-8s against Untertürkheim's in-line overhead-camshaft sixes. Mercedes wouldn't essay a V-8 until 1963, by which time their rivals were struggling back from the verge of bankruptcy with smaller quality models. Their Goertz-styled 3.2-litre 507 (answer to the 300SL) was, however, a thing of beauty, and it could move to the tune of 137 mph (220 km/h) with the highest available axle ratio. The hydraulic brakes were servo-assisted but, although some surviving 507s have discs, these were never catalogued. Only 250 of these coupés were built and, after a skirmish with a Bertone-bodied fixed-head development, BMW finally jettisoned their eight-cylinder line in 1965.

2.5 litres, not to mention well over 125 mph (200 km/h). A total production of 120–125 cars in eight years is understandable. The real breakthrough for overhead-camshaft systems, however, came with the quiet and inexpensive cogged rubber-belt drive, pioneered by Glas of Germany in 1961. These belts were inextensible and required no lubrication. Other users in our period were Fiat (in single and twin overhead-camshaft forms), Vauxhall, Pontiac, and Triumph, the last on an engine designed for Saab of Sweden and subsequently developed and manufactured in that country. The great advance of overhead camshafts in the touring-car field, though, is a phenomenon of the 1970s.

Two-stroke engines still belonged to the world of austere, minimal motoring. Simplicity and a small number of moving parts had their appeal, despite the messy petroil lubrication method (4 % of oil to every filling of petrol) and the exhaust smoke resulting from an incorrect mixture. With a free wheel incorporated in the transmission to eliminate snatch, the system worked well enough. Various DKW derivatives penetrated outside the two Germanies to Czechoslovakia, Poland, Spain, and Sweden, as well as to Argentina and Brazil in due course. Elsewhere, its image was indelibly that of the minicar. By 1957, Carl Borgward's cheap lines, Goliath and Lloyd, had gone over to four-stroke units. Auto Union themselves, by 1966, were phasing out the traditional DKW in favour of the overhead-valve four-cylinder Audi, and Saab's two-stroke line was being run down a year later. Tougher emission standards would speed the system's demise in the ensuing decade, although the two-stroke was to hang on for a while in eastern Europe and in some Japanese minicars.

DKW's cars invariably featured water-cooling, but the majority of minicars used air-cooled units of motorcycle origins: a good medium on grounds of simplicity and immunity from frost. Most devotees of air-cooling used it on small or utilitarian vehicles such as the VW family, Citroën's 2CV, and the flat-twin Panhard. The only big air-cooled cars were the Chevrolet Corvair and, of course, the Tatra. An interesting compromise manifested itself in 1961, on Renault's answer to the little Citroën. The new 4CV engine (R4-type) was water-cooled, but with a sealed-for-life system topped up via a tank on the bonnet side. Others would follow suit, and new air-cooled designs were rare in the later sixties. Honda had one in their 1969 catalogue, but it soon evolved into the best-selling Civic with water-cooling. DAF in Holland, while using developments of their overhead-valve air-cooled twin at the bottom of their range, preferred a version of the Renault in their bigger 55 (1968). Further, pump cooling gained steadily over thermo-syphon systems throughout our period. In the later 1960s, however, a regular adjunct of high-performance engines was the provision of one or two electric fans to assist cooling in slow traffic. Ferrari and Jaguar were among those who adopted such arrangements.

Carburettors were usually of downdraught type, both in 1950 and twenty years later, although America found single multi-choke instruments to be best when coping with the eight-cylinder offspring of the horsepower race. Two separate carburettors, a common practice in Europe, seemed more complicated across the Atlantic than a single body with two or four chokes. Such a device was also popular in the Old World: Ferrari used three dual-choke carburettors on their V-12 power units. Fuel injection, an essential technique in the diesel engine, made somewhat halting progress on petrol-powered types. Its attraction, already recognized in racing circles, was more precise metering of fuel. Its disadvantages were high underbonnet temperatures and formidable servicing costs, while—towards the end of our period—some systems proved difficult to adjust to the new American emission standards. Triumph employed fuel injection on home-market TR6 sports cars, but had recourse to carburettors again on the TR250 sold in the U.S.A.

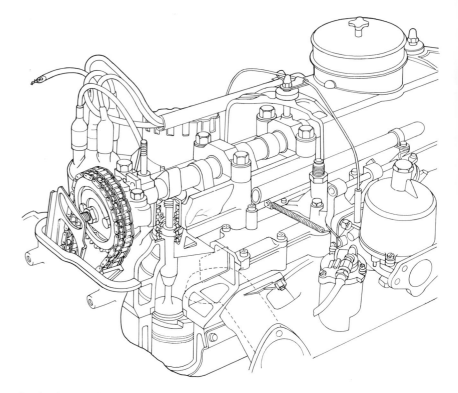

Overhead camshafts. The 1964 Rover 2000 four-cylinder (*above*) used the familiar toothed-chain drive, but already the cheaper and quieter cogged belts were known. Pioneer of this arrangement was the little-known Glas S1004 coupé, which went into production in May, 1962, and led to further, more powerful editions. Conventionally engineered, the Glas in its original guise used a 992-cc 40-horsepower engine and would do 130 km/h (80 mph). (*Below*) Cogged belts are applied to drive twin overhead camshafts on the Fiat 124 Sport of 1966, a successful and long-lived model. Open spyder developments with 2-litre engines were still being sold in the U.S.A. in 1982. Significant is the five-main-bearing crankshaft: in the earlier years of our period, three bearings would have been the norm for such a unit.

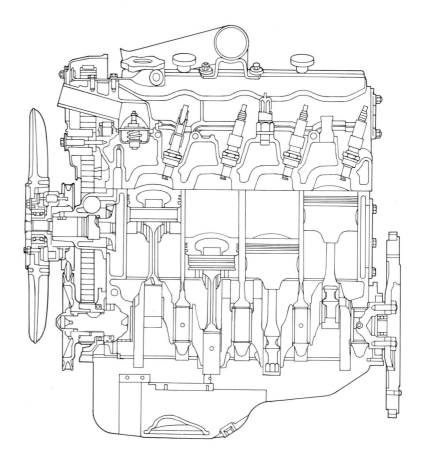

Most fuel-injection systems before 1968, though, were of mechanical type and confined to specialist sports cars. First in the field, as so often, came Mercedes-Benz: their 300SL sports coupé of 1954 featured a diesel-type jerk pump with one plunger for each of the six cylinders. Thence they progressed to a two-cylinder pump driven at engine speed, on which each plunger fed three cylinders, in spite of a reversion to the six-plunger type on the 230SL (1963). By 1969, the majority of their sixes were so equipped, while carburettors were retained on the cheaper fours. Triumph and Peugeot built fuel-injected engines as well. Bosch's electronic system did not appear until 1967 and was not widely used until the early 1970s. The acid test for this—like other innovations—was whether American makers would adopt it. They did, but only on a small scale in 1957–58, when it became an option in the V-8s of Chevrolet and Pontiac. Performance and fuel consumption were improved, but not enough to warrant the additional first cost of $550 (£200). The system persisted for some years, however, on the specialized Corvette sports car.

A curious absentee from catalogues of the 1950s and 1960s was the supercharger, although such a component was available on Pegasos of the early fifties, and a number of component firms built proprietary units which were applied to MGs, Volkswagens, and the like. (The centrifugal type of blower, used in the 1930s by Auburn and Graham, was revived in 1957 as an option on Studebaker's high-performance Golden Hawk coupé, mainly to extract some more power from the company's relatively small V-8 unit.) Nor was its replacement, the turbocharger, much used even in the sixties, except by truck manufacturers on diesels. We were a long way from the eighties, with many a range topped by a "Turbo" model. In turbochargers, a turbine driven by the exhaust gas powers a centrifugal blower which forces the mixture from carburettor to inlet ports. Its merit is, of course, that it turns waste gases to good use. Such a device was tried on the Studebaker Avanti, and became available on 1965 models of the rear-engined Chevrolet Corvair, boosting power in the flat-six engine from 140 to 180 horsepower and giving the car a top speed of 115 mph (184 km/h). The engine was not, however, offered after 1966, since the Corvair was already doomed by the published strictures of Mr. Nader and the success of the Ford Mustang in the sporty-compact sector of the market.

Bottom-end design had to receive serious consideration in the freeway era, when all major car-producing countries followed the original lead of Italy and Germany. In 1950, the normal quota of crankshaft bearings was three for a four-cylinder engine and four for a six. This allocation remained constant throughout our period on such well-established types as BMC's "A" unit, first seen in 803-cc form on the Austin A30 (1952) and applied, incidentally, to all standard Minis. As we have seen, the high-revving oversquare engine had also originated in Germany and Italy, and now other countries were emulating this fashion. But some long-stroke ancients lingered well into the 1960s: Citroën were still fitting their legendary 78×100 mm unit, the 2-litre 11CV, to advanced D sedans as late as 1965. At least one modern engine, the twin-cam Jaguar six, had the old-fashioned dimensions of 83×106 mm for a capacity of 3.4 litres—undoubtedly conceived in the shadow of the archaic British horsepower tax. At the other end of the scale, Ford of Britain's 105E engine, a pushrod 1-litre four, went to extremes with a bore of 81 mm and a stroke of 48.5 mm.

Soon, too, the five-bearing four-cylinder unit was back. Many big engines of the 1905–10 period had been so equipped—naturally without the benefit of pressure lubrication or a crankshaft balancer—and such a bottom end had been the recipe for the incredible longevity of the original 1921 Austin 12, although this one was never asked to exceed 2,500 rpm. All of Alfa Romeo's *autostrada*-bred post-war fours, from the

1900 (1950–51) onward, ran to five main bearings, as did the family launched by BMW ten years later. As old types came up for replacement, other makers made the switch: Ford of Britain on their Cortina, BMC with the B-type unit, Citroën on their long-overdue short-stroke models, and Rover on their overhead-camshaft 2000 (1964). In Japan, Mazda even built a tiny 356-cc five-bearing unit for minicars. The seven-bearing six-cylinder engine spread more slowly, if only because model changes were less frequent. Long-standing devotees of seven mains included firms as diverse as Jaguar, Nash, and Rolls-Royce. Mercedes-Benz confined the practice initially to their big 300 family, making their first smaller seven-bearing unit in 1967. By this time, others who had uprated their contributions included BMC, BMW, Chevrolet, Datsun, Holden, and Toyota, soon to be joined by Volvo.

Electrical ignition arrangements had been standardized by 1930, the effective watershed for the magneto, and coil systems had taken over in the U.S.A. as long ago as World War I. The coil and dynamo, universal in 1939, were equally so twenty years later, although 6-volt systems vanished from American cars between 1953 and 1956. These would survive another ten years in Germany, on the principle that what was good enough for VW would also serve lesser Fords and Opels. By 1969, however, the only car of any significance to retain the lower voltage was the 2CV Citroën: even its bigger 602-cc sisters had gone over to 12 volts.

This change, alas, did not solve an ever more pressing problem, the profusion of electrically powered ancillaries. A supply which sufficed for lights, ignition, and starting in 1950 simply could not cope with radios, heaters, power seats and windows, and electric screenwashers, especially at low traffic speeds where the charging rate decreased. On a cold morning, it was imperative to switch everything off before turning the key to start the engine, and also to remember that certain ancillaries—Renault's screenwipers, for instance—were not wired directly into the ignition circuit. Dynamos lacked enough low-speed output: hence the advent of the alternator (a dynamo working in reverse) on Chrysler Corporation's 1960 compact sedan, the Plymouth Valiant. In the ensuing nine years, there was a dramatic transition to the new system, headed by the entire American industry and its foreign associates, plus Leyland in Britain, Citroën in France, Ferrari and Fiat in Italy, and Auto Union and BMW in Germany. By 1975, the dynamo would be as dead as the magneto. Transistorized ignition was in use by 1969 on the four-cam V-6 Dino sports cars of Ferrari and Fiat, but would not see high-volume production until 1971, on Jaguar's 5.3-litre V-12.

Predictably, clutches saw little development, beyond the general adoption of diaphragm spring actuation and hydraulic assistance, the latter having been applied to most up-market cars with manual transmission by 1969. This state of affairs was the result of a great revolution in transmission arrangements, as important to a study of the fifties as was front-wheel drive to the automobile engineering of our second decade. Automatics had come to stay.

Shifting had been made painless by 1934, and dependable automatics existed even before America's entry into World War II, although only Cadillac and Oldsmobile fitted them. By 1951, some form of self-shifting was available on almost every model offered by Detroit. From then onward, manufacturers were confronted by a new class of knowledgeable motorists who knew what they were buying, had made the mental choice between manual and automatic, and wanted the best of either kind. What is more, the choice was there: while in America one had to opt for something cheap if one preferred "stick" (and at times to pay extra for it, whatever the catalogue might say), middle-bracket British cars such as Austin, Ford, Humber, and Morris could be had with either method. Gradually, too, automatic models spread down

(*Opposite, top*) The original owner of this 1957 Chevrolet Bel Air convertible probably paid around $3,000 (say £1,125) for it, allowing for freight and extras. Through European eyes, however, it looks an expensive car, all the more so for the elaborate grille, plated side sweep-spear, and fins which have yet to attain their ultimate in glory. With the top down, the aggressive effect of the dog's-leg windscreen is somewhat diminished, but the 14-inch wheels (new this year) hint at braking problems, especially with two-speed automatic transmissions and V-8 options giving 220 horsepower from 4.6 litres. As Chevrolet's only non-sporting ragtop in 1957, it drew over 47,000 buyers—more cars than Germany's Auto Union works sold during the whole season.

(*Top right*) From this angle, it's not apparent that the "works" of the 1964 Chevrolet Corvair Monza convertible live in the "trunk", or that the "hood" is reserved for baggage. Nor, as yet, had the crusading Mr. Nader vented his wrath upon this development of the Volkswagen theme with all-independent suspension and an air-cooled flat-six engine. It was, however, already clear that the car was more than a sub-utility compact sedan, and this year Chevrolet took a leap into the future by offering a turbocharger, using the waste gases of the exhaust to boost power. Until now, such installations were only seen elsewhere on heavy diesel trucks: their passenger-car applications would be a phenomenon of the early 1980s.

(*Opposite, bottom*) The 300 coupé of 1955 was surely the most exciting Chrysler in our period, though also one of the rarest—only 1,692 made. The recipe was simple: take Virgil Exner's long-overdue new shape in New Yorker hardtop form, lower it, give it the grille of the prestige Imperial line, and throw in a 300-horsepower V-8 with twin quadrajet carburettors, plus twin exhausts to make the right noises. Compulsory automatic and power steering might not add up to the European concept of a sports car, but then the so-called "muscle-cars" weren't competing against Ferrari and Jaguar. They would soon become a breed in their own right.

(*Bottom right*) Homologated stock-car racer, though it's still street-legal: the Dodge Daytona Charger 500 coupé, of which 505 were built in 1969. It is distinguishable from sedater offerings by the front spoiler, long nose with fully concealed headlamps, and a "tail unit" that would not shame a jet airliner. Power unit was the famed "426 Street Hemi", a descendant of Chrysler's original hemispherical-head V-8 of 1951. It gave 431 horsepower from 7 litres, and a four-speed manual transmission was regular equipment on this car.

from the category of 2–2.5 litres, to 1.5-litre sedans (Hillman, Ford) and even to the Mini by the end of our period. In 1969, indeed, among 132 major makers quoted in international buyers' guides, only 49 wanted no part of self-shifters. Notable holdouts were Alfa Romeo, Audi, Citroën, Lancia, Renault, Saab, and Skoda. All but the last-mentioned would soon give in to this ubiquitous pain-killer.

The main casualties of the automatic revolution were, of course, the semi-automatic systems. Chrysler's Fluidrive had given way to a proper automatic by 1954, while preselectors also became part of history. The electrically selected Cotal died because its principal French customers went out of business, and the same went for the Wilsons favoured by Talbot in France and Armstrong Siddeley in Britain. The latter firm, like Daimler, had in any case switched to proprietary automatics as being cheaper and less complicated. Armstrong Siddeley flirted briefly with electric selection of the gears in 1953–55, and another electric, the German Getrag used on the miniature Goggomobil in 1957, was an ingenious device actuated by a tiny lever. Sadly, this system did not work in bottom gear, and often expired altogether.

Automatic clutches flitted briefly across the scene in the later 1950s. Notable specimens were Renault's Ferlec, the German Saxomat offered on a diversity of makes, and the Lockheed Manumatic in Britain. On these, an electric switch, usually built into the gear-shift knob, disengaged the clutch when the lever was moved. Their balance could be upset by fast idling speeds with the engine running at low temperature. In fact, the auto-clutch was only a palliative to keep the manufacturers alive until small engines could be made powerful enough to absorb the inherent power losses of automatic transmission. Such arrangements were still around in the late sixties: On NSU's Ro80, driver-controlled manual selection was successfully combined with a torque converter, and Porsche used a rather similar device on their "Sporto-

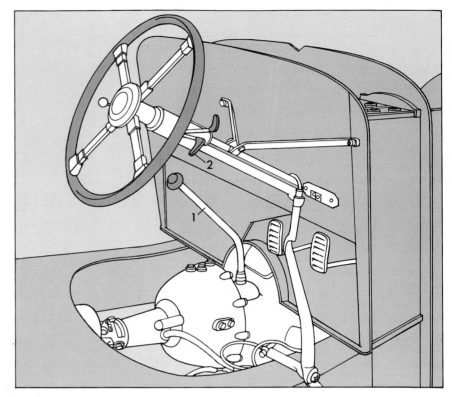

(*Top*) Complicated shifting. Still with us in the early fifties was the Cotal electromagnetic gear change, which used two levers: a floor-mounted forward/reverse selector (*1*), and a tiny finger-type gate (*2*) which selected the individual ratios electrically and, incidentally, offered four speeds in the wrong direction to the foolhardy. This picture shows a Salmson of the 1940s, but the Cotal's most dedicated users—Delahaye and Delage—favoured a smaller and neater floor lever.

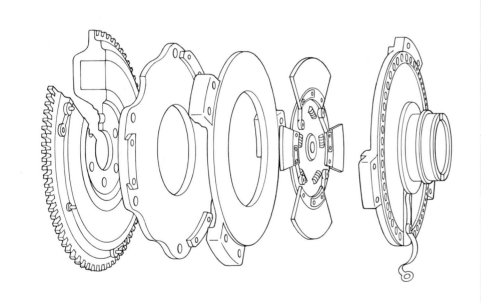

Painless, if not automatic, shifting—with full driver control. Two from the 1955–57 period were (*above*) the Ferlec electromagnetic clutch offered on Renault and some other French makes, and (*right*) Standard's Standrive as available on that company's small sedans. The French arrangement, seen here in exploded form, dispensed with a clutch pedal. Engagement was automatic, via current from the dynamo as the engine was accelerated, and disengagement was equally automatic, being controlled by movement of the gear lever. On the small 4CV, it cost only about £30 ($85) extra. The dynamo also powered Standrive, although disengagement of the clutch was obtained by pressing the button on the gear-lever knob.

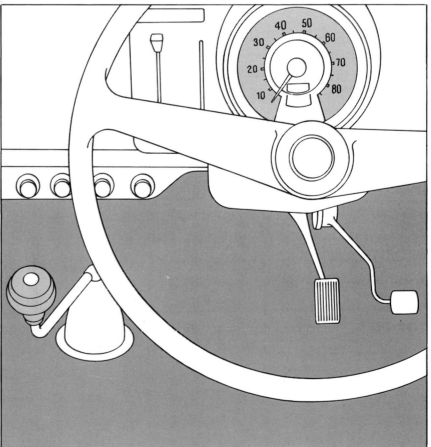

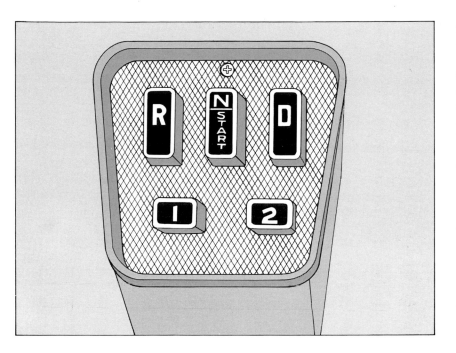

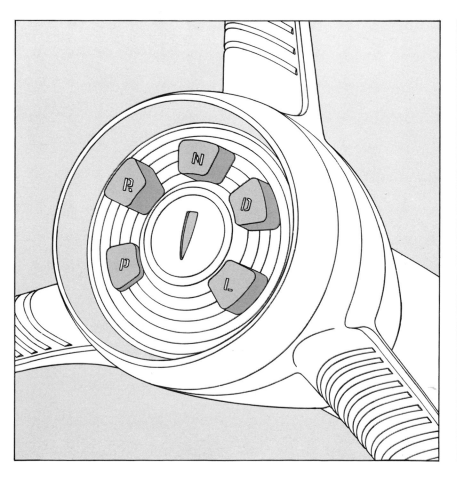

Automatic meant column-mounted selectors in the 1940s. Not so always in the fifties and sixties. The 1957 Dodge (*above*) and other contemporary Chrysler Corporation products used "pushbutton Torque-Flite", a self-explanatory device mounted to the driver's left on this left-hand-drive car. A year later, Ford's ill-fated Edsel featured what its makers called "Teletouch", with the buttons (*bottom left*) in the centre of the steering-wheel boss, a component which fortunately did not rotate with the wheel. By 1967 the trend was, however, towards a floor-mounted in-line quadrant (*bottom right*), here seen on Chevrolet's Corvette sports car. This had the advantage that the same centre console (and therefore the same sheet metal) could be used on cars fitted with "four on the floor" (four-speed manual).

matic" option. Fiat's Idroconvert was an old-fashioned automatic clutch, viable in Italy where people were wary of automatics.

Also a casualty was the three-speed manual box, a victim of the more sophisticated automatics. It survived on a modest scale in America, and on medium-sized American-type sedans (Austin, Datsun, Ford, Holden, Vauxhall) made elsewhere, usually in association with column-shift. This abomination reached its zenith in the first years of our period, when even sports cars (Jowett Jupiter, early DB2 Aston Martins) were thus afflicted. Its stronghold, apart from the U.S.A., was Germany. Yet it died, largely because of the virtual impossibility of arranging five gears (including reverse) in a vertical plane without the need for unnatural movements. Devious linkages encouraged wear in the selectors: hence the tiresome "two-finger exercises" familiar to all who have tried to hold an aged Hillman Minx in second gear. When the pony-car craze swept America in 1964, the public suddenly took an interest in manual boxes and, significantly, Detroit—back with four speeds for the first time in over thirty years—was careful to place the lever firmly on the floor and keep it there. On the other hand, the early five-speeders of Fiat and Alfa Romeo (1953–55) were column-selected, and one American critic summarized the 1900C Alfa as having "the most godawful shift ever made".

All-synchromesh boxes were, by contrast, a phenomenon of the sixties. True, by 1935 it was possible to buy an Adler, an Alvis, or even a Hillman Minx for £165, with such equipment. But high manufacturing costs, and—in the Hillman's case—a remarkable ability to "hang on" in top gear, defeated the object. After 1938, Hillman owners went back to double-declutching in and out of bottom gear, and they probably did not notice the difference. Be that as it may, the general rule in 1951 was to synchronize all forward gears save first. Main exceptions were the Standard Vanguard and the all-new six-cylinder Mercedes-Benz range.

(Opposite) "We are a poor country," said Pegaso's chief engineer Wilfredo Ricart, "and therefore we must make jewels for the rich." This Z102B made in the old Hispano-Suiza factory at Barcelona in 1954 is certainly exotic: four-cam, 3.2-litre alloy V-8 engine, four carburettors, five-speed non-synchromesh transaxle of de Dion type, limited-slip differential, and inboard rear brakes. Saoutchik of Paris and Touring of Milan produced bodies to suit—this example is by the latter firm and could well have inspired both the E-type Jaguar (1961) and the Z-series Datsun (1969). A $30,000 list price was mentioned in the U.S.A., which explains why only 125 Pegasos were made between 1951 and 1958.

(Below) Bubble-car heresy, or the one that preferred a four-stroke engine, in this case a 198-cc single. Heinkel, makers of this *Kabinenroller* (introduced in 1956) made such a unit and fitted it to their own cars. Here we see the British-built 1962 edition from Trojan with its front door open to show the interior. Unlike BMW with the Isetta, Heinkel kept the steering separate from this door and saved themselves some complicated linkages. The first cars had two close-set rear wheels, but in Britain, where both sales and road tax concessions favoured the three-wheeler, this latter version was more popular. Even on the smallest cars, the Germans liked the cabrio-limousine style. Trojan accounted for over 10,000 of the 200s, more than were sold in Germany.

Even in 1959, a synchronized bottom gear was regarded as a luxury, singled out for praise on such cheap European models as the Borgward Isabella (1954), the Peugeot 403 (1955), and the Vauxhall Victor (1957). Fiat's first similar box came on the relatively expensive 1800 and 2100 sixes in 1959, while that technical bellwether, the Volkswagen, was given one a year later. British and American makers did not change over for good until 1964–65, but the sole survivors of the old guard by 1969 were obsolescent machines like the Triumph Herald and the Fiat 600. As for the true crash-box, this was confined to Fiat's sub-utility 500 and a few minicars, although a "standard" Beetle could still be bought without synchromesh as late as 1964. It is significant that, two years previously, the latter firm had scrapped another long-standing crudity of the stripped People's Car, cable-operated brakes: safety already counted for more than an overworked clutch foot.

For those who wanted even more gear ratios, the choice lay between overdrives and "proper" five-speed transmissions (fifth being almost always an overdrive). In the high-performance field, Alfa Romeo preferred the true five-speeder, while Jaguar kept their prices down with an add-on overdrive. Ferrari tried both types before finally settling for the five-on-the-floor scheme which they, and Pegaso of Spain, had pioneered at the beginning of the 1950s. Five-speeders were costlier to make—although ZF of Germany offered a proprietary component, used by Alvis and Aston Martin among others—but they gave a greater degree of control, and eliminated the tedious switchgear of overdrives. Still, a proprietary overdrive bolted easily to the back of the existing gearbox, and it added little to the list price: £58 ($162) on a 1962 six-cylinder

British Ford, by comparison with the £110 ($308) asked for an automatic option.

Overdrives originated in America during the mid-thirties, but attained their zenith of popularity in Britain between 1956 and 1965. The extra gear was "switched in", to be disengaged by flooring the accelerator pedal. Jaguar invariably confined its operation to top gear, which made sense with about 200 horsepower under the bonnet. Lesser cars, however, came with triple overdrives and a multiplicity of overlapping ratios. While it was fun to play one's way up through seven forward ratios on a mundane Standard Eight or Singer Gazelle, this did nothing for efficiency, and the maddening habit of mounting the overdrive switch on the steering column—alongside the control for turn signals—could yield such embarrassing exercises as trying to signal a right turn and encountering the never-very-useful overdrive second! As for five-speeders, they remained essentially an adjunct of the sports car until 1969, only Alfa Romeo fitting them as standard to family sedans. They were, of course, standard on Italian supercars (Ferrari, Lamborghini, Maserati) and on later examples of the Aston Martin DB series, as well as on the fastest members of the Porsche family. In the last two years of the period, Fiat—who had tried such a box on their 1900 sedan as long ago as 1952—now applied all-synchromesh editions to their 125 sedan, and to their twin-cam 124 sports car.

Automatics were totally dominating the native American industry by the late 1950s: the overall share of new cars so equipped rose from 57 % in 1954 to 90 % in 1969–70. For all the glamour of "four on the floor", its use was very limited. Even if over half the sporty Pontiac GTOs

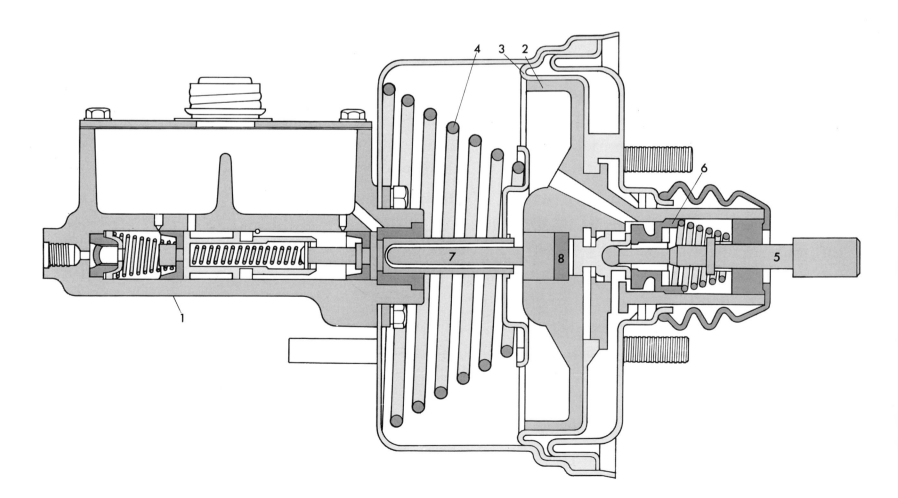

made between 1965 and 1967 came with "stick", this only added some 210,000 cars to the score. Early automatic problems were soon resolved and, after 1950, one heard little of curdling fluid, while the inherent power losses of the system were offset by the benefits of the horsepower race. A change in the law eliminated the endemic hazards of the original P-N-D-L-R (park-neutral-drive-low-reverse) selector quadrant with no protection against an inadvertent back-up. There was still, however, a variety of control layouts: column selection prevailed, but Ford's Edsel featured push-buttons on the steering-wheel boss. Buttons were also used on 1956 Packards and 1956–62 Chryslers. From 1964, though, the tendency was towards a floor-mounted T-handle. As an extreme, the true stepless transmission was ill-suited to cars, since it provided no engine braking, and the strange 1946 Invicta had no imitators until 1958. Then DAF came up with their Variomatic, the ultimate in simplicity, with final drive by twin belts—one to each rear wheel— from a transverse countershaft, thus dispensing with a differential. This was good only for small, low-powered vehicles designed to run in flat countries, and DAF remained its sole user, despite the recurrence of similar devices on 50-cc French minicars of the 1979–82 era.

Automatics, therefore, had to offer a choice of ratios, but how many? Two sufficed on early cheap systems such as Buick's Dynaflow and Chevrolet's Powerglide, the low ratio being necessary only for descending steep hills or manoeuvring in congested car parks. Unfortunately, the combination of powerful V-8 engines and smaller wheels—with less brake cooling and a limitation on drum size—posed headaches. On a standard transmission, second gear could be used to slow the vehicle down from around 60 mph (100 km/h). Not so with a two-speed automatic, where low might be held up to 50 mph (80 km/h) but was not engageable at more than 45 mph (70 km/h). What was ideally suited to a 140-horsepower six could become lethal on a 200-horsepower V-8. General Motors' Hydramatic had always offered four speeds, later reduced to three on 1964 and subsequent versions. Pontiac, Oldsmobile, and Cadillac favoured this system, although Buick developed their own two-speeder and retained it for many years. Ford, by contrast, started with three speeds incorporating an intermediate hold: this was a vital innovation, even if some of their later transmissions provided only two forward ratios. By 1965, the two-speed specialists had mainly gone over to the new type. Chevrolet's Powerglide saw its second decade out, but Turbo-Hydramatic was already available on their more expensive cars and would soon be GM's staple automatic box.

Acceptance came slowly in Europe, where smaller engines took less kindly to the new order. Setting aside Borgward's abortive 1950 experiments, the pioneers were Rolls-Royce/Bentley (1952), Jaguar (1954), and Armstrong Siddeley (1955), all large and expensive cars with capacities of at least 3.4 litres. Early Jaguars used the proprietary Borg-Warner two-speeder, the other makers favouring a licence-built version of GM's Hydramatic. In the main, American designs were adapted to European use, although intermediate holds became widespread rather earlier. There was a steady resistance to automatic on small cars but, by 1964, the loss of performance was apparent only to professional road-testers, who drove such vehicles to their limit. In the case of the 1964 Ford Cortina, the manual version was just 0.8 seconds quicker to

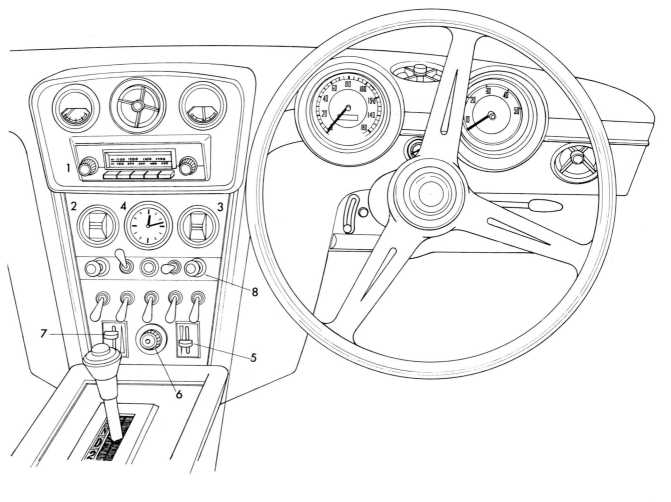

(*Opposite*) Vacuum servos up-to-date: Lockheed's 1961 version allowing for application to a split-circuit system. The servo cylinder is bolted to the master cylinder (*1*), with a direct connection between its piston (*2*) and the master cylinder's. The servo piston is sealed by a rubber diaphragm (*3*) and held against a coil spring (*4*) in the brakes-off position. Induction manifold pressure is applied through a valve to both sides of the servo piston, until application of the brake pedal acts on the pushrod (*5*), when air is admitted by the control valve (*6*). The servo piston then adds its extra thrust to the pressure applied by the driver's foot upon the pedal. Between the master cylinder pushrod (*7*) and the control valve is a rubber buffer (*8*). Fluid pressure built up in the master cylinder acts on the buffer, extruding it against the control valve, and moving it to the right to cut off the air supply to the servo.

(*Right*) Why alternators became a necessity. On the facia of a typical luxury car of 1967, the Jensen Interceptor with Chrysler V-8 engine, can be seen (*1*) the radio, (*2, 3*) controls for electric window lifts, (*4*) an electric clock, (*5*) the rear window demister fan, (*6*) selector for the electrically controlled rear dampers, (*7*) main heater control, and (*8*) screenwiper/washer switch (the latter now electric as well as the former). At the beginning of our period only the wipers would have been there for sure, although in the luxury sector one could reasonably expect that customers would specify both radio and heater. The other extras, however, lay in the future.

30 mph (50 km/h) and 2.8 seconds quicker to 60 mph (100 km/h), while fuel consumption increased significantly from 27.3 to 24.8 mpg (10.6 to 11.4 litres/100 km). On the Continent itself, small automatic-equipped cars took longer to arrive. Automatic Fords from Cologne were on sale by 1965. Opel, after an interval with automatic clutches, offered GM-built boxes on their six-cylinder cars in 1961, extending the option to their intermediate range in 1968. BMW adopted the ZF box in 1966, and Volkswagen had a rather inefficient three-speed "stick automatic" which sold well in America but was unpopular elsewhere.

A revolution in braking methods also characterized our twenty years. Statistical samples can be misleading, since they vary according to parameters: either the number of cars made, or the different types on the market. It would, therefore, be unfair to claim wholesale acceptance of hydraulic systems in 1938, when at least four of the world's biggest manufacturers—Austin, Ford, Peugeot, and Renault—were still firmly committed to rods or cables. But the latter arrangements were on their way out, while four British devotees of the mixed hydromechanical system—Austin, Daimler, Jowett, and Riley—were about to adopt full hydraulics. Only Rolls-Royce would hold out, with their great faith in the old gearbox-driven servo, destined to see them into the era of disc brakes.

The last bastions of mechanical brakes were the stripped-specification sedans, Ford of Britain's 103E Popular (1953–59) and the standard Volkswagen, which did not acquire hydraulics until 1962. The custo-

Remembered as the first mass-produced car to feature alternating rather than direct-current electrics, the 1960 Plymouth Valiant (*below*) was also important as Chrysler Corporation's first compact, and as symbolizing the switch from the old long-stroke side-valve six (made with little change since the 1930s) to a new and modest overhead-valve unit mounted in the frame at a 30-degree slant. Styling was restrained, too, apart from the usual "dustbin lid" pressing on the trunk. Although 2.8 litres were not enough for any real performance, the automatic Valiant managed 90 mph (145 km/h) and an 0–50 mph (0–80 km/h) acceleration time of 12.6 seconds, roughly the potential of a full-sized American straight-eight in 1939. With a length of 184 in (4.7 m), the Valiant was still a large car by European standards. (*Opposite*) Kaiser-Frazer's Henry J sedan of 1951 was, by contrast, a modest package measuring 100 in (2.5 m) between wheel centres, and 166 in (4.2 m) between bumpers. Conceived as a farmer's car to follow in the wheel-tracks of the Model-A Ford, it was a conventional affair with coil-spring independent front suspension, semi-elliptics at the rear, open propeller shaft, and hypoid rear axle. Engines were plain side-valves bought from Kaiser's future partner, Willys-Overland: the Jeep's familiar 2.2-litre four and a 2.6-litre six. Styling was uninspired, and the first Henry Js had no external trunk access. Alas, the American public wanted more car, more output, and more acceleration, while fuel was still cheap and plentiful. It took nearly four years to sell 120,000 Henry Js. The Valiant managed close on 200,000 units in its first season alone.

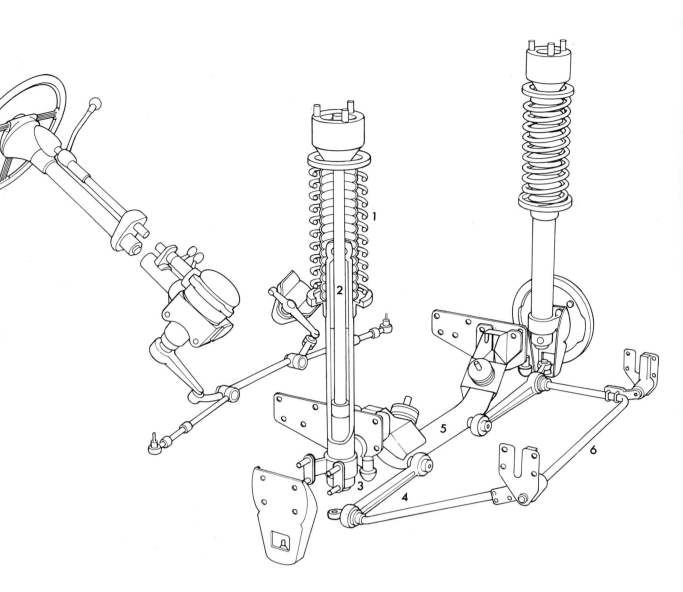

McPherson strut-type independent front suspension as used on French Fords from 1949 and later adapted to other members of the international family. Here is its application to the British Consul/Zephyr Mk. I family of 1951–56. The car's front end is supported on a flexible coil spring (1) on each side. These coils enclose telescopic guides (2) which keep the wheels straight and double as hydraulic dampers. The base of the sliding guide is held by a ball joint (3). This takes the main forces of both braking and cornering—and, incidentally, gives the system the name (ball-joint suspension) by which it is often known in the U.S.A. The ball joint is located transversely by a swept-back transverse wishbone (4), one arm of which is attached to a tubular-frame cross-member (5) and the other to a rubber-mounted anti-roll torsion bar (6).

mer who got a full-sized four-seater sedan for DM 4,000 (a bare 600 marks more than the 300-cc Goggomobil minicar cost) was unlikely to quibble over its crudities. Within a mere six years, however, he would be wanting to know why his "bargain" lacked disc brakes, and raising objections when he had to pay extra for them on such elderly designs as the basic Beetle and the Triumph Herald. While emergency braking systems remained largely unchanged, the deplorable plastic "umbrella" handle under the dash had almost had its day as well. Renault, who were content with one of these unpleasant devices on their otherwise excellent 16 (1965), returned to a floor mounting on their 12 in 1969, probably as a result of the safety drive. If one takes cars tested by the British motoring press as a fair measure, one may note that umbrella handles made up 45 % of the number in 1955, 40 % in 1960, and only 33 % in 1970. The foot-operated "handbrake" stayed an American preserve until Mercedes-Benz picked up the idea in 1968, although sudden-death devices working on the transmission had mercifully been dropped by both Fiat and Chrysler in the early sixties.

Anything made between 1951 and 1960, at all events, could be expected to have hydraulic drum brakes. Later examples were often less efficient than those of 1950–51, due to a new factor: decreasing wheel size. On sporting Classics of the early 1930s, brake-cooling problems had not existed, thanks to a 16-inch brake drum in a 19- or 20-inch wheel, especially since centre-lock wires were *de rigueur* in this class. But

wire wheels were dying out, replaced by the stronger and easier-to-clean disc, even on such traditional sporting machines as Alfa Romeo, Alvis, Bentley, Jaguar, Lagonda, and MG. The old order would return to favour, but not until 1956–57 when wires were a regular option on most British sports cars. Meanwhile, smaller wheels emerged, 16 in representing the standard European size in 1951. American cars then usually wore 15-in equipment, shrinking to 14 in by 1957 when the hairier V-8s were offering 300 horsepower or more—and some lesser models, still with V-8 options, were making do with 13 in four years later. By this time, 15 in was effectively the top limit in Europe, while the Mini, like the bubble-cars, wore tiny 10-in "boots". So there was less space for a brake drum and not enough for its cooling air. Drums heated up and expanded away from their shoes, just as linings lost their friction characteristics. Yet performance increased steadily: 75 mph (120 km/h) was now well within the compass of a stock 1.5-litre sedan, and a wide selection of 100-mph (160-km/h) sporting machinery was on sale. Thus, brake fade became a pressing problem.

The disc brake was the obvious answer. Essentially a development of the bicycle caliper brake, it had friction pads which moved axially to grip the sides of the disc. First fitted to Chrysler and Crosley cars in America as early as 1949–50, this method won prominence on Jaguar's competition sports models between 1952 and 1955. Pioneers of its application to touring models were Citroën (on the 1955 Déesse) with Jensen

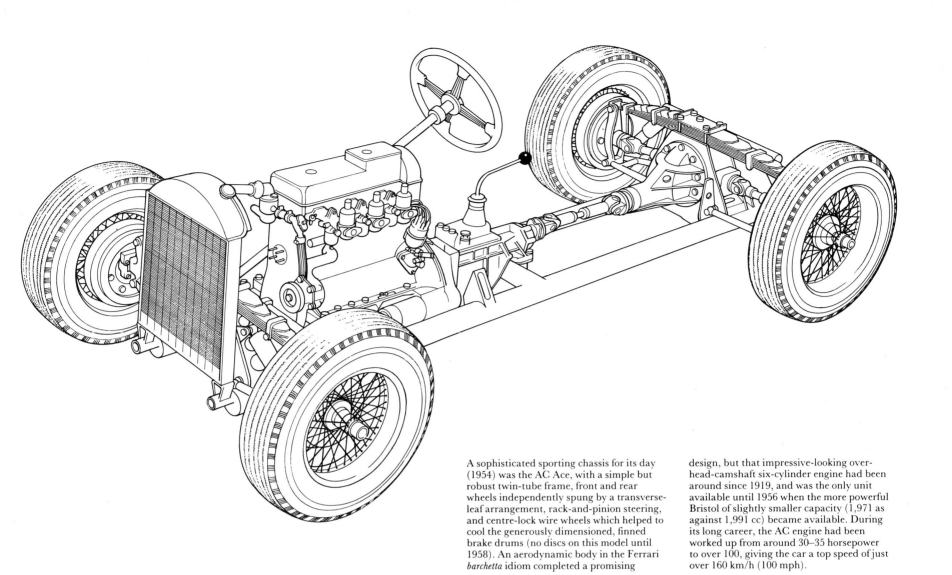

A sophisticated sporting chassis for its day (1954) was the AC Ace, with a simple but robust twin-tube frame, front and rear wheels independently spung by a transverse-leaf arrangement, rack-and-pinion steering, and centre-lock wire wheels which helped to cool the generously dimensioned, finned brake drums (no discs on this model until 1958). An aerodynamic body in the Ferrari *barchetta* idiom completed a promising design, but that impressive-looking over-head-camshaft six-cylinder engine had been around since 1919, and was the only unit available until 1956 when the more powerful Bristol of slightly smaller capacity (1,971 as against 1,991 cc) became available. During its long career, the AC engine had been worked up from around 30–35 horsepower to over 100, giving the car a top speed of just over 160 km/h (100 mph).

and Triumph a year later, although these firms—like most other initial supporters of the system—used discs only at the front. By contrast, Jaguar, whose XK150 (1957) was the next convert, insisted on a four-wheel installation and never offered anything else. A good proportion of the world's specialist manufacturers had taken the plunge by 1960 and, three years later, 24 makers listed front discs as either standard or optional equipment. All-disc layouts were found on Ferrari, Iso, Jaguar, Jensen, Lotus, Maserati, Mercedes-Benz, and Porsche. Fiat and Simca offered them only on sports models, but significant recruits in the family-car sector were Lancia and Renault. Even more interesting was the absence of any American brand except Studebaker, who fitted them to the sadly abortive Avanti sports coupé (1962).

American makers, too, were beginning to list front-disc options by 1966. Few European factories now relied on drums alone, and none of these made anything bigger than a 1,200-cc model. Alfa Romeo and Rolls-Royce had joined the all-disc brigade. At the end of our period, no quality machine (save the huge, ceremonial Phantom VI Rolls-Royce) lacked front discs, while Cadillac and Lincoln had standardized them in America. All but the smallest Fiats and Renaults wore them at the rear as well. In regard to brake actuation, dual master cylinders had long been a regular adjunct of hydraulic brakes, being seen on the big six-cylinder Fiats as far back as 1931. Safety, during our period, called for split-circuit systems with tandem master cylinders, isolating one pair of brakes from the other. These gained serious currency from 1966 onward, being general practice in America by 1969, and were also found on Alfa Romeo, BMW, Citroën, the latest European Fords, Lancia, Saab, and Volvo.

Keeping brakes cool and fade-proof was not enough. Servos were again engaging the attention of designers. They had long been used, the gearbox-drive Hispano-Suiza system (employed by Rolls-Royce) since 1919, and the Belgian Dewandre *servofrein à dépression* since 1923. The latter was applied to several popular makes, including Citroën and Hillman, in the 1920s, but was subsequently cast aside on the usual grounds of cost, not to mention the greater efficiency and modest pedal pressures resulting from the general adoption of hydraulics. By the outbreak of World War II, it had again become the preserve of luxury and sporting machines. More speed, however, calls for more braking effort. The driver of a Cadillac or Rolls-Royce was always in need of some assistance, and so might be the owners of 2-litre family sedans in an era when these were capable of 95 mph (150 km/h). Thus, vacuum servos came back into the picture during the 1960s. Citroën, predictably, preferred hydraulic pressure built up by the same engine-drive pump that supported their Déesse—as we shall see—and, in addition, furnished servo assistance to the clutch and gear change.

Servos were standard by 1960 on the heavier and more expensive American cars—not just Cadillacs, Lincolns, and Imperials, but also

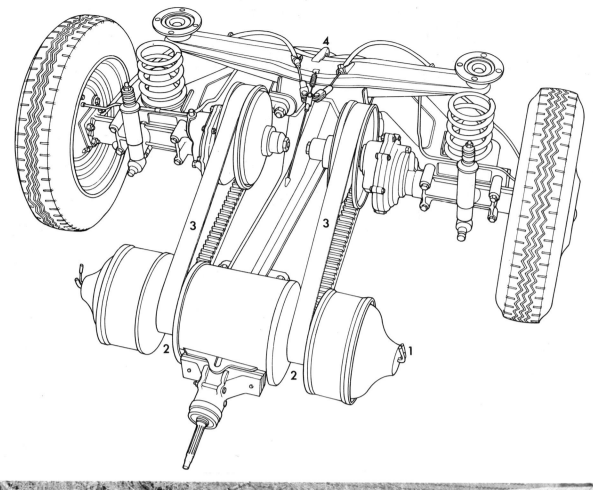

(*Top left*) Simplest of the automatics, DAF's Variomatic Drive, as used by this Dutch manufacturer from 1958 onwards. The drive was transmitted to a transverse countershaft (*1*) with the inboard halves of two vee pulleys (*2*) attached to it. The power was then taken by two belts (*3*), each driving a separate rear wheel. Movement of the pulleys altered the gearing by changing their effective diameter, while a reduction in manifold suction would widen the gaps between the flanges to lower the ratio. The transmission was entirely stepless, and free from the "hunting" of a normal automatic. The whole rear end is mounted on a separate sub-frame (*4*).

(*Bottom left*) Compact at 142 in (3.6 m) long, frugal at 40 mpg (6.5 litres/100 km), and innocent of frills, the 1964 DAF sedan gave no clues to its ingenious and painless Variomatic transmission. All-independent suspension and rack-and-pinion steering were to be expected on a small family sedan born in 1958. And if air-cooled flat-twins sounded a trifle barbaric in the age of the Mini—well, other respected users included BMW, Citroën, and Panhard, the last being a veteran with 73 years of car-making behind it. The DAF's 62 mph (100 km/h) were quite enough, since braking was not its strong suit, while 0–50 mph (0–80 km/h) took 22 seconds, or nearly as long as it took a standard Mini to reach 60 mph (100 km/h). But with only 746 cc under that short bonnet, there's a price to pay for not having to shift gears at any time.

(*Opposite, top*) Triumph switched to fuel-injected engines on their TR5 sports car of 1967, which combined the body and independent rear suspension of the superseded TR4A with a new 2.5-litre six-cylinder engine descended from the 1961 Standard Vanguard Six. Top speed went up from the old four's 109 mph (175 km/h) to around 120 mph (192 km/h). To meet American emission standards, there was a twin-carburettor six as well, the TR250. The interesting Surrey top—available either in metal or as a light frame with hooding—was an option on TR4s and TR5s, which anticipated Porsche's better-known Targa semi-convertible of 1967.

(*Opposite, bottom*) Power assistance for most things on a fine 1968 Euro-American from Jensen, who had built a luxury sedan with a Ford V-8 motor as long ago as 1936. This Vignale-styled Interceptor featured a 6.3-litre V-8 Chrysler engine, a three-speed automatic gearbox, dual-circuit power disc brakes with tandem master cylinders, power-operated windows, and heated rear window. Power steering would not, however, be part of the package until the 1970 season. Interestingly, too, Jensen, who had fitted glass-fibre bodies to sedans in the 1954–66 period, now reverted to all-steel construction. £3,742 was a lot of money to pay for a car in the late sixties, though 13 mpg (22 litres/100 km) was less of a worry while fuel was still cheap and plentiful. And a quiet 120 mph (196 km/h) appealed to nearly 4,500 customers between 1967 and 1973.

Rear suspensions of the fifties and sixties. On the Renault Frégate 2-litre sedan of 1953 (*centre, left*) coils are used in conjunction with trailing arms which oscillate around inclined pivots, running forward to mountings on a "chassis" cross-member. Also independent is the system used on the 1961 E-type Jaguar (*top*): this layout features a bridge-type sub-frame which attaches directly to the car's unitary hull. The springing medium consists

of combined coils and shock absorbers (two to each side) anchored to lower wishbones. The disc brakes are mounted inboard, as they are also on the 1964 Rover 2000 (*centre, right*). Here, however, we have the combination of vertical coils and, to keep the rear wheels parallel with each other, a de Dion "dead axle" tube. This variable-track device contains a telescopic joint with its own oil bath, which slides as the wheels rise or fall relative to each other (*bottom*).

the bigger Buicks and Ford's prestigious Thunderbird. Anything in the 120-mph (195-km/h) class demanded power assistance, too, as did such family machinery as Humbers, Datsuns, Mercedes-Benz, and Rovers. The next step was inevitable: small cars would need help as well. These were getting bigger, heavier, and faster. The 1951 Hillman Minx was 157 in (4.02 m) long, weighed 2,072 lb (945 kg), and could reach 70 mph (112 km/h). Its 1968 counterpart was only 11 in (28 cm) longer, but engine development enabled a mere 230 cc of extra capacity to deliver nearly double the output, plus a 15-mph (22-km/h) increase in top speed. The brakes were now too heavy in relation to performance, so a servo was added to the options list. Similar assistance was given to parallel models like the 124 Fiat, the Audi, and the Peugeot 403.

While wheel sizes went down, tyres were undergoing a major evolution. At the beginning of our period, speeds of around 125 mph (200 km/h) were within the compass of Jaguars, Ferraris, and Aston Martins, yet there were no tyres that could cope with such performance. The tubeless type, available in America by 1948, and in Europe some five years later, was a step towards simplicity but, in itself, contributed nothing to the need for better adhesion. During the 1950s, though, the radial-ply tyre started to make headway. This replaced the earlier cross-ply type, in which alternate layers of reinforcing cords are used at 45 degrees to the centre plane. On the new type, the cords run radially to the tyre, from one bead to another, while additional bracing plies—of steel cord on the Michelin version—were set under the tread. The result was a tyre of greater vertical flexibility, superior rolling resistance, better grip, and longer life. These virtues were won at the cost of a harsher ride and a higher noise level. It is also true to say that a radial induces a larger amount of breakaway when the latter occurs: still, the cornering speed limit is far higher than on a cross-ply. Radials were regular equipment on all high-performance cars by the end of our second decade, while even on family sedans a majority of motorists were specifying them.

Supporting the vehicle on a beam axle at each end was now virtually reserved for all-terrain models like the Jeep, Landrover, and Toyota Land Cruiser. We may pass quickly by such eccentricities as the early Bond Minicar, a three-wheeler on which "suspension" was limited to fat tyres and tiny wheels, albeit only at the back. Independent front suspensions in general use were the coil-and-wishbone type, usually with short and long arms that dispensed with the uncouth "curtseying" of 1930s versions; the transverse-leaf arrangement, where the springs are coupled to swivelling axles; and torsion bars, rigidly coupled to the lower wishbone at its chassis pivot and to a fixed point down the chassis length, a system favoured by Chrysler, Jaguar, Morris, and Volkswagen among others.

A variation on the coil-spring layout was the McPherson strut suspension, which used vertical coils and rigid stub axles. It was taken up by Ford for their French range in 1948, reaching the British models in 1951 and the German cars in 1952, although it would not attain a really wide currency until the 1970s. In the meantime, honours were generally divided between the traditional coil system and torsion bars. Longitudinal semi-elliptics at the rear remained common practice throughout our period, being still used on such makes as Chrysler, Datsun, Ford, Hillman, Oldsmobile, and Rambler even in 1969. The combination of a rigid axle and coils—as on some General Motors cars and on Volvos—called for a locating rod if the handling was not to suffer disastrously. On some cars with front-wheel drive, dead rear axles were supported by transverse torsion bars (the original Citroën *traction*, Audi) or by a rigid axle with transverse leaf spring (DKW).

True independent systems took a while to reach general acceptance but, of the German makers, Mercedes-Benz, Porsche, Volkswagen, and

Borgward used nothing else after the war. The swing axles and coils favoured by Mercedes-Benz and Triumph could create appreciable "hopping" in tight bends. A combination of coils and trailing arms was preferred by BMW, Chevrolet (on the Corvette), Fiat, Renault, and Hillman on the Imp. Volkswagen stayed with their swinging half-axles and transverse torsion bars. Lotus, on the 1957 Elite, adapted the McPherson strut arrangement to the back end. On their earlier sports models (1954), AC used the same transverse leaf and wishbone arrangement at both ends, but they discarded it in favour of coils when installing Ford's high-performance V-8s in the final Cobra series. Also converted to independent rear suspension (in 1961) were Jaguar, who mounted their whole assembly, including the inboard disc brakes, on a detachable bridge-piece. In this case, the actual suspension medium consisted of twin coil springs on each side, the wheels being located by parallel transverse links of unequal and longitudinal radius arms.

Ingenious, too, was the system applied to BMC Minis from 1959 onward, with rubber cones in torsion as the springing medium. This arrangement gave a variable rate, yet needed no lubrication. It would lead to the Hydrolastic interconnected springs found on the 1100 model in 1962, as well as on subsequent 1800s, with application to Minis after 1964. Here, interconnection was obtained by feeding hydraulic pipes into the cones, and the water-based hydraulic system ran down the sides of the car, incorporating the dampers. Not that it was the first such arrangement: on the 2CV Citroën, the simplest of self-levelling systems had been used. Leading arms and horizontal coils at the front were connected with trailing arms and another set of horizontal coils at the rear. This worked admirably, although the alarming roll angles caused by fast cornering would never have been acceptable on any vehicle of real performance. In its original 375-cc form, after all, the 2CV was capable of merely 40 mph (65 km/h).

Citroën soon passed on to better things. Their hydropneumatic suspension was first seen at the back of the old 15/6 in 1954. Two years later, it had been engineered into the remarkable Déesse. The car itself was a sensation, with shark-nose shape, plastic roof, "wheel at each corner" layout, and inboard front disc brakes. But the springing was a real *tour de force*, consisting basically of four oleo-pneumatic struts, with gas compression replacing the metal springs. The system was controlled by Lockheed brake fluid, metered through a regulator driven off the engine by a pump. This adjusted the height of the car from the ground, as well as providing power for jacking in the event of a puncture. Nor was the suspension the pump's sole responsibility. The hydropneumatics also lent assistance to the clutch, gear-change, brakes, steering, and gearbox—although the transmission was not an automatic, and no automatic member of the D family would be listed during our period. *The Motor* called it "the most complicated car made anywhere" and, perhaps wisely, Citroën soon backed the original DS19 with a simplified ID, on which hydraulic aids were confined to the springing. Yet it was certainly the most sophisticated car of the period, and only a sudden humpback bridge could catch it unawares.

Packard's contemporary self-levelling system used 9-ft (2.75-m) torsion bars running down the chassis, wound up anticlockwise to the front and clockwise to the rear, an electric motor being used to adjust the trim. It worked well but, by this time, Studebaker-Packard were in grave financial trouble, and the senior make was doomed to a speedy decline into a badge-engineered Studebaker, on which such devices would have been superfluous. Armstrong Selectaride electrically controlled rear shock absorbers with four settings, available in Britain by 1962, were taken up by Facel Vega, Gordon-Keeble, and Humber for their prestige Imperial sedan.

Air suspensions were tried by Cadillac in 1958, Borgward in 1960,

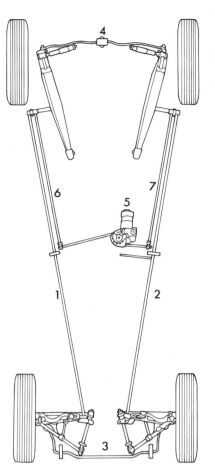

(*Top left*) There is no immediate indication that Cadillac's 1957 Eldorado Brougham is fitted with air suspension: it does not "squat" on its haunches when stationary with the engine switched off. But the new-fangled medium was leak-prone, and disappointing sales—704 in two seasons—high-lighted the common American preference for the safe and known way of doing things. For his $13,000-odd, of course, the customer got a lot more than just a 6-litre 335-horsepower V-8 engine, automatic, and power steering. Inclusive were air conditioning, separate front and rear heater units, radio, a six-way front power seat with built-in memory, power door locks, power trunk lid, tinted glass, a brushed stainless-steel roof, four horns, and such dainty touches as a full van-ity case (with six magnetized silver tumblers, lipstick, and stick cologne), and a perfume atomizer (by Arpège) in the rear-seat armrest. On this model 45 different interior colour/trim combinations were offered.

(*Top right*) Befitting an American luxury car was the sophisticated Torsion-Level inter-linked suspension system used on 1955–56 Packards. Its basis was (*1, 2*) a pair of torsion bars, 2.75 m (108 in) long, running the length of the chassis and attached to both suspensions with stabilizers (*3, 4*) at each end. To allow for changes of load, an electric motor (*5*) was coupled to a pair of shorter auxiliary torsion bars (*6, 7*). This motor cut in if the rear of the car was either higher or lower than its standard position, while a 5-second time lag ensured that the auxiliary system would not operate merely for a bump in the road.

(*Bottom*) Citroën's hydropneumatic suspension in its simplest form, as applied only to the rear of the traditional 15CV six-cylinder for 1954: later models used the hydropneumatics all round. Hydraulic pressure derives from a pump driven off the engine crankshaft (*1*) and supplied from a firewall-mounted reservoir (*2*). The fluid is delivered to a hydropneumatic accumulator (*3*) with a distributor valve which pressurizes the system when the pump is not working. With the pump in operation, the valve feeds the fluid under pressure to recharge the accumulator and feed the suspension system. The circuit passes to an automatic height corrector (*4*), from which single pipes run to each hydropneumatic spring unit (*5*), these being gas-filled spheres screwed to the end of the suspension cylinder. An isolation cock (*6*), between accumulator and height corrector, allows isolation of the front part of the circuit from the rear, thus locking the suspension at static height when the engine is turned off. This cock is reopened automatically by the first depression of the clutch pedal. In the car's boot is a manual override (*7*) to the height corrector, used to assist with wheel changes.

(*Right*) A shark shape—but not a predatory car. Citroën's Déesse wasn't noted for sheer straight-line speed or for fearsome acceleration. The top-of-the-range cabriolet has, of course, all the hydropneumatic aids to painless driving as well as the ingenious suspension. It was made in modest numbers from 1961 to 1971, Henri Chapron (famed for his superb pre-war coachwork on Delage chassis) doing the conversion. The car looks at its best with the top down: in closed form, the absence of rear quarter windows give it a heavy appearance as well as negligible rearward vision. This 1964 model retains the aged long-stroke 1,911-cc four-cylinder engine of a basic type used since 1934/35.

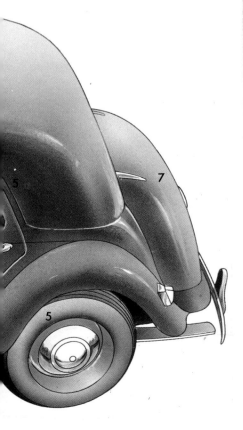

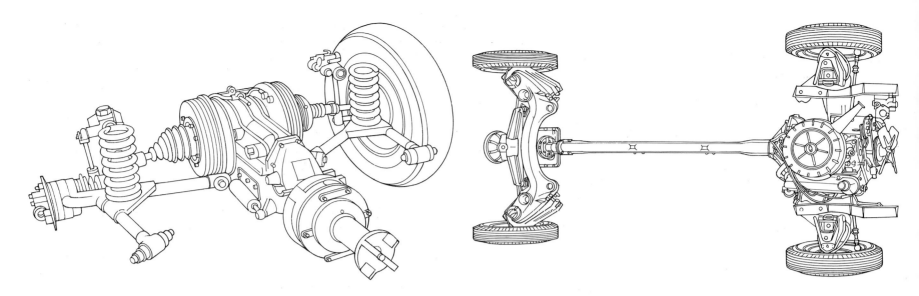

(*Above*) Transaxles. The V-6 Lancia Aurelia of 1950–58 (*left*) always wore its four-speed gearbox on the rear axle. This is the early version with fully independent rear springing by vertical coils which are located by diagonal swinging arms. Note also the mounting of the brakes inboard on the final drive assembly, which made for complicated maintenance. On the 1961 Pontiac Tempest (*right*), a transaxle was once again used, possibly because it shared its essential unitary structure with the rear-engined Chevrolet Corvair, and—like the Corvair—it featured swing-axle independent rear suspension. The Pontiac's oddest feature was, however, a curved flexible drive-shaft, said to damp out some of the vibration inherent in a big four-cylinder engine, in effect half of one of the Division's existing V-8 designs.

(*Below*) Power steering, as standard equipment fitted to the 1968 NSU Ro80 sedan with front-wheel drive and a Wankel-type engine. For safety, the steering box (*1*) is mounted high up on the firewall: the steering gear itself is of rack-and-pinion type. Power assistance is furnished by a vane-type pump (*2*) driven off the engine by two vee belts, and fed with hydraulic fluid from a tank (*3*). Thence it is delivered under pressure to a servo valve (*4*) adjacent to the steering box, and brought into action by movement of the steering wheel to left or right.

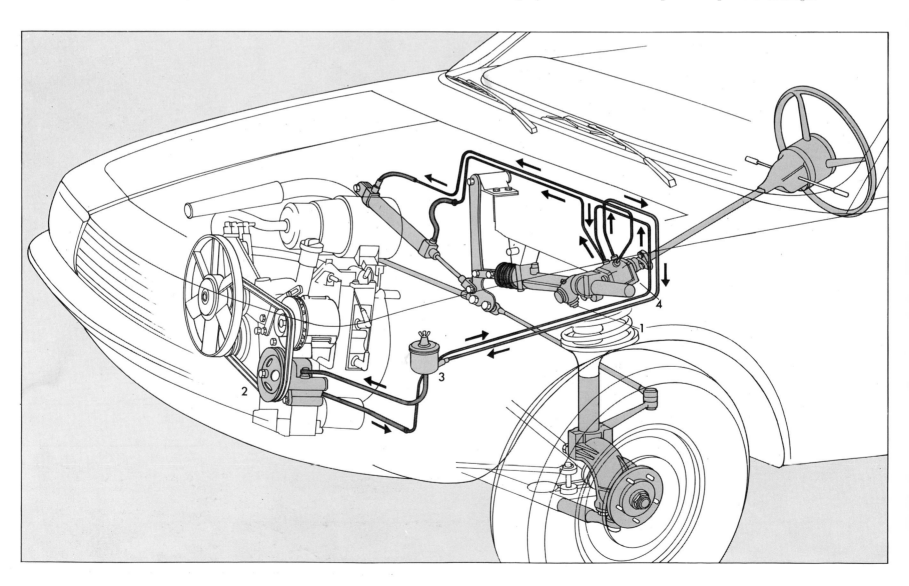

and Mercedes-Benz in 1963. Engine-driven compressors powered all these systems, although in the last case they were supplementary to the standard suspension—by coils and wishbones at the front, and by swing axles at the rear. The Cadillac used a rubber air dome at each corner, and no conventional springs whatever. This car, like the Citroën Ds, leapt into action with an obbligato of reproachful moans, but the main problem was that the system leaked. The Mercedes-Benz arrangements were simply too expensive in terms of the improvement they gave, though they survived on the ultra-costly 6.3-litre 600 limousine until it was finally withdrawn from production in 1981, and they were applied to some of the more expensive owner-driven sedans. The six-cylinder Borgward's two-year run was terminated by the maker's bankruptcy in 1961: few were made, and fewer still with the air springs. Perhaps significantly, when production was resumed briefly in Mexico in 1967, no mention was made of any suspension other than the orthodox type.

On cars with rear-wheel drive, the hypoid bevel reigned supreme. But on a number of models, notably Lancia and the Pontiac Tempest of 1962, there was a reversion to the transaxle, in which the gearbox was combined with the differential. While this helped to give a more even weight distribution, and was adopted by its American advocates for better front-seat legroom, it posed problems of maintenance and was never widely employed. A more lasting development was the limited-slip differential, which prevents wheel-spin when accelerating away

from a standstill. This was a valuable adjunct by the early 1960s, since many back ends were being made to transmit 300 horsepower or more. As early as 1951, it was standard equipment on the Spanish Pegaso sports car. By the end of our period, it was found on such rapid machinery as the Euro-American AC, Iso, and Jensen, all Ferraris and Lamborghinis, the E-type Jaguar, and the V-8 Morgan. It was also an option on the six-cylinder sedans made by BMW, Jaguar, and Mercedes-Benz. Meanwhile, the de Dion rear axle, a curved dead tube which carried the weight of the car but did not transmit the drive, reappeared on various models: notably Allard, Aston Martin, Frazer Nash, and Pegaso in the 1950s, besides the Rover 2000 of 1964 in conjunction with coil springs. On the Rover, it was selected to furnish a combination of good handling and low unsprung weight. It was never, though, widely used except on racing cars.

Power-assisted steering was more controversial than automatic transmission, largely because it took all the feel out of directing a car. In its more extreme forms, it gave the driver an impression that he was assisting the car, rather than the opposite. However, it was a necessary development in the U.S.A., where cars were growing in weight and bulk. There was also a limitation on the gearing-down which increased the number of steering-wheel turns from lock to lock. Five and a half turns were becoming the norm in America, but even the three and a half turns required by an average European 1.5-litre sedan felt undergeared by the standards of Vintage cars.

Backbone frames. Shown here is the classic Mercedes-Benz construction inherited from pre-war and still used on the big 300 sedans of 1951–62, though smaller models would switch to true unitary construction from 1953 onwards. This model featured a 3-litre single overhead-camshaft six-cylinder engine developing 115 horsepower, but higher outputs were extracted from later fuel-injected versions. Automatic transmission was available from 1956, and power steering from 1958. Also a legacy of the early thirties is the classic all-coil independent springing with swing axles at the rear. The 1959 Triumph Herald, a mass-produced sedan, reflected Mercedes thinking in chassis and suspension alike, though the body outriggers were longitudinally braced. Radius arms were used to locate the rear suspension units. The backbone was robust enough: unfortunately both outriggers and radius arms were rust-prone, sending many an outwardly sound Herald to the wrecking yard. The same backbone was applied to a sports-car derivative, the Spitfire (*photo page 199*), the idea being an entirely logical one for sporting machines on which any intrusion into the cockpit centre mattered little. Another user of the system was Lotus, on their superb Elan two-seater of 1962. The forked structure lent itself to front or rear engines, being subsequently applied to the Europa coupé with mid-mounted Renault unit (*photo page 51*). The Elan had all-independent strut-type suspension, a powerful twin overhead-camshaft four-cylinder Lotus-Ford engine, and all-disc brakes.

Cadillac and Chrysler were first in 1951 with a hydraulic system connected in parallel to the track rod, between the chassis and the steering arm. These principles were followed by all subsequent arrangements, although Citroën naturally linked the steering gear to their complex hydropneumatic circuit and Studebaker briefly tried a mechanical device driven off the crankshaft by a pulley. By 1953, the entire U.S. industry was offering this new form of assistance. It came on 93 % of all new Cadillacs and, even in the middle-class sector, 45 % of Chrysler customers and 40 % of Oldsmobile's had tired of sawing away at the steering-wheel. A year later, Cadillac fitted it as standard, while it remained an extra on Imperials until 1955 and on Lincolns until 1956. Nominally, it was still an extra on lesser breeds of American automobiles in 1969, but only 16 % of customers were content to do without it. Apparently, too, the sportier American motorist wanted acceleration, "performance packs", and illicit straight-line speed rather than precise handling, since 66 % of that year's Ford Mustangs were power-steered.

In Europe, Citroën led off during 1955, followed by Rolls-Royce, Bentley, Facel Vega, and the usual procession of up-market manufacturers: Armstrong Siddeley, Mercedes-Benz, and Jaguar. After this, it was the usual procession of semi-prestige sedans, with Rover in 1960, BMC in 1962, Opel in 1964, and Vauxhall in 1965. BMW's move back to six cylinders in 1968 brought them into the power-steering league as well. Assistance could also be had on super-cars in the Aston Martin/ Ferrari bracket, although normally as an optional extra.

The rack-and-pinion steering gear made great strides, yet it would not become nearly universal until the middle seventies. Always noted for its direct and positive action, it was quite widely used in the first decade of our century, but was discarded because of the backlash it transmitted to the steering-wheel. Intriguingly, it was an adjunct of one

Safety measures. This Alfa Romeo collapsible steering column dates from 1975, but typifies progress already apparent in the late sixties. Much promoted as a safe vehicle, the 1964 Rover 2000 (below) was built round a steel cage with a bulkhead strong enough to prevent the engine's working its way back into the passenger compartment in a collision: the skeleton version was drivable, with alarming-looking tubes on the rear quarter panel, namely the petrol-tank breathers.

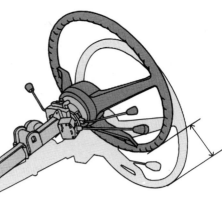

This diagrammatic view of the Rover's 3.5-litre automatic-transmission development (1969) shows some of the features singled out by the makers as "safety equipment": (1) resilient padding for the interior quarters, (2) front-seat belt anchorages (they were also furnished at the rear), (3) child-proof rear door locks, (4) softly padded sun visors, (5) switches "differing in shape, feel, and movement" to avoid pulling the wrong button, (6) heater air intake above the level of other vehicles' exhausts, (7) high-mounted steering box in a position where it cannot push the wheel and column up in an accident, (8) dished steering wheel, and (9) fuel tank mounted within the main structure and insulated from the passengers by a steel bulkhead. Also on the "safety" list was the linear speedometer, although a good few owners of the model (including the present writer) would regard this as a questionable asset.

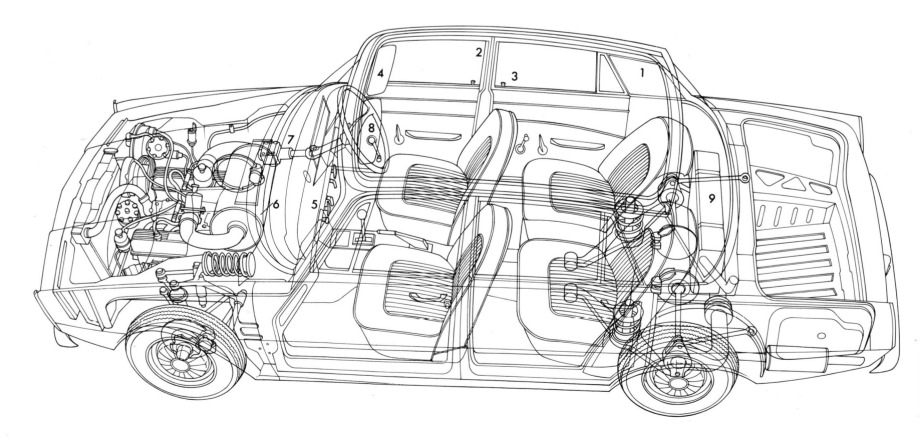

of the first successful independent front-suspension systems, that of Maurice Sizaire in 1905. In its modern form, the racks were damped by spring-loaded metal or plastic inserts pressing on their backs. Already in the 1930s, it had been successfully applied to the cars with front-wheel drive by Citroën, DKW, and Adler. By the late 1940s, it was found on two members of the new post-war generation, the Morris Minor and the Peugeot 203. The Saab had it from the start in 1949, as might be expected from the Swedish car's DKW ancestry. Jaguar, who had tried it on their competition models, applied the system to the touring line as well in 1955. Outside America, the industry was quick to spot its advantages. The first cars from DAF and a revived NSU company came out with such equipment in 1958, Mazda and Triumph being among 1959's recruits. Others fitting rack-and-pinion systems in the 1960s included Hillman, Opel, Porsche, and Vauxhall, joined at the very end of our period by Ford of Europe and Fiat.

The chassis frame was by no means dead. Although Americans preferred perimeter types to the old cruciforms, they still regarded unitary construction as a tiresome question-mark. Two of Ford's more expensive cars, the Thunderbird and the Lincoln, dispensed with separate chassis in 1959, but both were back with this older layout by 1969. Backbones were used by Volkswagen, Porsche, and Skoda, as well as by Mercedes-Benz on their pre-war "hangover" types. Triumph returned to traditional methods in 1959 by building the Herald on a double-backbone basis, which was said (correctly) to be stronger and (less correctly) to be rustproof. Except for Mercedes-Benz, Jaguar, and (from 1966) Rolls-Royce, the specialist makers tended to stay with separate frames long after the demise of a custom-body industry that cloaked the cars individually.

But otherwise the separate chassis was losing its grip. Austin quit in

1954, Standard in 1955, and Rootes in 1956, while on the Continent all post-1952 Fiats were unitary structures. Volvo reserved the old arrangements for their antiquated and ponderous PV800, a hangover from the 1930s which catered for the Swedish taxi trade and for chauffeur-driven executives until 1959. Unitary construction itself pursued the principles laid down at the time of its inception in the 1930s, although the Citroën/Fiat concept of a "wheelbarrow"—to carry the mechanical elements—was taken a step further on the Rover 2000 of 1964. This model was welded into a complete skeleton including the outlines of roof, bonnet, and boot, then was dressed with its mechanical elements and outer skin.

Tubular space frames were used to considerable effect on specialist competition cars, although fitting the machinery—or, for that matter, the crew—into the resultant structure was something of a problem. On 1954's Mercedes-Benz, a low profile was achieved by tilting the engine at 45 degrees, and this rendered a right-hand-drive option impossible, though it did not require the use of fuel injection instead of carburettors. A glance at the jungle of small-diameter tubing that made up the 1961 "Birdcage" Maserati was a clear indication of its unsuitability for all but racing, despite its undoubtedly optimum combination of strength and lightness.

We shall encounter glass-fibre techniques in detail when discussing bodies. Suffice it to say that the material was first adapted to car bodies in California in 1950, and initially applied to a series-production automobile on 1953's Chevrolet Corvette sports roadster. By 1956, however, Berkeley had built a small sports model around three sections of bolted-up glass fibre and an aluminium bulkhead, while Colin Chapman's Lotus Elite came a year afterward. The latter was constructed from three major mouldings bonded together, with only three important

(*Right*) What looks right is right—nearly 330,000 discriminating customers in a short decade can't be wrong. The shape suggests the Citroën Déesse, and Rover's 2000 of 1964 was nearly as awkward to work on. But even in 90-horsepower single-carburettor form with four-speed manual transmission, the 2-litre overhead-camshaft engine propelled the car at 105 mph (168 km/h), motorway cruising speed was a comfortable 90 mph (145 km/h), and with gentle driving one could average 31 mpg (9 litres/100 km). One was, of course, always conscious that the 2000 was a four: customers had to wait until 1968 for a V-8 alternative, and even then automatic was compulsory until 1972.

metal components—the front suspension frame, bonded-in mountings for the other mechanical elements, and the windscreen hoop which had built-in jacking points and supports for the door hinges. The final drive unit bolted directly at the rear onto the bottom moulding, with no structural problems at all. True, early shells did not line up very happily, and the finish of mouldings left much to be desired. But the Elite's misfortunes were not born of its avant-garde structure: rather, they were a result of the·maker's lack of experience with series production. Lotus chose a separate backbone chassis for their next car, because it was intended to have an open body and would therefore lack the reinforcement conferred by the Elite's fixed roof.

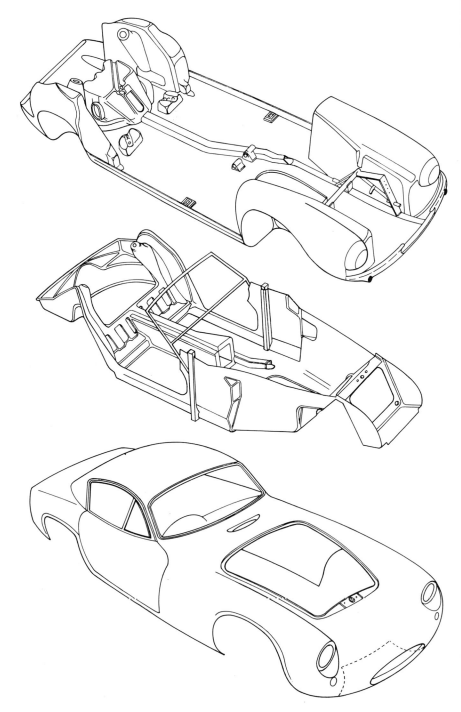

The marriage of glass-fibre and unitary construction, on the Lotus Elite sports coupé (1958). The whole structure is built up in three main mouldings. These consist of (top) the undertray with wheel wells, a front sub-frame to take the suspension units, and the differential mounting; (centre) the interior chassis/body panels, transmission tunnel, and engine bay; (bottom) the upper body with roof and wings. Doors, bonnet, and boot lid were separate mouldings, and the only metal elements were the front sub-frame and the tubular windscreen hoop.

Chapter 3

BODIES —BEAUTIFUL AND

OTHERWISE

The stylist had integrated the motor car long before it became truly unitary in construction. Radiators had vanished behind grilles, dumb-irons were casualties of independent suspension, spare wheels had been tidied into boots, and lamps merged into grilles or fenders. The greatest stylistic influence at the beginning of the 1950s, the Cadillac Sixty Special of 1938, retained a separate chassis frame, and so did the Cadillacs of 1969. Yet nobody, except the public-relations people, referred to these as Cadillacs with bodies by the Fisher or Fleetwood Divisions of General Motors Corporation. At a more exotic level, only students of the body beautiful were really concerned whether a Ferrari was clothed by Bertone, Pininfarina, or Scaglietti: it was a Ferrari. While almost every car out of Maranello in 1951 had been a one-off, such extravaganzas, when encountered, were no more than styling prototypes for the future. The rear-engined Berlinetta Boxer flat-twelve would not go on sale until 1973, and thus is outside our period of reference. However, visitors to the 1968 Turin Show were given a preview of its appearance, if not its mechanics, in the non-running P6 coupé displayed by Pininfarina.

As we have seen, the specialist car manufacturer was slower to commit himself to unitary construction. Alfa Romeo had taken the plunge in 1950, Mercedes-Benz in 1953, Jaguar in 1956, and Rolls-Royce ten years later. But Ferrari and Jensen still built on chassis frames, as did Triumph and Morgan at a lower level. Still, whereas in 1939—and even to a lesser extent in 1950—there had been Saoutchik Delahayes and Hooper Rolls-Royce (though not, alas, Le Baron Lincolns), the decline would end in death after a decade. Of eleven purveyors of *haute couture* who exhibited at London's Earls Court in 1951, only five survived into 1961. With the demise of James Young in 1967, the great British "coachbuilt" tradition came to a close.

During our period, the German custom-body industry was effectively reduced to the supply of limited-series cabriolets for the big battalions. In France, the house of Figoni ceased operations in 1955 with a small series of Simca convertibles, there being no more Delages or Delahayes on which to exercise their craft. Chapron's decline was even more poignant. A special 15CV Citroën limousine—built for the President of the Republic, no less, in 1955—incorporated assorted hardware from French Fords, Chevrolet stop-lights, Bentley door handles, and a 1949 Buick rear window! The demand for "specials" on more mundane chassis was fading away: Plymouth shipped 20,762 cars without bodies between 1930 and 1942, but only 10,645 in the more prosperous years from 1951 to 1955. As for Cadillac, the 1938–50 chassis shipments, apart from specially lengthened "commercials" for ambulance and

hearse builders, amounted to 128 units. Thereafter only 44 were delivered, the last of these in 1963.

Not all was gloom. There was the shining exception of Italy. Before the war, connoisseurs of the exotic went to Paris or London according to taste, with an occasional glance at Berlin or Brussels—Belgian coachbuilders outlived the nation's chassis-makers by several years—but now they flocked to Turin. We shall meet the actual work of the Italians in a later chapter: let us note for the moment that they either devoted themselves to the creation of inspired shapes for volume production, like Bertone's Alfa Romeo Giulietta coupé (1954), or quietly transformed themselves into car builders in their own right, just as William Lyons of Swallow Coachbuilding had done in the 1930s with his SS and later with Jaguar. The line of demarcation was narrow, and sometimes a maker backtracked. Moretti, for instance, switched at the end of the 1950s from costly and none-too-successful twin overhead-camshaft miniatures, to Fiat derivatives which were not obviously Fiats.

Styling was sometimes subordinated to engineering. Arguably, with elaborate testing programmes extending from the Arctic Circle to the Sahara, it was becoming ever more difficult to produce a bad car. Mistakes, when they happened, were the result of poor market research or, alternatively, of premature release which reduced the customer to an unwilling member of the experimental department.

Disasters were nevertheless possible. At Chrysler in the early fifties, a constant battle was waged between the stylists and Corporation president Kaufman T. Keller, who dismissed the shapes of GM and Ford products as "jello-mold" and insisted that car boots should be able to carry a milk-churn in the vertical position. Hence, a style just about acceptable in 1950 had run its course by 1953, losing Plymouth two places in the sales-race list and, worse still, a quarter of a million sales in one year. The necessary and overdue reaction, masterminded by stylist Virgil Exner, went too far. Tail fins could be forgiven in 1957, when everyone else was adding them, but the abominable "dustbin lids" of 1957–61 could not.

Also to be laid at the stylist's door were wheel spats (fender skirts), smaller wheels and their alarming side-effects on braking performance, deep alligator bonnets with tricky access (the Jaguar Mk.VII was a bad offender), and large areas of non-detachable sheet metal capable of turning apparently superficial damage into an insurance write-off. Those who derided the 2CV Citroën's "garden shed" look should remember that, by contrast, almost everything save the basic skeleton was demountable for quick and cheap replacement. Not that the stylist

(*Below*) A tradition fades. Britain's first razor-edge sedans were seen in 1935–36, and the idiom persisted through the 1950s, with Austin and Triumph applying it to volume-production cars. By contrast, the Empress body created by Royal coachbuilder Hooper for the 2.5-litre Special Sports Daimler chassis was a true special-order item, and a clever blend of the traditional shape with the latest in fender lines. A single-panel curved screen is used, though the headlamps are only half-recessed and even a minor parking incident would lead to alarming repair bills. This example from 1953 is mounted on the later 3.5-litre Regency chassis, a bigger six retaining Daimler's fluid flywheel preselective transmission as used by the company since 1930. Only about thirty such cars were built.

(*Opposite, top*) When this Tipo 410 Superfast coupé was exhibited at the 1956 Paris Salon, Ferraris were still being built on a truly bespoke basis. Created by Pininfarina (who else?), it was strictly a one-off, but total production of the 410 series did not exceed two dozen units, all with 5-litre V-12 engines delivering 340 horsepower at 6,000 rpm. There was still only one overhead camshaft per bank of cylinders and four forward speeds, while Enzo Ferrari—like most specialist makers—was content with a beam-axle rear end and drum brakes. Price? The 67,000 francs quoted in Switzerland for a "standard" 410 would have all but bought two Aston Martins, or three XK Jaguars with all the optional extras.

(*Opposite, bottom*) Not quite the ultimate in conventionally engineered "street" Ferraris—the Daytona was yet to come—but the best you could buy in 1966, a 275 GTB/4 *berlinetta* on the short, 2.4-m (7.9-ft) wheelbase. Split-circuit power disc brakes are becoming the norm for super-cars, but now Ferrari have switched to independent rear springing and a five-speed transaxle incorporating a limited-slip differential. The V-12 engine has the familiar dimensions of 77×58.8 mm (3,286 cc), but now there are twin overhead camshafts per bank of cylinders, six Weber dual-choke carburettors, and 300 horsepower, to give the happy customer 155 mph (250 km/h) and an acceleration over a quarter mile (0.4 km) in 14.7 seconds from standstill. Despite a production run of only two years, 280 such cars found buyers.

always had things his own way. An integrated body design could be changed only after it had paid for its tooling, and the weaker brethren suffered accordingly. Kaiser's "1951" shape (actually on sale early in 1950) would probably have seen the firm beyond their collapse in 1955, but there was nothing Singer could do with the SM1500 of 1948, outmoded by 1952 and still with four more laboured years ahead of it. For the devotees of unitary construction, the going was even harder: no wonder Nash scrapped Hudson's six-year-old Stepdown when they took over in 1954.

To show the problems of a unitary shape, let us consider that hardy perennial, the Hillman Minx, from a company that kept free of financial stress for at least the first eleven years of our period, with an annual sales potential of 50,000 or more at all times. Having gone unitary ahead of the rest in 1940, it lasted for the whole of our relevant twenty years. Yet, during this interval, it had precisely five shapes, one being the supplementary "Super" line produced alongside the basic Minx from 1962 to 1966. The final pre-war idiom took it through to 1948, when the slab-sided "squashed Plymouth" type took over. By dint of extensive juggling with chromium strip, enlarged boots, new grilles, and two-toning, this type held up until the summer of 1956. Detroit's latest "sculptured line" then enjoyed a ten-year heyday, while tail fins

came and went. The design was stretched into 1966 by giving it a razor-edge roofline (not unattractive), and a similar treatment was accorded to the bigger Supers for their last two seasons. The final wedge shape, common to both junior and senior models, emerged in 1966 and had a run of over ten years. Indeed, it was still being made in 1982 from British-built units in a state-owned factory in Iran.

Even such ingenious methods called for some sacrifices. There were no convertibles after 1964, and the operation was kept profitable by the intrusion of the badge-engineering element. Almost everything made after 1955 had close relatives which were either Sunbeams, Humbers, or Singers. Confusion might arise: the Super Minx-based Humber Sceptre of 1963 looked as if it had started as a Sunbeam only to be diverted into the prestige family by the addition of quad headlights (a Humber hallmark) and overdrive as standard. But to Britons, the Hillman Minx was an institution—it was not to anyone else, despite a healthy export performance from 1948 until the early sixties. Alas, it was too British in concept to challenge true world cars like the VW, the 403 and 404 Peugeots, or even the Mini. Further, the Minx had no stylistic continuity. Even had the final version less painfully resembled the latest in European Fords, it was by no means clearly a descendant of the 1950 car, let alone of its 1940 ancestor.

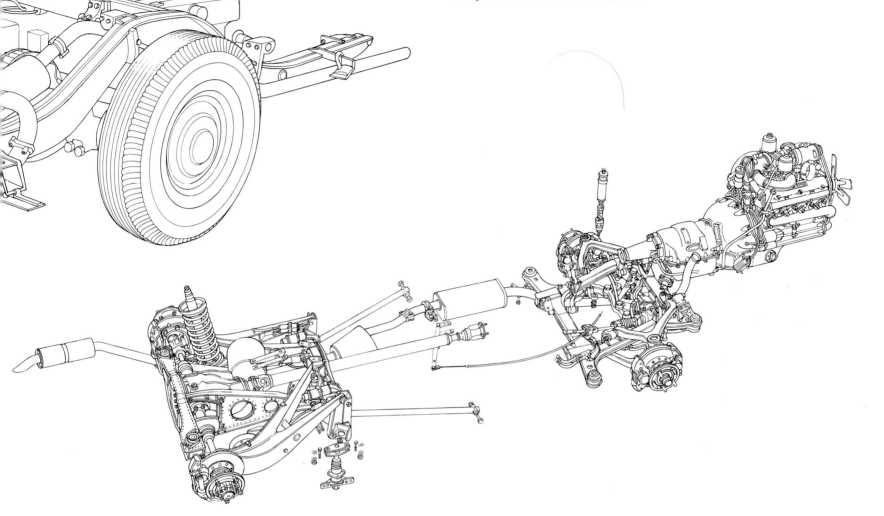

The changing face of craftsmanship. A traditional cruciform-braced chassis frame was used by the 1959 Rolls-Royce Silver Cloud II (*left*). Viewed in section (*below*) is the unitary Silver Shadow which replaced it in 1965. Almost the only features common to both are the 6.2-litre overhead-valve V-8 engine, the four-speed automatic transmission (soon to be replaced by a three-speeder on the Shadow) and, of course, the classic radiator shape, without which the chassis somehow has a naked look. Power steering had already appeared on Silver Clouds in 1957, but with the Silver Shadow came disc brakes and self-levelling, all-independent suspension.

Those who achieved an immortal shape—such as the Morris Minors of 1949–71, or the Volkswagen (born 1938 and still going strong in 1982, though not in Germany)—had to go into a great deal of detail work in keeping it up-to-date. Surviving specimens of Adolf Hitler's original KdF-Wagen in museums are unmistakable cousins of the latest models from Mexico or Brazil, but no part is interchangeable. A closer look reveals that the only common elements are the general shape, the "phut-phut" exhaust note, and the base engineering except for post-1969 suspensions. Even if we take the Beetle as it was in 1950, ignoring purely technical developments like synchromesh and disc front brakes, we begin with a small-windowed sedan, innocent of ventipanes or scuttle-vents. The thin bumpers sprouted overriders of dubious utility, the windscreen was straight rather than curved, and the rear window was of divided type, while the car rode on 16-in wheels. Scuttle air-vents came in 1951, front-window ventipanes in 1952, and an oval one-piece rear window in 1953. The latter gave way from 1957 to something bigger, no longer oval, and the window area was substantially increased in 1964. Anything made from 1954 onward had twin exhaust tailpipes, sliding roofs replaced the original canvas-insert option in 1962, and the "spine" on the rear engine cover disappeared in 1963. This is only a very abridged account of the changes.

The Morris Minor story is simpler: the shape was even more inflexible, and world demand had fallen off by the later 1950s. Changes made after 1949 included raised, semi-exposed headlamps (to conform with American law) in 1950, a new grille in 1953, and a single-panel curved screen from late 1956. The engine alterations of 1952, 1956, and 1962 had, in themselves, no significant effect on the Minor's appearance. Other long-lived shapes existed, too, in a period of stylistic change. The Alfa Romeo coupé and spyder of 1954–55, Fiat's 600 and 1100–103, the compact Jaguar sedans, the original Saab: all were at least fifteen years old by 1969, although both Fiats and the Jaguar were near the end of their careers. Oddly for such a period, it is a list as impressive as that of pre-war ancients still with us in 1955—the Citroën *traction* (1934), the IFA F8 *née* DKW Meisterklasse (1935), and that quartet from 1936, the Fiat 500, Type 170 Mercedes-Benz, T-type MG, and four-wheeled Morgan.

As we moved into the middle sixties, the stylist's function changed. In the early years, it was a case either of prolonging an outmoded shape's career, or ensuring that next year's model didn't look too like last year's. Pontiac's famed Silver Streaks, still around in 1956, had come into being twenty-two years earlier as a hurried add-on, for just this reason. But as the safety lobby moved in, the stylist's aid was

Sorrows of a stylist, or what can happen on a low budget. John Reinhart's new shape for the 1951 Packard was fine at its introduction, and still acceptable in 1952 (*left, top*): unfortunately it had to suffice, in essence, until 1956 and the end of the firm's independent technical existence. This one is, of course, a side-valve straight-eight, and the presence of only three ventilating ports in the rear fenders identifies it as the relatively inexpensive 4.7-litre 200 rather than the up-market 400. On this car, a three-speed manual transmission was standard, though over 85 % of Packards (less than 63,000 this year) preferred the company's own painless Ultramatic, and most of them would have chosen the servo-brake option, too. Still visible are traces of the traditional Packard radiator shape, crowned by the proud Cormorant mascot. Star of the 1954 range was the Caribbean convertible (*left, bottom*), still a straight-eight, though they'd extracted a startling 212 horsepower from 5.8 litres of engine, and there were nine main bearings as on the first of the family way back in 1923. The sporty Continental spare wheel kit was not the only built-in luxury—you also had power brakes, steering, top, seats, windows, and radio antenna, as well as automatic, a screenwash, and genuine wire wheels. At over $5,000 delivered, this monster attracted precisely 400 buyers.

(*Opposite, top*) Measures of desperation. Stuck with the ageing and whale-like Stepdown shape on their full-size cars, Hudson tried their luck with the compact Jet in 1953, on a 105-in (2.7-m) wheelbase. At long last, the traditional wet-plate clutch gave way to a dry-plate unit, but the engine, though now pressure-lubricated, was a modest 3.3-litre side-valve six giving only 114 horsepower even with a twin-carburettor ("Miracle H-Power"!) option. Sales of 35,000-odd in two seasons were not encouraging and, when Hudson merged with Nash to form American Motors, the new combine discarded the Jet in favour of Nash's established Rambler.

(*Opposite, bottom*) Unkind critics likened its styling to a "squashed Ford Consul", its unitary hull was corrosion-prone, and the transmission-type handbrake was an anachronism. But the 1100–103 Fiat unveiled in 1953 was one of the best small sedans of its era, good for over 75 mph (120 km/h), cruising at 70 mph (112 km/h) on its native *autostrade*, and turning in a frugal 38 mpg (7.4 litres/100 km). It was also fun to drive, and more flexible than the original *millecento*, on which skilled bootcraft had been necessary to sustain anything as low as 20 mph (31 km/h) in top. The central spotlamp identifies this as a second-series car from 1956–57.

invoked to supply the odd sporty touch that could no longer be worked into mechanical specifications. At the 1968 London Show, the cynical, diehard *Veteran and Vintage* amused itself at the expense of such purveyors of "safety and scriptitis". Singled out for comment were vinyl tops (every sedan a hardtop), "Ro-style" wheels, and a lovely assortment of chromium strip within and without. To make an artificial "GT" out of up-market trimmings was much cheaper than an extra carburettor.

One could also pool components cleverly across a range, and still make the end product look different. Until they branched into specialty items (Corvair, Toronado) in the 1960s, General Motors of America purveyed family sedans in five grades, from Chevrolet at the bottom to Cadillac at the top. In the mid-fifties, at any rate, one recognized a Cadillac by its tail fins, a Buick by the portholes in its bonnet, and an Oldsmobile by its missile motif. Chevrolet had a bow-tie emblem, and Pontiac the legendary Silver Streaks. These "signature tunes" (no milder term suffices) were so engraved upon public consciousness that nobody paused to reflect that, within this wide range, GM made do with exactly three basic bodies. While there were occasional shufflings and interchanges, in principle the "A" body served for Chevrolet and Pontiac; "B" covered Oldsmobile, Buick, and the cheaper Cadillacs; and "C" was a Cadillac exclusive. On Oldsmobiles, an element of difference could be injected by altering the rear wing line. Up to 1953 Buick, as the only member of the medium-range group still using a straight-eight engine, had a longer bonnet which could be turned to good use. At the top of the range, Cadillac's current Sixty Special, its name a symbol of stylistic progress, had to look different. The original 1938 car had been neither a "B" nor a "C": not so in the 1950s, when the transformation was effected by lengthening the C body's rear deck, and adding some extra luggage space as a bonus. Nor was this the limit to which the "C" could go. Add an extra 22 in (56 cm) of roofline and rear quarter-lights, and you had another Cadillac institution, the lengthy Model 75 limousine.

America was, of course, the only manufacturing nation still committed to yearly models. But the process was relatively painless, thanks to a regular drill. Unless finances were truly chaotic, one updated the mechanics and the styling in alternate years. Ford, who had entered the 1950s with Harold Youngren's long-overdue 1949 shape, left everything firmly alone till 1952, when they came up with a new body shell and compromised on the mechanical side with a new overhead-valve six, leaving the established V-8s unaltered. Whereas 1953 was a year of no change, 1954 was devoted to the technical side, and the bodies got the treatment again in 1955. In 1957, the rules were broken to let the tail fin in, with mechanical changes, and 1958 was a styling year which bred the infelicitous six-passenger Thunderbird.

After 1960, the new multiple ranges—everything from compacts to muscle cars—upset the situation appreciably. With more different chassis/body combinations to play with, one could spread restyling across these. The 1964 Ford line-up embraced the compact Falcon (1960), the intermediate Fairlane (1962), and the all-new Mustang pony-car, as well as the regular full-sized models and the specialized Thunderbird. With the Mustang's advent came restyles for the Falcon and Thunderbird, and a facelift for the regular Fords. The Fairlane was left alone until 1966, in which year the Falcon altered its shape for the last time. In 1967 it was the Thunderbird's turn, and so on ...

Throughout our period, certain rules governed U.S. styling. Grilles, as the most flexible and easily changed items, were also the most variable, although 1950's "teeth" had resolved into egg-crate treatments by 1956, these being fully integrated with lamps and bumpers. Headlamps, already tucked away in the wings by 1950, were hooded by 1954–55, while quad installations took over from 1957–58: Plymouth, however, reverted to the old single type on Valiants from 1963. Curved windscreens, still with vee-type dividers in 1950, had lost this adjunct three years later—while within a year Detroit had gone over to the deplorable "dog's leg" pattern, fashionable until the early sixties, though less aggressive in their later manifestations. Thereafter, screens tended to become deeper, and pillar treatment more restrained. Side chrome was fairly moderate until 1953, due to shortages accentuated by the Korean War. Then it burst into full glory between 1954 and 1959, before giving way to sculptured mouldings which divided up the slab-sided masses without the rust hazard that could develop unnoticed beneath a chromium-plated "spear". Towards the end of our period, the decorations were surprisingly modest. The 1969 Chevrolet Caprice

was the Division's most expensive sedan, priced above the cheapest Buicks, yet it made do with a single sculptured lower belt moulding and some cleverly flared wheel arches.

Three-window (six-light) sedan bodies, the norm of the 1930s and indeed on most American cars until 1948, made a brief reappearance between 1955 and 1960, after the 1938 Cadillac Sixty Special and 1941 Packard Clipper themes had worked themselves out. This trend was duly echoed in 1965 by Britain's Detroit-oriented Rootes Group, long after America had gone back to two side windows. Fins, the hallmark of Cadillacs since 1948, were in vogue between 1956 and 1961, with fearsome galaxies of tail-light installations. Chevrolet's 1959 version had to be seen to be believed. The wrap-round rear window, a 1947 innovation by Studebaker, lasted about ten years before giving way to something less productive of glare. As for the rearward-inclined "breezeway" back light, first seen on Mercurys in 1957, this remained a preserve of the Ford Motor Company, though it occurred on such European products of the empire as the 105E Anglia (1959) and the Classic (1961)—this last an appalling parody of obsolescent American styling, and an awful warning to those who thought that it could be scaled down successfully.

While the stylist nibbled at ends, wrapped his bumpers round, and decorated his body sides with non-structural chromium and sculptured lines, all to compensate for this year's lack of a new automatic transmission or revised brakes, the badge engineer pursued his own uneasy

More unitary-construction headaches. Britain's Rootes Group were better off financially than Hudson, and their competition was less fierce. Thus, their popular Minx light car could manage with the same front-end treatment from 1949 to 1952, the changes being rung on chromium trim and more efficient engines. The next grille shape (*above*) saw them through from 1953 to mid-1956, although from 1955 the car had an overhead-valve power unit and top speed was up from a laboured 112 km/h (70 mph) to around 130 km/h (80 mph). Essentially, however, the 1955 Minx's side elevation (*opposite*) was the same as it had been seven years before—something like a squashed and abbreviated 1949 Plymouth. This one dates itself only by the combination of a chromium-plated strip on the front fender and an extended boot.

One class of vehicle was immune from the march of styling and technology: the taxicab. We may think instinctively of London's Austins, but other countries had their specialist machinery. Throughout the 1950s, Sweden's standard cab was the good old Volvo PV831/832 (*below*) with a 3.7-litre side-valve six-cylinder engine dating back to 1929, and authentic 1942 American Ford styling given a few local overtones. Though the model was catalogued as a private car, private owners and export customers were equally uninterested, yet between 1950 and 1958 Volvo managed to sell 4,135 complete limousines and 2,081 chassis, not to mention specialist 4×4 military derivatives.

If there was a car to symbolize our period—socially if not technically—this was it. Theoretically on sale in 1939, and with deliveries over the six-figure mark by 1951, the Volkswagen *Käfer* would achieve its first million in August, 1955, and its tenth million just over ten years later, by which time rear engines were out of fashion and air-cooling was less popular as well. Exactly when it broke the Model-T Ford's production record is still a matter for debate, but by late 1981 world-wide deliveries exceeded twenty million units. Here (*above*) is a 1958-model chassis as today's kit-car fraternity sees it: a tubular backbone frame with torsion-bar springing at either end, rack-and-pinion steering, and the familiar cranked central gear lever controlling four forward speeds, although it will be another two years before buyers are

offered synchromesh on bottom. At the back, the air-cooled flat-four engine still looks the way Ferdinand Porsche conceived it, albeit with some extra cc (197 of them, to be precise, since 1939) and 30 horsepower instead of 23, which spell maximum *and* cruising speeds of 112 km/h (70 mph). Brakes are hydraulic, too, though until 1962 the parsimonious could order a "stripped" model with mechanically actuated cables! The sectioned side view of a complete car (*opposite, top*) is a trifle claustrophobic by 1980s standards, and the maker's ideas of luggage accommodation also seem a little optimistic. They did stress the value of proper weight distribution with a low centre of gravity, and the better traction obtained by placing the engine directly over the drive wheels. The rear window, which had still been divided in

1952 and was a one-piece oval affair by 1954, now ran the full width of the body, while the engine cover had been redesigned and the ventilation slats were of continuous type, illustrating the host of minor changes which marked the Beetle's steady evolution. The 1954 power pack (*opposite, centre*) shows the big shrouded cooling-fan mounted in front of the engine, with its driving-belt at the rear. The carburettor is very accessible: the lower spark-plugs less so. Ten years later, the rear window was even larger, you could open the engine cover by pressing a button rather than turning a handle, and the tail-light cluster had been revised too. There wasn't a lot of space under the frontal "bonnet" (*opposite, bottom*), either, after allowing for the spare wheel and the fuel tank—but accessory roof-racks were quite cheap.

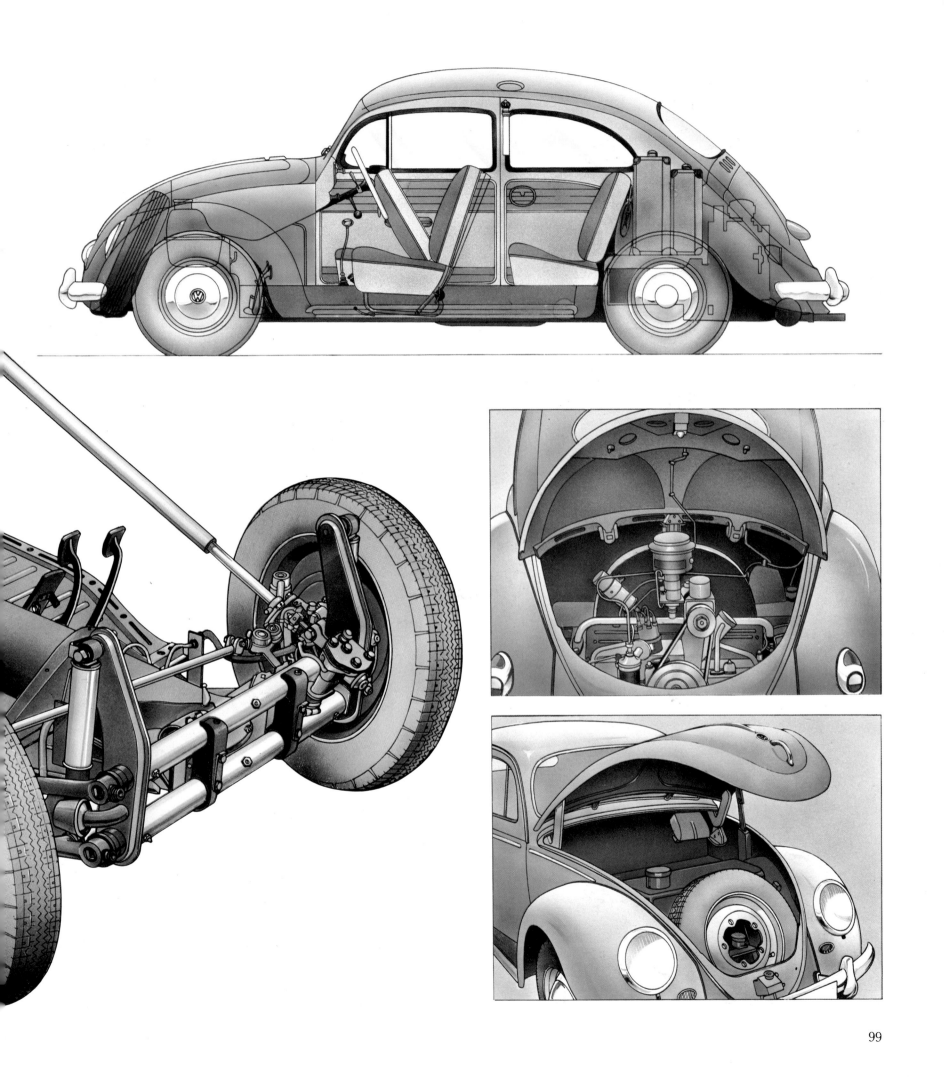

path. His motives were technical and sentimental rather than stylistic. If one had to market three family sedans under three different names in the same group, it was cheaper to play with grilles, interior trim, and two-toning than with engines, suspensions, and body shells. The British Motor Corporation, the worst offenders of this kind, entered 1955 with four distinct 1,500-cc family sedans. Admittedly, they used the same engines and transmissions, but they ran to three totally different chassis/body structures, while front suspensions were divided between the Austin type (coils) and Morris's torsion bars. Sometimes, badge engineering was of the crudest sort: the sole difference between the original 1959 Austin Se7en (*sic*) and the Morris Mini-Minor (again *sic*) was the grille-bar pattern (straight on a Morris, wavy on an Austin), though the colour charts were not the same.

Carried to its logical conclusion—and one that was inevitable, given two dealership chains and two sets of entrenched *marque*-loyalty (in Britain, at any rate)—we reach the strange state of affairs which obtained from 1965 onward in the front-wheel-drive 1100/1300 line-up. Here we find five different grilles, three stages of engine tune, three levels of interior appointments with some further internal variations, and the ultimate nuisance of body permutations. The inflexibilities of unitary construction limited the choice to two- and four-door sedans and to station wagons, but all styles were not available on all brands of 1100 or 1300 and, at times, a variation permitted for export never appeared on the home market. A certain degree of "difference" was achieved, yet it must have been a nightmare for the stylists, and a worse one for production engineers who had to feed all the permutations down the assembly line. In the long run, one wonders if it was all really necessary.

The disease would naturally spread into Europe during the 1970s, with cross-pollinations of Audi/VW and Peugeot/Citroën among others. But it was never as uncontrolled as in Britain, and sometimes it even made sense. A joint development programme shared by Peugeot, Renault, and Volvo would breed an excellent V-6 engine which, in all probability, none of the individual contributors would have considered viable without outside backing. It is fair, however, to add that this went into three completely different cars.

As in America, so in Europe. Bumpers, grilles, lamps, running-boards, boots were gathered up and merged into harmonious wholes. The traditional running-board had all but gone by 1953 and, henceforward, the only excrescences to mar the shape of the motor car were wing mirrors and radio antennae, while even the last could be wound electrically out of sight by the mid-sixties. Fuel fillers were set flush in the rear quarters. The windscreen wipers, on 1967 American cars, were not only self-parking but vanished into a slot at the lower edge. Retractable headlamps, last seen on 1942's De Sotos, were back again in 1963 on the British Lotus Elan sports car, appearing on a variety of Americans—led by Buick—from 1965 onwards.

European sedan shapes generally followed the basic American idiom. Typical variations on the GM/Ford theme came in the early 1950s from Alfa Romeo, Austin, Fiat, British and German Fords, Mercedes-Benz, Opel, the Rootes Group, Rover, and Vauxhall. But Mercedes and, to a lesser extent, Alfa Romeo retained their traditional radiator grilles. Full wrap-round rear windows were not so popular, and largely confined to such American-controlled companies as Ford, Opel, and Vauxhall. These were, however, applied to a number of coupés, a fine example being the three-cylinder DKW of 1954 which, in its final form, boasted a dog's-leg windscreen as well.

European contributions to the quad-headlamp craze included an

(*Opposite*) Styling features as marque identification. Plated "silver streaks" were first applied to Pontiacs in 1934: without them, too many people might have noted an overly close outward resemblance to the superseded 1933s. By 1937 (*left*), they had been integrated into a continuous bonnet/grille motif, and there was good publicity to be gained from a label shared with one of America's crack diesel-electric expresses of the period. The lowered grilles of the 1950s meant that by 1956 the streaks (*right*) had to be confined to the bonnet top. By this time, however, "Silver Streak" no longer signified speed in the public eye, and the Pontiac was regarded as something of an old ladies' car. Hence they (and the Indian Head of Chief Pontiac, who had sat atop the bonnet for thirty years) were consigned to limbo for 1957.

(*Right*) Making the most of the same body, or how General Motors' stylists coped with 1951 Oldsmobiles (*top*), Buicks (*centre*), and Cadillacs (*bottom*). To the customer, the end product is not at all similar. The plated belt line kinks upward on the Olds and down on the Buick, while it terminates halfway across the front door on the Cadillac. Oldsmobile's rear fenders have a missile motif to match the hood ornament, Buick's are graced by an elaborate continuation of the belt moulding, and Cadillac's incorporate non-functional air intakes. Buicks are recognizable by their bonnet portholes, and the rear-quarter light treatment on Oldsmobiles is different from the other two breeds. But in factory parlance, they share the same "B" body, and the differences are not too expensive to fit in. We encounter a further headache (*below*): Buicks, still straight-eights, are not too impossibly long in the hood with the smaller of the two engine options, but some extra length is needed up front when it comes to the monstrous 5.2-litre Roadmaster version, or things will get out of proportion. So one just adds an extra porthole . . .

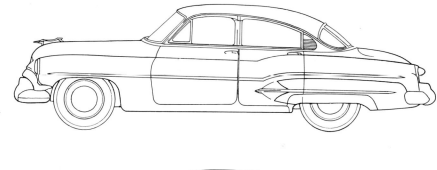

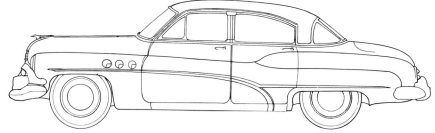

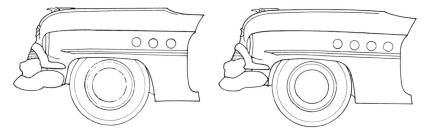

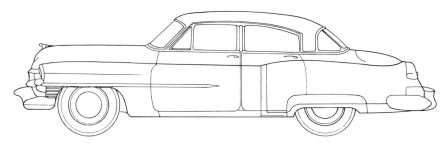

attractive variation, the vertical cluster used on Facel Vegas from 1954. Among imitators of the American configuration were Humber, Ford of Britain, Jaguar, and Lancia—plus, surprisingly, the Prince from Japan—in 1961, and Alfa Romeo in 1962. By 1963, even the aristocratic Rolls-Royce and Alvis had succumbed to the fad, which was still strongly supported in 1969. Fins, however, did not really fit in, and none of the more outrageous interpretations from Detroit crossed the Atlantic. Rootes, predictably, produced a watered-down variation on the theme, as did Simca on their later V-8 Vedettes. Some rather depressing appendages were found on such 1959 sports models as the Auto Union 1000 Sp (a species of mini-Thunderbird in the original 1955 spirit) and Daimler's SP250, but they had no imitators.

Alongside the American echoes, old shapes lingered on for a few years, especially in Britain. In 1951, the standard models from Alvis, Citroën, Daimler, Lea-Francis, MG, Morgan, Riley, Rolls-Royce/Bentley, and Singer (on roadsters only) retained both a traditional shape and an unmistakable radiator grille. The same, to a lesser degree, went for Lancia's sedans. Right up to 1955, Mercedes-Benz continued to make the good old 170, complete with running-boards, exposed lamps, and bumpers which looked like afterthoughts. The clean-up, however, was on the way. Already Alvis ran to rear wheel spats and semi-recessed headlamps, while the last of the traditional Jaguars, Mk.V, was phased out during the summer of 1951 in favour of the slab-sided, integrated Mk.VII. By 1952, integrated headlamps characterized the latest Daimlers and Lanchesters, the Lea-Francis' headlamps having already retreated into the wings. Catalogues for 1954 featured slab-sided sedans from Mercedes-Benz, MG, and Riley. MG's new 1956 sports car, the MG-A, dispensed with running-boards, individual wings, and a traditional radiator. Even Morgans acquired mildly

streamlined grilles, although their one attempt at a full "streamline"—the Plus Four Plus coupé of 1963—met with such resistance from customers that it was withdrawn after a very short run. The classical *tractions* outlived Citroën's Déesse by only twenty months, being dropped in the summer of 1957.

Even some of the surviving "traditionals" were not as traditional as they looked. Apart from its recessed headlamps, the 1951 Type 220 six-cylinder Mercedes-Benz might have stepped straight out of the 1938 Berlin Show, but the conventional bonnet was afflicted with fixed sides and an alligator top. In any case, the side-opening bonnet was ill-suited to the new high wing lines, thus leaving motorists stuck with the tiresome alligator and its linkages: either via a wire protruding through the grille, by pressure on the radiator badge, or by a remote-control knob under the dash, this last being perhaps the commonest in later days, if only because it was thief-proof. Better accessibility was sought on Aston Martins and the post-1958 Triumphs (Herald, Vitesse, Spitfire) by making the whole bonnet-wing assembly tilt forward, at the same time exposing the front suspension. Alas, it let in road dirt, was prone to distortion, and scarcely guarded against the ministrations of careless filling-station attendants. The idea was not new—it had been used on air-cooled Tatras as long ago as 1924.

But whatever the shape, there remained the question of amortization. How many cars can one unload, how long will it take to unload them, and will the whole concept be out of date before the appointed target has been reached? By 1930s standards, tooling costs were horrific. True, in 1932 Chrysler expended $9,000,000 (say £1,500,000) on rebuilding the Plymouth plant, but this was a prelude to the switch from four cylinders to six, and they would still be using essentially the same engine twenty-six years later. At a simpler level, Daimler, unable

Three shapes of the 1950s. The original 1950 Saab 92 (*opposite, top*) is still a triumph of perfect aerodynamics over most other considerations, to be expected from one of Europe's leading aircraft manufacturers. Its engineering is improved DKW: 764-cc water-cooled twin two-stroke engine driving the front wheels, three-speed synchromesh transmission with free wheel, rack-and-pinion steering, and hydraulic brakes. Debits are poor headroom, negligible rearward vision, and fender skirts which are built-in mud traps, while customers could have it in any colour so long as it was this green. The shape, if not the engine, had nearly another thirty years to go, whereas Fiat's 500C (*below*) would be dropped in 1955 after a career dating back to 1936. With its hydraulic brakes, adequate legroom, four-speed

synchromesh transmission, and independently sprung front wheels, the Fiat had been the baby-car to beat before World War II, and even in 1950—as seen here—it was still competitive, thanks to a redesigned 16.5-horsepower version of the old 570-cc engine with overhead valves. It could outrun the original side-valve Morris Minors of 1949–52, yet it was strictly a two-seater and something of a home mechanic's nightmare—everything looked so accessible, but fingers were not small enough! The "other Swede", Volvo (*opposite, bottom*), would go on making fastback variations on the PV444 theme (a 1944 debutante) into the mid-sixties. By 1957, this car was showing its age, too, with 1942 American styling (more Ford than anything else) and a three-speed transmission controlled by a long, willowy lever in the

1935 idiom. What it had, however, was a new performance image: capacity had been increased from the original 1,414 cc to 1,583 cc and, with an extra carburettor, there were 85 horsepower and 90 mph (145 km/h). The proof of the pudding was in the eating—this was the model that would spearhead the Gothenburg factory's successful onslaught on the tricky U.S. market.

Badge engineering, or pandering to out-moded marque loyalties. Throughout the 1960s, Britons—and some export customers—could buy this dull and dependable piece of Pininfarina styling with 1.5-litre engine, or 1.6-litre from 1961. The options listed included automatic, though never disc brakes, and in a few export markets the basic Austin/Morris version was available with a diesel engine. Here (*right*) we see the Austin Cambridge so beloved of family man and rural hire-car operator. The Morris Oxford was exactly the same thing with a different badge. But add a traditional grille, an illuminated radiator emblem, and some wood and leather within, and you have a Wolseley (*below*). More grille swapping and an extra carburettor give you a Riley or MG. The Australians lengthened the BMC-Farina theme and fitted their own brand of short-block six to produce local Austins and Wolseleys—and the strangest things happened in Argentina, including a "Riley Rural" pickup!

(*Opposite*) What concealed headlamps can do. Both cars are 1968 Chevrolet Camaros, General Motors' belated answer to the best-selling Ford Mustang coupés and convertibles. The SS (*left*) has a conventional installation, while the Rallye Sport (*right*) tucks its

illuminations away electrically into the grille when they are not in use. For all the names, the Rallye Sport was a "personality package" (mouldings round the wheel arches, special emblem on the fuel-filler cap) rather than a sporting one: you had to specify one of the hairier V-8s if you wanted speed and acceleration. The SS, by contrast, came as stock with a 5.7-litre or 6.5-litre V-8, the latter rated at 325 horsepower. With this engine, you also had your rear body panel painted black, presumably to alert the Highway Patrol!

to subsist on chauffeur-driven limousines in the Depression years, spent a mere £30,000 ($180,000) on tooling up for their small 1.2-litre Lanchester in 1932, giving themselves a natural seller in the retired-colonel market.

Daimler's economics were entirely healthy. They could reasonably hope to sell 3,000–4,000 a year, and the clientele was conservative. It appreciated the preselective gearbox—for which, in any case, Daimler were tooled—but was disinterested in sophisticated suspensions or in the impending "streamline" craze. History records that the first cars had hydraulic brakes, scrapped quite soon in favour of cheaper mechanicals, but it is unlikely that the customers noticed. With a fairly wide range of body styles on a straightforward chassis, Daimler made it through to World War II with a single major restyle in 1937, although a full updating was planned for 1941 and was duly released as a post-war model in 1945. This sufficed till 1951, but the next step would have to be unitary construction—with some improvements in transmission, meaning an automatic. Worse still, the planned size of 1.6 litres implied that there could be very little interchangeability of parts with the next larger model, a 2.5-litre six. Thus, on top of an untried mechanical recipe, they were saddled with a complete retooling programme, which would have cost £500,000 ($1,400,000) with no guarantee of selling enough cars before the shape became outmoded. The limit seemed to be 8,000 a year in the overcrowded and capricious English upper-middle-class market, and this car was hardly something for the export customer. So the Lanchester Sprite went to the wall after about ten prototypes had been built. The cost per copy is best left to the imagination.

As an indication of what a mass producer could spend, Plymouth's next big factory update in 1955 cost $40,000,000, and a reorganization of the Buick plant took $500,000,000 in pursuit of a million-a-year production schedule as yet unrealized in 1982. Even facelifts called for deep pockets. It cost Jaguar £250,000 to bring the E-type into line with the American safety and emission standards enforced in 1968. Hence, spending the money on the wrong car could be catastrophic: classic instances of this were Kaiser's Henry J compact (1950), Borgward's 1959 big six (confronting Mercedes-Benz), and the Hillman Imp (1963).

People still wanted a choice of bodies. Convertibles were a constant source of worry, as a maker had no room for side-issues even where he was responsible for his own pressings. Ford used Carbodies in Britain and went to Karosserie Deutsch in Germany, while VW drew on Karmann, Opel on Autenrieth, BMW and Auto Union on Baur. The British Jensen company, originally coachbuilders, revived their old love to supplement a meagre production of cars, building ragtops for BMC (Austin, Austin-Healey), the open Alpines of 1959–68 for Rootes, and Volvo's P1800 coupés until 1963 for the Gothenburg firm.

The convertible would become a major casualty of the decade. Even a separate chassis required some reinforcement to circumvent scuttle-shake, and unitaries were far trickier—as Citroën had discovered to their cost in 1934, when they offered a roadster in the original *traction* range. One way out, long favoured in Germany on both separate-chassis and unitary models, was the cabrio-limousine, on which the body sides were fixed, leaving only a roll-top roof. In our period, such a style was marketed by Fiat, Nash, Opel, Peugeot, and Renault, while examples with chassis included the original Fiat 500. It was an acceptable compromise, but the lines were still the sedan's. Further, the demand for convertibles was limited: in 1955, the all-car/ragtop totals produced by Chevrolet, Ford, and Plymouth were respectively 1,830,029/66,121, 1,451,157/41,966, and 742,991/8,473. The market was being eroded from various directions. In America, the two-door hardtop coupé, with all the style and none of the snags, sold better—for all the "wind in your hair" nonsense purveyed by advertising agencies, the ladies did not care to subject their hairdos to freeway speeds. Even the soft-topped sports car was disappearing. Where Lancia had begun, others carried on the good work. Jaguar and Porsche, who offered both styles of body, always did better overall with closed models. The conclusion was obvious before the safety-propagandists stepped in.

Open sports cars, of course, saw the second decade out. The Triumph Spitfire and TR6, the E-type Jaguar roadster, and the MG-B were still going strong in 1969, as were Italy's open Alfa Romeos and Fiats. The defection of Datsun and Porsche, however, did not pass unnoticed, while the non-sporting convertible was fading out. Such cars as the Singer Roadster (1951–55) and the Austin A40 Sports (1951–53)

(*Below*) Ford of America's new look—Phase One, the 1951 Mercury Club Coupé, complete with coil-spring independent front suspension (new, incredibly, as late as 1949) and hypoid rear axle. The cruciform-braced frame on this car is of course Lincoln rather than Ford in origin, while already the divided windscreen and bulbous fender treatment are looking a trifle outmoded. And whereas GM and Chrysler have V-8s with upstairs valves and oversquare dimensions, Mercury's engine is still an antiquated side-valve offering 110 horsepower from 4.2 litres. Further, GM have now had automatics for eleven years, but this is the first season they will be available on either Ford or Mercury.

(*Opposite, top*) Amazing grace—or a stylistic elegance seldom achieved by Americans—on the second-year edition of Raymond Loewy's brilliant 1953 Studebaker Commander coupé. The 1954 is hard to distinguish from the earlier models, and chromium-plated ornamentation is kept to a minimum. The company's V-8 (3.8 litres, 120 horsepower) was modest if adequate, but triumph was turned into disaster by problems of corrosion, poor quality control, costly experiments with mechanical power steering (some assistance was needed, for the Commander required nearly six turns from lock to lock), and bad planning. Studebaker intended the coupé as a limited-production "come on" to attract customers into the showroom—and then sell sedans. When the demand arrived, there were not enough coupés to go round. And by 1955, the chromium plate was moving in . . .

(*Opposite, bottom*) American Motors sought escape from their "common sense" image in the 1960s, this Marlin (originally badged as a Rambler in 1965) being an entry for the personal-car market. Looks of this 1966 version were individual enough, but it was a big car on a 112-in (2.85-m) wheelbase, and its length of 195 in (4.05 m) made it a handful beside Ford's Mustang. The standard engine was, predictably, a staid 3.8-litre pushrod six, but with the optional 5.4-litre V-8 the Marlin was a respectable performer. Its whale-like styling was, however, against it, and steadily diminishing sales told their own story. In three seasons, only 17,500 customers chose this one.

were not very saleable in their heyday and would have been dead ducks in the climate of, say, 1966.

In 1960, most relevant German and American manufacturers still had something in this class, as did Fiat in Italy, BMC, Ford, and Rootes in Britain, or Peugeot and Simca in France. But the market was dwindling, and a maker committed to unitary construction was likely to think twice about tooling for a convertible the next time a redesign became due. Few firms did so, and even in America the boom was almost over. If Chrysler's ragtop sales remained steady throughout the sixties at 4,000–5,000 a year, Buick—the top American builder of convertibles—saw orders slip from 41,528 in 1962 to 22,616 in 1969. Ford, admittedly, disposed of 33,874 cars in the latter year, but this was only just over half 1962's showing. Most indicative of the decline is the story of the Ford Mustang, a car which seemed a natural for the "sporty ragtop" clientele: 73,112 convertibles were sold in 1965, the model's first full year, but less than 15,000 found buyers in the last season of our period. European factories encountered the same picture. In the Triumph Herald/Vitesse family, the convertibles accounted for about 11% of sales (with no ultimate competition in Britain), but Peugeot's 2% ration of coupés in the 204 and 404 ranges included hardtops as well, and the same went for Mercedes-Benz's statistics at 6% of all medium-sized sixes up to 1965.

Colour was assuming greater and greater importance. It was used to inject an extra year of life into the ageing 1949 Hillman Minx shape, and now the dual aids of colour and chromium were pressed into service: plated strip, sweep-spears and, later, sculptured lines could divide one shade from another. Sometimes the results were alarming, as on Ford of America's 1955 Crown Victoria, "with a crown of chrome

sweeping down from roof to belt line at center pillar level". On the 1956 De Soto Fireflite, something resembling an attenuated rifle (in contrasting colour) started low down by the rear bumper, taking in the rear wheel arch as a "trigger guard", the "barrel" terminating in a stylus-shaped "head" just behind the front wheels. This set off the new six-window styling and tail fins quite well, but was hardly beautiful. Chrysler's colour-influences spilled over into later Simca Arondes, although Citroën did it better on the Déesse by painting their glass-fibre roof section in a lighter shade. In Britain, two-tone treatment was skilfully applied to some of the uglier examples of slab-sided styling—Austin's A105, Ford's Mk.I Zodiac, and Standard's Pennant and Vanguard. Here the lily was sometimes gilded by minor engine tuning, in addition to a goodly quota of accessories. Ford's 1954 Zodiac package included white-wall tyres, heater, screenwash, wing mirrors, clock, and reversing lamps, as well as two-tone paint. The little Standard Pennant was embellished with a wider grille and headlamp hoods.

A lot could be done with wheels, almost invariably plain discs except where brake-cooling problems dictated otherwise. Perhaps the most fashionable accessory of the 1940s had been the "beauty ring" (Britons called it a "rimbellisher"), a painted or chromed rim trim, originally devised in the U.S.A. at a time when white-wall tyres were still hard to get. Wire wheels were too expensive, and chromium plating on the spokes was liable to weaken them, so America succumbed during the middle fifties to a fad for clip-on dummy wire trims. On the 1953 Buick Skylark, however, genuine wires with "40 individually set chromed spokes" were standard equipment, which explains why it cost $1,000 more than any other car in the range and sold in tiny numbers. Also imitated were the cast magnesium-alloy spoked wheels used on compe-

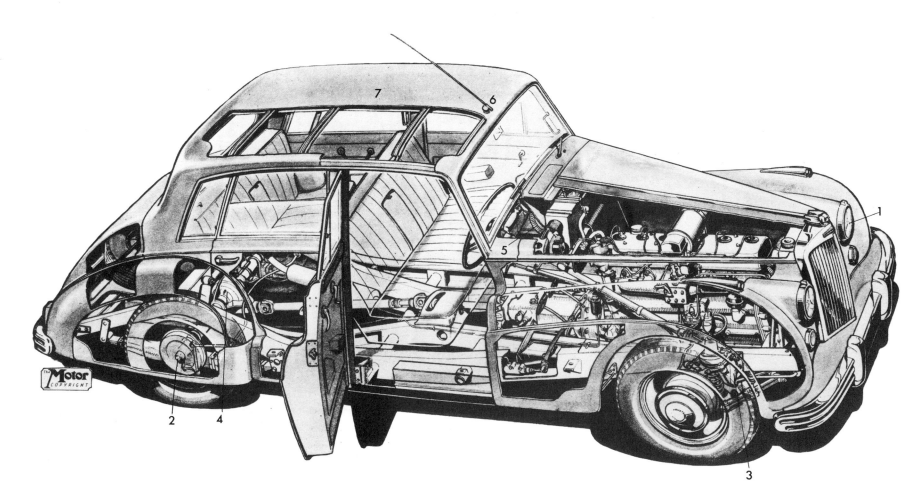

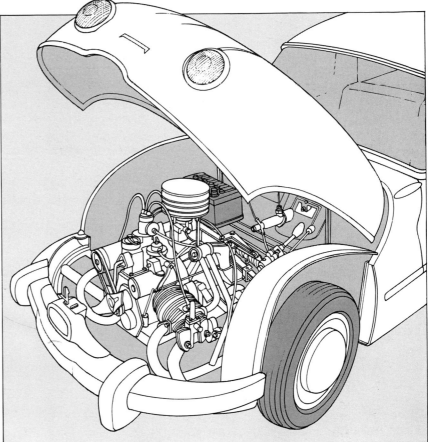

(*Opposite*) Eliminate (*1*) the recessed headlamps, (*2*) the hydraulic brakes, and (*3*) the coil-spring independent suspension, replacing the hypoid rear axle (*4*) with an old-fashioned spiral bevel, and we could be back in the Britain of 1938 with this 3.4-litre Armstrong Siddeley Sapphire as made from 1953 to 1958. True, the six-cylinder engine has hemispherical combustion chambers and the "square" dimensions of 90×90 mm, and by pre-war standards 120 horsepower would be a lot from a power unit of this capacity. Students of creature comforts will note the heater trunking (*5*) and radio antenna (*6*), while the roof (*7*) lacks that sliding panel found on almost all British sedans of the 1930s. But one did get two-speed wipers, a fuel reserve, a map-reading light, and wood and leather trim, while Armstrong Siddeley's preselective transmission (still available as an alternative to synchromesh) now had its ratios electrically selected. From 1955 there would be an automatic option, too. Rover, Jaguar, and Mercedes-Benz would, however, be the death of the smaller specialist makers, although Armstrong Siddeley also tried their luck in 1955 with a seven-seater limousine on which radio and an electric division were standard. Alas, there were not enough mayors and company presidents to keep the order-books full, while undertakers tended to buy secondhand.

(*Above*) Better under-hood access, but for road dirt as well as the home mechanic. On the 1959 Triumph Herald (*left*) the entire hood/fender assembly tilts forward, being secured by fasteners at its trailing edge. By contrast, that of the 1954 Dyna-Panhard sedan (*right*) hinges fom the back, in a fashion pioneered by Tatra of Czechoslovakia a good twenty years previously. This is a real boon on a front-wheel-drive car, and in any case the air-cooled Panhard has no "plumbing". Better still, the inner "wings" keep some of the dirt out. This remarkable little car featured all-aluminium unitary construction, which produced a full six-seater capable of 120 km/h (75 mph) and a frugal 7 litres/100 km (40 mpg) all on 850 cc and two cylinders. Heavy manufacturing costs, alas, caused a switch to steel bodies in 1957, and the extra weight didn't help the handling. The Panhard was always a noisy little car and, though *la marque doyenne*'s annual sales were up to over 30,000 in the late fifties, this wasn't enough for a small, cheap family model. A Citroën takeover in 1955 was only the prelude to the disappearance of the Panhard name twelve years later.

tition cars from the later fifties. A prevalent disease of the 1970s, these were very much with us from 1967–68 onward, finding their way onto MG Midgets among others. The "Ro style" label commemorated their initial use by Rover on the 1968 eight-cylinder line.

Britain's Ford Zodiac and its fellows sparked off another strong trend of the 1960s. If a body programme was inflexible and restricted one to sedans and station wagons, one could still offer quite a wide range of models by graduated trim packages, with or without mechanical modifications thrown in. When hanging a "GT" label on a car, something would have to be done to the engine, but a good deal of variety could be achieved by the French-type graduations of equipment. *Affaires* gave a minimal specification, and *Confort* was not always very much better. At the other end of the scale were GL (*Grand Luxe*) and GLS (*Grand Luxe Special*, or maybe *Sport*—one consulted the catalogue to discover which it was). On Simca's front-wheel-drive 1100 (1968), a GL model came complete with rear overriders, two vanity mirrors instead of one, armrests at front and rear, a parcel shelf, child-proof door locks, and a grab-handle: a judicious mixture of safety and luxury. In the GLS grouping, you got some ornament as well—mild scriptitis at both ends, plus reclining front seats, rim trims, through-flow ventilation, a thermometer, a clock, a second grab-handle, rear-seat ashtrays, coat hooks, a lockable glove-compartment, and floor carpets instead of rubber mats.

Vinyl roof-coverings were fashionable from about 1961, to make a sedan look like a hardtop. They were standard on Humber's 1965 Imperial to distinguish the car from the cheaper, but otherwise identical, Super Snipe. On the 1968 Dodge Charger, however, you could have your vinyl in "black, antique white, or antique green", this being but one of a whole series of dress-up kits offered. As the Dodge could be had with engines giving over 400 horsepower, sporty items predominated. Comprehensive (extra) instrumentation included a rev-counter "large

(*Left*) Secondhand American influences. On Vauxhall's Cresta PA, marketed from 1958 to 1960, we encounter a 2.3-litre six-cylinder overhead-valve engine and classic unitary construction of the type used by this company since 1938. But now the stylists have added a dog's-leg windscreen—though a neater one than on the companion four-cylinder Victor family—along with tail fins, and even the three-piece wrap-round rear window found elsewhere only on 1957 Buicks. The PA family ran through to 1962, but during a fairly brief life it used two different wheel sizes and three patterns of radiator grille, while in 1961 it was given bigger fins and a bigger engine. By this time, too, over-drive and automatic were available as well as the all-too-familiar three on the column.

(*Opposite, bottom*) The British Ford Consul II convertible as made from 1956 to 1962 (this is a '59) looks less spectacular in the metal than it did in the company's catalogues. The shorter hood, of course, does not help: the more expensive Zephyrs and Zodiacs had 2.6-litre in-line sixes instead of the Consul's 1.7-litre four. Ford managed a unitary convertible by having Carbodies of Coventry do a top chop. On the cheaper four-cylinder cars, this component went up and down by hand. As power assistance on the sixes took it only halfway, not a lot was lost, though in an affluent society the sixes now outsold the fours. In Mk. I days (1951–56), the ratio was 4-to-3 in favour of the Consul.

(*Opposite, top*) Last new Jaguar model with a separate chassis, the Mk. IX sedan (1958). There's not a lot to distinguish it externally from the original Mk.VII of 1950 save the single-panel windscreen, and nothing to show that it's not a 1957 Mk.VIII. But in eight years, power has gone up by 40 % to 220 horsepower, top speed up by 10 % to 113 mph (179 km/h), and 0–60 mph (0–100 km/h) acceleration figures have improved by 20 %. Add power disc brakes on all four wheels (no mixed systems for Jaguar!) and power steering, and you have a luxury carriage that will still keep pace with the American opposition even if it lacks tail fins. Automatic, compulsory for the U.S. market, is only one of three options (the others are manual and manual/overdrive) elsewhere. Sales of 10,000 Mk.IXs in three seasons were entirely satisfactory: after all, the makers had their profitable compact sedans, and the XK150 sports car destined to give way during 1961 to the advanced E-type.

(*Right*) A touch of Pininfarina made all the difference to Austin's small conventional sedan announced at the 1958 Shows, a year ahead of the Mini. The A40's mechanics are copybook British: 948-cc (or 1,098-cc from 1961) pushrod four-cylinder engine, four-speed synchromesh transmission, unitary construction, coil springs at the front and semi-elliptics at the rear. The wider track not only improved the looks—it eliminated the old A35's penchant for lying down on its door handles! The two-tone finish helped to make up for what the little Austin lacked in character, and so did a modest 42-mpg (7 litres/100 km) thirst for fuel. This was the first British Motor Corporation design to be made under licence in Italy by Innocenti.

enough so you can read it", as did "mag-style covers" (our old friend the Ro-style wheel again) and "bold, brash bumblebee stripes on the tail". A steering-wheel in "simulated woodgrain" was an attraction at a time when wood-rim wheels were regularly worn on Maseratis and the like.

The package business reached its zenith on the sportier Fords of the 1960s, the American Mustang and the Anglo-German Capri (1969). "Packs" were not to be classed with accessories, which had to be ordered individually and were supplementary to a wide choice of engine/transmission combinations (six in Germany). There were cosmetic and performance "packs". With the XL order came reclining front seats, separately contoured rear seats, an extra rear lamp, and an anti-dazzle mirror. XLRs were XLs with leather-rimmed steering-wheels, simulated black leather gearshift knobs, and map-reading lights. It must have been some compensation to a client who could not help being aware that his Capri was one of a million look-alikes with the same chassis/body, the same wheelbase, and essentially the same instrumentation.

Italy had her dress-up industry, too, although this was secondary to the nation's vast influence on overall styling from the early fifties onward. Up to 1950, America had been the style leader in the mass-produced sector. Formal car ranges might be inspired by the British razor-edge idiom of 1935 on; the beautifully made, if somewhat ponderous, German cabriolet style had its echoes in Sweden and Switzerland; and the splendid, if impractical, sporting roadster with flowing wings and a windscreen of letterbox-slot proportions hailed from France. But when it came to cheap sedans, be they Renaults, Opels, or Austins, they still reflected secondhand U.S. thinking, usually distorted by its adaptation to shorter wheelbases and abbreviated bonnets. Italy's main influence so far had been confined to open sporting bodywork: Zagato's magnificent Gran Sport Alfa Romeo of 1929 remained the exemplar of this type of coachwork up to 1936–37.

The new "tin" of the forties and early fifties was still strongly Detroit-oriented. Singer aped Kaiser, and so did Volvo on a V-8 prototype which never saw production. Standard and Rootes drew their inspiration from two successive generations of Plymouth, the original Austin A40 was a stunted 1940 Chevrolet, and the Borgward 1500 was a deplorable mixture of American and German thinking. Renault's Frégate and Fiat's 1400 had no obvious American prototypes, yet were clearly non-European in concept. Ironically, Hudson would borrow back from Fiat for their unsuccessful compact Jet sedan of 1953. Volvo mixed GM grilles, Ford front wings, and Chrysler's body shapes to produce some astonishing mock-Americans: a definite style would not emerge until the 140 series (1966). Even the successful and well-loved 120 series (1956 onward) had front ends which were pure 1955 Chrysler. The Japanese, handicapped by a sheet-steel shortage, continued to build bodies by hand, the end product having assorted Chrysler, GM, and Crosley overtones. The 1951 Datsun, indeed, could have been confused with one of Powel Crosley's diminutive overhead-camshaft sedans.

This state of affairs made up in variety for what it lacked in elegance or cohesion. That is, until the Italians moved in, adopting the British razor-edge idiom and refining it beyond the narrow confines of Anglo-Saxon imagination. Given separate wings and headlamps, and a proper radiator, Britons could achieve low-cost miracles, such as the big Triumph sedans of the 1946–54 era. But let the concept of integration take over, and one encounters disasters like the 1.3-litre Triumph Mayflower, summarized by an unkind woman journalist as having "a Queen Anne top and a Mary Anne bottom".

Led by Pininfarina, the Italians championed the retreat from the shibboleths of the chassis maker's front-end treatment. Some of the

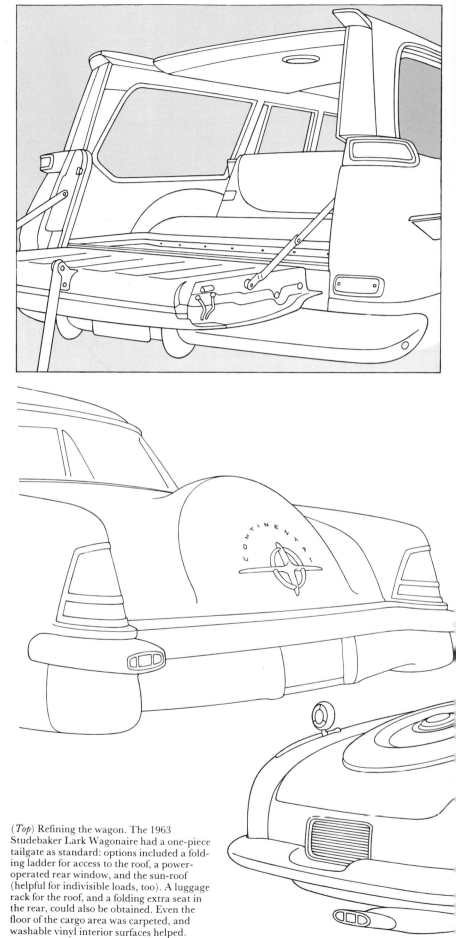

(*Top*) Refining the wagon. The 1963 Studebaker Lark Wagonaire had a one-piece tailgate as standard: options included a folding ladder for access to the roof, a power-operated rear window, and the sun-roof (helpful for indivisible loads, too). A luggage rack for the roof, and a folding extra seat in the rear, could also be obtained. Even the floor of the cargo area was carpeted, and washable vinyl interior surfaces helped.

early outbursts of rebellion were fairly horrible, since they drew on such unsuccessful purveyors of grille-work as Buick, Lincoln, and Studebaker. Nonetheless, the vee-grilles used—with a marked lack of discrimination—by Ghia and Pininfarina on Alfa Romeos, Lancias, and Fiats in 1937–39 were standardized on 1940's bigger Fiat models, and would survive on the old-school 508C Millecento until early 1953. But while the seller's market remained, the Italians had little chance to work on foreign chassis. They could neither import these, nor export bodies to European clients, except for subsequent re-export to hard-currency countries. Before 1951, the sole signs of outside work had been bodies by Touring and Pininfarina on British Bristol chassis, both of which were modified and commercialized by that firm.

The floodgates were opened in 1951, when Pininfarina created a new body for the ugly Anglo-American Nash-Healey sports car, being subsequently hired to restyle the domestic Nash line. In fact, series-production Pininfarina Nashes existed only in the firm's press releases: his ideas did not lend themselves wholesale, and only some of them were used. It was, however, good publicity for Nash, and even better publicity for the Italians. Over the next few years they moved in on Europe. Pininfarina signed up with Peugeot in 1954, doing the 403 and 404 sedans. He then lent his talents to the British Motor Corporation, applying his razor-edge shape first to the Austin A40, and then to a rationalized 1.5-litre sedan. Austin got an unexpected bonus out of this deal, since Innocenti of Milan acquired a licence to build A40s in Italy, an exercise unthinkable in the 1930s (even forgetting Mussolini's anti-British sentiments).

By the end of the 1960s, the Pininfarina influence extended as far as Argentina, where he styled the six-cylinder Torino coupé for IKA. Nor was he the only Italian stylist to leave an imprint on foreign makes. Volkswagen's sports coupés and cabriolets (1956 on) were built in series by Karmann of Osnabrück to Ghia designs. Ghia also enjoyed a long association with Chrysler, building a whole generation of dream-car prototypes which would influence the standard product in coming years. Produced in limited series were the Chrysler-based Dual-Ghia sports coupés and convertibles, and some very expensive limousines (90 between 1957 and 1960) on extended Imperial floorpans. Boano had a major hand in Renault's Dauphine (1956). Michelotti of Vignale worked with Standard-Triumph in Britain, starting with a tidy-up of the 1956 Standard Vanguard, and progressing to the Herald-Vitesse family. The "fine Italian hand" would penetrate as far as Japan, where Michelotti refined Hino's version of the small rear-engined Renault into the Contessa series of 1964. He was also responsible for the later Dutch DAFs.

The Pininfarina style in its ultimate form was severe and, by the early sixties, critics were complaining of a new uniformity. After all, the same influence was now detectable in the latest Fiats and their French cousins, the Simcas, as well as in the Peugeot 404 and the Austin/Morris clan. The Austin and Peugeot were especially close in appearance. The trend was nevertheless here to stay, and the seventies would see such developments as a Pininfarina Rolls-Royce and a Bertone Volvo.

Alongside these international relations, Italy continued with Fiat *elaborazioni*, a sure line of business in a market where imports were heavily restricted until 1960, and where—at least in the earlier part of our period—90 % of all new cars came from a single factory. An *elaborazione* was exactly what the word implied: one took a standard Fiat and jazzed it up with chromium strip, a new facia and, in the case of the rear-engined 600 and 850, more doors than Fiat themselves considered suitable. One could, of course, go well beyond the bounds of mere beautification, and some staggering things were done to 600s and 850s by Abarth, for instance. The tiny coupés, with their 90–95 mph (145–

Nostalgia before the nostalgia-car, or the cult of the Continental spare wheel kit, looked right on the original Mk.I Continental Lincoln, styled by E.T. Gregorie for Edsel Ford, and current in the 1940–48 period. Typical of the revival was Nash's version (*above*), widely applied to their cars in the 1950s and here seen on the British-made 1.2-litre Metropolitan coupé of 1954. But when Lincoln went nostalgic and revived the Continental theme as Mk. II for 1956, (*opposite, centre*), it was merely a trunk lid pressing, and looked it.

Chrysler (*below*) approached the theme from a sportier angle, with a realistic and not unattractive pressing on the K310 "dream car" created for them by Ghia of Italy in 1952. This one came close to actual production, though one wonders if the Corporation could have afforded the wire wheels—genuine, not clip-on trims. The only concrete result was, of course, 1957's infamous "dustbin lid", or "sportdeck", as Chrysler preferred to call it.

(*Left*) Dyna-Panhard sedan from France, 1954 style—or almost the exact opposite of Dante Giacosa's small-car philosophy at Fiat. Two cylinders and front-wheel drive (where Giacosa settled for an in-line four at the back) add up to carrying six people at 75 mph (120 km/h) on 850 cc, 42 horsepower, and a weight of only 1,568 lb (710 kg). What is more, none of this was won at the price of low gearing (top was 4.71 to 1) or excessive thirst: consumptions of the order of 40 mpg (7 litres/100 km) were possible with give-and-take driving. The key to all this was all-aluminium unitary construction—on Panhards the only steel structural member was the tube supporting the front end. Weaknesses were noise, poor synchromesh, an inefficient petrol heater, and the high cost of the lightweight carcass.

(*Opposite, top*) BMW's determined attempts to challenge Mercedes-Benz in the 1950s were financially disastrous, for all the lovely overhead-valve V-8s that it bred. The sedans used updated 1936 styling and looked bulbous, but Munich's answer to Stuttgart's 300S—this Type 503 cabriolet made from 1956 to 1959—was more attractive. Both rivals had four-speed all-synchromesh transmissions with the column shift beloved of Germans, but the BMW retained a beam rear axle, and played safe with carburettors while Daimler-Benz adopted fuel injection. Hence output (at 140 horsepower from 3.2 litres) stayed lower than that of the 300's in-line overhead-camshaft six. The BMW was, however, cheaper in the home market, and annual sales ran at about the same level.

(*Opposite, bottom*) Peugeot made few mistakes in our period. The stolid 403 would account for over 1,100,000 units beween 1955 and 1967, in a range which also embraced the 403/Sept with the old 203's 1,290-cc unit, a diesel variant, a convertible, a station wagon, and a line of light commercials. If rust took over in the end, the 403 proved very tough indeed, with a win to its credit in the 1956 Australian Ampol Trial, and a good record in the East African Safari—this last destined to be almost the preserve of the model's successor, the 404. Pininfarina styled the older car as well as the 404, but he managed to keep the French look, lost by later models which could easily pass for Fiats or Austins from the same drawing-board.

(*Right*) The spyders created by Pininfarina for Alfa Romeo are familiar. Less usual is the four-seater Giulia GTC (1965), one of the last designs by Carrozzeria Touring of Milan. Only 1,000 were made. The car used the famous 1.6-litre five-bearing twin overhead-camshaft four-cylinder engine, and by this time a five-speed all-synchromesh gearbox with well-chosen ratios and floor change was standard. So were servo-assisted disc brakes on all four wheels. The result was expensive—2,395,000 lire in Italy as against 1,570,000 for a sedan—but pleasing, and tremendous fun to drive.

155 km/h) of top speed, really came under the heading of a separate make—but 850TC versions of the 600, still with the regular body, were bored and stroked out from 633 cc to 847 cc and 80 horsepower (standard engines gave 24.5 hp), with a lowered suspension, stronger clutch, special exhaust system, and radial-ply tyres. In its ultimate form, the 850 ran to a twin overhead-camshaft unit with double the original capacity, a nose radiator worthy of a 1920s fighter aircraft, and a top speed of 132 mph (211 km/h): it could stay level with an E-type Jaguar up to 100 mph (160 km/h).

The next stage was to circumvent the problems of custom bodies, when there was no chassis on which to mount them. One could buy a non-running set of mechanical elements—floorpan, engine, transmission, brakes, and suspension—and build a car around them. This practice was followed by Abarth, Siata, Lombardi, and Moretti among others. Abarth also worked on French Simcas, while a parallel industry was developing in France around Panhards (DB were the principal exponents), Renaults (Alpine) and, from 1967, the Simca-based CG. What emerged could be strange. Siata started our period with a conventional MG look-alike based on the Fiat 1400, and ended their career in 1970 with something externally similar, yet having 850 mechanics at the rear. The open Lombardi, also rear-engined, had Morgan and Lotus overtones, the same firm offering an odd little square-tailed sports coupé. At the other extreme, Ghia's Vanessa was a "shopping coupé" for ladies, complete with built-in parcel trays and a two-pedal transmission.

The Italians worked with new components. In Britain and America, however, the novel glass-fibre techniques were originally devised to furnish fresh, cheap bodies for elderly chassis. Despite Ford's dedicated early-1940s experiments with soya derivatives (never, incidentally, applied to coachwork), glass-fibre bodies were a post-war phenomenon, surfacing quietly in southern California in 1950. Early examples were usually adapted to elderly Ford V-8s, and we shall meet these again when we explore the panorama of the kit-car. The new form of construction, though, entered regular chassis-makers' catalogues for the first time on the 1953 Chevrolet Corvette sports roadster, followed a year later in Britain by Jensen's 541 two-door sedan. The pioneers of glass-fibre unitary construction, as we have seen, were Berkeley (1956) and Lotus (1957).

Glass fibre has much to commend it for small production runs, since tooling is cheaper to balance a higher unit cost. Moulds for complex shapes are cheaper than elaborate machinery, and this method of construction also obviates the need for spot-welding in awkward places. It will stand considerable punishment without deformation and, in the event of an accident, one can cut out the damaged section and "knit" another into place. It can be made fire-resistant, and it may also be self-coloured to cut out multiple-cost spraying, although its great durability in such cases has been somewhat offset by the advent of hard, deep, and durable acrylic celluloses from 1964 onward. Plastic bodies have been used successfully by makers in countries like Turkey and Israel, where runs are unlikely to exceed 4,000 a year and there is no presswork industry.

Against the system is the relatively short life of a mould. A run of several thousand can be the limit, as many small specialists have discovered when taking moulds over from defunct firms. One cannot repaint a self-coloured body when it eventually starts to discolour: and one of the tougher glass-reinforced materials, Expanded Royalite (used on the original 1966 Cord replicar in America), was reluctant to hold a coat of paint for any length of time. Individual panels are occasionally difficult to align, and on open cars there is the problem of door apertures. On the Lotus Elan (1963), internal framing had to be welded up

and incorporated in the mouldings. Thus, in mainstream car manufacture, the chief use of plastic has been confined to individual mouldings—the roofs of D-series Citroëns, the bonnets of Singer Hunters (1955), and the boot lids of Honda minicars from 1968 onward. The material has, of course, been in wide use for dashboards since the later 1930s.

Not that many manufacturers have not used glass-fibre bodies: there were 19 such users in 1963, and 26 in 1969. What is significant is that few of them were true volume producers, and those who were did not apply the material to their best-selling items. The highest annual production rate recorded—about 30,000 at peak—stands to the credit of the pioneering Chevrolet Corvette, but such an output is a drop in the ocean to a company with a total potential of two million units a year. Of other major makers, Studebaker used glass-fibre on their exciting Avanti coupé (1962), yet were frustrated by failing finance as well as the usual headache of panel-fit. Saab's contribution was the short-lived, low-volume Sonett sports car. As for the rest, they consisted of firms in emergent countries (Anadol in Turkey, Sabra in Israel); Reliant, the British makers of three-wheelers and sports cars; and an assortment of kit-cars and specialist machinery employing British Leyland, Ford, GM, Renault, Rootes, or VW mechanical elements. Most of the latter were British, but there were also manufacturers in the U.S.A., Belgium, Germany, and France, plus a Greek minicar—the Alta—based on the German Fuldamobil.

With the convertible on the decline, a situation had been reached in 1969 when only one major European maker, VW, was still building the style in real quantity. Their plain Karmann-bodied four-seater had always outsold the Karmann-Ghia with its sportier lines. However, some interesting variations were seen. Power tops had long been common in America, although for the less expensive European models this was an unnecessary complication. Austin offered one on their big four-cylinder Atlantic and Hereford types (1949–52), while the later Daimlers and Dagenham Fords had an infuriating system in which the hydraulics were applied only to bring the top into a half-erected position. The four-door convertible was largely dead, Kaiser's version barely lasting into 1951: the only other contenders were the Mercedes-Benz 300, current throughout most of our first decade, and the huge Lincoln of which less than 15,000 were built between 1961 and 1967.

An unusual compromise between the fixed-head coupé and the convertible was tried by Ford of America in 1957. On this steel-roofed five-seater, the entire roof section retracted into the boot. Alas, the loss of luggage space and rear-seat legroom were as nothing beside the 6,000 feet of assorted wiring, ten power relays, ten switches, eight circuit breakers, and seven electric motors required to operate this mechanical marvel. The model was dropped after three seasons, despite respectable sales of 48,000 units. A sadder solution, albeit one to catch on strongly in the 1970s, was Porsche's 911 Targa (1966), a coupé with only the roof section detachable. Storage problems were simplified, while the solid rear quarters not only gave structural stiffness but also served as a crash pylon. In a safety-conscious world, this was a necessary compromise, although it is significant that Porsche returned to real convertibles in 1982!

The station wagon—roomier than a sedan, less discriminatory than a limousine, and adaptable to unitary techniques—went marching on through both our decades. True, it had yet to become a five-door, dual-purpose sedan, but equally it was neither servants' transportation nor the plumber's best friend. Indeed, station wagons embraced a vast range from the stripped *commerciales* of France (seats and not much else) to the luxury nine-seaters of Buick or Oldsmobile. As late as 1970, the most rudimentary class was represented by Britain's Bedford Beagle, a

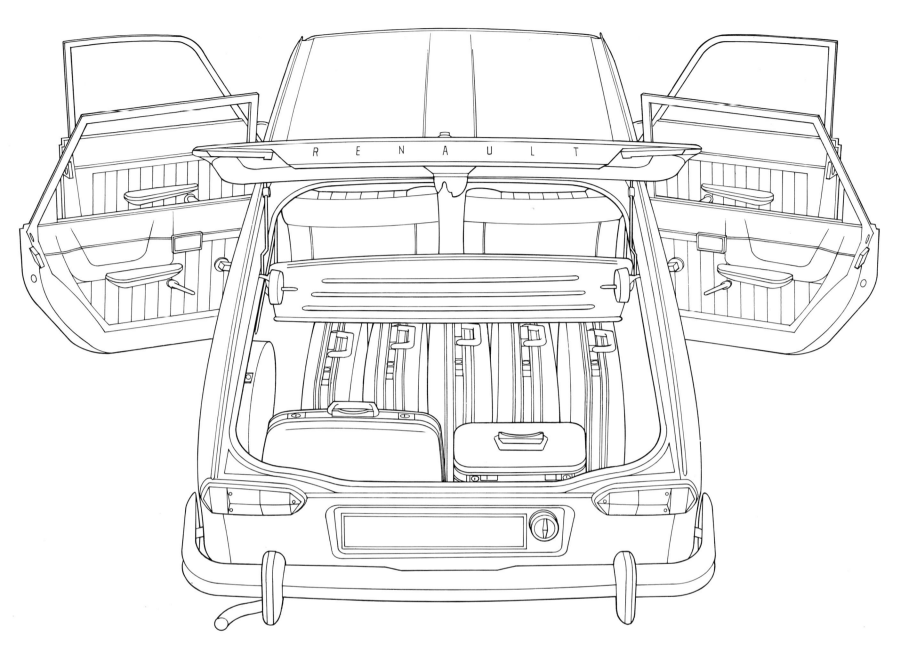

Enter the hatchback, or what can be done with a new style, given the flat floor conferred by front-wheel drive on the 1965 Renault 16 sedan with 1,470 cc. Interior accommodation could be arranged with any combination from free bedroom for two to enough luggage for a sizeable expedition. And even as a four-door family sedan, there was plenty of space, with no access problems for either passengers or their bags. The handy volume at the rear in normal use (*above*) could be doubled by tilting the rear seat forward and suspending its backrest on straps (*below left*). The latter might also be tilted so as to meet the backrest of the front passenger's seat, forming an enormous inclined lounge-chair, until both front seats were arranged flat for sleeping (*below right*). Adjustment was manual by means of locking levers, the seats sliding on ball-bearing runners. Fortunately, a heavy load in the boot did not result in a higher headlamp beam when driving, as a switch was available to lower the beam.

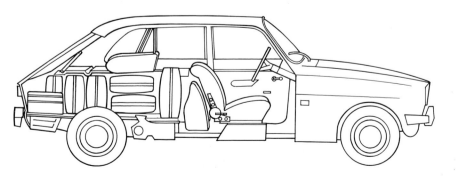

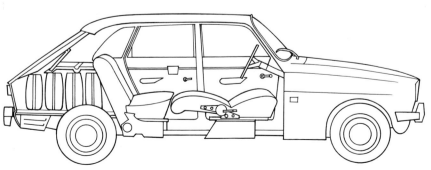

(*Above*) The Great American Norm, or one of 128,582 Chevrolet Bel Air Hardtop Coupés of 1956, a production statistic that would be creditable for any European maker's *whole* range—in Germany only Volkswagen and Opel would surpass it that year. The 4.3-litre V-8 engine was not particularly powerful (165–170 horsepower, or 205 with all performance options), and the base specifications still spelt a six-cylinder unit and three-speed manual. One could, however, "load" one's Chevy with automatic and power steering, brakes, seats, and windows, besides air conditioning and (from this year) seat belts.

(*Opposite, top*) Apart from Mercedes-Benz and a few cars from Kaiser-Frazer, Lincoln was the only firm to market a four-door convertible during our period, whereas in 1938 there was a diversity of offerings from GM, Chrysler, and Ford. Stylistically, the 1961 Lincoln had affinities with the six-passenger Thunderbird, and it was also unitary, but its wheelbase was 10 in (25 cm) longer, while the engine was a huge 7-litre V-8. The power-operated top was a real necessity, as anyone will know who has grappled with the opening and closing of a large British or German formal cabriolet of the 1920s or 1930s.

(*Opposite, bottom*) Colour used to break up slab-sided masses: the poor little Metropolitan 1500 (this is a 1961 model), made by Austin for American Motors, certainly needed it. Comparisons with Neapolitan ice cream were inevitable, but it has never been easy to scale a sixteen-foot (say 4.9-m) sedan down to a mere 149 in (3.8 m) of length. What looked right on a straight-eight in 1933 looked stunted with the shorter bonnet of a six, and the rules hadn't changed. Over 95,000 Americans, however, fell for the little Anglo-American, and it had quite a following in Britain, too.

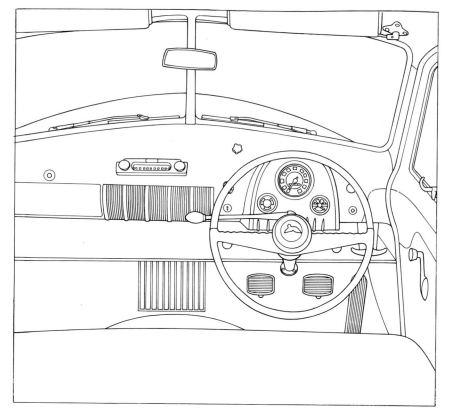

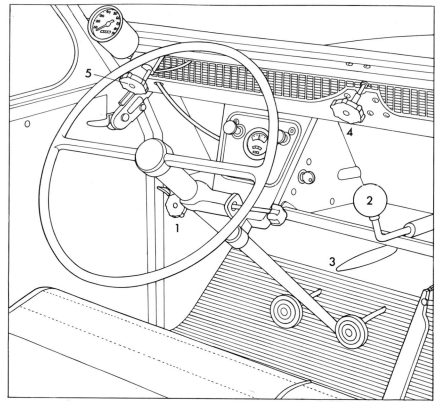

conversion of a light van using the mechanics of the Vauxhall Viva, though not the current styling, the sheet metal being a holdover from 1964. This had seats and windows, but little sound damping, while the combination of the latest engine and high-ratio back axle allied to indifferent drum brakes made it an exciting vehicle to drive in the wet.

The wagon's share of the U.S. market remained steady at about 11% overall, and it became an essential element in makers' programmes elsewhere. Offerings were limited in 1951, coming from Austin, Hillman, and Standard in Britain, Ford and Opel in Germany, Peugeot in France, Fiat in Italy, and Skoda in Czechoslovakia. All were van types except the latter two. In fairness, the French 2CV Citroën, nominally a convertible sedan, counted as a dual-purpose vehicle, but choice was restricted. By 1955, however, there were wagons by such firms as Borgward, DKW, Morris, Renault, Simca, and Volvo, soon to be joined by Citroën, Humber, and Vauxhall. On the other hand, the "woody" was a thing of the past, and extinct in America after 1953. We were also heading away from the van-with-windows school of thought, even if this persisted in Japan right into the late sixties. Bodies were still truckish, rear seats were uncomfortable, and not a few makers considered two doors and a tailgate sufficient.

Gradually, though, the concept of a sedan with an additional tail section began to take over. Rambler led this trend in the U.S.A. in 1957, and more and more refinements followed. Studebaker's 1963 model with sun-roof was not copied, nor was the rearward-facing extra back seat on Saab 95s. But by 1966, American wagons featured tailgates that opened either sideways or downward, and the power-operated type made their appearance a year later. By the end of our period, anyone with the right money could take his pick of a huge range, from the tiny Mini (still with a wood-straked option for the traditionalists) up to the colossal nine-seaters of Ford, Buick, Oldsmobile, and Pontiac, 18 ft (5.5 m) long and good for nearly 125 mph (200 km/h) on 6.5 litres of V-8 with the usual power options.

From this it was only a step to the true "combination car". This label conjured up visions of the *camionettes normandes* (farmer's tourers) offered by Citroën and others in the twenties. Citroën had in fact revived the theme on their 2CV in 1948, since it featured quick-detachable seating and a canvas one-piece top extending down to floor level at the rear. Thus it could double as a car or delivery van and, with the hood furled, a wardrobe or a grandfather clock could be carried. Sedans with rear tailgates were offered by Chrysler and Kaiser in the early fifties. A one-piece, swing-up tailgate made Citroën's last long-wheelbase *traction* (1953–57) into an old-school *commerciale*, if an unwieldy one. A further advance was the Farina-styled Austin A40 (1959), although in sedan form it was no hatchback, as the rear window was fixed, even if the boot-lid gave access to the rear of the body: only on the later Countryman version did the whole rear panel open. The real breakthrough, however, came with such cars as the Renault 16 (1965) and Austin Maxi (1969), using a true five-door sedan configuration with proper seating. In both these cases, front-wheel drive permitted an unobstructed flat floor at the back. A trend was being started—by 1982, 29 makers in seven European and Asian countries were listing three- and five-door styles as well as (and sometimes instead of) the traditional two- and four-door types.

Chevrolet and Pontiac had already produced sporting two-door wagons in 1955, but these did not catch on, and the true "sports" model arrived only in 1969 with the much-imitated Reliant Scimitar. This part of the story belongs to the seventies. Not that the van-type wagon was finished—it merely assumed a new and more apposite direction. Volkswagen's Transporter (1950) and Fiat's Multipla (1955) exploited rear-engine techniques to the full, with maximum carrying capacity crammed onto the shortest possible wheelbase, and true forward control in the commercial-vehicle sense. In due course, there would be a parallel development of the Chevrolet Corvair: its 1965 replacement, the Chevyvan, would adopt the layout despite a return to a front-mounted, water-cooled engine. While many vehicles in this class were used as station wagons, their main impact, as we shall see, would be in the realm of the mobile home.

Limousines, landaulettes, and sedancas were in decline, largely because the wealthiest motorists tended to opt for up-market editions of regular sedans (Cadillac, Jaguar, Mercedes-Benz) or drive themselves in the new generation of GTs and sports coupés. Of fourteen firms offering assorted formal carriages in 1951, only seven were still quoted in 1960. By 1969, those who preferred not to drive themselves, and also required the snob features of a division and occasional seats, had a simple choice: mainly Cadillac, Daimler, Rolls-Royce, and Mercedes-Benz, not to mention a price tag in excess of £6,000. Of these, the Phantom VI Rolls-Royce was strictly tailor-made, and the 6.3-litre V-8 Grand Mercedes by no means a regular showroom item: only 336 were delivered that year. Daimler's production ran at about 200 units annually, while Cadillac's fluctuated between 1,500 and 2,000 regardless of the *marque*'s overall sales performance. That other specialist vehicle, the up-and-coming 4×4, was not geared to any particular body type, and will be dealt with elsewhere in this book.

Of the accessories, the spare wheel remained a permanent headache. The side-mount had long gone, and external rear stowage was used only on traditional sports cars (pre-1956 MGs, Morgan, Lotus Seven). An odd and persistent hangover was the Continental spare wheel, a strange euphemism for what had, after all, been general practice up to 1934. Its new sobriquet stemmed from the vertical, exposed rear mounting used on that splendid if slightly misguided Classic, the Lincoln Continental of 1940–48. Suddenly in 1952 this became a cult object, and accessory makers started to offer "Continental kits" for almost any American car. Kaiser and Nash standardized it on some

models, the latter's including the curious little Austin-built Metropolitan, while all the big three manufacturers listed installations in their accessory catalogues. The cult spread to Britain, where Dagenham Fords started to sprout such excrescences, albeit not as factory options.

It was all over by 1959, though there were some peculiar side-effects. Lincoln revived the Continental theme in 1956 and, while the spare wheel was no longer outdoors, its presence was commemorated by a moulding in the boot lid. Even worse was Chrysler's "sport deck", a disease either optional or—occasionally—standard on various models of the 1957–61 era. This consisted of the impress of a spare wheel and its cover on the nearly horizontal deck lid, and the resemblance to the top end of a dustbin was only too obvious. Mercifully it died, but the third redesign of Lincoln's two-door Continental coupé (1968) featured a near-surrealist tail bustle, last flowering of a strange fad. Otherwise, spare wheels tended to live in boots, except on rear-engine cars where they helped to limit the space available under the frontal "bonnet". Odd locations were in the front wings (Bristol) and over the engine on such cars with front-wheel drive as the D-series Citroën and the Renault 16: as the former was cramped anyway, not much accessibility was lost, and indeed a little was gained by mounting the tool kit inside the wheel. Honda claimed that their under-bonnet mounting protected the passengers. The older idea of a separate access tray under the boot—usually behind the number plate—was dropped quite early in the 1950s, being prone to rust, although some such systems survived to the end of our period, as did those in which the wheel was mounted

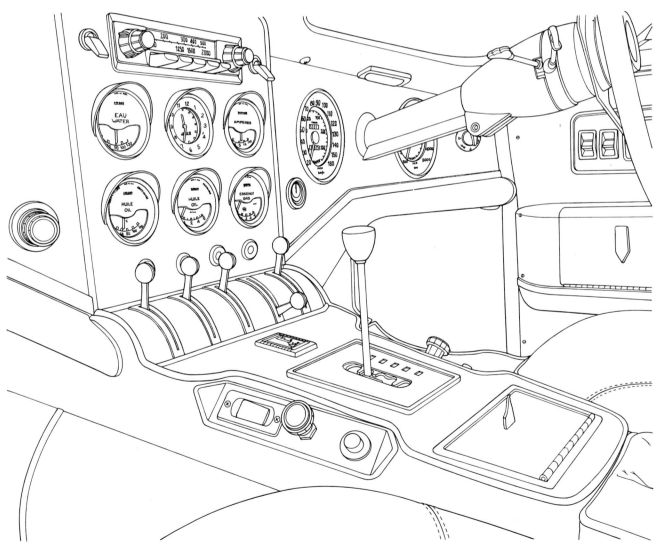

Facias of the fifties, not a good period for instrument displays. Very American was the original 1948–53 Holden from Australia (*opposite, left*) (the absence of a heater is to be expected in a country where snow is virtually unknown) though other influences are detectable in the circular dials. There is precious little on the dash of the 2CV Citroën (*opposite, right*) as originally marketed (this is a 1953 model), which offered only an ammeter and a speedometer, the latter apparently an afterthought. The headlamp tilt control (*1*) was necessary to adjust the lights to the self-levelling suspension. The gearshift (*2*) is the now-traditional Citroën dashboard-mounted type, and the handbrake lever (*3*) lives on the dash as well, like the air control (*4*). Twin wipers (*5*) are provided: they can be worked by hand if the power source fails.

(*Right*) Birth of the console—although this Facel Vega with 6.3-litre Chrysler engine is the 1962 model, rather than the original 1954. The theme is light aeroplane, with speedometer (angled inwards) and rev counter in front of the driver, secondary dials and radio grouped in the middle, and aircraft-type tumbler switches underneath. The floor-mounted automatic gearshift (or the "stick" for the alternative four-speed manual transmission) lives in the centre of the console, with six controls alongside. To the driver's right on this right-hand-drive car are the controls for the electric window lifts. Not all the walnut cabinet-work is, however, of wood.

Styles change, even on Lancias, though differences go far beyond the traditional grille of the 1953 Appia (*above*)—this is a 1957 *berlina*—and the modern Pininfarina shape of the 1960 six-cylinder Flaminia (*left*). Both are unitary, but the Flaminia's basis is a punt-type frame with deep box-section side members. Both retain the narrow-angle vee engines used on all Lancias since 1925. On the Appia, however, the famed sliding-pillar front suspension is retained, whereas the later car features more conventional coils with short and long arms. On a popular 1,100-cc sedan, too, there are attempts to cut costs by dispensing with the complex transaxle and inboard rear brakes of the parallel Aurelia six: a conventionally located four-speed synchromesh gearbox and semi-elliptic springs take their place. Doors lack pillars, while both weight and corrosion are kept at bay by using aluminium for these, the trunk lid and hood. The engine is almost incredibly compact, but the car had to compete against Fiat's *Millecento* in Europe, and it took ten years to sell 100,000 units. The Flaminia came with 2.5-litre or 2.8-litre engine: all but the first few cars had disc brakes as well, but there was little market at that time for big family sedans in Italy, and the big Lancia offered no international competition for Mercedes-Benz, Jaguar, and the even more complicated Citroën. Sales of 3,386 *berline* between 1957 and 1970 told their own story, although the short-chassis sporting Flaminias fared somewhat better.

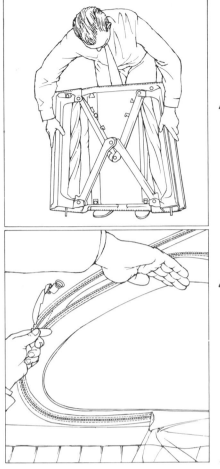

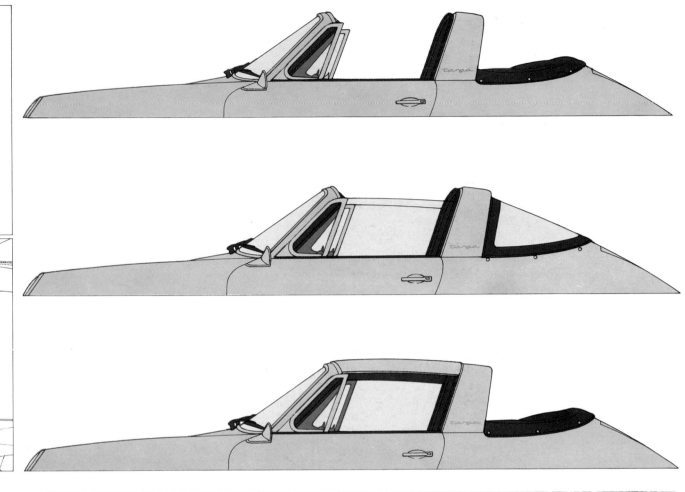

(*Above*) "Four in one", said the 1967 Porsche catalogue of their then-new 911 Targa. Top and rear window were detachable, and the side windows could of course be lowered, giving passengers the choice of fresh air plus safety, sun without draughts, fresh air without rain down one's neck, or sedan protection. The price? Where does one put the detachable bits when one is not using them? The roof folded, to occupy "minimum space" in the front luggage compartment, and the zip-up rear window lived on the parcels shelf. What one did in a sudden shower isn't stated.

(*Right*) Here is how the complete Porsche looked in 1972, by which time the flat-six engine had a capacity of 2.3 litres and was available in various states of tune, with either twin carburettors or fuel injection, and outputs from 130 to 190 brake horsepower.

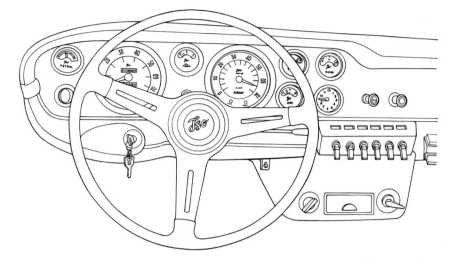

vertically in the boot itself. A less happy notion of GM's was to locate it in a well above floor level at the front of the luggage space, leaving plenty of room for suitcases, but requiring the services of a contortionist to extract the wheel. Fortunately, improved tyre technology meant fewer punctures ...

In-car living was taken seriously, as Chevrolet's 1953 accessory catalogue shows. Heater/defroster units were still extra, and would not become generally standardized for another ten years. But also available were seat-covers, radio (with or without rear-seat speaker), trunk lamp, screenwash, glare shade, automatic headlight dimmer, electric clock, cigar lighter, tissue dispenser, and plug-in electric shaver. The 1958 list had one serious addition—air conditioning—and one comedy item, the vacuum ashtray ("Cigarettes placed in this tray vanish like magic when the lever is pressed"). Heaters were mainly of fresh-air type, although air-cooled Panhards came with a petrol-fired device of somewhat dubious efficacy.

Real air conditioning—Nash's much-plugged system was merely a form of controlled ventilation and heating—arrived on Packards as far back as 1941. This was revived after the war as an option of 1953 Cadillacs, costing $619 (£221), and the other American makers followed soon afterward. It was taken up in the Old World by Rolls-Royce in 1956, and Jaguar were offering it on their prestige sedans by 1965. In most parts of Europe, however, such a refinement was superfluous, and even in 1969 the option was confined to the more expensive cars, like Ferrari and Mercedes-Benz.

Radio tended to be an extra throughout our period, and stereo—a 1960s phenomenon—even more so. Apart from Rolls-Royce (who invariably fitted a radio as standard) and oddities such as the Russian Volga, a radio was inclusive only when an importer wanted to justify the higher price with superior equipment. The Japanese were especially adept at this: all *de luxe* Toyotas sold in Britain included in-car entertainment. Nonetheless, more and more cars had radios. In 1935 approximately 1.2 million cars were so equipped in the whole of the U.S.A, whereas 7.5 million new models (91% of national production) were sold with radio in 1969. In Britain, however, of 341 cars tested by *Motor* between 1961 and 1967, only 174 offered in-car entertainment, and only 17 of these had it as standard.

Of other amenities, Nash had offered seats convertible into a bed on

their 1930s models, and in the 1950s their accessory catalogues included plastic blinds for the rear windows on such occasions. From the early 1960s, reclining back-rests began to catch on, and in the later sixties they would be standardized on a number of the more expensive European cars. In 1950 the screenwash was very much an extra, even though it could be specified as factory equipment. By 1960, its use had become almost universal, and most motorists were wondering how they had managed without it. Refinements of the system included electric operation—a great improvement on the squeegee which could shower water over the driver's knees if pressed too energetically—and an intermittent wash/wipe device which had reached the better middle-class cars by 1966.

Sunroofs were also coming back into prominence by the later sixties, a direct result of the convertible's declining popularity. Originally they had been a British preserve: the only major European firm to adopt them was Peugeot, although General Motors had tried such an option in 1939–40 and found few takers in America. A number of British factories persisted with the theme after the war—but as sliding roofs let in monsoon rain and dust with equal lack of discrimination, Britons bowed to the exigencies of the export drive and went without. Even Rolls-Royce ceased to offer it on their standard bodies after 1955. The Golde canvas-insert type, however, continued to sell well in Germany, while certain standard bodies (Fiat's twin-cylinder 500 of 1957, for instance) were a compromise between the full-length cabrio-limousine and the old-school sunroof type. Volkswagen's adoption of metal sunroofs in 1964 presaged a return to the old idiom in a more reliable, metal-panel form, with or without electric operation. BMW, Ford in Europe, Peugeot, and Renault offered manual versions in 1969: on a Mercedes-Benz, one got power assistance.

Power windows had been a regular option on Cadillacs as early as 1953, and 1957's Mercury Turnpike Cruiser carried matters still further with a power seat incorporating a built-in "memory": once set in the appropriate position, it would slide back when the ignition was switched off, returning to its pre-set point when one restarted. By 1963, most Cadillacs had seats with powered six-way adjustment, while similar types were recognized options on other American cars. On Cadillacs of the later sixties, one could have power assistance for door locks, trunk lids, and ventipanes as well. However, most of these aids were extra,

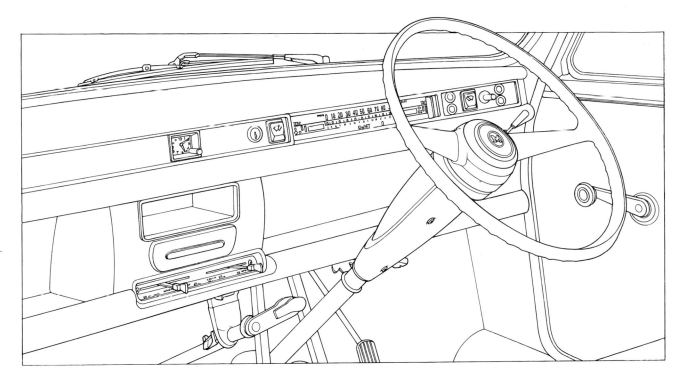

panel light, interior light, heater fan, rear-window demister fan, and fog lamps). As for the dials, the larger ones (for revs and speed) are easier to distinguish than the smaller ones (clock, water temperature, oil temperature and pressure, ammeter, and fuel gauge). The panel itself is crash-padded in anti-dazzle material, as is that of the contemporary BMW 1800Ti (*centre*), on which the gearshift really does "fall conveniently to hand". Typically German is the horn-ring, but wood-graining will be simulated on a relatively inexpensive sedan. There is some bogus wood, too, on the front-wheel-drive Austin/Morris 1800 of 1968 (*right*), with clock, ashtray, and radio space grouped neatly in the centre. Less pleasing are the linear speedometer and that deplorable 1940s hangover, the umbrella-handle handbrake. As these facias show, one advantage of having a simpler car was to remove some distractions from the driver's field of vision.

and in Europe they were reserved for prestige offerings. Power windows, for example, were found on cars such as Iso, Jaguar, and Rolls-Royce. Heated rear windows, those essential adjuncts of 1980s motoring, were regularly available by 1961, but only just beginning to penetrate beyond the executive-car market in 1969 on cars like Rover and BMW. Further, they were still on the extras list. We were a long way from the days when it would be possible to buy a European Ford model inclusive of headlamp wash/wipe, stereo, tinted glass, and power windows.

Wholesale acceptance often breeds a dreary uniformity, but the one place where this never occurred on a motor car was, perhaps, where it was most needed—on the dashboard. There can be nothing so infuriating as minor controls which work in an unexpected manner. True, in the inter-war period there were some oddities, such as the back-to-front gear gate of Vintage Buicks and Dodges and certain 1930s Wolseleys. The French multi-purpose stalk control for lights and other ancillaries was not very common outside that country, and turn-indicators could be maddening afterthoughts on cars from countries where they were not compulsory (they were illegal in some states of Australia, so Holdens dispensed with them altogether). Even starters could be difficult to find, although the "pedomatic" (foot-operated) types beloved of Americans in the thirties were on their way out. Key-starting, a Chrysler innovation of 1949, had attained wide currency by 1961, and was virtually universal six years later. This eliminated some of the less pleasant devices, notably Fiat's plunger-type key, which was pushed in for ignition and rotated for lights!

Facias did, however, move slowly towards the ergonomic. The lunatic rectangular displays of the forties and early fifties, inspired by some weird whim of the stylist, became less frequent by 1960. Prime horrors of the initial years were the strange binnacles of Nash and Panhard, set on the steering column. This meant that the driver had to re-focus his eyes every time he consulted his instruments, not to mention the electrical risks of a profusion of wire extending down the column. Among the few obvious merits of the late-1960s safety legislation was that the demand for collapsible columns led to the removal therefrom of many items which should never have been there in the first place.

After 1959, there was a welcome reversion to circular dials, and from the early 1960s they tended to have black faces. Nonetheless, the linear

speedometer continued to earn its adherents—at the end of our period, it was found on a number of American cars, as well as on models from Leyland, Renault, Simca, and Skoda. It was certainly an improvement on the white-faced, arcuate instruments of certain Rootes cars in the early and middle fifties. Instruments were also uniformly grouped in front of the driver: even the Mini had fallen into line by late 1969.

What went on the panel? Here, two warring factors were at work, the desire for simplicity and the need to furnish information to a more knowledgeable generation of drivers. To some extent, the information required was not the same as in the 1930s, when the dials to watch were the thermometer and the oil-pressure gauge, both potential harbingers of expensive noises. Sealed-for-life cooling systems and stronger crankshafts, however, had changed the situation, and a rev-counter was probably more useful on small units which were safe up to 6,000 rpm. This was certainly necessary on a Wankel, which would give no audible warning of stress when approaching its safe limit. Ammeters, in some form or other, were likewise more important, since the march of the ancillaries was faster than the march of the alternator. Indeed ammeters, thermometers, and oil-pressure gauges continued to be found on the majority of up-market cars throughout the fifties and sixties, with the thermometer as the last to vanish when a maker had to economize. Rev-counters were usually adjuncts of the sports car, although they also appeared on sedans with a "GT" label and featured in the "performance packs" of American makers.

At the bottom end of the market, facias were almost bare. Early VWs offered merely a speedometer, but the 2CV Citroën also had an ammeter and, on the sub-utility antiquated British Ford Popular (1954–59), you got a fuel gauge. Simca's Aronde had an "oil-pressure indicator" (something, it would seem, rather less than a gauge), though it featured warning-lights for low oil pressure, low fuel, and dynamo charge. Early Minis had a single central dial supplemented by warning-lights, and these devices gained in quantity and complexity from the mid-fifties onward. A fairly expensive 1962 model, the Alfa Romeo 2600, had lights for the choke, generator, fuel reserve, ignition, and lamps. Mercedes-Benz and others threw in one for the handbrake: on the Rover 2000, this light also showed if the brake-fluid level fell too low. Perhaps the extreme case of "idiot lights" was found on Fiat's 2300 S coupé (1961), a poor man's Ferrari and an early user of power windows. What drivers

Thunderbird development. Here (*opposite, top*) we see the 1956 edition of Ford of America's original two-passenger "personal car" in soft-top guise, with the famed Continental Spare Wheel Kit as standard equipment. Like Chevrolet's Corvette, this was little more than a shortened standard chassis, but creature comforts were more carefully studied, and automatic was not compulsory although power brakes, steering, and top were. The automatic variant set the later fashion for floor-mounted gear selectors. The original 4.8-litre "Thunderbird Special" V-8 was exclusive to this Ford model, but was available in Mercurys—as was the 1956

5.1-litre development, though you could only have this latter with automatic. By 1963 (*opposite, bottom*), the breed had degenerated into just another large American two-door car, available with hard or soft tops, and without any of the elegance of the rival Buick Riviera. An odd variation that year was this Sport Roadster with its wire wheels and racing-car-style headrests. The latter had no more than an add-on glass-fibre "tonneau cover" concealing the rear seats, and most people were disinclined to pay the extra $650 asked. Standard engine in this one was a 6.4-litre, 300-horsepower V-8, and there was no manual transmission option.

(*Below*) You can't call Buick's 1953 Skylark convertible a sports car, for all those genuine wire wheels, the plunging belt-line, and the 188-horsepower edition of the brand-new 5.2-litre V-8 engine with its quadrajet carburation. The car was, however, loaded with equipment usually reserved for the extras

list: power steering, brakes, and radio antenna, besides tinted glass and whitewall tyres. At $5,000, too, it cost nearly twice as much as the regular Roadmaster ragtop with the same engine in detuned form. Sales of this Skylark and the less attractive 1954 version totalled only 2,526 cars.

remembered was, however, a battery of ten warning lights, plus two bells, to signal overheating or an engine speed of over 2,000 rpm with the choke out. It was only a step away from buzzers which sounded when seat belts were unfastened.

Although suction and camshaft-driven systems survived into the 1960s, especially on American cars, the electric screenwiper was standard practice. Twin installations were universal, and triple wipers would arrive with the vast panoramic screens of later mid-engined GTs. Two-speed devices, if not general practice, had reached the upper echelons of the 1.5-litre sedan market by 1969.

Another dilemma, then, was being faced by designers. Idiot lights were confusing enough, but there was also the problem of an increasing number of items which did not properly belong to the conduct of a car—the heater and its fan, the power-window switches (usually on the driver's door), the radio, the cigar lighter and, eventually, the stereo cassette. Standard 1950s practice had been to "style" the radio into the dash, or to park it underneath as a chronic knee-barker.

One of the brighter ideas of our period was to build a console below the main facia, to take this overflow of ancillary devices. Here the pioneer was the French Facel Vega of 1954, with its instrumentation likened to that "of a classy private aeroplane". The large-diameter speedometer and rev-counter sat in front of the driver, leaving the centre clear for the other dials and the radio. On the console itself was a row of aircraft-type switches for heating and ventilation, with the gear lever, ashtray, and controls for lights and washer/wipers. Others followed: in many cases, the "console" served merely as storage space for oddments, although on new models of the sixties (Rover, Triumph) it housed the radio, and the Chevrolet Corvette kept its heater unit and clock there. On medium-sized European Fords of the last years, what

went on it depended upon the detail specification. The 1967 Cortina GT received an ammeter and an oil-pressure gauge (not found on cheaper versions), plus space for extra instruments, thus saving amateurish and unsightly private modifications at a later date.

But even with all these improvements, ergonomic groupings were not as common as they should have been. Of the Ford Capri, one critic observed: "Minor controls are scattered about with apparent disregard for ergonomics; the handbrake warning light being paired with the light switch." Odd things happened. In the early 1950s, there was a craze for bonnet-mounted bug deflectors, and another for huge tinted sun-visors. An accessory peculiar to Australia was the kangaroo guard, desirable for night driving in the outback, but looking most peculiar when affixed to the front end of a VW. An irritant on some small rear-engined sedans was the arrangement of the heater ducts to follow the gear-linkage tunnel. This would not have been so bad, had not Fiat and Renault fitted flip-up starter and choke levers behind the gearshift, where they became near-incandescent to the touch after a long winter run. In hot weather, cheaper plastic upholstery adhered to the driver's posterior—leather was reserved for *de luxe* models, and not always then. One could, in theory, be sure of it on the more luxurious European cars, and also on American convertibles, but in 1968 even Jaguar turned to plastic on their least expensive 240/340 series.

Beyond an increasing interest in energy-absorbing steering columns, and tougher rules from America, safety had not moved in to the alarming extent so characteristic of the 1970s. Nowhere in Europe was the wearing of seat belts compulsory, although Britain and several other countries required these to be fitted on all new cars from 1967 onward. There had long been a conspiracy of silence over inbuilt safety. Two American makes—the Nash and the obscure Muntz—had been available with seat belts in 1952, and they were actually standard on the latter breed, along with padded dashes and padded roofs on hardtop versions. But 394 Muntzes sold in three seasons made little impression, even in the car's native California. Just as unsuccessful was Ford's 1956 "safety

package" of belts and padded dashes. The idea had an adverse psychological effect, and was quietly dropped. A survey taken in England in the summer of 1966 showed that only 26.7 % of all cars were fitted with belts, and only 17.7 % of motorists wore them. Some of these, too, limited their active use to motorway work.

Improvements were on the way. The new models of 1968–69 almost always featured padded dashes, although, as one cynical observer put it, "some people's ideas felt harder than the old burr-walnut treatment". There were also instances in which the instruments were carefully recessed into the facia, yet the old, hard projecting surround was not only retained, but extended all the way across to allow for left- or right-hand steering. Safety was also breeding brighter colours: for too long, drab shades had been an integral part of mass-produced motoring. If not everyone was following the uniform black of Citroën's pre-1952 *tractions*, the 1955 Fiat 600 had come in four chaste colours—green, light or dark blue, and grey. In Britain, the black-with-brown-leather of the late forties had given way to wishy-washy pastel shades, so much so that, when U.S. servicemen brought their Austin-built Metropolitan coupés to British bases, their two-tone strawberries-and-cream paintwork stood out in car parks. Only sports cars and the more expensive American machinery featured bright colours. Now the need for cars to be more visible gave us Fiats in gamboge, Renaults in lime green, and Hillmans in brilliant blue.

All of which was at naught beside what Detroit could do when she really tried. AMC's performance offerings for 1969 were the Javelin and AMX coupés, and they could indeed move when endowed with quadrajet-equipped 6.4-litre V-8s. They were loaded with safety equipment—seat belts, deep-dish steering wheel, energy-absorbing column, padded dash—and the extras list included eight-track stereo, tinted glass, and rally stripes running up the bonnet and over the roof. Who, however, could resist the season's special colours: Big Bad Orange, Big Bad Blue, and Big Bad Green?

Chapter 4

HAVE *YOU* A TIGER IN YOUR TANK?

"It's dashing, road-hugging, exciting to drive, proudly styled, beautifully made, and it handles like a sports car."

"It is a car that one never tires of driving. Extremely lively, economical, a joy to handle on the road because of its responsible manoeuvrability."

Yes, they are the same car, though "road hugging" conjures up the image of a low-slung convertible, and "responsive manoeuvrability" suggests a 1920s delivery boy rocking his Model-T van out of a congested space by alternate kicks to the low-speed and reverse pedals.

The former version is American, and sacrifices truth for effect. The latter is British (by the car's actual maker, Austin) and injects an element of respectability that was never part of the poor little Metropolitan's make-up. Like the "strawberries and cream" Rover Nine of 1926, and the early pre-Jaguar SS, it was never "quite nice". In any case, there was a world of difference between the enterprising image of Nash in the U.S.A.—first on the home market with Anglo-Americans, first with unitary construction, first with a modern compact—and the stolid picture of Austin, "Britain's dependable car".

Herbert Austin might be long dead, and the vituperative Leonard Lord firmly in the saddle at Longbridge. The company's early post-war output might, and did, include a poor man's Bentley (the 1947 Sheerline sedan), an abortive convertible mini-Pontiac (the 1949 Atlantic), and a genuine sports car (the Healey 100) for the first time since 1932. By having an all-new car on the road in March, 1947, they were more than one-up on their traditionally more progressive rivals, Morris, and they intended to stay that way. Like it or not, Austin were the senior partners in the British Motor Corporation. Unfortunately, they had an image to kill, and they did it in the least inspiring way possible, as their handling of the Metropolitan shows.

Slogans were a danger, in that they reinforced an image which had outlived its usefulness. Packard's "Ask The Man Who Owns One" and De Soto's "The Car Designed With You In Mind" had acquired an ironic tinge by 1956–57, the former because nobody was much interested in up-market Studebakers, and the latter because the "You" in the agency doggerel was becoming visibly less and less plural. If MG's "Safety Fast" was to fit even better into the mood of Nader's America than it had into that of Stanley Baldwin's England in the 1930s, Vauxhall must have regretted their 1961 slogan—"Everybody Drives Better in a Vauxhall"—especially as it coincided with the nadir in handling characteristics. (The writer recalls a cynical colleague who scrawled, under the magic words on one of Luton's stamped envelopes, "They . . . well have to"!)

The winged wheel of Austin dogged their career right up to 1972, when Lord Stokes ordained that the name be reserved for cars with front-wheel drive, of the school of Issigonis. The code-name for the Mini might be ADO (Austin Design Office) 15, but attempts by sentimentalists at Longbridge to christen it the Austin Seven foundered at birth, with visions of pram-hooded Chummies driven by jolly maiden ladies. "Mini-Minor", the Morris label, stuck. Even the Austin-Healey, which had nothing remotely Morris about it, acquired a Morris publicity image late in life. The moment the badge engineers slapped an MG label on the little 948-cc Sprite (born 1958), sales went up, and the car earned a happy sobriquet, "Spridget". Company critics may have dictated the discarding of the old designation after 1971—but even had Donald Healey not dissociated his name from the Leyland Group, one suspects that the change would have happened.

Austin fought a long battle against a *marque* image. They were not the only ones. American Motors took time in 1965 for some self-congratulation in an "I didn't think you were that kind of car" display, and this certainly applied to their advertising, if not to the vehicle itself. Only six years earlier, they were indulging in a dreadful comic-strip showing how a basketball player seven feet tall at last found the right length and width of automobile.

An even worse case was Pontiac. Originally a cheap companion car to General Motors' middle-class Oakland, it outstripped its senior running-mate from the start in 1926, encompassed the Oakland's death in 1931, and thereafter sat happily in the top six. After 1936, it was usually in the top five. What it lacked was a genuine image. The famous plated Silver Streaks had appeared in 1934: a year later they hit the bonnet top, though they still had some significance, as the name commemorated a streamlined diesel railroad express which made the headlines. Also there, and on the radiator cap from the beginning, was the "Indian head" of Chief Pontiac. Railroads, however, were old hat in the 1950s, and everyone was bored with the Chief in an era where Oldsmobile decorated everything in reach with missile motifs, Cadillac's tail fins commemorated the Lockheed P-38 fighter aircraft of World War II, and "jet" became an epithet associated with anything from quicker automatics to the latest in multi-choke carburation. Pontiac had, in any case, lagged behind with side-valve engines only as late as 1954, and even the industry's last cheap straight-eight when everyone else was stuck with sixes or had made the switch to vees and upstairs valves.

New Division head S. E. Knudsen was determined to change all this, and he did. For all the stylistic potential of those plated streaks on the wide bonnet of 1955's new V-8, they had to go, and go they did. From 1959, the Pontiac image centred round their "wide track" chassis, while the publicists even took the risk of using the European term, for reasons of euphony and to avoid unwise associations. After all, "wide tread" would suggest a stair carpet . . .

By way of introduction—the clean, classic lines
of the Ford convertible range ... Long, low, splendidly
luxurious, perfectly proportioned, with
just the right amount of chrome and sparkle.

(*Opposite, top*) The performing midgets are on their way out, although much the same effect is available by playing with perspective. The interior of Austin's 1959 3-litre Westminster sedan was not quite as roomy as this press illustration would suggest.

(*Opposite, bottom*) Danger, elongators at work. You could almost land a helicopter on that rear deck, and the illustrator has cleverly suggested tail fins that don't exist in the metal. The worm's-eye front view suggests an enormous car, too, while the minimal text on this catalogue page keeps the prospect's eye on the vehicle. It is Ford of Britain's top-of-the-range Zodiac convertible as depicted in their 1960 catalogue: a modest 2.5-litre six, smaller than contemporary American compacts. It didn't look so pretty with the top up, so there is only one illustration (later on) of the car in this form.

(*Right*) German publicity, whereas the use of colour against a dark background was a favoured Swiss technique in the 1960s. The skill here is in hiding the boxy outlines of the 1965 Simca 1500 sedan, and giving it a beauty and individuality which it so signally lacks in the metal. (The "French *chic*" derives, in any case, from an Italian-inspired shape, one of Pininfarina's less felicitous efforts, and largely shared by products of Fiat, Peugeot, and British Motor Corporation.) The copywriter has been clever enough to give a recital of the car's features which never sinks to nuts-and-bolts level, and yet conceals the vehicle's surpassing ordinariness from the reader. The policy worked, too—Simca sold over 1,300,000 of the 1300/1500 family, their last conventionally-engineered models, between 1963 and 1976, though in the mid-1960s German sales of the whole range were running around 15,000 a year, for all the appeal to local patriotism implied in that "Porsche-type synchromesh". It is also intriguing to see how translation can breathe new life into an old slogan. In 1939 "The Car that Knows No Frontiers" had been the British Wolseley, cunningly prompted by a cut-off view of the rear end with a GB plate prominent. This was at least honest, in that it admitted that the car crossed frontiers on a *triptyque*, not on an import licence! Few Europeans were buying British cars before World War II.

Sein guter Ruf kennt keine Grenzen - SIMCA aus Frankreich

Wie elegant kann eine komfortable Limousine sein?

SO!

Der erste Eindruck – französischer Chic, formbewußte Eleganz, stilreine Linie. Ein Wagen an dem alles stimmt: SIMCA 1500 GL. Betont tief liegt die Gürtellinie. Sie läßt Platz für große Fenster und gibt der Karosserie die gestreckte rassige Form.
Der zweite Eindruck – vollendeter Komfort. Ein Wagen, der Fahrer und Mitfahrer verwöhnt: SIMCA 1500 GL. Vier breite Türen öffnen sich bis zum rechten Winkel. Die fülligen Polster bieten fünf Personen großzügige Bequemlichkeit (vorn Einzel-Liegesessel, in der Mitte der Rücksitze versenkbare Armlehne, Klima-Anlage mit schwenkbaren Frischluftdüsen und eine Fülle individueller Attribute). Und dann zeigt der SIMCA 1500 GL, was in ihm steckt: Leistung und Fahrtüchtigkeit. Die 66 DIN-PS des 1500er Motors bringen ihn mühelos über 145 km/h. Seine hervorragende Straßenlage, seine Kurvenstabilität (SIMCA-Ankerachse) und seine verläßlichen Scheibenbremsen geben jede Sicherheit.
Typisch für jeden SIMCA: 4 Türen, der ungewöhnlich große Innenraum, die freie Sicht nach allen Seiten, die fünffach gelagerte Kurbelwelle, das 4-Gang-Vollsynchrongetriebe System Porsche, die hydraulisch betätigte Kupplung, Ölwechsel und Abschmieren alle 10000 km.
SIMCA 1500 DM 7450,–*, Grand Luxe DM 7950,–* zuzügl. Überführung (*empf. Preis)

5400 Servicestellen in Europa,
600 in Deutschland
Deutsche SIMCA, Neu Isenburg

SIMCA 1500

Had Austin's stolid Metropolitan catalogue appeared in 1950, it would have been comprehensible. Paper was still short in Europe and, as yet, a new car was either a dream or something to be glimpsed through a dealer's showroom window—maybe even two dealer's showrooms, as there were not enough demonstrators to go round, and the odds were that the vehicle would move to the next town in a fortnight's time. Even in America, the backlog of orders had scarcely been worked off in 1949: and in the rush to make cars, there was neither the time nor the need to indulge in good copy or typography. Catalogues had to be issued in foreign languages, and a firm as small as Lea-Francis burst into French. Not that this was any problem for the big companies, who had been doing it before the war. MG issued a brochure in German (complete with Gothic script) for the benefit of their Swiss customers in 1933, and most major British and American firms were proficient in Flemish and Dutch. French was not always their strong suit, and sometimes it looked as if translators had never seen a car or, at any rate, studied the technical jargon. The genius who, confronted with the word *exhausteur* (the standard French term for a vacuum fuel-feed), decided that it was a case of fractured *franglais* is only too well known. His final version (*pot d'échappement*, or exhaust pipe) must have prompted some strange theories on the working of an internal combustion engine! Early Japanese essays into English included such solecisms as "two-stoke".

In any event, there seemed little point in wasting good copy on something the public could not buy, and writers—usually of the "exaggerated" school of thought which translates three metres of motor car into four or five—had to work for their living. True, the British motoring press let itself go once a year in the Show Numbers of *Autocar* and *Motor*, with their colour supplements. The results, however, were messy and a tribute only to the professional elongators. It took some concentrated effort to transform the Kaiser-like Singer SM1500 into something even longer than its American stylistic prototype.

Four themes had stalked the primitive era of automobile advertising: the testimonial, the illustrious client, the competition awards list, and the "nuts and bolts" approach. None of them fitted the post-war years. Testimonials were out, if only because a car was now supposed to work properly, and nobody bothered to write to the factory unless it did not. Instead there came "knocking copy", either the indignant letters to more critical sectors of the motoring press ("all four big-ends failed within a month of purchase") or the consumer's-report style of comparative analysis, which was popular in the U.S.A. by the early sixties and spreading rapidly to Europe. American Motors ran their own version of it, distributed along with their regular catalogues.

These great adva
most exc

No need for any artifice to depict the 1957 De Soto Fireflite Sportsman—the photograph is by the factory press department, and the gowns by Magnin. Not a nut or bolt in the copy, plenty of emphasis on the low build, and no word to suggest that the car is a good 216 in (5.5 m) long. It's not always clear what is standard equipment and what is optional at extra cost, and there's a hint of snob appeal in the words "priced just above the lowest". And where else, in 1957, would there be a plug for radio and TV commercials? The message in tiny print at the lower right, that De Soto sponsors a programme called "You Bet Your Life", sounds almost ironic.

New *Flight Sweep* styling. For 1957 De Soto presents the new shape of motion! Long, upswept tail fins that add stability at modern highway speeds. Sleek, lower-than-ever lines. 40% more glass area for a super-safe view of the road.

Barely 4 feet 7½ inches from ground to graceful roof—yet inside, this exciting beauty has generous head room with lots of length to stretch.

New *Torque-Flite* transmission. This year De Soto introduces the most advanced transmission ever built—*the new*

Torque-Flite. It gives you breath-taking getaway, tremendous passing acceleration and velvet-smooth power surge at any speed! No shift delay, no annoying "clunk."

New *Push-Button* control. Simply touch a button of De Soto's new Triple-Range push-button control—and you're on your way!

New *Torsion-Aire* ride. For the smoothest ride you've ever had in an automobile, try De Soto's new Torsion-Aire ride. Cobbled streets seem smooth as silk. You take corners without lean or sway.

DE SOTO

ces make the '57 DE SOTO the
ing car in the world today!

is level as a table top, even from ceds. Positively no nose-dive! secret? A completely new suspen-t combines torsion rods, super-soft afety-Sphere control joints, outrider orings, and a rubber-cushioned spension.

Torsion-Aire ride is *standard equip-* every 1957 De Soto.

uper-powered V-8 engines. '57 engine designs are the most l in the industry! These deep-ng giants respond instantly for safer

passing, loaf quietly at superhighway speeds. Here's "take-charge" perform-ance that won't take a back seat to anything on the road.

There are three new and powerful De Soto V-8's to choose from…with higher-than-ever horsepower for safer passing!

New 4-Season air conditioner. This advanced and compact unit—mounted out of the way under the dash—*cools* in summer, *heats* in winter. It filters out dirt and sneezy pollen…wrings moisture from muggy summer air. One flick of a simple

set of controls keeps the interior of your new De Soto ideally comfortable and quiet every mile you drive.

New interior features. Each '57 De Soto interior features exciting new fab-rics with smart accenting trim, and a beau-tiful new flight-styled instrument panel.

Your choice of every advanced power feature: Full-Time power steering—Feather-Touch power brakes—6-Way power seat—Electro-Lift power windows. See the most exciting car in the world to-day at your De Soto-Plymouth dealer's.

Be sure to see the new
De Soto FireSweep
Priced just above the lowest!
The Most Exciting
Value in the World Today
See it! Drive it! Price it!

De Soto dealers present **Groucho Marx** in "You Bet Your Life" on NBC radio and TV

133

In an increasingly democratic era, the maharajahs had been eliminated long before 1956, when the Indian Government clamped down on car imports and cut the potentates off from their custom Bentleys. In the main, the cars they used to buy no longer existed, and one air-conditioned Cadillac looked very much the same as the next. If a V.I.P. ordered something especially exotic—as in the case of the Papa or other Mercedes-Benz limousines from 1963 on—a discreet release might secure a photograph in the weekly press.

"Class" advertising existed, albeit in a toned-down form, applicable to executives rather than to persons of title. Lincoln and Cadillac were consistent adepts at this art, and so, latterly, was Lancia ("One name stands out of the herd")—backed by an emphasis, in Britain at any rate, on strictly limited imports and a small, select band of dealers. Limited editions, however, were more a 1970s phenomenon, being sale-boosters in times of recession, and used (by British makers certainly) in the same way as school-children dream up improbable reasons for an extra half-holiday. American Motors were among the first to explore this field when, in 1967, they ran three station wagons with unusual side trim: the Briarcliff for the East, the Mariner for coastal areas, and the Westerner for the Midwest and Southwest. The total run was 1,500, with rather more Mariners than the other two—a "special" would, after all, draw more attention in vacation-land. Another happy hunting ground for limited editions would be the nostalgia car and the replicar, but these, as we shall see, had made little impact, and the market was light-years away from 1982's saturation point.

More typical of attempts to capture the new executive sector was Jaguar's "Grace, Space and Pace", combining dignity and performance

Rolls-Royce went unitary for 1966, and tidied up their quad headlamp installation, but these—and several others—were qualities shared with American Motors' full-size Ambassador sedans and coupés, and AMC weren't letting this pass. The punch is undeniable: it is also undeniable that Rolls-Royce were still making prestige V-8s in 1982, whereas AMC dropped the Ambassador line at the end of 1974.

with euphoria and a re-run for the virtues promoted (in a different order) by MG on their big sixes in 1936. ("The Car of Grace that Sets the Pace" was, however, none other than that Vintage Classic, the 30/98 Vauxhall, which had both those qualities, albeit a thumping 4.2-litre four-cylinder engine!) At a comic level came Avtoexport's 1953 attempt to promote their 3.5-litre ZIM limousine as "a comfortable middle-class car". Quite apart from the improbable suggestion of a Russian manufacturer's catering for the *bourgeoisie*, it was certainly not a car that any Western middle-class family would have bought, although they might have voted one for their mayor or even hired one for a daughter's wedding.

There were, of course, snob elements in the knocking copy of the 1960s. Ford, while still capable of inverted snobbery on occasions, promoted the 1965 Falcon as "first class at low economy fares" against the background of a jet airliner: a reminder that there was a world of difference between the basic six-cylinder sedan and a hardtop V-8 with all the performance options. In 1965, they had a go at Rolls-Royce, claiming that their top-of-the-range LTD was quieter than a Silver Cloud. American Motors would carry this a step further. Their Ambassador, indeed, shared many features with a late-sixties Silver Shadow costing six times as much: coil-spring independent suspension, air con-

SPRINT

This is the wonderful interloper that looks like it was designed in Italy, acts like a European road machine, and costs so little you'll think we left out the engine. Which, of course, we couldn't have because that outrageously efficient 215-hp Overhead Cam Six is the heart of it all – even if the car does corner like we did. The Sprint Option is available on all Le Mans, Tempest Customs, Tempests except station wagons. Interested? Who isn't. Turn the page.

TEMPEST CUSTOM HARDTOP COUPE WITH SPRINT OPTION

TEMPEST SPORTS COUPE WITH SPRINT OPTION

SPRINT

LE MANS CONVERTIBLE
WITH SPRINT OPTION

Killing the maiden aunt image—it's 1967, eleven years since either Silver Streaks or an Indian Head graced a Pontiac's bonnet. They're in the performance business now, and using this ingenious combination of straight artwork with close-photograph illustration to sell, not a model, but a performance option. The car measures 207 in (5.3 m) from bumper to bumper, so no exaggeration is called for.

ditioning, individually reclining front seats, unitary construction, and deep-dip rustproofing. That such characteristics were common to a great many medium-category and luxury cars was supremely relevant—but in their final paragraph, they could not resist a dig at General Motors. "The Rolls-Royce has less headroom than a Cadillac. The Ambassador has more." Ford's British masterpiece came in 1967 when they asked the executive market, "Would you let your daughter marry a Ford owner?" As a means of killing the maximum number of birds with the minimum copy, this was a stroke of genius. The Ford in question was the limited-edition, near-racing GT40 coupé (31 made for street use), the price was £7,540 and, observed the economically minded press office at Dagenham, "If you're a bit worried about your future son-in-law, just ponder over the trade-in value: 5 Escorts, plus 3 Cortina Estates, plus a Corsair 200. You could become the first 9-car family in your road."

In the fifties, competition successes were still viable copy, and they cropped up throughout the sixties in the more sporting papers, usually to the detriment of layout. To sporting-minded customers, in Britain and also in Italy, they helped sales. They were, moreover, a useful booster for lesser foreign imports in the U.S.A., and were sometimes employed to back acceptance of a controversial model. A full page was

devoted to assorted wins in the 1963 Australian Mini catalogue. Unfortunately, specialization and professionalism were taking their toll. When Bentley trumpeted a win at Le Mans in the 1920s, or Alfa Romeo in the early thirties, the elite who read the motoring weeklies knew that—given the right bank balance—they could go out and buy a similar car, even though it might not stand up to twenty-four hours flat-out on the Sarthe Circuit without benefit of a bevy of racing mechanics. But no truly "street" sports car had won Le Mans after Delahaye's 1938 victory. A D-type Jaguar could be driven on the road, yet the only motive for doing so would be to save the cost of a transporter *en route* to the circuit.

Likewise, in 1953–54, Hudson's big side-valve six-cylinder Hornet dominated American stock-car racing, but Hudson's sales went on falling: everyone knew that it was a six and not a V-8, and that the body looked just like its 1948 counterpart. Porsches were by no means always bought on the strength of their racing record—the RSKs which brought the trophies home were no more stock than Jaguar's D-type. Panhard and Renault derivatives fought it out in the Index Performance at Le Mans, and a flat-twin Panhard even won an Ulster TT, but these successes sold—if anything—just a few more base components to the small specialist makers.

That the manufacturers felt the same was only too apparent. Talbot in France and Lancia in Italy compounded their financial troubles with racing programmes. Bugatti's transverse-engined Formula I straight-eight (1956) was a built-in guarantee of their demise, especially when they had sold precisely ten roadgoing Type 101s in the whole post-war period. Mercedes-Benz and Jaguar, who could afford it, quit as soon as

135

A Most Unusual 'Ten'

"The roomiest, best-sprung 'Ten' I've sat in!"

Your comfort is well catered for in this new Lanchester 'Ten.' It is excellently sprung. All occupants sit well within the wheelbase. There is no roll or sidesway. The interior dimensions are more than ample; upholstery and fittings are excellent; luggage space is liberal. Yet the Lanchester is by no means 'over-bodied.' Its performance alone — 55 m.p.h. cruising and a capacity for 65 m.p.h. — proves this.

LANCHESTER 'TEN' with the **Daimler Fluid Transmission**

BY APPOINTMENT
MOTOR CAR MANUFACTURERS

(LICENSED UNDER VULCAN SINCLAIR AND DAIMLER PATENTS)

THE LANCHESTER MOTOR COMPANY LIMITED · COVENTRY AND LONDON

they had proved what they had set out to prove: a renaissance from the ashes of 1945 in the former case, and "the fastest scheduled service round Le Mans" (to quote Lord Montagu) in the latter. Aston Martin gave up racing after winning the sports-car Constructors' Championship in 1959. Even rallying was a question of "survival of the fittest". Did the results justify the retention of an expensive competition department, and did it sell cars? After 1960, in fact, rallying began to lose its publicity value. While the amateurs in their home-tuned cars still stood a chance, it was relevant that Delahaye, Allard, Ford, Lancia, Sunbeam, Jaguar, Renault, and Citroën, in that chronological sequence, had won the Monte Carlo Rally. Most of the cars were relatively "stock", even Sydney Allard's Pl Allard sedan, 1952's winner. It was ironic that this small and struggling firm, which needed the honours so badly, found their triumph forgotten in a Britain mourning the death of King George VI.

Now all this was changing. Professionalism and the back-up circuses were moving in, and television commentators stalked the course. Everyone knew that Carlsson's Saab or Hopkirk's Mini was a works-entered car, and as non-standard as the regulations permitted. True, most firms with a foot in the rally camp offered factory-sponsored tuning kits, but they could hardly be expected to list everything that made their own cars into winners. Some capital could still be made out of the classic car-busters: the East African Safari, the one-off London-Sydney Marathon, and the various Round Australia rallies. The Japanese, indeed, had anticipated their onslaught on the Commonwealth with entries in the 1957 and 1958 events. Toyota took a third place in 1957, and the following year Datsun mopped up the 1-litre category, beating Morris Minors and Renault Dauphines. By contrast, Liège-Rome-Liège, which the drivers themselves regarded as the toughest challenge of all, was just another European rally. Victory might swing a few enthusiasts towards Jaguar (who won it once) or towards Mercedes-Benz (with four wins to their credit), but it was not a safe bet.

Nuts and bolts, in their old-fashioned form, stood little chance, although British advertising clung painfully to such themes throughout the fifties. ("The large boot at the rear of the Standard Vanguard gives 14 cu.ft. of space for luggage. Spare wheel and tools are neatly fitted in a separate compartment and the lid, which is spring balanced, encloses and locks both"—this, mark you, in a colour advertisement, not a catalogue.) Generally, therefore, the method should have been, and latterly was, valid only in the case of kit-cars, to convince the client that he or she could cope with the vehicle. It also obtained in the case of sub-utility items intended for the handyman. The makers of the 1966 Lightburn Zeta, "Australia's Own Second Car", devoted four pages of their catalogue to earnest technicalities and to a full description of the two-stroke Villiers engine, a device unfamiliar to Commonwealth motorists.

The philosophy did, however, assume a new dimension. While technical data were often somewhat sketchy, technical illustration became a strong point. The Americans discovered the photogenic qualities of a wide range of alternative power plants. If the "cooking" six always came out as a lump of iron, V-8s with multiple quadrajet carburation were most impressive, especially when divorced from their usual sheet-metal surroundings. The prospective customer remained blissfully unaware that, in real life, few of those splendid ancillaries would be accessible to him, or that, if he opted for the full-house V-8, he would pay a lot more, both in the showroom and at the filling-station.

If the general public was becoming bored with "unibodies"—one looked very much the same as the next—it was good policy to show a chassis, as proof that it was still there. One of Triumph's most successful advertisements depicted just such an item, complete with trade number plates and a factory test driver at the wheel, alongside a com-

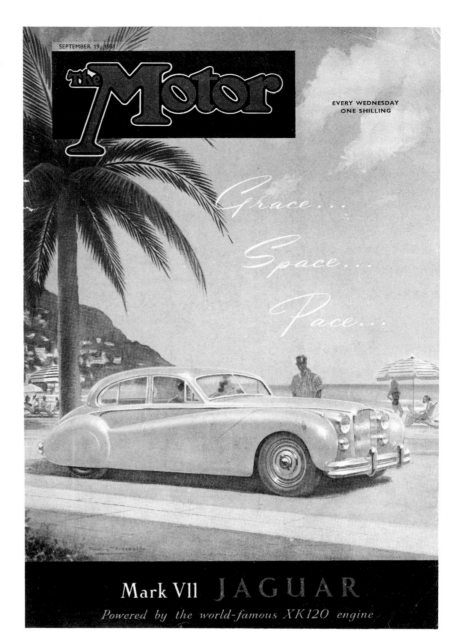

THE TOTAL PERFORMANCE FALCON **FUTURA** HARDTOP

Falcon flies you First Class
—at low economy fares!

First class? Falcon's ride is the plushest in the compact class. Smoother, too – thanks to its lively new standard Six. *Economy?* There's Falcon's low initial cost, easy twice-a-year (or 6,000-mile) service schedule. And, when you couple its standard 170 cu. in. Six to a 3-speed Cruise-O-Matic option, Falcon delivers up to 15% more gas savings. Take a test drive. Find out how beautiful economy can be.

Best year yet to go Ford!
Test Drive Total Performance '65

MUSTANG · FALCON · FAIRLANE
FORD · THUNDERBIRD

138

(*Opposite*) Cashing in on the jet age. The Germans had favoured aeronautical backgrounds in the 1930s, and Ford could legitimately become nostalgic about their famous Tri-Motor airliner made from 1927 to 1931. This time, however, they were right up to date with an apt theme. Although automatic was more popular than manual on the Futura, costliest of the Falcon compact range, most customers would surely have favoured the optional V-8.

(*Right*) How a Swedish car maker went after the public in 1966. One drove a Saab for fun, and there was a whole host of rally victories to prove it, plus the splendid figure of Erik Carlsson, perhaps the greatest rally-driver of the post-1945 era. Unfortunately, the design was getting a trifle old-fashioned: if the basic shape had another twelve-years of life in it, the three-cylinder two-stroke engine most certainly had not, even in its latest three-carburettor Monte Carlo guise with 55 horsepower and dry-sump system. The latter was mainly sold abroad, but this standard Swedish home-market 96 had also now replaced its single carburettor with three, "for still better acceleration" according to the copy, and was up to 42 horsepower although retaining petroil lubrication. The mention of new colours was a refreshing reminder that the days of unabated green were gone. There was no need to drape blondes over the scenery, for the Saab had that "rarin' to go" look anyway.

SAAB 1966

vassare... sportigare...

Ni kanske tycker att SAAB-ägarna är alltför kategoriska i sitt lovordande av det egna märket. Men dra Er inte för att lyssna — det kan löna sig. Ni får då höra om hur trivsam bilen är att köra, om framhjulsdriftens fördelar och mycket annat. En stund bakom ratten på nya SAAB 1966 övertygar Er om att det var fakta Ni hörde. Nya SAAB 1966 har fått trippelförgasare för ännu bättre acceleration. Nya färger: malmgrått och gult. Besök närmaste SAAB-ANA-återförsäljare och se på alla nyheterna. Be samtidigt att få närmare fakta om 2/5-garantin — marknadens mest prisvärda — och om hur billigt det är att köra SAAB. De exceptionellt låga milkostnaderna framgår av ett flertal opartiska tester. Välkommen!

139

plete car, pointing out that the frame was "so strong and sturdy... you could build a compact truck around it". A chassis was also a natural for the "circular tour" type of commentary, from front disc brakes to rear anti-roll bar, though such a technique was best applied to catalogues. In a display advertisement, the small islands of type were merely messy.

Exploded views sometimes misfired. Honda used a roof-off shot of their N360 in 1968 with the caption "spacious interior assures riding comfort". The slightly elliptical English did not matter: what did was that the passengers were four small Japanese, and the car would have been much less comfortable with four full-height Europeans aboard. DAF's simplified technical analyses of their belt drive undoubtedly countered customer resistance, reminding the prospect that belts had an expected life of 30,000 miles (50,000 km), a sure defence against the strictures of the older generation with their memories of motorcycles and cyclecars from World War I days. In general, however, any feature with an old-fashioned ring about it was ignored. One has to search through independent technical articles to discover that the 1966 Oldsmobile Toronado had a chain primary drive, with all its motorcycle associations.

The democratic element was creeping in. Where once one was adjured to buy even a simple family sedan because the aristocracy favoured it—Fiat thus listed an Ethiopian grandee among owners of 509As in 1928—one was now urged to acquire Ford's austere 1954 Popular, "because it was a real working man's car, a real car designed to fill your empty garage or that piece of road in front of your house". In the sixties, this would have been an unwise approach: congestion had supervened, and local authorities were wary of street parking.

Nonetheless, the odd nut or bolt helped. Willys' 1952 Aero was promoted for its 35-mpg thirst (less impressive when translated into Imperial gallons or litres/100 km), on the ability of the driver to "see all four fenders" (not a common attribute then in America) and on seats 61 in (1.69 m) wide. A few semi-technical drawings in 1939 style filled in the story, while Willys reminded readers that they made Jeeps. Rover, with an up-market image, would never have dragged the Landrover into publicity for their P4 sedans.

Ford played the game of "horses for courses". By 1960, they were no longer concerned with filling "empty spaces" as most people had cars and congestion was a pressing issue. They still, however, had a bargain-basement automobile to sell in the shape of the 100E Anglia (demoted to the rank of Popular) while they also had the latest Anglia to plug. This latter was "a new shape, jet-sleek from headlight to tail, a new, spacious sense in light-car design" which helped its owner "to discover a zest you'd forgotten". The four-speed gearbox, Dagenham's first ever on a private car, understandably merited the epithet "magic", whereas the Popular's three speeds rated only a passing mention.

With the Popular, however, we ran into the artificial testimonial: the young bride who could afford a car as well as a mortgage (and, if pictures were to be believed, the latest fashion in slacks and head-scarves) or, with a delectable touch of 1900 snake-oil, the grey-haired senior citizen. "Many years ago, when I was a young doctor, I bought my first low-priced Ford. Now I find I need two cars, one for my scattered country practice, the other for my wife." All very democratic, but wait for the affluent sting in the tail, which comes from Junior, smirking in his school tie. "Dad takes the Zephyr to work every day, and Mummy drops us off at school on her way shopping." Thus the two-Ford family was established, and another prospect for an over-drive-equipped six was garnered in.

Volkswagen went after the working customer by showing Beetles in deserts, in streams, in polar regions. ("Are you looking for roads in

Up to 35 Miles on a Gallon!

The Aero Willys

7.6 COMPRESSION HURRICANE 6 ENGINE

DRIVER SEES ALL FOUR FENDERS

61-INCH-WIDE SEATING, FRONT AND REAR

Record mileage is only one reason this car is a sensation!

Some cars sacrifice mileage for performance... others are designed for economy at the expense of passenger space and comfort. But in the *Aero* Willys, for the first time, you get a ride so smooth and silent you feel airborne... spacious seating for six... surging pickup and thrilling speed... and mileage up to 35 miles per gallon with overdrive*! To get *everything* you want... get an *Aero* Willys.

Equipment, specifications and trim subject to change without notice. *Optional equipment, extra. White side-wall tires, optional when available.

MADE BY THE MAKERS OF THE WORLD FAMOUS **Jeep** with billions of miles of tough service

Aerodynamic Design and low 5-ft. silhouette minimize wind drag, adding to both speed and fuel mileage.

New Hurricane 6 Engine, F-head design with 7.6 compression, one of the world's most efficient power plants.

Panoramic Visibility and low (23-in.) center of gravity make the *Aero* Willys safer to drive and easy to park.

Production for Defense is our business, too—military Jeeps, jet-engine parts and many other products.

these pictures? Don't: you won't find any. Because there aren't any there.") Citroën stuffed Victorian wardrobes and grandfather clocks into 2CVs, secure in the knowledge that an unbeliever had only to motor a few kilometres down a *route nationale* to see the French doing just that. A 1975 catalogue, admittedly from the energy-crisis era, told buyers that "you have the independence of a car for less than the price of a bus ticket".

American advertising was sophisticated, even to the point of the subliminal. Lincoln-Mercury were among the star exponents of the "you haven't lived if you don't drive our car" school. Pony-cars were "the password for action in the 70s. The mood is upbeat. The spirit is untamed. The car is Cougar." Such copy was easily adjustable to the aura of Wall Street, as witness this specimen from 1956. "Good taste and good judgment are the essential attributes of the man for whom we designed and built the Continental Mk.II. Such a man", continues the copywriter, "inherently rejects the ordinary." This was a comedown from Duesenberg days, since such publicity called for a commentary—and pictures of a car. It was, perhaps, disappointing that Lincoln did not show the car in a gateway, either: a favourite Rolls-Royce trick of the thirties, and still used in the sixties by Alvis and Lancia. The Lincoln had to be illustrated, of course, because its prime merit was that it was not just an outsize Ford, like the firm's sedans. Unfortunately, too, there was a merit within a merit, so a second picture showed the deplorable bustle at the rear, a vestige of the Continental Spare Wheel.

(*Opposite*) Nuts and bolts—in America, too. But then the Aero-Willys was an undistinguished automobile from a firm which had concentrated on modest fours since 1933 and, from 1941 to 1951, had been too preoccupied with Jeeps to build any orthodox cars at all. Add uninspired styling and not a hint of a V-8 anywhere, and it is apparent that Willys-Overland's press department would have to focus on the less fashionable virtues.

(*Right*) Where competition publicity is permissible. The Mini *did* win the 1964 Monte Carlo Rally outright, the first time a British car had done so since 1956. There were supplementary trophies to record, too. Not mentioned, though interesting, was the fact that the winning crew started from Minsk, the first time that the U.S.S.R. had figured in a "Monte" itinerary. But then there was no prospect of selling Minis in Russia . . .

(*Below*) Nuts and bolts, 1968 style—but Industria of London had to promote a relatively unknown East German car. Two strokes, in any case, were unpopular in Britain, and they couldn't cash in on the Wartburg's DKW background, since the latter name belonged to Auto Union in the *Bundesrepublik*, who in any case had dropped these cars in favour of the four-stroke Audi. The nostalgic appeal of the 1898 type can't have helped much: this was a licence-produced French Decauville, and Britons always got the native French strain. As for suggesting that the Decauville had served as Henry Royce's initial inspiration . . .

In Europe, Volkswagen were undoubtedly the cleverest exponents. "The Car That Turned The Head Of The World" was one of the star performances of the 1950s—closely matched by the later "quality control" advertisement, in which a car festooned with graffiti symbolized the countless inspections a Beetle had to pass. As for the equally famous ice-covered radiator (absent, to be sure, from any VW), this was almost knocking copy, especially as the offending component bore a marked resemblance to a certain illustrious British make of the thirties and forties.

One had to think international, and this meant not only mere semantics. Slogans had to translate, and so did specifications. The constant battle between the cubic centimetre and the cubic inch verged on the illogical. The British, still wedded to feet and inches even in 1969, thought in terms of them, but quoted in litres when building an engine: consequently, a unit built by their own manufacturing methods involved three or four decimal places in millimetres for cataloguing purposes. Americans used litres only to "sound foreign"—the biggest Ford V-8 was "seven-liter" by 1965. Conversely, a European contemplating the potent 4.7-litre unit under the bonnet of a Ford Mustang would probably refer to it as a "289" (its displacement in cubic inches). Tyre dimensions were still quoted in inches throughout our period, and "overdrive" was an international word. Germans tended, latterly, to reserve *schnellgang* for the complex Maybach system favoured by their luxury-car makers in the 1930s.

The best copy did not always translate. At their peak, Renault could rival Detroit's finest in French, but their English sounded mundane. The delightfully permissive 1960 Floride catalogue headed "*Ils s'aimaient*" carried a hint of masculine domination, whereas the English version "They Were In Love" suggested a corny film-trailer. American press-office jargon was untranslatable and, fortunately, it seldom had to be given the treatment, beyond the mandatory French for *Quebecquois* and the occasional outbursts into Spanish.

Internationalism did not stop at mere copy. Cars had to be launched, and it was no longer the inflexible rule that one unveiled an American car in New York, a British car in London, or a German car in Frankfurt (which had replaced Berlin as the venue for the *Bundesrepublik*'s show). With yearly models largely a matter of the past, a new car was sent upon its way when it was ready, and not when the next show turned up in the calendar. Thus, the good publicist thought his way round a year which opened in January at Brussels, and progressed via Geneva (March), New York (April), and Frankfurt (September) to London and Paris in October, and Turin in November. For domestic items such as the latest Vauxhalls or Opels, the native show would do—but if one were after international business, where better than Brussels or Geneva, with no local industry to steal the thunder and the best stand sites? The Americans tended to favour the former, since Belgium was their best market in Europe. Other nations chose Geneva, which saw such

standouts as the Austin Sheerline (1947), the Fiat 600 (1955), and the E-type Jaguar (1961).

Still others to plump for Switzerland were Mercedes-Benz for their 230SL sports car (1963), Renault with their 16 (1965), and Ferrari with the definitive 2.4-litre edition of their mid-engined Dino in 1969. A year later, the revolutionary Citroën SM sports sedan would join the ranks of Geneva's debutantes. By contrast, Mercedes-Benz preferred Paris for their vast 6.3-litre V-8 limousine in 1963, and Rolls-Royce revived a tradition two years later by launching their Silver Shadow in France: the first public showing of the make in 1904 had, after all, been in Paris and not in London. But Switzerland was an excellent bet. In 1957, the country harboured agencies for cars from Austria, East Germany, and Czechoslovakia, as well as from more familiar sources. By 1969, the choice ran alphabetically from Abarth to Wolseley, embracing the products of Holland, Japan, and the U.S.S.R. There was naturally a linguistic nightmare, for Switzerland had three official languages and English was a desirable adjunct for the international set. Some people were unworried—Chrysler issued annual press guides in English, French, German, Italian, Spanish, and Arabic, all in one volume.

If you did not wish to wait for a show, there was the alternative of an international press party, set against a suitably scenic background. Such exercises in public relations were common practice in the sixties, but the pioneers were Renault in 1956. In fact, the launch of their

Appealing to the world's masses, 1967 style—and more than one style at that. Egypt (*below*) and Germany (*opposite*) may be only a few thousand kilometres apart, but light-years still separate their advertising methods, at least on the surface. Not that the Ramses is a very different kind of small car

than the Beetle, having origins in the same country (*see page 229*). Yet its presentation by a painting allows one to imagine anything from American cartoons to the sacred Pharaonic sun, and even to expect that the vehicle is wider than it actually was: these proportions don't fit the data inside the same

catalogue. Combine this with the unmentioned price and the vague maker's address ("Motorcycle Factory, Desert Road") and you realize that what sold a car in such lands was simply its local manufacture if not design. Volkswagen, with photographic precision and technical persuasion, had to ring a

clear, new, practical note while citing almost no innovations in the product. They did so time and again, in this instance by intoning the low cost and playing up safety features to a nation which lacked neither money nor courage on the *Autobahnen*.

الشركة المصرية لصناعة وسائل النقل الخفيفة
إحدى شركات المؤسسة المصرية العامة للصناعات الهندسية

EGYPTIAN LIGHT TRANSPORT
MFG, Co.
ELTRAMCO

Dieser Wagen kostet nur 4485 Mark.

Aber das allein ist kein Grund, 4485 Mark für ihn auszugeben.

Der Preis allein sagt Ihnen noch garnichts. Solange Sie nicht wissen, was Sie dafür bekommen.

Und das ist beim VW 1200 eine ganze Menge.

Zum Beispiel eine Menge Komfort. Sie bekommen tiefgepolsterte Sitze, die mit luftdurchlässigem Kunstleder bezogen sind. Und eine Fußraumverkleidung aus Noppenteppich. Und Gummifußmatten. Und einen abwaschbaren Kunststoffhimmel. Eine pneumatische Scheibenwaschanlage. Drehfenster vorn und eine Extraheizung hinten. Und noch einiges mehr.

Weiter bekommen Sie eine Menge Sicherheit: Die Sicherheits-Lenksäule, die sich bei einem Aufprall ineinanderschiebt. Das Sicherheits-Lenkrad aus ungewöhnlich elastischem Material. Die neuen Scheinwerfer mit senkrechter Streuscheibe. Sicherheits-Türgriffe und -Fensterkurbeln. Und die Schraubanschlüsse für Sicherheitsgurte, an denen alle Gurtsysteme angebracht werden können.

Und schließlich bekommen Sie alles, was den VW 1200 zum VW macht. Den unverwüstlichen, luftgekühlten Motor mit Startautomatik. Die einzeln aufgehängten, einzeln gefederten 15-Zoll-Räder. Und die stabile Karosserie mit durchgehender Bodenplatte.

Der günstige Preis ist also nur ein Vorteil unter vielen.

Aber auch nicht zu verachten.

National Benzole's Getaway People of 1963 were the rivals of the Esso Tiger, and their euphoric aura was entirely permissible in a Britain with no overall speed limits—and, better still, where a 150-mph (240-km/h)

E-type Jaguar still cost less than £2,000. But even more American than the euphorics were the car's whitewall tyres and chromium-plated wire wheels, a combination that no Briton would ever have ordered.

Pale sunrise and purple evening . . . getaway hours! Sleek, beckoning roads and away-from-it places…getaway playgrounds! Put your right foot down! Relish the power of Super National. Getaway people get Super National.

GETAWAY PEOPLE
GET SUPER NATIONAL

Dauphine highlighted the whole new outlook. Its pre-production models had done over three million kilometres of testing—in the mountains of Switzerland, in the U.S.A., in the Arctic, in tropical Africa—and now the car was being unveiled in Corsica. So "try it for yourself" parties were fast replacing the old vogue for "end to end" drives by professionals.

More use was being made of the sneak preview and the slow leak. Traditionally the industry guarded its secrets. Vauxhall fitted anonymous grilles, Jaguar used plastic to camouflage the body lines, and the prototype Rover 2000s bore "Talago" emblems—anagrams of the designer's initials. Masking tape was liberally used, even on the stylized badging of steering-wheel bosses. But the public was seldom fooled. The present writer recalls driving a pre-release Hillman Imp in the winter of 1962–63. One was asked to drive it at night as far as possible and, when a minor defect developed and a dealer had to be contacted, a huge sheet was thrown over the car while it was still manoeuvring into a corner of the workshop. Though the Imp was flashed up by several NSU-owners who had mistaken the shape, one also has clear memories

of seeking the dimmest small filling-station in the wilds of the Wiltshire Downs to top up the tank. "Would it be Apex?" enquired the pump attendant, and this at a time when the code-name was almost as secret as the car.

The slow leak was better. Occasionally it even paid to show a prototype openly, as in the case of Nash's N.X.I. (1950)—the first bid at an American baby car since the Crosley (1939), which was foundering even then, despite the post-war adoption of an efficient little overhead-camshaft four-cylinder engine and primordial disc brakes. If the Edsel (1957) must go down in history as the worst instance of misguided market research, a lot of work went into its conception and even into its naming. Further, press and dealer previews consisted of tantalizing shots of odd parts of the car, projected onto a screen by a Ford public-relations man. By the later 1950s, the public were indeed being subjected to mild "come on" hints. Pontiac ran an advertisement in the *Saturday Evening Post* to preview the "off the shoulder" look of their 1957 line, but a mere glance at the interior gave little away. The same held for Chrysler's 1958 effort captioned "Can this be the 1959 Plymouth", a shot concentrating mostly on a huge tail fin which everyone expected, anyhow.

Road testing became a serious art, even in America. No longer were polite euphemisms used to skate around serious sins of commission, or around deadly normality. To illustrate the change of attitude within our period alone, let us compare the first road test of the Mk.VII Jaguar (1952) with what the same paper had to say eleven years later about Mk.X, the earlier model's lineal discendant. With the 1952 car, the only hints of criticism concerned the low-geared steering (with the proviso that 4.75 turns from lock to lock would be entirely acceptable in America), mild brake shudder, some noticeable brake fade ("but the loss of power which occurred was of an unusually moderate amount"), and a little too much lost movement in the gear lever. Alas, Mk.X, for all its power steering and 120-mph (192-km/h) top speed, received harsher treatment. "The decorative woodwork", began the summary, "has a skin-deep quality, revealed by close inspection". Nor was this all. "The gracefully bulbous sides" made for thick doors rather than interior space, the seats lacked lateral support, and the heating and ventilation "fell short of many cars costing a third as much". The manual gearbox, still innocent of synchromesh on bottom gear, was "elderly in design and, to most drivers, out of place in such plush surroundings".

The manufacturer's woes were not over. Where, hitherto, he had only to submit his wares to a brief work-out of perhaps 250 miles (400 km), plus performance testing, he was now at the mercy of the long-term assessment. Not that he was thrown in immediately at the deep end. In Europe, cars were being taken across frontiers on test as soon as fuel restrictions were lifted at the close of the forties. A favourite British routine for a high-performance model was a fast run to some Continental event—the Geneva Show, say, or a Grand Prix—followed by performance tests on the *Jabbeke* autoroute in Belgium. The *pavé* of the Low Countries, after all, would reveal suspension weaknesses, while pass-storming in the Alps was still a better trial of water pumps than end-to-end in London at rush hour. But though alarming things could happen in ten days, it was the factory's responsibility to put them right. Back the car would go for rectification, and then the trial would continue. Astute readers, confronted with photographs of two different vehicles in the same article, sometimes drew the correct conclusion: a second car had been needed!

For long-term testing, the car became the magazine's property, was assigned to various staff members, and was serviced at office expense. Thus, readers had the opportunity to watch the march of rust, to find out who had good dealers, and to learn how much labour costs added to the advertised prices of replacement units. *Motor Trend* in the U.S.A. and *Motor Sport* in Britain ran owner-surveys of best-selling models. Volkswagen emerged with flying colours, 85% of owners indicating that they would buy another Beetle. The Mini fared less well, with a high proportion of defective clutches, 44% of drivers disliking the poor synchromesh, and only 64% opting for a second example—though of the defectors, the largest proportion proposed going up-market to the new, high-performance Mini-Cooper.

Dealers came under fire. *Marque* loyalties remained strong, and it was said unkindly that BMC's badge engineering was there because the dealers wanted it. Certainly there could have been no other valid reason for the continuance of Riley after 1956, or Wolseley after 1965. A good dealer network was the key to success, especially in a foreign market, and that is why VW prospered in the USA and the British, ultimately, did not. And poor service or dealer coverage spelt poor trade-in value. This is why Ford and GM always topped the published lists in the U.S.A., and why Studebakers fetched "orphan" secondhand values long before the *marque* faded from the lists in 1966.

A new make or a new market posed grave problems. It has been said that Volkswagen's immediate success in Germany—where, remember, they had sold virtually no civilian cars before the war—was in part due to the fact that they were able to move in on Adler's dealer network after that firm abdicated from car manufacture. In foreign markets, however, the native manufacturers had all the plums, and exclusive one-make or one-group dealerships were now the order of the day. In one small British town, the BMC and Ford agencies were owned by one holding company, and servicing went on (discreetly) under one roof, but two showrooms and two sets of accounts had to be used, to avoid the wrath of either manufacturer.

Sometimes the dealer became the tail wagging the dog. The British Motor Corporation furnishes the classic instance of this. As of 1951, when Austin and Nuffield merged, there were two entirely separate networks, with the added complication that Nuffield's two most recent acquisitions—Wolseley (1927) and Riley (1938)—still had dealers who did not sell the other makes in the group. As Austin customers did not usually buy Morrises, and vice versa, this worked reasonably well before model-rationalization was set in hand, while it also gave BMC two outlets in a town to Ford's one.

But with the Austin customer reluctant to buy a Morris—any Morris—and the Austin dealer reluctant to sell it, an impossible duplication resulted, which was perpetuated into 1968. From the dealer's standpoint, matters were exacerbated when BMC invented the artificial prestige make, Vanden Plas, and forced all the dealers to stock it. Having done so, they then persuaded the factory that Vanden Plas' prestige sedan, the Princess R with automatic transmission and a 4-litre engine built by Rolls-Royce, merited production at the rate of a hundred per week, which it did not. Not that badge-engineering to please the dealers was a British preserve: Canada had her fair share of cross-pollinated Ford/Mercurys, Chevrolet/Pontiacs, and Dodge/Plymouths to ensure that garages in a smaller, poorer market than the U.S.A. had something to sell to every potential customer.

By the end of our period, if not in 1951, old-car enthusiasm was becoming a nuisance, too. The sport was by no means new. The Veteran Car Club of Great Britain had been formed in 1930, and the U.S.A.'s three principal Clubs of today (Antique Automobile Club of America, Veteran Motor Car Club of America, Horseless Carriage Club of America) were all firmly established by 1941. These, however, catered for pre-World War I vehicles, while Britain's VSCC took the story up to 1930. But already the picture was beginning to widen. By

1949, the VSCC let in "approved" cars made up to 1939, and the new Classic Car Club of America catered for the True Classics of 1925–42. They also decided that any Mk.I Lincoln Continental, even the post-war models of 1946–48, merited Classic status.

Thus the gates were opened. Though no classification of post-World War II cars existed even in 1969, certain models (XK120 Jaguar, early Ferraris, the 300SL Mercedes-Benz coupé) were recognized as collectable. The Citroën *traction* was becoming a cult object in France and Holland. An alarming prospect was opening for the manufacturer: where hitherto a car took perhaps ten years to depreciate from "low-mileage, off-new" to a $50 or £20 bargain with no warranty implied or given, and then became junk for some ten years, certain cars now never even got as far as the back row of a suburban used-car lot. They became collectable first.

This was more a development of the seventies than of the sixties, but it posed the question of who was responsible for parts and service. No problem arose in the U.S.A.: in 1965, more than a quarter of a million Model-A Fords from the 1928–31 era were said to be still running, and

There's nothing like creating qualities that aren't there in order to emphasize those that are. Anyone studying this 1967 effort by Renault would think that their utilitarian 4 had a separate chassis and superlative brakes. In fact it had neither, and when this publicity was issued it was the only Renault model without a disc brake at each corner. Nobody, however, was going to measure lining area, least of all a Frenchman in quest of a reliable hack capable of handling passengers or goods. And that the 4 assuredly was, being a roomy station-wagon-type vehicle with front-wheel drive and a dependable 845-cc pushrod four-cylinder engine whose ancestry went back to 1946. Announced in 1961, the 4 was Renault's first attempt at the front-wheel-drive configuration which they would standardize by 1973. Unlike BMC and Peugeot, Renault arranged their engines longitudinally, and the 4 was no compact, though oddly it was 6 in (16 cm) shorter than the established 2CV Citroën. And it slotted into a gap in the native market which theoretically didn't exist. Initial reaction to the car was that it merely offered more complication (water-cooling, twice the number of cylinders) than the Citroën and wouldn't sell. It was, however, still going strong in 1983. The "Parisienne" mentioned in the copy was something that only a French maker would risk: its side panels were covered in imitation canework!

427 cm² de garniture ! voilà pourquoi l

Elle obéit... au pied et à l'œil, la Renault 4 !
Ses nouveaux freins - encore plus puissants -
répondent au quart de seconde.
Et elle s'arrête pile, bien en ligne :
un répartiteur de freinage «dose» l'effort
sur les roues de façon à conserver une adhérence
maximum à chacune d'elles. Quelle que soit
la vitesse, la violence du coup de frein,
le poids supporté,
la Renault 4 freine en toute sécurité.

Et la Renault 4 «67» ne vous offre pas seulem
la sécurité de ses nouveaux freins.
Pour vous être agréable, elle est devenue
plus jolie, avec son nouvel habillage intérieur
encore plus confortable avec ses sièges garn
de drap mousse de jersey ; encore plus pratic
avec sa tablette arrière amovible (en option).
Venez vite découvrir toutes ses nouveautés.
Elle vous attend chez tous
les concessionnaires et agents Renault.

146

Renault 4 freine si bien

Moteur 4 CV
(30 chevaux réels)
ou moteur 5 CV - Traction avant.
Plus de 110 km/h chrono,
5,5 l aux 100 km.
Intérieur drap
ou simili cuir au choix
Toit ouvrant optionnel (120 F)
3 versions : Luxe, Export, Parisienne,
à partir de 5 580 F*

c'est Renault qu'il vous faut

On the way:

Cars that can do what they look like they can do

Can this be the new 1959 Plymouth? Believe it or not, it is and it's just a sample of the all-around newness you have to look forward to in the 1959 cars from Chrysler Corporation.

—and they look like they can do more than any other cars on the road

New 1959 Cars of The *Forward* Look from Chrysler Corporation

PLYMOUTH · **DODGE** · **DE SOTO** · **CHRYSLER** · **IMPERIAL**

no high price on luxury here—just sport and sparkle...breeziness and breadth...and jet-smooth luxury!

countless parts houses catered for anything that could not be found in a wrecking yard. For European manufacturers, the headache was worse —the number of surviving cars was smaller, the demand lower, and storage space more at a premium. Nostalgia did not sell cars. The tendency was increasingly to sell off obsolete parts to specialist garages, or to the growing ranks of the one-make clubs. Even Rolls-Royce would follow this course in the case of their pre-1940 cars, although Alvis—to the end in 1967—advertised that they were willing (and usually able) to supply spares for any car they had ever built.

And if the car makers wanted no part of elderly models, they did not regard these as good advertising copy, either. Such publicity campaigns tended to be the preserve of component makers. One remembers especially Lockheed's "We Put a Stop To All this", a clever series based on early users of hydraulic brakes. Lancia occasionally devoted some catalogue-space to their earlier achievements, as well they might, being the fathers or godfathers of independent front springing, modern unitary construction, narrow-angle V-4 engines, and the GT coupé as it was now understood. Ford, mindful of their splendid museum at Dearborn, trotted out the odd antique in their publicity, with the latest creations shown against a background of Model-A phaetons and late-1920s Ford Trimotor airliners. Firms as diverse as AC, American Motors, and Citroën issued competent company histories, and so did Mercedes-Benz and Fiat. Jowett's Golden Jubilee volume, published in 1951, talked hopefully about "the next fifty years" when they had barely three years to go.

One could sometimes evoke past glories without being too specific. In 1967, Dodge reminded readers that the name "evokes special respect. To the professional, in the United States and abroad, Dodge means unequivocally that rarest of all syntheses, advanced engineering combined with meticulous attention to detail." Which sounded better than "Dodge is the car you buy if you have outgrown your Plymouth and cannot afford a Chrysler".

If there was one aspect of advertising that improved, particularly in the 1960s, it was truthfulness, if within certain limits. Among the limits was advertised engine output which, unless qualified with DIN (*Deutsche Industrie Normen*), meant exactly what the press department wanted it to mean. An advertised increase from 180 to 200 probably reflected one from 150 to 170 by the time the unit was installed in the chassis—but there was nothing to stop anybody from taking the net rating in 1955, and the gross in 1956, to make the rise sound more impressive.

It was also desirable to keep one's eye on the small print, since this year's new power steering (in bold italic) was certainly an optional extra and, in all probability even then, applicable only to the top of the range. We have already encountered Willys' remarkable 35 mpg from a six-cylinder sedan in 1952, but the warning asterisk (probably unnoticed) qualifies it to explain that such frugality was available only with "optional extra automatic overdrive". The headline, "Dodge says yes to Power Steering and Power Brakes" (1967), was perfectly true, but if you wanted them it added at least another $200 to the invoice. Sometimes one had to read the small print thrice to realize what was going on. All 1951 Lincolns came with automatic transmission, yet it figured in the extras list. The reason was simple, and equally unfit for general release. Ford's new automatic was not ready, so Lincoln had to buy Hydramatic from their arch-rival, General Motors. And it would never do to admit that this was the only acceptable means of connecting engine and driving axle!

Occasionally there were moments of blazing honesty. Pontiac's GTO, the "ultimate tiger" of the later sixties, could not be camouflaged beneath a welter of jargon and power-assists. "Its purpose in life", the

Save the Cost of Changing Automobile Body Styles Every Year

Studebaker's beautiful modern style doesn't need yearly styling changes. The money saved is passed on to you, in added comfort and quality, and in continuing engineering improvements. And, because Studebaker styling won't become obsolete, your car will look new year after year. See your dealer. Now!

Studebaker

THE COMMON-SENSE CAR

Triumph introduce the new Spitfire Mark 3
The big news is under the bonnet!

(*Opposite*) If you've nothing new to sell, you can't beat the old theme of a good trade-in value: after all, it sold Austins right through the thirties. It couldn't, however, sell Studebakers in 1965, once the famous *marque* had been relegated to the role of a foreign import (from Canada), using Chevrolet engines, and lacking the cost of even a facelift. The 1966s would be the last of the line.

(*Above*) Even when the car looks the same as last year, you can open with an eye-catching illustration. Triumph were adepts with technical subjects, as the front page of their 1967 Spitfire Mk.III catalogue shows. Six men under a forward-opening bonnet rate almost as high in the publicity stakes as nine adults crammed into a 2-litre station wagon. The jealous blonde is a welcome change from the usual female occupants of sports cars.

press office warned, "is to permit you to make the most of your driving skill. Its suspension is firm, tuned more to the open road than to wafting gently over bumpy city streets. Its dual exhausts won't win any prizes for whispering, and unless you prefer it with our lazy 3.08 low ratio its gas economy won't be anything to write home about." Having thus dismissed all the little old ladies from Pasadena, the punch line is ready. "If this dismays you, then you're almost certainly a candidate for one of our other 27 Pontiacs and Pontiac Tempests." What wanted explanation, alas, was a prime piece of motoring jargon that would have confused our prospect, especially had he or she been nurtured on the motoring press. It would have been kinder to point out that a *numerically low* rear-axle ratio confers high gearing. One wonders how many customers with leanings to freeway economy expected an even higher axle ratio of positively Edwardian concept!

Pontiac were not the only honest ones. Ford of Britain summarized the GT40's fuel consumption as "wicked" and its boot space as "laughable", while DAF admitted cheerfully to "a considerable use of synthetic materials" at a time when a favourite journalistic quip on the subject of hide-like seats was "all that's leather does not breathe".

In the fifties and sixties, copy could be fabricated from anything. The comedies of the thirties—Daimler's attempt to justify both pull-on and push-on handbrakes in the same year's range, and Chrysler's defence of the transmission brake as leaving the main drums free to cope with normal stops—were as nothing to the cheerful support of anything that happened to be on sale. Take automatic transmission and the typical, early (1941) approach of Oldsmobile: "The lever you see ... is not a gear shifter. It's a direction control. Set it in HI and leave it there. The gears shift automatically through all four forward speed ranges. The clutch pedal that you *don't* see on the floorboard is gone for good. With Hydramatic Drive, there's no clutch to press—no work for your left foot to do."

By 1951, of course, Americans knew how the device worked, and not a few of them had forgotten how to cope with stick-shift. Hence Studebaker, in their first year with the new arrangements, adopted a different tack. Automatic drive merely "takes over most of the physical effort of car operation for you". It was a little naughty, although continued with a comment on "the brilliant triumph of nearly fifteen years' research by the most exacting technicians in the automotive industry". True, but the technicians were Borg-Warner's, not Studebaker's. Europeans knew how the system worked, too—but when one has set up extra plant to manufacture self-shifters, people have to be coaxed into buying them. Thus, Opel asked plaintively in 1968: "Do you have anything against the full automatic because it shifts faster than you can?"

There were new jargon words—Hydrolastic, Sportomatic—but as always, such language was used to suggest novelty where no novelty existed. Ford's 1955 "K-bar" frame sounded exciting until one looked at the accompanying picture. All they had done was to revise a common 1930s practice, that of reinforcing the central cruciform bracing with a K-shaped brace at the rear. The term "X-K" type had been used before the war, but now Jaguar had pre-empted those initials. When you drove "in hushed luxury, with constant fresh air" on a Datsun, it merely meant that they had adopted the through-flow ventilation system, already in general use by the time this 1968 advertisement appeared. And sometimes a translator could produce jargon where no jargon was intended, as witness this from a 1965 Daihatsu catalogue: "Gear shift lever of left handled model is provided on the floor in the right side of the driver".

To restyle or not to restyle? The advertising department was right either way. In 1965, Oldsmobile's new cars had "not a line borrowed from last year", which gained them an extra 140,000 sales on 1964. Studebaker, teetering on the edge of limbo, and with a budget to match, told customers that "our beautiful modern style doesn't need styling changes every year. The money saved is passed on to you, in added comfort and continuing engineering development." One wonders how they explained that they had just stopped making their own engines and would henceforward buy from Chevrolet—but then the rules did not specify that, if one bought parts elsewhere, one had to declare them (this came later). Checker of Kalamazoo, whose main business was taxis and who had no use for tail fins, were even more forthright. Their cars had "no useless overhang in the front or the rear, all usable space is inside to provide more room". This reminded one of Dodge's favourite catch-phrase in 1949–50: "Lower Outside—Higher Inside—Shorter Outside—Longer Inside", as good a justification as any for K.T. Keller's over-vertical shapes.

Chromium plate was a plus or minus, according to whether it was there or not. In 1955, Ford made much of their "tiara line", with its plated vee neck to the belt moulding, while their *pièce de resistance*—the Crown Victoria—featured a "crown of chrome sweeping down from roof to belt line at center pillar level". Dodge, in a less ornate mood fourteen years later, summarized their Charger coupé as "the car that doesn't need the chrome treatment to look new". The British could sound impressive, too, if the product had to be sold. In 1963, Riley's 4/72 was "a distinguished motor car with irrepressible spirit", not to mention "clean and dignified styling", "exceptional interior grace and high-speed safety", all adding up to "a brilliantly worthwhile heir to an illustrious name". A subsequent allusion to "the unmistakable Riley grille" was salutary: the rest of it was BMC out of Farina, and therefore indistinguishable from four other makes.

Americans took warning lights for granted, except when extra gauges were part of an "appearance pack" or "decor group". Not so in Britain, where Rover rose to their defence in 1962. "There are indicator lights to warn that oil pressure is low, that the cold start control should be returned to its normal position, that the handbrake has been inadvertently left on, or that the fluid in the braking system needs replenishment"—in other words, look what good care Rover takes of its cars. Triumph referred to their clustered idiot lights on the 1300 (1965) as "all systems go".

Typographically, advertising techniques improved. In the early 1950s, we were back with the obsession for using every bit of column space, not with continuous text, but with boxes: specifications, irrelevant minor illustrations, even—in Britain—the odd competition success. While AC, with commendable economy, abridged their pre-war slogan ("The First Light Six and Still the Finest") to "The World's Finest Light Six", Austin ruined a two-page colour spread by depicting their entire range, and Citroën used nuts-and-bolts. Drawings were the rule rather than photographs, especially when colour was used, and the elongators were hard at work, making Auntie Rover look as big as a Cadillac and transforming Humber's big Pullman limousine into a motor-coach. This technique would outlive the adoption of colour photography from 1958. It was astonishing, too, what could be done, even with a full-sized American sedan, if one took it from slightly above and three-quarter front. The performing midgets, designed to make the interior of a car look enormous, had been very largely retired: when the elongators decided to show the inside, they now preferred to show it empty. But colour photography put the elongators out of business and produced a higher standard of catalogue, as well as some splendid advertisements—notably British Leyland's "The Cars That Hold The Road" (1968), a close-up of a driven front wheel doing its work at high speed.

Radio and TV advertising were still essentially an American preserve, though music was not, as any visitor to an international motor show soon discovered to his cost. With DAF churning out the *Van der Valk* theme (Dutch only to followers of the silver screen), and Lotus countering with *Land of Hope and Glory*, it was a relief to escape to

La nuova Opel Kadett
una macchina buona divenuta ottima
adesso anche a 4 porte

La Kadett ha fatto suo lo stile delle sorelle Opel più grandi: frontale, coda, fiancate. È il nuovo profilo Opel: moderno e dinamico.

Ed è divenuta più potente, veloce, sicura. Aumentato a 1078 cc. il motore: 60 CV nella versione potenziata, disponibile su tutti i modelli; 55 CV nella versione normale. Velocità massima, rispettivamente: 138 km/h e 130 km/h. Fino a 146 km/h col motore potenziato sul Coupé.

Freni a disco anteriori a richiesta. Impianto elettrico da 12 volts. Aumentati carreggiata e passo: migliore tenuta di strada. L'abitacolo è più ampio in larghezza e in lunghezza.

Un vasto assortimento di colori, rivestimenti, accessori, fa della Kadett la vettura su misura per ogni automobilista, ora più che mai con l'aggiunta di un modello a 4 porte.

La Kadett è una vettura «Made in Germany», per le nuove esigenze del Mercato Comune.

Kadett Berlina a 2 e 4 porte: accelerazione da 0 a 80 km/h in 11,5˝ con motore potenziato, in 13,5˝ nella versione normale.

Kadett Lusso a 2 e 4 porte e Caravan Lusso offrono ben 30 extra in più, tra cui: tappeti in moquette, faro di retromarcia, rostri gommati ai paraurti, dischi copriruote, accendisigari, orologio elettrico.

Kadett Caravan e Caravan Lusso: pianale di carico lungo m. 1,57, largo m. 1,25. Carico utile: 340 kg. Capacità di carico: 1,57 m³.

Kadett Coupé: coda filante aerodinamica. Cambio sportivo a cloche con leva corta. Una vera 5 posti con spazio abbondante anche per i 3 passeggeri sui sedili posteriori e capacissimo vano portabagagli posteriore.

Prezzo a partire da L. 975 000* franco sede Concessionario in condizioni di marcia, compresi dazio e I.G.E. *Prezzo suggerito

Chiedete una documentazione completa sulla Kadett ai Concessionari Opel o direttamente alla General Motors Italia S.p.A., Milano, Via Tito Speri 8

Opel Kadett
la 1000 che va forte
Un prodotto della General Motors GM

Sie finden 38 neue Ideen
in den großen Sechszylindern
von Mercedes-Benz

Die neue Form ist nur eine davon

Gestrecktes Profil, niedrige Gürtellinie, größere Fenster für bessere Sicht (12% mehr Glasfläche) und noch mehr Raum für die Fahrgäste.

Dazu 37 weitere Neuerungen und Verbesserungen: Hochleistungsmotoren von 130, 150 und 170 PS, 7fach gelagerte Kurbelwelle, Scheibenbremsen an allen Rädern, neue

Heizungs- und Lüftungsanlage. Weiterentwicklung aller wichtigen Aggregate. Aber das ist nur ein kurzer Blick auf die neuen großen Sechszylinder von Mercedes-Benz. Fahrsicherheit, Fahrkomfort und die ungewöhnliche Fahrruhe dieser Wagen können Sie nur selbst erleben. Auf einer Probefahrt.

Die Mercedes-Benz Klasse

Das wird Sie interessieren: die Mercedes-Benz Dokumentation

Typ 200 4-Zylinder, 2 Vergaser, 95 PS bei 5 200 U/Min., Spitze ca. 160 km/h

Typ 200 D 4-Zylinder Diesel, 55 PS bei 4 200 U/Min., Spitze ca. 130 km/h

Typ 230 6-Zylinder, 2 Solex-Vergaser, 105 PS bei 5 200 U/Min., Spitze ca 170 km/h

Typ 230 S 6-Zylinder, 2 INAT-Vergaser, 120 PS bei 5 400 U/Min., Spitze ca. 175 km/h

Typ 250 S 6-Zylinder, 2 INAT-Doppel-Register-Vergaser, 130 PS bei 5 400 U/Min., Spitze ca. 180 km/h

Typ 250 SE 6-Zylinder, 6-Stempel-Einspritz-Pumpe, 150 PS bei 5 500 U/Min., Spitze ca. 190 km/h

Typ 250 SE Cabriolet 6-Zylinder, 6-Stempel-Einspritz-Pumpe, 150 PS bei 5 500 U/Min., Spitze ca. 190 km/h

Typ 250 SE Coupé 6-Zylinder, 6-Stempel-Einspritz-Pumpe, 150 PS bei 5 500 U/Min., Spitze ca. 190 km/h

Typ 300 SE 6-Zylinder, Einspritz-Motor, 170 PS bei 5 400 U/Min., Spitze ca. 185 bis 200 km/h

Typ 300 SEL 6-Zylinder, Einspritz-Motor, 170 PS bei 5 400 U/Min., Spitze ca. 185 bis 200 km/h

Typ 300 SE Cabriolet 6-Zylinder, Einspritz-Motor, 170 PS bei 5 400 U/Min., Spitze ca. 185 bis 200 km/h

Typ 300 SE Coupé 6-Zylinder, Einspritz-Motor, 170 PS bei 5 400 U/Min., Spitze ca. 185 bis 200 km/h

Typ 230 SL 6-Zylinder, 6 Stempel-Einspritz-Pumpe, 150 PS bei 5 500 U/Min., Spitze ca. 200 km/h

Typ 600 8-Zylinder, Einspritz-Motor, 250 PS bei 4 000 U/Min., Spitze ca. 205 km/h

Typ 600 Pullman 8-Zylinder, Einspritz-Motor, 250 PS bei 4 000 U/Min., Spitze ca. 205 km/h

MERCEDES-BENZ

Ihr guter Stern auf allen Straßen

Refinement of an established concept versus new style-packaging: two displays from 1965, Mercedes-Benz (*opposite*) and Ford of America's Mustang (*right*). From merely reading copy, it is hard to realize that the German car commands far more technical interest than the American one, which is probably why Stuttgart shows a full-face, whereas Dearborn prefers careful posing. Against its background of instant, spectacular sales success—plus the hurried pursuit of similar themes by General Motors, Chrysler, and AMC—one doesn't easily accept the Mustang for what it was: a cleverly styled, short-wheelbase, occasional four-seater edition of the American norm, aimed at the man or woman with individual tastes but no particular enthusiasm for the motor car. The Mustang was Protean—you made it what you wanted—and that amounted to anything from a shopping runabout of indifferent performance to a V-8 "bomb" that could out-drag a Jaguar, though only in the lower speed ranges and in a straight line. Disc brakes aren't mentioned in this ad, as they weren't yet listed, but already Ford felt confident enough in their "pleader for the open road" to quote the visual differences between a "cooking" six and a V-8 with their "Rally Pac". There are echoes of a Model-T-oriented past, too, in the "more for your money" by-line. Daimler-Benz, by contrast, were preaching to the converted. Their family sedans showed a continuity of design going back at least to 1932, and the 1965 cars were merely logical developments of what they had been making since 1954. In Stuttgart, styling didn't matter: it was "just one of thirty-eight new ideas" incorporated in the latest sixes, and with the "good star" atop the (admittedly dummy) radiator-filler cap, everybody knew a Mercedes-Benz when they saw one. And while Ford plugged variety through the art of "personalizing" one's Mustang, the press department at Stuttgart wasted no space on purple prose. They just gave one a potted survey of their entire current range—some of which was continued without alteration—to show that there was a car for all customers from the middle-class sector to the petro-dollar millionaires: a price spread, in fact, from 11,000 to some 65,000 Deutschmarks. The ad wasn't meant to sell SL sports cars or 600 limousines, or even diesel-powered taxicabs—it merely reminded the public that big family sedans weren't the only product.

1965 Mustang hardtop on "Main Street" of a Western town, U.S.A.

Meet America's most successful new car
Mustang by Ford—a spectacular four-seater
at an unexpectedly low price.

With the all-new four-passenger Mustang—Ford springs the most exciting surprise ever wrapped in steel! Hours after its American introduction, it had taken the country by storm! Come closer, see why.

The styling is distinctive, lean, swift. Even at rest, Mustang seems to plead for an open road . . . to anywhere. But Mustang is more than motion. It is practicality, too. The unexpectedly low price proves it. So does Mustang's fabulous wealth of *standard features:* Like deep-foam bucket seats, wall-to-wall carpeting, padded instrument panel, floor-mounted shift, 200 cubic inch Six, ample trunk, sports steering wheel, wheel covers, courtesy lights, even more, and it's all standard!

But it is *choice* that makes Mustang practically magic. There are three models—hardtop; convertible; and the 2 + 2 fastback with a rear seat that folds down to create extra loadspace. In the equipment department, Mustang options are all but endless. There is a special "Rally Pac," red line sports tires and styled steel wheels, two different V-8 engines, vinyl roof covering, 3-speed automatic and 4-speed manual transmissions, console, power brakes and power steering, even air conditioning!

So make of Mustang what you will—a practical family car—a high-performance sports car—a personal luxury car. Mustang can be any of these. And Mustang can be yours at an unexpectedly low price. See it at your local Ford Products Dealer today!

You get more for your money in _any_ Ford-built product

MATRA EST DANS LA COURSE!

Riche de l'enseignement tiré de ses succès en compétition (1er à Reims, 2e à Rouen, 1er à Cognac...) MATRA-SPORTS met à votre disposition, avec la "DJET", un ensemble de solutions techniques qui ont fait leurs preuves. ✳ **Le moteur central**, placé en avant de l'essieu arrière, représente une sécurité exceptionnelle : tenue de route inégalée, freinage progressif et équilibré par la juste répartition des charges, réaction neutre aux effets latéraux.

✳ **Un aérodynamisme étudié** : l'avant profilé englobant les phares, la ligne surbaissée, l'arrière tronqué, permettent à la "DJET" de rouler plus vite que toute autre voiture de puissance égale. Sécurité et performance font de la "DJET" une voiture étonnante à un prix sans concurrence sur le marché. Certains modèles dépassent le 200 km/h et vous pourrez vous offrir une "DJET" à partir de 16.900 Francs ! D'un prix intéressant, la "DJET" est économique à l'usage : 9 à 10 l. aux 100 kms avec la sécurité d'une mécanique de grande diffusion. ✳ **Demandez à votre concessionnaire un essai... vous serez stupéfié !**

156

Je ne sais quoi as a commercial property: wooing the Gallic Jet Set in 1965, as done by a native maker, Matra (*opposite*), and by an importer, Alfa Romeo (*right*). In advertising, the known way isn't just the safe way—it's the easier one, too, and any Frenchman knows what an Alfa is, since he's still blushing over four Italian victories in a row at Le Mans in the early 1930s. And despite the occasional styling gaffe (the Giulia *berlina* was no oil painting), the Alfa with its lively twin-camshaft engine and "seat of the pants" steering is a car that sorts out the men from the boys. Thus he is already half sold when he's informed that the art of conducting such a car is inborn, not acquired. Sex doesn't have to be mentioned—the two envious gents quizzing the owner in the picture are already on their way to the local friendly dealer (over 250 of them in France, please note, so you don't have to phone Milan for parts). In the case of the Matra, though, the public is less well informed as to the product: the company name spells rocketry, and the racing record is associated with machinery that is definitely not for street use. Further, past history is a little confusing, for the *marque* has had two previous identities in fifteen years (DB, René Bonnet) and what started with a flat-twin Panhard engine driving the front wheels now has an amidships-mounted Renault four transmitting its power to the back end. Besides, for every 75 new Alfas to come out of Portello, there is precisely one new Matra issuing from the shops at Vélizy. Hence the copy is a bit mixed up. It starts magnificently with a couple, surely the original Beautiful People, hurtling out of the rather awkward doors—that leg show would never have done in the 1930s—*en route* for a suggestive destination, and ends with a truly T.S. Eliot whimper (before a long, tedious recitative of dealers, like Jean-Paul Sartre reading from the Paris telephone directory).

non, cette tranquille assurance ne s'achète pas...

Cette confiance en soi, cette manière d'être à la fois passionné et sage, cette décontraction naturelle, cet art de rire à la vie... C'est le «savoir-vivre-Alfa» que nous regrettons de ne pouvoir vous vendre!

Nous ne vendons que la voiture. Pas le style!

Sinon, comment expliquer qu'une Alfa Romeo puisse allumer une lueur d'envie dans les yeux de ceux dont la voiture coûte autant et parfois plus. Non, on ne devient pas conducteur d'Alfa comme on devient chauffeur, en s'asseyant au volant de n'importe quelle voiture. En fait, il faut être né comme ça!

Parmi ceux qui ont cette chance, certains ont une Alfa dès le début, d'autres restent insatisfaits jusqu'au jour où par hasard, ils essaient une Alfa...

Peut-être êtes-vous de ceux-là...

Pour vous permettre de vous «découvrir», nos concessionnaires tiennent une Alfa Romeo à votre disposition: ne vous refusez pas le plaisir d'un essai!

GIULIA SUPER Berline 4 portes - 5/6 places - moteur 1570 cc - 4 cylindres en ligne à double arbre à cames en tête - 9 cv fiscaux - 112 cv SAE - 5 vitesses synchronisées (+ marche arrière) - 4 freins à disque assistés - poids à vide: 1.000 kg - vitesse maximum: plus de 175 km/h.

alfa romeo

Sté Française Alfa Roméo - Magasin d'exposition: 150 Champs Elysées - Centre d'essais: 25 rue Cardinet - Tél. 267 31-00 + - 250 points de vente et service en France 1200 en Europe.

157

Glamorous new quality-built Mercury Park Lane 4-door Hardtop Cruiser—the liveliest, most luxurious Mercury.

Wider doors, softer seats, more leg room —Mercury's style is <u>planned for people</u>

MERCURY PROVIDES 6 INCHES MORE ENTRANCE ROOM. It's easy to keep hips and knees at a dignified level when stepping in or out. See how Mercury's cornerpost is moved out of your way. Mercury prices won't cramp your style either—easily fit the new-car budgets of two out of three. Why wait?

MERCURY REMEMBERS PEOPLE HAVE KNEES—and legs, hips, heads and shoulders, too.

You step, *not crawl*, into a Mercury. You sit up, *not crouch*, in your seat. It carries six people, *not four*, comfortably.

There's more room before you, beside you, beneath you. Nine inches more knee room up front. Almost double the foot room and cushioning in the middle because Mercury cut the floor hump in half (while other cars made it bigger than ever). There's even more room *behind* you (31½ cubic feet!) in a wide, open, easy-to-get-at trunk.

Now look again at the styling. What other '59 car offers you so much beauty—and without sacrificing comfort!

'59 MERCURY

Planned for People

SEE IT   DRIVE IT—

AT YOUR MERCURY DEALER'S

158

Cutlass S.

Break the routine. Let your hair down and swing (for) a little!

Routine. The same old thing. There are a lot of cars like that—and one that isn't.

Cutlass S. The freshest fastback on the road today.

One look at those great new lines and up goes the old pulse rate. Sporty new hood with raised pods. Chromed louvers at the cowl. Concealed wipers. Ventless side windows (Holiday Coupe and Convertible). New flared sculpturing toward the rear.

Take the wheel and you leave the routine far behind. With standard Rocket 350 V-8 or big Action-Line 6 (take your pick), you light out pronto. With smooth coil springs at each wheel and sporty 112-inch wheelbase, handling and parking are a breeze. You can change directions as quickly as you change your mind.

Which is exactly what you should be doing about all those (ho-hum) routine cars. This year, give them the slip by slipping into a Cutlass S — still priced with or below many of the low-priced names!

The old 9 to 5. Hurry. Worry. Crank out the work. Wouldn't it be nice to have an Escape Machine?

Cutlass S Holiday Coupe.

Mercury were not always devoted to "man's car" advertising, and here is how they went after the ladies in 1959 (*opposite*). They picked on just about the only genuine virtue of dog's-leg windscreens, though portlier people coped less well. No attempt was made to sing the praises of the deplorable tail fins.

(*Above*) Oldsmobile woos the fair sex, 1970. Maybe it's a little patronizing to suggest that "you can change directions as quickly as you change your mind", and the male chauvinist pig behind in the traffic must have blessed General Motors . . . Interestingly, the girl second from the right in the background is Black, something that would not have been seen in automotive publicity even three years previously.

Chrysler Corporation territory, where on this occasion the sale of Australian cars in Britain was being commemorated by a corralled and somewhat distraught kangaroo.

There remain the triple themes of sex, safety, and euphoria: of these, the greatest was undoubtedly euphoria. Sex was still something to be treated in low-key fashion. Not so women. The only surprising factor was that they took the wheel less frequently than one might expect. Only in Japan did girl drivers consistently predominate. But female views were certainly canvassed. Secretaries were urged to "break the routine, let your hair down, swing a little" in a Sporty Oldsmobile Cutlass. Buick picked six top fashion models to sing the praises of their 1967 range. It was usually a dainty feminine foot that sampled the minimal pedal pressures of power braking systems. The Triumph Herald was "the masculine car that delights women"—and in 1964 Cadillac, no less, suggested that "the finest compliment that can be paid to a lady is to provide her with the company of a Cadillac". The car would "gratify her practical nature with its low maintenance expenses and universally recognized high standard". Somehow this rang a bell: in 1930 Chrysler had commended the Plymouth Four to women for "its ability to spend more time on the road than in the service station". The ladies had moved up from the bargain basement to the top of the class.

But while the girls were told that they drove better in a Triumph, and posed in bikinis on its bonnet, they still seldom actually took the wheel, except in one memorable specimen: "The girl gets dated—the Triumph Herald doesn't." Attitudes were still patronizing. Porsche called their least potent model the *Damen*, and Daimler's Ladies Model (1956) featured, among other things, simplified wheel-changing tools and specially labelled control knobs. Panhard, after inducing a smart young executive to "gallantly open the door for his wife" as they enter their 24CT coupé, hints that this sports model is a little too much for her to

159

självväxlande!

1966

daf 66

Fitting one's copy to local needs, or how to sell (*left*) Dutch cars to Swedes and (*opposite*) Italian cars to the French. There's no need for "reverse-block" techniques in 1966, for Sweden is about to change to a right-hand rule of the road—and France has always followed it, even if Lancia themselves featured right-hand drive for almost all their cars until they started to explore the U.S. market. DAF, of course, were after the town runabout market, where they were up against things like the Mini: faster, better-handling, more compact, and infinitely better-braked. Their one great strength was that they marketed not only the smallest car with fully automatic transmission, but the only car anywhere with a stepless system—and this at a time when Saab offered no automatics, and Volvo were just getting into the game. Hence the headline "Self-Shifting" which wouldn't have caught the eye of a Briton, Frenchman, or German, and would positively have deterred an Italian. With long and cold winters, good traction on ice and a three-year guarantee against rust are stressed, while the little twin-cylinder sedan is shown in *de luxe* form with two-tone paintwork and whitewall tyres, the perfect shopping mount for *madame*. Lancia had no problems of image in France: they had assembled there in the 1930s, and the Augusta (Belna) and Aprilia (Ardennes) had enjoyed a steady sale. Here "class" is being sold rather than euphoria. St. Moritz and the Cresta Run are the epitome of the sporting *homme d'élite* (the girls presumably stayed in the passenger seat). Also a recognized hallmark was styling by Pininfarina, though anyone who paused to think would realize that such a label also applied to any Peugeot model launched since 1954. It is fair to add that the quoted performance figures were obtainable only with the optional-extra fuel injection, though this tended to be standard on export cars. And the package, if rust-prone and complicated, was quite impressive: a 1.8-litre flat-four with superlative handling, and all-disc brakes. Plus front-wheel drive, of course . . .

Ni behöver bara gasa, ratta och bromsa — aldrig växla. Växlingen sköter DAFs steglösa kraftöverföring, Variomatic, som gör kopplingspedal och växelspak överflödiga. Körningen blir enklare och säkrare. Lugn och avspänd körning, alltid med båda händerna på ratten och ena foten på golvet? Sportig, snabb och rivig med en fot på gasen och en på bromsen? Vilket körsätt Ni än väljer är DAF bekvämare — inte minst i stadstrafik.
Där vinner Ni också på de snabba starterna och upplever att DAF är en billängd före — inte bara i tekniskt avseende. Självväxlingen inbegriper även differentialspärr för riktigt väggrepp i halkigt väglag och tvära kurvor. De små ytterformaten, ringa vändradien och direktstyringen gör DAF lättparkerad. DAF har alltså oslagbara egenskaper som stadsbil.
För långkörning erbjuder DAF god ekonomi och komfort. Bränsleförbrukningen är låg och rundsmörjning obehövlig. 3 års rostskyddsgaranti. Bekväma sittutrymmen för 4 vuxna. Genomströmmande ventilation med stängda rutor. 400 l bagageutrymme (nästan som två ordinära badkar!).

daf -en billängd före . . .

handle. ("She also seems to appreciate the high performance of their car when normally high speed frightens her.") When she asks to drive, the copywriter tactfully changes the subject. Mercury, the prime euphoria merchants, stressed masculinity: "the friendship between a man and his car is a very special thing, a passport to adventure, an open road beckoning, and a well travelled trip to work". One feels that the girl by his side is purely incidental, and that he would not have welcomed the young lady who competed against her husband in sprints to help sell Triumphs in America in 1978.

For the truly patronizing, nothing can match this gem from Anadol of Turkey. "Men, let there be no sleepless nights if the wife can drive. Anadol is made with safety in mind. It has a beefy steel chassis under the elegant fibreglass body, disc brakes in front, and large drum brakes at the rear, face level vents to ward off drowsiness. It all adds up to a car you can rely on to get her out of trouble—safely." Not the brightest of copy, but an exercise in how to cram nuts and bolts, male chauvinism, and the 1967 safety theme into a couple of sentences.

Euphoria multiplied. Oldsmobile's 1952 convertible was "the supreme stylist of the highway". The sky seemed "closer, friendlier when you're cruising easily up a mountain highway" in a 1956 Sun Valley Mercury: understandably, since it had a glass panel in the roof to let the passengers look up at the mountains. With an MG-B the driver was "the man with the advantage (press it home)", and enthusiasts were adjured bluntly to "get into an Austin-Healey and see what you get out of it", an approach which would have been more effective had it not also been applied to mundane Austins of the same era. Australian Mini advertising was headed with the surfers' call, YABBADABBADOO,

and the cars were depicted with surfboards on their roofs. Oldsmobile's 1970 "escape machines" got one "away from the daily grind, be it office, plant or kitchen". The Renault Dauphine brought an air of "springtime, year in, year out". Plymouth Valiants "take you where the fun is and always add their additional zing to the fling". Pontiac, safely entrenched by 1965 in their new wide-track image, appealed to those "who have made up their mind that wagons can't be beautiful to look at and fun to drive", though there was a practical side to this dose of euphoria: the women would appreciate "upholstery that stands up to the patter and batter of tiny feet".

"Trees flashing by a grey ribbon of road" sufficed in a humble 1960 English Ford. But the heights of prose could still be scaled, and in a manner worthy of the great Edward S. Jordan. Here is Buick in 1967. "These are the melodies that build our Buick convertible rhapsody. The first caress of summer sun, the vaulted roof of stars, the sight of wind in the trees, the rhythmic chuckle of rolling tires on warm pavement, all are preludes to that certain time when you climb into your new Buick convertible and drop the top. It's a great, free feeling that must be experienced. It's a feeling that truly puts a song in your heart." Enough, indeed, to make one march out of the office and point the car's nose down the nearest freeway. Europeans, however, never quite managed such eloquence. In 1959, Borgward assured their clientele that you would "enjoy and admire your Isabella coupé, even more in mountain climbing". But just as you were ready to roam, fancy-free, in the Black Forest or the Jura, they brought you down to earth with "thirteen-inch tyres for better traction and a lower centre of gravity". The magic was lost.

LE COUPÉ FLAVIA PININFARINA EN STYLE DE VAINQUEUR

Entre deux murs de glace, rien que le froissement de l'acier:
Plaisir pur des reflexes aiguisés par la vitesse. Sur la
route, à 185 à l'heure. Le silence du coupé LANCIA
Une mécanique racée pour des hommes d'élite.

COUGAR XR-7
...ITS INTERIOR THE PURIST'S DELIGHT.

Cougar's proud pedigree is evident at a glance in the lavishly fitted cockpit of the XR-7 hardtop or convertible. You see it in tawny tones of warmly burled walnut vinyl appliqués on instrument panel and sporty steering wheel. In hi-back bucket seats tailored in vinyl with accents of richly grained leather. In the authoritative layout of rocker switches and instruments, replete even to tachometer, trip odometer and clock with elapsed time indicator. All standard in XR-7, as are the left-hand remote-control racing mirror... distinctive XR-7 wheel covers... rear seat armrests... seat-back map pockets... map and courtesy lights... the visual check panel with lamps that signal low fuel or door ajar... deep-loop carpeting wall-to-wall.

XR-7 instruments include tachometer and trip odometer, cove-inset to permit extra legibility.

A center pod houses rocker switches for map, panel and courtesy lights, defogger or convertible top.

Mercury on top form: it's actually 1970, but could be from any of their mid- or late-sixties publicity. Here you have the lot—the sultry blonde, the contoured figure-hugging seats, the convertible body (seen as it would be by lesser mortals pottering along in stock sedans), even the gloves and sunglasses which show that Madame has annexed this particular automobile. Scenery was superfluous: it could be the Rockies, the Adirondacks, or Palm Beach, but never a place like Coney Island.

162

KANGAROOS...

DRJ·151

don't need Datsun

Kangaroos have their own built-in means of getting places fast — so why should they care about cars.

But Australia is a good deal more than kangaroos.

Most of all, it's a lot of forward-looking, down-to-earth practical people, plus a good many bustling cities surrounded by plenty of wide-open space where people are building and growing.

That's why we're not at all surprised to see the folks from Down Under calling for more and more DATSUN Bluebirds—the choice of practical people in more than 70 nations, besides being Japan's most popular passenger car.

To Australians, as well as to practical people

everywhere, the charm of the DATSUN Bluebird is its all-encompassing compatibility.

It's trim, solid and compact but with sleek, low big-car lines that give just the right touch of dynamic beauty.

An extra-efficient, highly economical engine plus the unitized body and well-balanced suspensions provides 5 comfortable passengers with new dimensions in stability, maneuverability and all-round motoring satisfaction—in crowded city streets, on the open highway, on country backroads.

Long admired for their practical approach to transportation, the kangaroos probably aren't the least bit surprised to see more and more practical

people rolling by in the DATSUN Bluebird the compatible compact.

Even the sheep seem to be showing interest in these sleek and snappy newcomers.

DATSUN
Bluebird

Japan's Largest Exporter of Automobiles
NISSAN MOTOR CO., LTD. / Tokyo, Japan   NISSAN

precedere i tempi

Per noi della Bertone precedere i tempi vuol dire applicare con intelligenza i concetti costruttivi e stilistici più avanzati per creare forme nuove, valide nel tempo.
La 850 Convertibile è un concreto esempio dei nostri criteri di lavoro.

La sua eccezionale profilatura ci ha consentito di ottenere una velocità di oltre 145 Km/h, con 52 HP e 720 Kg. Ed abbiamo risolto il problema del doppio impiego: una razionale soluzione tecnica permette di trasformare rapidamente la 850 Convertibile da perfetto coupé in brillante spider. Ma la nostra opera non si limita a questo: noi vi diamo una vettura accogliente, curata in ogni dettaglio con il gusto artigianale che da sempre ci distingue.

Rifiniture di lusso - Tinte metallizzate
Organizzazione di vendita in tutta Italia
Assistenza **FIAT**.
Versione Convertibile L. 1.285.000
senza hard-top L. 1.175.000
BERTONE - GRUGLIASCO (Torino)

850 CONVERTIBILE

BERTONE

Typographic art from the Great Outdoors (*opposite*)—if not quite the Outback—and from Italy (*right*). The 1965 Datsun advertisement did not originate in Australia: its purpose is merely to demonstrate the adaptability of the breed, besides creating a background into which the then-mandatory Caucasian models would fit. The Commonwealth was the best place to locate such publicity, the environment is authentic Australian, and the car wears correct New South Wales registrations. All of which is splendid cover for a thoroughly uninspired vehicle, with a 1.2-litre pushrod four-cylinder engine developing 60 horsepower, three-on-the-column (though four forward speeds were available in some export markets), and an advertised top speed of 78 mph (125 km/h). In Australia, unlike America, one wouldn't equip one's Datsun with either whitewall tyres or a radio antenna. But what dates this piece of copy, apart from the Bluebird's 1950s shape, is Nissan Motor Company's modest claim to be "Japan's largest exporter of automobiles". With barely 100,000 passenger cars sent abroad (Australia got about 36,000 of them), the Land of the Rising Sun was still a long way from the Big League. As for Bertone's 1967 effort on the open sports 850 Fiat, it was an instance of letting a coachbuilder promote his own wares, thus leaving the "chassis" maker free to spend a budget on the high-volume sedans. Hence there is no hint whatever of nuts and bolts, beyond a truthful statement of maximum speed (if not of the revs required to attain it). But Bertone's faith in the shape is shown by depicting the car with the detachable hardtop in position, and there's also a necessary reminder that this particular "special" is Fiat-approved and thus to be serviced through Fiat's dealer network. (Some of the exotics weren't, and some were only "approved" at home in Italy, as owners would discover to their cost.) The graphics at the foot of the copy recall McKnight Kauffer's efforts for Chrysler in the late 1920s, only this time they aren't used to conceal the boxiness of the car in the metal.

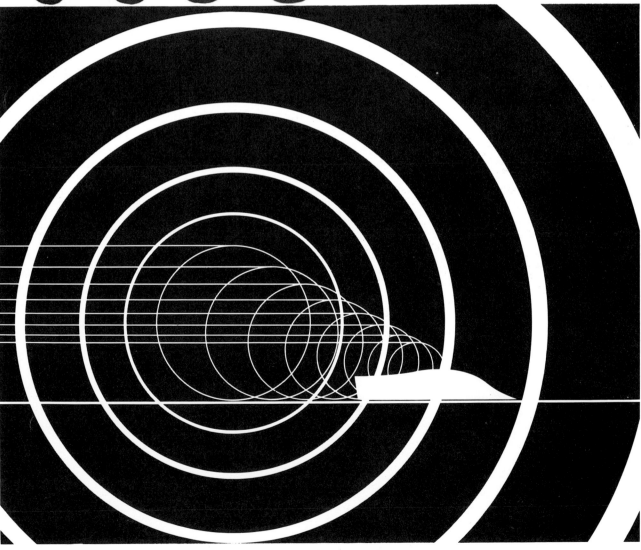

Interpretazione grafica degli effetti delle vibrazioni: propagazione delle onde sonore in funzione della velocità

165

(*Left*) Price is the spur—we're back with Chevrolet's 1929 slogan, "A Six for the Price of a Four". Germans in 1965, however, are more specific, and scrupulously honest: this is the cheap model of the six-cylinder Ford range, and the closest competition is the Opel at DM 9,310 (if you want a Mercedes six, there's no change out of DM 12,000). Borgward are long defunct, and BMW offer only fours. *Grosse* is a relative term, of course: all Cologne had done was to insert a V-6 engine into the space once occupied by an in-line four, and now normally used for V-4s of 1.5 or 1.8 litres' capacity—but then this went for their rivals, too. The car was certainly roomy, and the performance claims could be substantiated, while the front view showed German customers that the local product now had the stylistic edge on contemporary efforts from Dearborn and Dagenham alike, both available in the *Bundesrepublik*. And, as in America, there was always the art of "personalization" to play up—your 20M could be had with three speeds, four speeds, or automatic: floor or column shift: bench or separate front seats: and a choice of four bodies with two- and four-door sedans, an attractive sports coupé, and the seldom-seen cabriolet (a semi-series top-chop by Karosserie Deutsch). Sadly, by the end of our period, the German Ford would be transformed into merely a Ford made in Germany—the 1968 Escort line was almost identical with its British counterpart, and 1969's Capri coupé was conceived along the same lines.

(*Opposite*) It's surprising what a good typeface will do. Fiat had their own, shown to excellent purpose in this page from a 128 sedan catalogue of 1969–70. First-class reproduction and a clear layout of technical data make up for the absence of other gimmicks. The catalogue itself was a trick of design: you unfolded it once for this view, twice for details of the interior space for five people, a third time to look at the front-wheel-drive power unit (both on its own and, with the spare tyre, under the bonnet), and finally to get a poster covering half a square metre of wall with the car for "a changing world".

Taunus 20M

Der große 6-Zylinder unter DM 8000

Der Taunus 20 M ermöglicht Ihnen den Aufstieg zum 6-Zylinder, ohne daß Sie 8000 Mark auszugeben brauchen. Sein Preis mag nur der erste Grund sein, aber längst nicht der einzige.
Seine 85 PS beschleunigen Sie in nur 15,5 Sekunden von 0 auf 100 km/h.
Ihr Dauertempo im Taunus 20 M liegt bei 160 km/h.

Der Taunus 20 M hat Breitspur-Fahrwerk und serienmäßig großvolumige Sportreifen – das ist Sicherheit!
Er hat als einziger Wagen seiner Klasse Vollkreis-Ventilation. Sein V6-Motor hat die serienmäßige lange Lebensdauer aller V-Motoren, die Ford baut. Vieles, was dieser Wagen serienmäßig an Luxus

bietet, müßten Sie bei anderen extra bezahlen. Und Sie haben viele Möglichkeiten, aus einer Vielzahl von Modellen, Ausstattungen und Farben Ihren ganz persönlichen Taunus 20 M auszuwählen. Sind das genügend gute Gründe?
Nun, dann vereinbaren Sie recht bald mit dem nächsten Ford-Händler eine Probefahrt.

Den Taunus 20 M gibt es ab DM 7990 a.W.

FORD
die Linie der Vernunft

4 doors
2 doors

overall length: 12 ft. 7$^{13}/_{16}$ in. (3.85 m). Nearly 4 in. (10 cm) shorter than the Fiat 1100.
visibility: all round, from a very low waistline.
tyres: 145 x 13 radial ply.
protection: compact and rigid passenger compartment, highly resistant to longitudinal and transverse loads.
Front and rear structures designed for differential deformation to absorb the effects of possible impact.
door locks: three way locks plus safety catches.

167

From simple euphoria, we approach the tiger spirit, that furious one-upmanship which burst upon the motoring world in the early 1960s, when Esso exhorted motorists to "put a tiger in your tank". Panhard's high-performance flat-twin engine was a *Tigre*, and soon Pontiac's GTO would be promoted over the radio networks as "the ultimate tiger" in a voice of the type usually reserved for ghost stories. The bestiary was filling up: Ford's Mustang was a best-seller by 1965, and Dodge countered medievally with a Charger. Plymouth had a maritime predator, the Barracuda. Mercury joined the felines with their Cougar—and persuaded a live specimen to pose uncomfortably on the boot lid for publicity pictures. By the beginning of 1970, de Tomaso of Italy had a Pantera coupé, and Lincoln-Mercury were lined up to market it in the U.S.A.

Suddenly it was all go. In 1951, Jowett had said of their Javelin, "take a good look as it passes you", but nobody was going to pass the tiger-car brigade. The Mustang "grabs you, turns you on, creates a new you". Mercury's Cyclone was "the high performance spirit of Daytona", and the mere sight of a Pontiac GTO would breed "an uncontrollable urge to plant yourself at the wheel". The Cougar, of course, remained in an upbeat mood, but if you opted for the Eliminator version (7 litres, 345 horsepower) caution was advised, for "Spoilers hold it down. Nothing holds it back". It was hard to believe that, only twelve years earlier, Chrysler had said "goodbye to rock and roll" purely on the strength of new torsion-bar front suspension.

But times were changing. The same Cougar's publicity included an unlikely picture of a man at the wheel, wearing a seat belt. Now safety outranked convertibles, sex, or even euphoria. In 1967, Mercedes-Benz pontificated: "Safety is the foremost requirement on the road". DAF and Honda insisted that putting the spare wheel under the bonnet gave the front-seat passengers extra protection. Ford's Highway Pilot roof-console (on deluxe Thunderbirds) included a seat-belt warning light, while the Mustang had thirty brand-new safety features. Rover offered shaped and marked switches which "can be reached while a properly adjusted seat belt is being worn".

Sex played second fiddle to euphoria. Housewives were wooed with reclining seats, power steering, and "magic tailgates" for their station wagons. It was the wife who acted as spokeswoman when "together we chose a Morris" in the early sixties. Live-in lovers were not catered for: within a few years one would be able to "do it in an MG", but 1969's prospects were merely urged to "get the old magic again", and this referred to driving and nothing else. The girls might be scantily clad on occasion, but they were still wives or fiancées. The only brave statement of emancipation was Renault's *Ils s'aimaient* brochure for the Floride convertible (1960), the delightful story of a weekend which was (by implication, if in no other sense) extramarital.

Colour was not yet an issue, though a curious situation arose in 1969–70. By this time Americans were beginning to use black as well as white models to promote their cars, whereas the Japanese were turning towards "Western" backgrounds (the U.S.A. for left-hand drive, Australia for right) and also towards Caucasians to pose with the product. In 1981, astonishingly, Mazda would publish a Japanese-language brochure set against a Swiss background.

If we were not permissive over sex, we were permissive over smoking. Extra cigar—never, please note, cigarette—lighters were news, and an extra one could uprate a French car's specification from GL to GLS. And in 1967, Volvo were still proud of their outsize ashtray, "because the seats are made to sit in for a very long time".

With all this strange jargon circulating, publicity had not yet killed a car. Semantics, however, did—in 1963. That summer, the last Standard left Coventry, the line terminated because of the debasement of a word. The qualities inherent in the Union Jack badge were forgotten in a world where "standard" was the opposite of "de luxe".

Chapter 5

LUXURY GOES SELF-DRIVE

In 1939 Croesus rode in a Cadillac 75, Maybach Zeppelin, Delage D-8-100, Lancia Astura, or Phantom III Rolls-Royce, according to his nationality or political prejudices. The President of the United States favoured Lincoln, the President of the French Republic a straight-eight Renault, the King of England—like his three immediate predecessors—a Daimler, and Germany's Nazi hierarchy the monstrous 7.7-litre supercharged *Grosser* Mercedes-Benz. Whatever the car, it would have a wheelbase of at least eleven feet (3.38 m) and be chauffeur-driven. Neither heads of state nor their wealthier subjects took the wheel, and probably the only people who actually handled these formal carriages were paid drivers and inquisitive motoring journalists.

Thirty years later, Croesus' executive limousine was unlikely to be a Cadillac. The thing was 244 in (6.2 m) long and took up too much space in parking lots. His business interests would be international, so he would use a Lear Jet or Piper Twin Comanche aeroplane. When on the ground, he would drive himself—in a Porsche 911, Aston Martin DBS, Lamborghini Miura, or Ferrari Daytona.

He could, of course, have been his own chauffeur in 1939, but it would have been hard work. Chassis were massive, and bodies coachbuilt. Apart from France's famed *grandes routières*, which were fairly cheap at £750 ($3,500) in their homeland and £1,100–1,200 (somewhere between five and six grand U.S.) in Britain, the super-cars of that period came heavy. The sophisticated V-12 Lagonda weighed in at 4,500 lb (well over two tonnes), and the magnificent Mercedes-Benz 540K was *avant-garde* only in that it featured all-independent springing. Beautiful it certainly was, and one could not deny the splendour of its proud vee-radiator set well back behind the Bosch headlamps—but it was a big car some 210 in (5.35 m) long, turned the scales at a good 2.5 tonnes (2,600 kg), and was still frequently made as a pure two-seater. Nor was the performance really impressive: the Mercedes would do 105–108 mph (165–170 km/h) with the blower engaged, but the blower was not supposed to be used for more than half a minute at a time. And for all this it required a 5.4-litre straight-eight engine, giving 180 horsepower at 3,400 rpm.

One could hardly compare the 540K with its 1954 successor, the 300SL. This car was a closed two-seater, yet it managed 140–145 mph (235 km/h) on three litres, two fewer cylinders, and a formidable 215 horsepower, without the limitations of a blower, for emergency use only. This added up to 70 hp/litre as against 30 (or 22, running unblown) for the 1939 car. As for 1969's form, the best offered in that season was the Ferrari Daytona, 4.4 litres of four-camshaft V-12 disposing of 350 horsepower, or 80 hp/litre, with a top speed in the region of 175 mph (280 km/h). Such true driver's cars would not be entrusted

to one's chauffeur, and in any case they were strictly two-seaters.

We have already noted the decline of the specialist coachbuilder. First to go were firms catering for "different" bodies on medium-priced chassis, if only because such medium-priced cars (favourites had been Vauxhall in Britain and Opel in Germany) no longer had chassis. The *haute couture* brigade took a while to fade away, but their demise was only a matter of time. Outside Italy, they closed their doors, or allied themselves with a "chassis" maker: H.J. Mulliner and Park Ward (who ultimately merged) with Rolls-Royce, Vanden Plas of London with Austin, Tickford with Aston Martin Lagonda. Thrupp and Maberly, long a Rootes subsidiary, abandoned custom bodywork in favour of such "in-house" jobs as Humber's touring limousines. Abbott devoted themselves to the conversion of Ford sedans into station wagons, and Martin Walter to mobile homes. The surviving provincial builders—Rippon in Huddersfield and Vincent in Reading—sold and serviced cars where once they had clothed them.

What happened in Britain was paralleled elsewhere. In Germany, small-run jobs for the big battalions were the order of the day, although Spohn worked up a brief American connection by customizing Cadillacs for U.S. servicemen and building bodies for the Gaylord specialty car in 1955. It was effectively all over in France by the mid-1950s, while the U.S. carriage trade had been a pre-war casualty. Only Derham in Pennsylvania, plus a few small Californian firms, were still active in 1969—and Derham's modest operations were a mixture of upper-class customizations (turning big sedans into "formals") and restoration work on the older Classics. Switzerland's coachbuilders, headed by Hermann Graber in Berne, remained active into the sixties, Graber keeping his firm alive by designs on the 3-litre Alvis chassis. Alvis themselves would organize manufacture of these in Britain from 1958 onward.

But the whole concept was doomed, and had been so even in 1939. The absence of a separate, drivable chassis on which to build was, of course, the ultimate deciding factor, but almost equally responsible was the decline of traditional craftsmanship. The wartime skills learnt in aircraft manufacture were best adapted to mass-production techniques, although in Italy the use by Touring of aluminium panelling over a tubular frame took a leaf out of the aeronautical book. In any case, once the era of austerity faded and affluence returned, the mass-producers were quick to raise their standard of interior appointments. Even if leather was too expensive, and polished wood too vulnerable to extremes of climate, the public were quite happy with radios, heaters, reclining seats, electric window lifts, and the other refinements of the new age.

(*Opposite*) The immortal gullwing, one of 1,400 Mercedes-Benz 300SL two-seater coupés made between 1954 and 1957. It suffered neither the amateur mechanic nor the inexperienced driver gladly, and its complexities were the space frame, the canted six-cylinder engine with dry-sump lubrication and fuel injection, and those strange doors which were a structural necessity. However, what price 135 mph (216 km/h) in top gear, 98 mph (157 km/h) in third, and 70 mph (112 km/h) in second? The car looked its best in "works" silver, a reminder of the prototype's dramatic impact on the 1952 sports-car racing season.

with the firm's 1939 prestige limousine, the straight-eight Grosser. The latter needed a supercharger to extract 230 horsepower from 7.7 litres, or about 32 % less power for 20 % more capacity. Further, it could weigh as much as 7,500 lb (3,400 kg), so 105 mph (170 km/h) was hard work, especially on the ultra-heavy versions used by the Nazi hierarchy.

(*Right*) Tailor-made for heads of state and oil millionaires: the interior of a Mercedes-Benz 600 Pullman, 1966, showing the rearwards-facing jump-seats and trim worthy of a first-class carriage at the zenith of the railroad era. For this ultimate in chauffeur-driven automobiles, with 6.3-litre fuel-injected V-8 engine, power steering, automatic transmission, and air suspension, the makers used a longer-than-standard wheelbase of 3.9 m (154 in), adding up to something like 6.2 m (246 in). Weight was 2,630 kg (5,800 lb). Between 1964 and 1981, production ran to 2,677 of all types, long and short.

(*Below*) The sedan version of Mercedes-Benz' super-car, the Grand Mercedes 600 introduced in 1963, does not look quite so enormous from this angle, though it is 218 in (5.5 m) long and weighs 5,380 lb (2,440 kg) dry. Top speed was 127 mph (205 km/h), and this one forms an interesting comparison

And the non-sporting "Classic", basis of the specialist coachbuilder's art, was on its way out. At the outbreak of war, quality cars aimed at the non-enthusiast were being built in Britain by Alvis, Armstrong Siddeley, Daimler, and Rolls-Royce; in the U.S.A. by Buick, Cadillac, Chrysler, Lincoln, and Packard; in Germany by BMW (their new 3.5-litre Type 335), Maybach, and Mercedes-Benz; in France by Delage and Delahaye; and in Spain by Hispano-Suiza. Twelve years later, Maybach were no longer producing, the Hispano-Suiza works were committed to the new idiom in the shape of the exotic Pegaso, Delage and Delahaye were near the end of a long slow decline, and the surviving German contenders had barely recovered from war and defeat. Corporation politics had pushed Buick down-market and out of the carriage trade, and the only new recruit was—surprisingly—Austin, whose big 4-litre cars, first seen at Geneva in 1947, were poor man's Bentleys rather than Daimlers.

Subsequent developments were predictable. Alvis' image grew steadily more sporting, right up to their demise in 1967. The true Packards vanished in 1956, and the Armstrong Siddeley four years later. BMW, after a spell with prestige V-8s, discovered only just in time that this did not pay. Daimler fell into the fatal trap of challenging Rover, Jaguar, and Rolls-Royce at the same time: their production of super-cars was always very small (205 of the 5.5-litre straight-eights between 1946 and 1953), and by 1968 anything with the famed fluted radiator grille was a

Jaguar in all but name. Chrysler, though they gave their costly Imperial line the status of a separate make in 1955, never managed to give it a corresponding individuality. In 1969, the market was effectively bounded by Rolls-Royce/Bentley in Britain, Cadillac and Lincoln in the U.S.A., and Mercedes-Benz as the status symbol of western Europe—not to mention its role as the recognized "car of state" in emergent republics. The vast ZIL limousines made in the U.S.S.R. were badges of rank and never on commercial sale to anyone, and the same went for China's rather similar Honq-Qi. As for the big V-8s at the top of the Nissan and Toyota ranges, these were seldom encountered in their native Japan, and never anywhere else. In any case, they were less than impressive. One could not regard the 3-litre Toyota Century, with its 112.5-in (2.86-m) wheelbase and "mass-production" specification, as a super-car: a Japanese with a taste for luxury would probably have imported a Mercedes-Benz.

Nor was the sports car always the killer. The executioners of Alvis, Armstrong Siddeley, Hotchkiss, and the others were neither Ferraris nor Maseratis (too cramped and too complex for the everyday driver), nor even more manageable sporting cars like the XK Jaguars—they were the new high-performance sedans. Initially, Jaguar's twin overhead-camshaft line fought it out against the single overhead-cam models of Mercedes-Benz, but other contenders hovered in the wings. Rover's P4 of 1950–64 (always "Auntie" to her friends) was a stodgy piece

172

(*Right*) Evolution of the grand tourer: the BMW 2800CS four-seater coupé of 1969 (*top*), with a seven-bearing overhead-camshaft six-cylinder engine developing 170 horsepower at 6,000 rpm. The use of twin Zenith carburettors rather than fuel injection stamps this car as a creation of the sixties and not of the seventies, although even before World War II one is entitled to expect all-independent springing on a quality car from Germany, and of course one gets it, including the now-fashionable McPherson struts at the front. Coils and semi-trailing arms are used at the rear. Brakes are disc/drum, with dual circuits and servo assistance, and on a car with a dry weight of 1,275 kg (2,811 lb) the power steering is a welcome refinement. Performance contrasts interestingly with that of the 1955 Mercedes-Benz 300SL, bearing in mind that this is a car any layman can handle. The BMW isn't much slower, at 207 km/h (128 mph), it is actually quicker to 80 km/h (50 mph) which it manages in 6.4 seconds, and the magic 160 km/h (100 mph) comes up in a respectable 24.3 seconds. A fuel consumption of 12–15 litres/100 km (19–23 mpg) is reasonable for this class of car. The interior (*centre*) of a left-hand-drive example shows a good instrument layout, central control for the four-speed gearbox (one doesn't really need five speeds on a flexible touring six), well-shaped individual bucket seats, and the now-familiar overflow of controls (wiper speed regulator, cigar lighter, electric window lift) into the console. Boot space (*bottom*) is generous, thanks to a separate underfloor mounting for the spare wheel, while the huge tool kit is something that one has learnt not to expect normally, except on Russian cars.

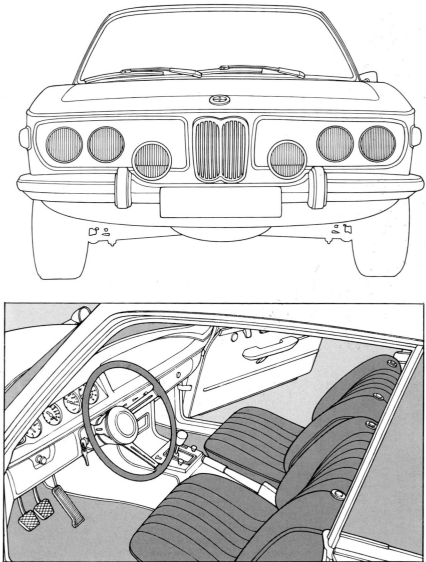

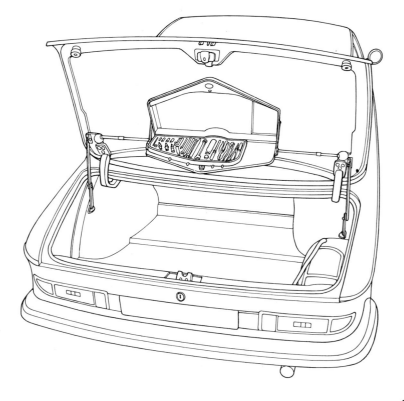

of British tradition hidden under a modern skin, but from 1958 an element of performance intruded into Solihull's wares: first on the 3-litre six, then on the 100-mph (160-km/h) overhead-cam 2000 of 1964, and finally with the 3.5-litre V-8s current from late 1967 onward. If Alfa Romeo's 2600 (1962) was something of a damp squib and notoriously rust-prone, they were still a force to be reckoned with, especially when it came to modestly-priced sporting coupés. Other challengers who moved in on this sector were BMW and Volvo, adding fast sixes to their repertoire in 1967 and 1968 respectively.

Production was formidable. Mercedes-Benz delivered 455,000 of their key 220 series between 1951 and 1965, with production building to 65,000 in a good year. Jaguar, working on a more modest scale, contributed 145,000 compacts and 71,500 full-size sedans between 1951 and 1970. Volvo's overall production climbed steadily from 118,464 in 1964 to 181,500 in 1969, all of these cars using engines from 1.8 litres upwards, and therefore always on the fringe of the market, if not actually in it. Even BMW, the latecomers, had added 75,000 sixes to the score by the end of our period.

Of course, this sector of the market was almost as capricious as it was in America. Since European makers seldom put all their eggs in one basket, there were few total casualties of the calibre of Edsel and De Soto after 1960. Nonetheless, several models fell by the wayside, including Italy's three contenders, the Alfa Romeo 2600, Lancia's Fla-

(*Left*) After the gullwing Mercedes-Benz 300 SL coupé, perhaps the most collectable Classic of the 1950s is the original R-type Continental Bentley (1952–55), of which only 207 were made, almost all with H.J. Mulliner's lovely fastback two-door sedan bodywork. Mechanically, it used the familiar overhead-inlet-valve 4.6-litre Rolls-Royce six-cylinder engine, mated to a superb four-speed synchromesh transmission with right-hand shift (though, alas, the lever was on the column on left-hand-drive cars). Moreover, a 3.08 axle ratio spelt a top speed of 115 mph (186 km/h), three-figure cruising speeds around 100 mph (160 km/h), and the possibility of 21 mpg (13.5 litres/100 km) in gentler driving. But the price—about £5,000 or $14,000 even without sales taxes—was a daunting prospect in 1953.

An even better view of the Bentley's shape as seen from its front end (*below, left*) shows the ingenuity with which the traditional radiator grille has been blended into the scenery. (Italian coachbuilders tended to discard such make-identity wherever possible.) A high fender line gives poor underhood accessibility, but then Bentley owners were not expected to do their own maintenance. The side elevation is interesting as it indicates a surprising degree of rear-seat headroom, thanks to the hypoid rear axle. The back seats (*below, right*) were extraordinarily comfortable, and more room can be gained by folding the central armrest. Except with two very tall people in front, there was reasonable legroom, too, and especially memorable was the almost total absence of wind noise even at 90 mph (145 km/h).

(*Top*) Last of a famous line, the 1959-type Armstrong Siddeley Star Sapphire perpetuated the *marque*'s vee radiator. A sphinx emblem still crouched atop the hood and, in addition to the British wood-and-leather trim, there were an automatic transmission, power disc brakes, and power steering. Externally, the painted radiator shell distinguished this 4-litre from the earlier (1953–58) 3.4-litre cars. Armstrong Siddeley could not, however, withstand the combined onslaught of Jaguar and Rover, and in the summer of 1960 the parent Hawker-Siddeley company decided to concentrate on aircraft.

(*Centre, left*) Wood and leather for the British professional classes on the 1965 Humber Imperial, top of the Rootes line. Also in the package are quad headlights, power steering, automatic transmission, electrically controlled rear dampers, and a vinyl top to distinguish the car from the cheaper Super Snipe. You wouldn't find power front disc brakes (except as an extra) on the Imperial's American contemporaries, although Americans would have expected a V-8 rather than an old-fashioned 3-litre in-line six to propel 3,616 lb (1,640 kg) of car. While 100 mph (160 km/h) were there, the big Humber pitched alarmingly if pushed to the limit.

(*Centre, right*) Introduced at the 1950 Geneva Salon, the 3-litre Alvis upheld traditional British craftsmanship until 1967—by which time it had acquired bodywork styled by Graber of Berne, power disc brakes, a choice of five-speed manual or automatic transmissions, and a useful 150 horsepower from its short-stroke (84×90 mm) six-cylinder pushrod engine. Alas, it had little appeal outside its homeland, and had little to offer that a Jaguar lacked, save scarcity: Alvis' total post-war production was a mere 7,072 units. This TE21 convertible of 1965 was bodied by H.J. Mulliner/Park Ward, a Rolls-Royce subsidiary who bridged the gap after Mullin-

ers of Birmingham and Tickford—Alvis' regular sources—had been taken over by Standard/Triumph and Aston Martin respectively.

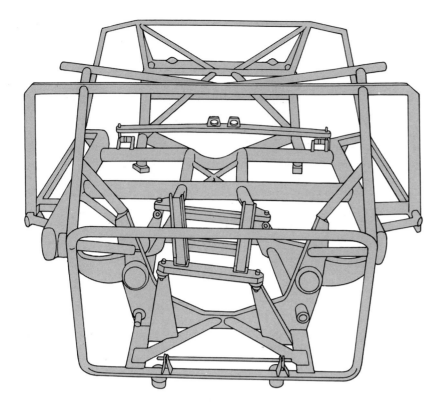

minia, and Fiat's 130 with 2.8-litre V-6 engine. The latter struggled on into the mid-seventies, but production fell short of 20,000 units.

On the lower fringes of the market, one found such truly mass-produced items as the austerer Mercedes, BMC's luxury sedans, and the straight-six and V-6 Fords churned out by Dagenham and Cologne. France, as ever bedevilled by fiscal problems, was stony soil for an anti-Jaguar, but *de luxe* editions of the immortal D-series Citroën catered for her wealthier citizens. By 1969, the ageing but still wholly modern shark-shape had been given an engine worthy of it, a 2.2-litre short-stroke 115-horsepower unit with hemispherical combustion chambers. To its familiar "power assistance for everything" could now be added swivelling headlamps and a heated rear window, if not as yet automatic. Renault's 16 was also evolving into a luxury car.

Civilizing influences were already apparent in sports-car design by the end of the 1940s. They no longer had to be open: Alfa Romeo's six and eight-cylinder *berlinette* by Touring and Fiat's 1100S had shown the way pre-war, and by 1951 Lancia's *Granturismo* Aurelia coupé was in full production. The GT idiom, as we now know it, had been launched.

The prostitution of the GT label from the early sixties onward has been something of a red herring. It has come to be associated with family saloon cars, loaded with all the performance and luxury options, plus a surfeit of external scriptitis. In 1955, however, the meaning was clear to all motorists: a car of sporting specification and driving characteristics, with a 2+2-seater closed body. It did not matter how "occasional" the rear seats were: thus the Lancia, all the Porsches, and the XK140 and XK150 Jaguars qualified, though not the E-type which was unavailable with extra seating until 1966. But even outside the GT category, it is immediately observable that all the great sporting cars of our period were conceived with a roof over their heads, even when ragtops were listed. The Facel Vega, the E-type Jaguar, the DB Astons, the 300SL Mercedes-Benz, and the 3.5-litre Maseratis all fall within this class. The rare American Cunningham (1951–54), while raced in open form, was sold to the public with fixed-head coupé coachwork by Vignale. At a less exotic level, AC soon had an Aceca coupé in production alongside their Ace roadster, Lotus made their international name

with the closed Elite before essaying the open Elan, and Reliant's Scimitar coupés won far wider acceptance than the earlier open Sabres—although this was largely due to some curious suspension geometry on the 1961 roadsters. The specialist TVR was always a closed car, and even the mass-producers were beginning to recognize that not everyone fancied wind in their hair.

Detachable hardtops were generally on sale from 1952–53. But MG had a coupé edition of their A on sale from 1957, and a true GT eight years later, in the B range. Triumph's GT6, a closed Spitfire derivative, came in 1967. Sweden's first commercially successful sports car, the Volvo P1800 (1961), was never offered in open form. That the Swedish climate was ill-suited to roadsters is not in itself a valid reason, for by this time Volvo were firmly established in the U.S.A. Further, the public liked it this way. If American demand lifted Jaguar's open-car sales to 48,456 of all six-cylinder sports types, as against 39,211 closed models, it should be remembered that in pre-E days there were two open types, the drophead and the roadster. More typical is the case of Alfa Romeo, who offered only one variation of each—and still coupés outsold spyders roughly 3-to-1.

Sports-car engineering tended to be a jump or two ahead of main-stream design: limited-slip differentials in 1951, fuel injection in 1954, disc brakes in 1956, radial-ply tires in general use by the beginning of the sixties, and transistorized ignition by 1968. At the very end of our period, Citroën's SM—a true GT—offered a remarkable package. Under the bonnet was a Maserati-built alloy V-6 with four overhead camshafts, driving the front wheels via a five-speed gearbox. The power steering was of variable-ratio type, its assistance decreasing as speed went up, and thus restoring a satisfactory degree of feel at high speeds. Suspension was the now-familiar hydropneumatic, and the end-product was capable of transporting four people at 135 mph (218 km/h), and of wafting them up to 100 mph (160 km/h) in just over 26 seconds. By GT standards, too, it was roomy, if not quite comfortable enough for four large adults.

Independent rear suspension was found on all Mercedes-Benz, on Fiat's semi-experimental 8V (1952), and on Jaguars from 1961. Ferrari was to use beam rear axles until the mid-1960s. De Dion rear axles featured on Aston Martins, Pegasos, Isos, and Gordon-Keebles. Disc brakes had been accepted across the board by 1961, applied to all four wheels on anything with a potential of 120–125 mph (200 km/h) or more. Most cars stayed with a separate chassis, the exceptions being the space-frame of the 300SL Mercedes-Benz and the monocoque structures of Lancia and the later Jaguars.

In the transmission department, Ferrari and Pegaso were early users of five-speed gearboxes (without synchromesh!). Alfa Romeo followed in 1954–55, and towards the end of our period they would be adopted on all the great Italian cars, and also by Fiat for their twin-cam sporting type. They were standard on Aston Martins, and optional on Mercedes-Benz and Porsche. Lamborghinis had the unique refinement of a synchronized reverse gear. The Euro-Americans, however, tended to stay with four forward speeds, since gearboxes—as well as engines—came directly from Detroit. The demand for automatic had scarcely developed, and Mercedes-Benz did not list a fully automatic transmission until 1962. But Jaguar, with an eye on American customers, had automatic XK140s on sale by the end of 1956. Aston Martin's first automatic came a year later, yet the Italians stayed away with a firm hand on the shift.

All in all, the super-car was a far more interesting and enjoyable package than any long-bonnetted "formal" of the 1930s. In 1969 form, it was good for over 150 mph (240 km/h), with acceleration to match. It

was, of course, expensive. In Britain, 1968 prices ranged from Jaguars at £2,117, through the Aston Martin (£4,497) to imported Maseratis from £6,553, Lamborghinis from £7,400, and Ferraris from £7,797: the little mid-engined Dino had yet to cross the English Channel. The money asked for a Ferrari would buy ten VW Beetles or six DS Citroëns. In those days of cheap petrol, 14 mpg (19.5 litres/100 km) was no embarrassment, and in any case a Lamborghini owner could afford a Mercedes for the family and a Mini-Cooper for town work. But servicing could be an embarrassment. While Mercedes-Benz made do with six cylinders and a single overhead camshaft, and Aston Martin, Jaguar, and Maserati with the same number of "pots" plus twin overhead cams, the Ferrari and Lamborghini were the period's only V-12s. The Pegaso, the short-lived Fiat, and the Euro-American brigade were V-8s. Four-overhead-camshaft engines were used by Ferrari, Lamborghini, Pegaso, and the hottest Porsches.

In the midst of all this sophistication, however, one did note an odd, seemingly retrogressive trend—a return to assembled cars, not in the modern sense, but in the sense of cars like the Clynos and Jordans of the 1920s. The difference lay in the type of vehicle itself. Small specialist firms lacked either the facilities or the resources to design or manufacture major mechanical elements. Jaguar, Mercedes-Benz, and Alfa Romeo were big enough to be self-contained, while Aston Martin and the Italian super-specialists were geared to annual runs of 500 cars or less a year and costed accordingly.

(*Opposite*) Maserati had been making racing and sports-racing cars since 1926, but they did not venture seriously into "street" models until 1958 with the 3500GT. This was quite a car, with a 3,485-cc twin overhead-camshaft six-cylinder engine developing 220 horsepower at 5,500 rpm. Originally it had a four-speed synchromesh gearbox and drum brakes: later came an extra forward ratio, fuel injection, and discs (at first only on the front). Some 2,000 of the basic type were built, the last in 1964. But six-cylinder models were still offered in 1969 and, by then, 275 hp were being extracted from 4 litres, while four-cam V-8s had appeared. All the sixes retained conventional semi-elliptic springing at the rear. Seen here are (*left*) the oval-tube chassis frame, (*right*) one of the original Touring-bodied coupés with a superb engine-room beneath the bonnet.

(*Right*) Hardtops for roadsters: a British example from 1956–57, the self-coloured glass-fibre hardtop on the Austin-Healey 100/4, is a proprietary after-market item. Such extras added £45–55 ($125–155) to the price of the car. But even with the late-1960s swing towards closed sporting models and the compromise *targhe* of Porsche and others, factory-fitted hardtops survived. (*Below*) The master touch of Pininfarina's styling is unmistakeable on the Alfa Romeo 1600 Spyder (1966), a characteristic twin overhead-camshaft four with five-speed gearbox and all-disc brakes.

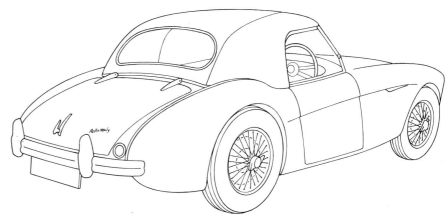

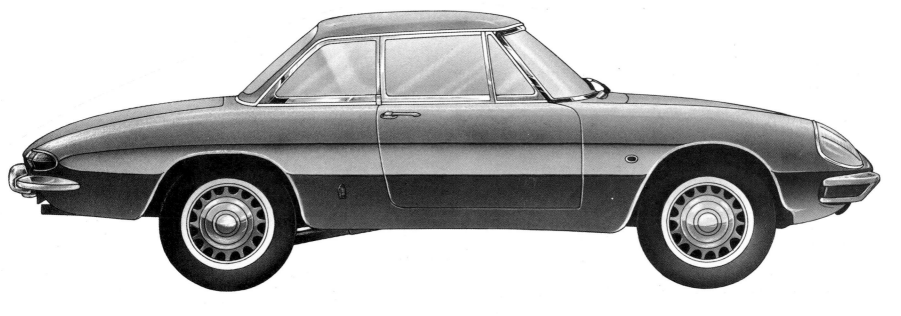

(*Right*) Not a true GT is the Bristol 404 of 1954—it seats only two. Families bought either the two-door 403 or the four-door 405, the latter sharing the 404's "hole in the wall" grille and single-panel curved windscreen, and also carrying its spare wheel in the left-hand front wing. Mechanically, the Bristol was an update of the 1938/39 BMW 327/80 with the same 2-litre six-cylinder overhead-valve engine. For the man with £3,543 to spend, there were few pleasanter ways to enjoy cruising at 100 mph (160 km/h). For the American market only, the Arnolt firm offered a Bertone-bodied open variant at a modest $4,250.

(*Left*) The frog-eye look, or the Austin-Healey Sprite in its original 1958 form. Twin-carburettor BMC A-type four-cylinder engine giving 43 horsepower at 5,200 rpm, straightforward four-speed gearbox, drum brakes, quarter-elliptic rear springs, and a simple unitary structure, the lot weighing 1,463 lb (about 660 kg) on the road, good for over 80 mph (130 km/h) and capable of rushing up to 50 mph (80 km/h) in 13.7 seconds. Driven gently , it's as frugal as a small sedan, and the whole bonnet/fender assembly lifts up to give access to the works. The ride is harsh, admittedly, and directional stability isn't quite what it might be, while the top has to be wrapped round its frame before you put it up: but can you expect more for £679? Some 49,000 customers felt that one couldn't.

(*Right*) Touring of Milan styled the standard Aston Martin DB4 sedan of 1959, a 2+2-seater, which offered 240 horsepower and 140 mph (225 km/h) from a 3.7-litre twin overhead-camshaft six-cylinder engine. For even more enthusiastic drivers there was the GT version, with three Weber carburettors, bigger disc brakes, a shorter wheelbase, and a limited-slip differential, plus the performance to be expected from an extra 62 horse-power. More aggressive still, though suitable for street use, was Zagato's 1961–62 version seen here, strictly a two-seater, and produced in small numbers—25 in all.

(*Above*) Perhaps the most delightful small Italian of the 1950s, and ancestor of the classic Alfa Romeos of the two ensuing decades—Orazio Satta's inspired 1956 Giulietta Sprint Coupé. Bertone did the styling, the mechanics were classic Alfa with a 1,290-cc twin overhead-camshaft four-cylinder engine giving 65 horsepower, and all the great Alfa virtues were there: superb brakes, sensitive handling, and an "in or out" clutch. Better still, the unpleasant column shift of contemporary sedans had given way to a floor-mounted lever, and there was a spyder version for open-air enthusiasts. Failings were a notably rust-prone hull, a nasty umbrella-handle handbrake, and (for British customers) no right-hand-drive option for several years to come.

(*Right*) When is a Fiat not a Fiat? Certainly when Austrian-born tuning wizard Karl Abarth laid hands on a rear-engined 600 floorpan, and added a streamlined body by Zagato. This Abarth *Mille* was a popular Italian small sports model of the early 1960s. Suspension is lowered Fiat, and all the other Fiat elements are suitably reinforced. But where the standard article stood 1.4 m (55 in) off the ground, your Abarth is only 1.1 m (43 in) high. How fast it went depended on the degree of tune: 109 mph (170 km/h) with pushrods and single carburettor, but 130 mph (210 km/h) with a twin overhead-camshaft head and twin dual-choke instruments by Weber. The all-disc brakes of later *Milles* were a necessity.

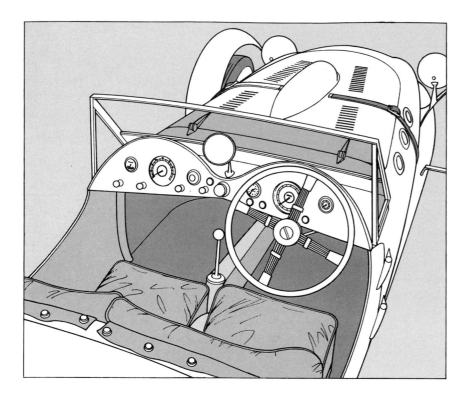

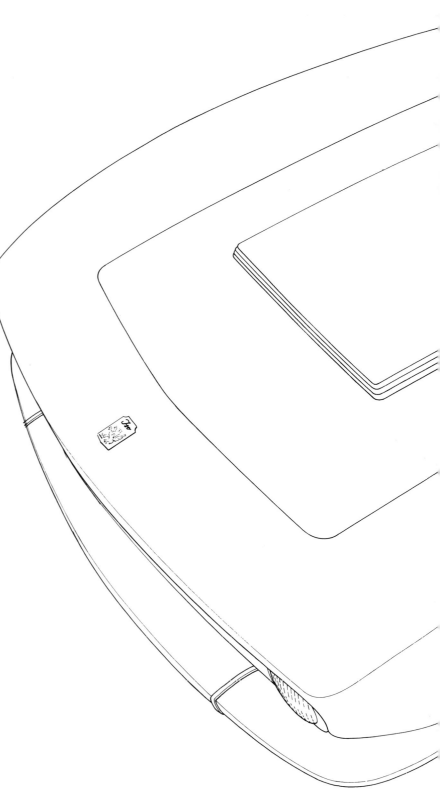

The problem was less acute when the car itself was simple and modest. Morgan bought engines from Standard-Triumph, Ford, and Rover during our period, Lotus from Coventry-Climax and other sources, and Frazer Nash and AC from Bristol. The end-product was individual enough to escape the "assembled car" label, and its sponsors were certainly better off than the unhappy Facel Vega management in France, who wanted a 1.6-litre *petite routière* in 1959 and had to create an engine from scratch. It was probably no more of a "travelling oil leak" than two of its contemporary rivals, MG's Twin Cam and Fiat's 1500S. The difference was that Fiat and BMC could afford a small-production mistake, and Facel could not. By the time they had recognized the error of their ways, and gone shopping for a reliable engine with Volvo, it was too late to save the company. This was ironic, for Facel's revival of the French *grande routière* tradition—launched in 1954—had followed a safer route with a fair degree of success, confirmed by the number of their imitators. Their engines and automatic transmissions, if not the manual boxes, had been purchased from Chrysler in America. The Anglo-American sports hybrid of the 1930s had been reborn, albeit in France this time.

It was inevitable. The French specialist manufacturers were dying on their feet, hence Jean Daninos' determination to redress the balance. Firms like Jaguar would not sell engines, and in any case a complex straight-six was not the answer. By contrast, the new American V-8s were cheap and powerful—they were also constantly being uprated. Not for Facel the problems of Railton in 1935, having to take whatever engines were available, with no prospects of many more horsepower in the near future. The breed had never, in fact, become extinct. In Britain, Sydney Allard had stayed in the game, using the British-built 3.6-litre Ford V-8 for home-made cars, but shipping engineless vehicles across the Atlantic, there to be fitted with the latest overhead-valve creations from Cadillac, Oldsmobile, and Chrysler. Other less successful attempts to marry American engines and Continental chassis had been the front-wheel-drive Rosengart (1946) and the Italian Italmeccanica (1950). Healey had built Nash-engined roadsters for the U.S. market from 1950 onward.

Euro-American crossbreds. The 1951 Allard J2 from Britain (*opposite, top*) was a legacy of the 1930s, conceived by Sydney Allard as a tough mount for English-style "trials", sprints, hill-climbs, and sports-car racing. Even in post-war guise, there were few civilized amenities, as this cockpit view shows—but with a weight of 1,063 kg (2,342 lb) and a 5.4-litre Cadillac V-8 engine, acceleration was staggering. Currency problems forced Allard to ship J2s engineless to the U.S.A., where customers could fit the V-8 of their choice. Britons got the faithful old Dagenham-built 3.6-litre Ford, with or without an overhead-valve conversion. The more civilized Allards sold well in the car-starved 1940s, but they were putting on weight by 1952, when the P2 sedan was announced with a forward-tilting hood (which antici-

pated the later Triumph Herald, though Triumph did not mount the spare wheel underneath, nor did they use hydraulic rams to raise it), also returning to the 1920s with a right-hand gearshift. Home-market cars (there were very few) still had to make do with the aged Ford motor. Representative of a new and more sophisticated generation was the 1966 Iso, using a 5.4-litre Chevrolet V-8 unit which fitted rather tightly under the hood, simpler than an Italian V-12 but not very accessible. If, however, one was content not to look at the power pack, the external appearance of these hybrids was authentic Italian, as in the case of Iso's 1968 Grifo (*above*) with the same 400-horsepower Chevrolet engine that was used by contemporary Corvettes. The alloy wheels were genuine, too.

181

(*Left*) *Doyenne* of the new Euro-Americans, one of the last Facel II coupés made in 1964 shows off its unmistakable vertical headlamp clusters and centre-lock wire wheels. The angular roofline gave better all-round vision, the disc brakes were improved, and (for the British market, at any rate) the rear shock-absorber settings were electrically controlled. The 6.3-litre Chrysler V-8 engine could be mated either to its regular Torque-Flite automatic transmission or to a four-speed all-synchromesh box by Pont-à-Mousson. In this latter form, a brutal 390 horsepower were available, but the makers' finances were tottering, and only 184 Facel IIs were delivered in three seasons.

(*Right*) Alongside Italy's Fiat-derivatives, France had her Renault-based sports cars, and Alpine's link with the parent firm paralleled that of Abarth on the other side of the Alps, the *marque* being handled through the Renault sales organization in a number of foreign countries. Jean Rédélé's coupés based on various rear-engined Renault themes dated back to 1956, and typical of their mid-sixties offerings was this Alpine A110 with, basically, R8 mechanics. Servo disc brakes, all-independent springing, and rack-and-pinion steering were part of the package, but buyers could have four or five forward speeds, and four-cylinder pushrod engines in the 1,100–1,300-cc bracket giving anything from 65 to 120 horsepower. The 1,255-cc version was credited with 127 mph (205 km/h), and the *marque* was a major force in international rallying during the later 1960s.

(*Right*) After 1963, there were no true Mercedes-Benz sports cars, only a line of refined and beautifully made roadsters with six-cylinder overhead-camshaft engines. From the original 230SL, they progressed to this 250SL (2.5 litres, seven main bearings) in 1967, and ultimately to the 280SL which saw our period out. Fuel injection was standard, and the new low-pivot swing axles at the rear eliminated most of the handling defects of earlier Mercedes-Benz cars. All these models could be bought with power steering and automatic transmission. Speeds of 115–120 mph (185–195 km/h) were possible, and sales of these admirable luxury tourers were good—44,312 units between 1963 and 1971.

(*Left*) Euro-American brute force: the AC-Shelby Cobra 427 of 1967. The body is that of the AC Ace of 1954, and the car uses the same twin-tube frame, but all-coil independent suspension replaces the earlier transverse-leaf arrangement, while greater traction means wider rims and flared wheel arches. With AC's aged 2-litre six, the car did just over 100 mph (160 km/h)—but with 7 litres and 425 horsepower from Ford of America's hairiest V-8, one is thinking in terms of 150 mph (240 km/h), and it doesn't take long to get there. Some 1,500 Cobras of all types (earlier ones had 4.3- and 4.7-litre engines) were made between 1962 and 1969, and the theme would become a favourite with the replicar industry in the 1980s.

(*Right*) Purpose in every line: the Lamborghini Espada of 1968 looks as if it's doing 150 mph (240 km/h) even when it's standing still, and is in fact quite capable of such velocity. It was the company's best seller, with 1,277 examples sold up to 1975. The need for four seats dictates a conventional engine location, but the 3.9-litre V-12 engine has four overhead camshafts and the six carburettors are fed by twin electric pumps. There are five forward speeds with Lamborghini's usual synchronized reverse gear and, for a driver's car such as this, power steering is not an option, much less automatic. Power windows and air conditioning, however, come as part of the package, as do centre-lock wheels.

The Facel, however, represented a short cut into the super-car bracket. Chassis and styling were uniquely European. Further, Facel would be the only purveyors of Euro-Americans forced to make their own manual transmissions. Four on the floor were generally available with most high-performance American V-8s by 1963, and the engine/gearbox package came cheap: £400 (say $1,100) for a complete 5.4-litre Chevrolet unit delivered in Britain. Thus, the Facel's imitators came in droves during the early sixties. They themselves were forced to suspend operations in 1964, and the British Gordon-Keeble, perhaps the best of the hybrids, ended a chequered career three years later—but in 1969 the contenders included three Britons (AC, Bristol, Jensen), three Italians (Bizzarrini, de Tomaso, Iso), and a solitary Swiss (Monteverdi). Monteverdi, Jensen, and Bristol shopped with Chrysler, while the others used Chevrolet or Ford units. Their wares extended from that Spartan "motorcycle on four wheels", the AC Cobra, to the luxurious Bristol, conservative in line, beautifully made, and available only with automatic.

The power, too, was there. On European cars credited with 300 horsepower or more in 1966, four out of seven (two AC models, the Bizzarrini, and the Iso) had U.S.-built engines, the 7-litre AC topping the league with 425 hp, by comparison with the 400 of the most potent roadgoing Ferrari. And if, on paper, nobody could match the Ferrari Superfast's 174 mph (280 km/h), the AC, Bizzarrini, and Iso Grifo two-seaters could all top 150 mph (240 km/h). Price-wise they were competitive as well. In Switzerland in 1963, the small-production AC Cobra was only marginally more expensive than an E-type Jaguar, and actually cost less than a Chevrolet Corvette at 28,900 francs. In 1969, cheapest of the big four-seater sports sedans on the Swiss market was the Chevrolet-powered Iso, at 44,500 francs, less than was asked for Ferrari's little rear-engined 2-litre Dino.

In the long run, of course, such scissors-and-paste jobs could not compete against Ferrari, and their vogue was curtailed by 1973's energy crisis and the ensuing shrinkage of American engines. A really big V-8 with quadrajet carburation and four-speed all-synchromesh gearbox could deliver Italian performance: not so its stifled, automatic-only successor with 150 dubious horsepower. Only Bristol and de Tomaso were still cataloguing Euro-Americans in 1982, and their combined efforts accounted for around 250 cars a year.

Front-wheel drive had few recruits in the true sports-car field, apart from the Panhard Junior Sports, its close relative the DB, and a few other minor French makes using the same mechanical elements. The fashionable small sports sedan of 1962–69 was, however, the Mini in its ultimate Cooper S form with 1.3-litre engine, capable of around 100 mph (160 km/h) with the usual Mini handling, backed by BMC's service network. Many people hoped for an MG derivative, and prototypes were built. But they never reached production, leaving Abingdon to close in 1980 after building obsolete designs to the last.

By contrast, rear-engined sports cars had a considerable vogue even before the mid-position came into fashion from 1966. This was largely because the specialists had three eminently suitable base-vehicles on which to work: Fiat, Renault, and Volkswagen. The immortal Porsche had first seen the light of day in 1948 as a VW-based special using secondhand bits and pieces, and its layout—if nothing else—remained Beetle right up to the demise of the 356 series in 1965. The success of this formula can be gauged from Porsche's production: 335 cars in 1950, but 5,000 in 1956, and 10,000 in 1964, the last year before the flat-six 911 came in fully.

With its engine mounted over the rear axle and nearly 60% of its weight on the rear, the Porsche could corner very fast, although alarming oversteer set in if the limit was exceeded. Once the knack was acquired, however, the cars were uncatchable on a twisty mountain road. Porsche's mid-1950s catalogue read rather like a driver-training course: one won one's spurs on the sedate 44-hp *Damen* (note the semantics!), capable of 90 mph (145 km/h), and worked one's way— bank balance permitting—to the Carrera, externally the same car, but with a four-cam 2.2-litre power unit in its tail. This would do 124 mph (200 km/h) in the right hands. Porsche stayed with horizontally opposed rear engines throughout our period and well beyond, the fiercest of their 1969 line being a 2.2-litre six with dual-circuit disc brakes and five forward speeds. From 1965, Fiat offered some delightful coupé and spyder developments of their little 850 sedan.

Mid-engines, with their superior weight distribution and safer handling, were only beginning to gain ground at the end of the sixties. First of the new generation was the short-lived Italian ATS (1963) with a 2.5-litre twin overhead-cam V-8 engine mounted ahead of its gearbox, in a tubular frame with all-coil springing. Lamborghini's Miura with its transverse V-12 unit came in 1966, while also transversely engined were the original Dino Ferrari (1968) and the British Unipower which utilized, in effect, a Mini power pack at the "wrong end". Other small cars in this class were the Lotus Europa with a Renault engine at the rear of

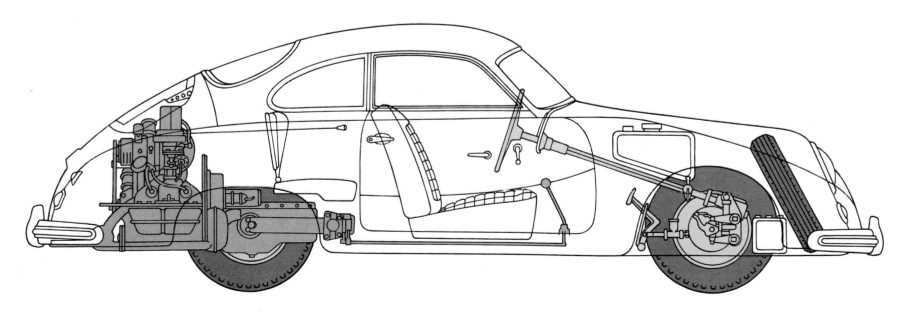

a backbone frame, the French Matra with V-4 Ford engine, and the Ginetta G15 on which the Hillman Imp unit sat in front of, rather than over, its driving axle.

Attractions were short bonnets, a low centre of gravity, and a low frontal area. The Ferrari's height of 44 in (1.11 m) compares interestingly with the 52 in (1.32 m) of Fiat's similarly powered, front-engined coupé. The little Unipower stood a mere 41 in (1.03 m) off the ground, and this, with the weight saving, made it both faster and more frugal than a Mini-Cooper in the same state of tune. Failings were, of course, poor rearward vision and a high noise level. Insulating the engine room was a headache, as was cooling. Nose radiators called for some very elaborate plumbing. There was also the problem associated with true rear-engined cars: long and woolly gear-shift linkages, which militated against the whole concept of a machine built for the pleasure of driving.

It was almost comforting to step down into the world of the popular sports car, where—Fiat apart—the *système* Panhard reigned unchallenged from 1951 to 1969, where pushrod engines still sufficed (they had to: anything else would have ruined budgets), and where most customers were resigned to side-curtains rather than wind-up windows.

In the 1930s, cheap sports cars had been British, they had small-capacity engines—thanks to the then prevailing horsepower tax—and they were suspended on beam axles with semi-elliptic springs and friction dampers. The Morgan's sliding-pillar independent front suspension was an exception. The formula was not very different in 1951, although MG had gone to coil-spring independent front suspension in 1950, and Jowett's Jupiter (never a volume seller even if one of Raymond Chandler's anti-heroes drove it) had educated the sports-car public into full-width body work, space frames, and—alas!—column shift. There was, it is true, a sign of tax-emancipation in Morgan's adoption of the 2.1-litre Standard Vanguard unit (18 hp under the old formula), replacing the 1.3-litre engine of the old days. And while MG stayed with 1.25 litres, there was a move towards bigger units better suited for American road conditions. Hot on the Morgan's heels came the first TR Triumph (1952) using the same Standard engine in 2-litre guise, the Austin-Healey 100 with the Austin Atlantic's 2.7-litre unit, and the less successful Ford-powered Palm Beach from Allard. The 1955 Shows saw the streamlined MG-A, by 1957 Triumphs had disc front brakes, and unitary construction arrived on the MG-B (1962).

There was also Colin Chapman of Lotus, whose space-framed sports cars had paved the way to the unitary glass-fibre Elite coupé. The

Seven continued all through the 1960s, attaining 100 mph (160 km/h) with a 1.5-litre Ford engine, not to mention the maximum of discomfort for the crew—but by 1963 it was also possible to buy a more civilized open model, the Elan with twin overhead-camshaft engine, backbone frame, all-independent springing, and all-disc brakes. A cheaper contemporary, Triumph's Spitfire, likewise had all its wheels independently sprung (though the Herald-type swing-axle back end did not help the handling), while from 1965 the big TR family received independent rear suspension as well. There was even a Euro-American in the group: between 1964 and 1967 the second-generation Sunbeam Alpine, yet another Hillman Minx derivative, became the Tiger when a Ford V-8 engine was shoehorned under its bonnet. And whereas the Germans cornered the European prestige market, Britain hung on to her favourite sector. During our twenty years, MG made 426,890 sports cars, and Triumph more than 340,000, less than one in every ten TRs going to a home-market customer. Even Lotus managed to produce some 12,000 Elans between 1963 and 1973.

Nobody else had much of a chance. France had little to offer, and the German Porsche—while compact—was never cheap or suitable for the uninitiated. The small twin-cylinder coupés of BMW and NSU had little international impact, and Glas' later efforts with four-cylinder engines and cogged-belt overhead camshafts were seldom seen in foreign lands. Alfa Romeos were always priced well above the British opposition, though the 1.3-litre Giulietta was a delightful little car, streets ahead of an MG. Fiat catalogued small sports models almost from start to finish, but their faster 1100s never recaptured the promise of past years, while the early twin-cam convertibles burned oil in alarming quantities. It was not until 1965 that they would start to make inroads into British territory, first with the rear-engined 850, and then with the twin-cam 124 series.

As for the Japanese, they had nothing to offer before Datsun's Fairlady (1964). The Australian quip that "it was a great MG-A replacement, only MG invented the B first" was not wholly unjust, since specifications closely paralleled the B's—even down to the visibly Austin origins of its 1.6-litre twin-carburettor pushrod engine. However, it lacked the magic of a name. The tiny twin-cam Honda was too much of a toy, while Toyota's double-cam six-cylinder GT and the twin-rotor Mazda-Wankel Cosmo were merely interesting harbingers of a future no one could yet foretell. In fact, the world's best-selling sports car of all time was around in 1969, although not many people had seen it. This was, of course, the Z-series Datsun coupé with all-independent springing and six-cylinder overhead-cam engine, a clear indication that the Japanese knew that the days of the roadster were over. Three quarters of a million units later, they had been well and truly vindicated.

A curious sports-car renaissance was under way in America, though the true enthusiast—who bought foreign *faute de mieux* in 1950—was still buying foreign, albeit from choice, in 1969. Of the home-grown items, only the Chevrolet Corvette approached anywhere near his ideal. The other native products were "personal cars" (Henry Ford II's own label for the original Thunderbird in 1955): "pony-cars" like the Mustang and the other sporty compacts, or, in the ultimate development of the theme, "muscle-cars" (Dodge Charger R/T, Pontiac GTO).

Europeans would have been horrified by some of the earlier efforts. The original Corvette of 1953 was the marriage of a shortened standard frame, a tuned but still basically standard six-cylinder engine, and a glass-fibre body. Door sealing was a constant nightmare and, for some unaccountable reason, two-speed Powerglide was compulsory. The Corvette, however, was raced, and racing lessons were learnt. The new short-stroke V-8 arrived somewhat tardily in 1955, a manual transmis-

Porsche's 356 spanned the first fifteen years of our period and accounted for over 75,000 cars in regular pushrod form: the four-cam Carrera versions were made in very limited numbers, starting in 1955. This sectioned side elevation reveals the car's Volkswagen ancestry, and indeed the earliest Porsches were pure VW from the mechanical standpoint, though the Beetle's original cable-operated brakes were an immediate casualty. They were out of place on a motor car which, even in its 1,100-cc touring guise of 1951, was capable of 140 km/h (87 mph). The low centre of gravity is very apparent, while the front-mounted tank could affect the handling as fuel supplies were used up. The battery is mounted below and behind the spare wheel. The platform chassis has a very rigid bulkhead aft of the fuel tank, and heavy box-section sills. Authentic Volkswagen in concept is the front suspension by torsion bars and trailing arms: its ancestry goes back to an even more illustrious piece of rear-engined machinery, the sixteen-cylinder Grand Prix Auto Union of 1934, another Ferdinand Porsche creation. The rear seats on the 356 are very occasional indeed, though well trimmed: the backrest folded down to give extra luggage accommodation.

America's sports car, the Chevrolet Corvette, was less than inspiring in its original 1953 guise: a shortened stock chassis with Hotchkiss drive, and three carburettors boosting a standard in-line six to 150–160 horsepower. Two-speed automatic was compulsory until 1955, so the Corvette was no threat until an overhead-valve short-stroke V-8 arrived. Then things started to move: except for the side sculptures and the factory-extra hardtop, the 1959 looked rather like the 1953, but its 225 hp and the same basic chassis, suspension, and brakes gave you Jaguar performance without Jaguar roadholding. (*Opposite, top*) The 1961 Corvette had 11-inch drum brakes (*1*) which couldn't cope despite cooling slots in the wheels, (*2*) semi-elliptic outboard rear suspension (though the opposition, Jaguar apart, admittedly had yet to go "independent"), (*3*) a box-girder frame, and (*4*) a smooth-sounding dual exhaust. Transmission was three-speed all-synchromesh (four speeds or automatic remained options) and, with the fuel-injected version (315 hp) of the latest 4.6-litre V-8, top speed was well over 200 km/h (124 mph).

From 1963, as shown by this Sting Ray (*above, opposite bottom*), the Corvette was redesigned with a shorter wheelbase, all-new styling in a shark-like idiom, retractable headlamps, and (most important) all-independent suspension. (*Left*) The engine's fuel-injection equipment fitted neatly between the two banks of cylinders, with the radiator's separate header-tank filler at the side. Four-wheel disc brakes were added for 1965, and by 1969 a standard Corvette (5.7 litres, 300 hp) was good for 225 km/h (140 mph): with the 7-litre 435-hp unit, 257 km/h (160 mph)

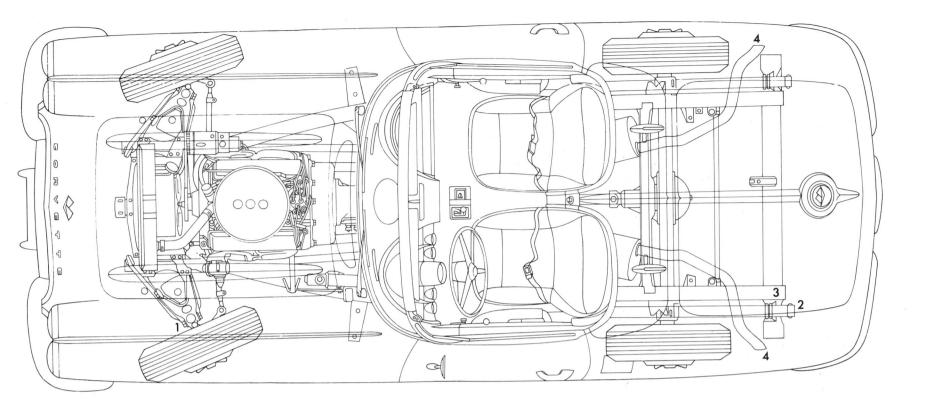

were claimed. Open and closed models were listed—the new line did not lend itself to detachable hardtops—and the year's production was 38,762 units, an interesting contrast with the 12,727 Porsche 911s delivered that year, or Jaguar's total output of 57,240 six-cylinder E-types between 1961 and 1970. Just about the only factor common to all these Corvettes is the glass-fibre body, holding the production record for this form of construction. But one should not forget the ever-impressive interior (*see page 69*) and, for pedestrians who could not enjoy its improved luggage accommodation, the recurrent view of that disappearing rear end with an emblem of crossed race-flags.

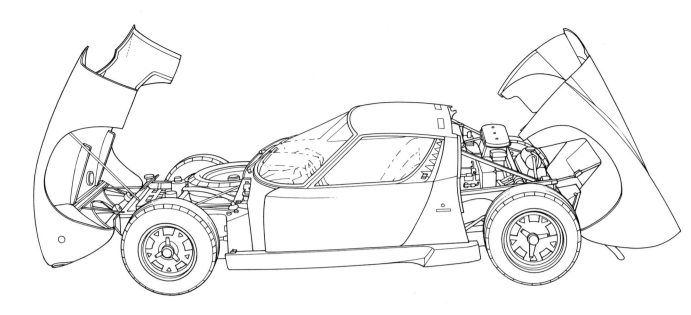

Circumventing some of the problems of a mid-engined layout, on the Lamborghini P400 Miura coupé first seen at the 1966 Geneva Salon. The power was provided by a transversely mounted 3.9-litre four-cam V-12 unit, with a five-speed all-synchromesh transaxle (even reverse was synchronized), all-coil independent suspension, and dual-circuit disc brakes. The advertised top speed of 300 km/h (186 mph) was certainly on the optimistic side, but 270–280 km/h (170–175 mph) were within the car's compass. Price varied from country to country, but a fair indication is furnished by Switzerland, where you paid as much for a Lamborghini as you would for two and a quarter E-type Jaguars or one and a half Cadillac sedans. Tilting up the front end gave access to the spare wheel and front suspension units: with the rear section raised, the effect was that of a tilt-cab on a heavy truck.

sion option was listed in 1956, and fuel injection was available a year later. The 1960 model could be had with "four on the floor", and 1963's redesigned Stingray series had all-independent suspension. Four-wheel disc brakes were standard in 1965, years ahead of the rest of the industry, and latter-day Corvettes were good for 140 mph (224 km/h) when fitted with the biggest optional V-8, of 7 litres capacity.

The original Thunderbird, by contrast, was a triumph of styling over design, via some clever chassis shortening. It sold on such touches as its Continental spare wheel, its "Thunderbird Special" engine (a Ford exclusive, though you could have it in some quite ordinary Mercurys!), and the detachable hardtop with oval portholes. The early cars were quite fast, if under-braked, but after 1957 the label was attached to a lumbering, six-seater unitary device which had nothing to distinguish it from other full-sized Fords save a formidable price-tag and a lot of equipment that would normally be "extra".

The 1955 Chrysler 300 was perhaps more important as the forerunner of the true muscle-cars. Seen through European eyes, it was not a sports car at all, merely a lowered New Yorker hardtop coupé with a special grille and an outrageous 300 horsepower, extracted with the aid of quadrajet carburettors. Automatic transmission was compulsory, and the drum brakes were fairly inadequate, but to haul 4,400 lb (2,000 kg) of automobile with five people aboard at 140 mph (224 km/h) was no mean feat. The series was continued into 1965, with output reaching its zenith in 1961.

Buick developed the "personal car" theme a stage further in 1963 with their elegant Riviera coupé, while Studebaker's Avanti with a glass-fibre body was a bid for a four-seater extension of the Corvette theme. There were also high-performance editions of regular sedans. Chevrolet's Impala SS was typical but, although the specification embraced a four-speed manual transmission, stiffer suspension, stronger brake linings, and "quicker" power steering, as well as the biggest V-8s, there was nothing sporting about a sedan built to the standard U.S. length of 210 in (5.3 m).

The pony-cars and muscle-cars were rather more fun. The fashion was set in 1964 by Ford's best-selling Mustang. In its basic form, it featured an undistinguished 3.3-litre six, but even at the beginning the V-8 options ran up to 4.7 litres and 271 horsepower, which gave the car a potential the right side of 120 mph (190 km/h). Handling was by no means in the Triumph or Jaguar class, but dimensions were compact—a wheelbase of 108 in (2.74 m) and a length of 181 in (4.61 m). All the

components used were stock Ford, and any dealer could service it. As for price, the 1966 "factory-delivered" quotation on a V-8 Mustang was $2,522—$100 more than an MG-B, but below a TR Triumph at $2,703—and one got four seats, too. Jaguar E-types started at $5,400-odd and lived in a totally different world.

The Mustang sparked off a whole generation: rival "ponies" like Plymouth's Barracuda and the Chevrolet Camaro, as well as "muscle" offerings in a slightly bigger class. Mercury's variation on the Mustang theme, the Cougar (1967), had three inches (8 cm) of extra wheelbase and concealed headlamps to distinguish it, while there was no six-cylinder option, a 200-hp V-8 being standard. Oldsmobile had their 4-4-2, and Buick a GS (Gran Sport). Even the conservative and economy-oriented American Motors had come up by 1968 with the Javelin and AMX coupés, available with V-8s of up to 315 hp.

Pontiac's challengers were the splendid GTO muscle-cars, supported from 1967 in the smaller category by the Firebirds—Camaros with some stylistic variations and their own range of engines. Together, the Mustang, Camaro, Barracuda, and Firebird accounted for nearly a million cars in 1967. Even in 1969, when the force of unbridled power was nearly spent, their share of the market amounted to nearly 750,000 units. That year, too, would see perhaps the ultimate development, Dodge's Charger Daytona. Its 7-litre "street hemi" engine gave over 400 hp, the extended aerodynamic nose incorporated a spoiler, and from the rear deck there sprouted "twin fins and rudders" in aircraft style. This one was never seriously for sale—an $8,000 price tag was sufficient deterrent—but it was catalogued, if only to ensure homologation for stock-car racing, and it could be driven on the road. Most of these muscle-cars, though not the Dodge, could be had as convertibles, but sales were relatively low. The GT idiom had taken over here, too.

Not as yet an important part of the automobile scene were the replicars, destined to become so fashionable in the ensuing decade. Such vehicles were styled, with varying degrees of accuracy, on the lines of Classics from the twenties and thirties, only with modern running gear. Here glass-fibre was in its element, but even then such contraptions were very expensive to make, and would become economically viable only when their prototypes had become gilt-edged investments in the auction world. The Achilles' heel of the whole concept was footwear: no problems attended the manufacture of a nineteen-inch wheel, but nobody built modern-type tyres to fit it!

In 1964, the Oklahoman Glenn Pray replicated the 1937 Cord convertible on a four-fifths scale, using a Chevrolet Corvair flat-six power pack to drive the front wheels. Three years later, he had progressed to the easier task of making a mock-1935 Auburn speedster on a modern Ford floorpan. Brooks Stevens' Excalibur SS was a convincing reproduction of a 1928 supercharged Mercedes-Benz based on Studebaker (later Chevrolet) running gear. Initially, only those smaller wheels and the unmistakable V-8 beat gave the game away, but closer inspection would reveal automatic, power steering, and even—occasionally—air conditioning. In Italy, Zagato ran off a small batch of imitation 1930 Gran Sport Alfa Romeos using the works of the same firm's current 1.6-litre Giulia, while the ill-starred Studebaker Avanti was back in production as a replicar within eighteen months of its demise at the beginning of 1964. More of a "nostalgia car" was Vignale's comic Gamine (1967), almost an Enid Blyton creation with its twin-cylinder Fiat 500 unit tucked away in the rounded tail.

Kit-cars were, however, firmly entrenched on both sides of the Atlantic. They were uncommon outside the U.S.A. and Britain, and their origins in the two countries were more than somewhat different. In Britain the target was purchase tax, a wartime impost which survived right through until the era of E.E.C. membership. The rate fluctuated from as low as 30 % to a swingeing 66.7 %, but it was charged only on *complete new* cars, which explains the profusion of uncouth and amateurish station-wagon bodies found on quite expensive chassis (Allard, Alvis) in the later 1940s. These happened largely because on such exotics the waiting-list was short, but even when the sellers' market had receded, purchase tax was still there. It could, though, be evaded by buying the necessary kit of parts and assembling these oneself. It also saved a small maker money, since if he assembled nothing, he needed no assembly line, or even a conventional factory. In Wales, the Gilbern operation was run in its early days from above a slaughterhouse, while in America the King Midget—most persistent of all the nation's minicars—was sold as a kit because complete cars could not be lowered from the second-floor workshop!

Price comparisons make interesting reading. Elva sold their 1962 Courier kit for £650, as against £1,000-odd for a complete car. The cost of an MG-powered TVR coupé was inflated from £880 to £1,299 for those unblest with mechanical skills, and there was a £700 differential in the case of the Lotus Elite.

Small mid-engined sports cars. The French Matra M530 (*below*) came at the end of our period, and featured a glass-fibre body bolted to a welded steel floorpan. The all-independent suspension, rack-and-pinion steering, and all-disc brakes were predictable on a specialist offering of 1969. Matra, still without the Chrysler-Simca connections they later acquired, have abandoned the Renault power units inherited from their predecessors, René Bonnet, in favour of a German engine already used by Saab: the Ford V-4, in this case of 1.7 litres and 90 horsepower. Fixed-head and Targa-roof versions were available, but at 18,510 francs the M530 was more expensive than a 2-litre D-series Cit-roën sedan with all the power assists. In Britain, the 1965 Unipower (*left*) came from a small company in the London suburbs whose normal products were forestry tractors. There was, however, nothing ponderous about their GT coupé, which used a Mini power pack at the "other" end of a space frame to which glass-fibre bodywork was bounded. The rear section of the body swung up to give access to the engine-room, and the Unipower stood a mere 1 m (40 in) off the ground. With a 1,275-cc Cooper S engine installed, 192 km/h (120 mph) were possible: competition versions were some 32 km/h (20 mph) faster. Manufacture ceased in January, 1970, after some 75 cars had been built.

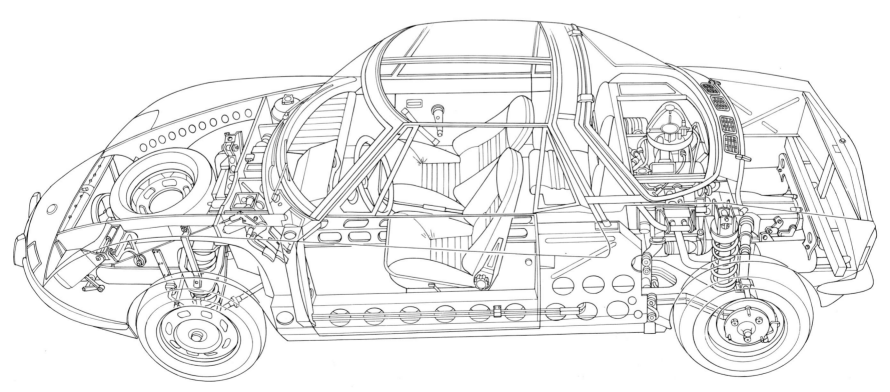

(*Above*) Buick's 1963 Riviera was a "personal car" of the type pioneered by the Ford Thunderbird, but it had a grace totally lacking in later six-passenger editions of the Ford, and chromium plate was strictly rationed. The proportions are so good that one is not conscious of the length of 208 in (5.3 m) or the width of 75 in (1.9 m). Brakes and steering are servo-assisted and, on 6.6 litres and 325 advertised horsepower, 120 mph (193 km/h) present no problems. Early ones, sadly, retain developments of the inefficient two-speed Dynaflow automatic transmission, and front disc brakes are not yet even on the options list.

(*Left*) Mustang by Ford, 1965: the pony-car has arrived. Nearly 700,000 were sold in the first ten months of production—and over a million of this coupé style in less than two years. With the optional 4.7-litre V-8, the car was good for 115 mph (184 km/h), but the stock six-cylinder type was hardly a brisk performer, handling was always uncertain, and the Mustang sold on its image. There was also the useful combination of sporty looks, simple mechanics, and an options list which offered limitless permutations. Further, imitation is the sincerest form of flattery—hence such rivals as the AMC Javelin, Chevrolet Camaro, and Plymouth Barracuda.

Nostalgia triumphant. First of the replicars—planned as a show exhibit for Studebaker in 1964—was Brooks Stevens' Excalibur SS, marketed with Chevrolet running gear after Studebaker closed their engine plant. Here (*right*) is the 1971 roadster version, closely modelled on the 1929 SS-model Mercedes-Benz. With servo disc brakes, power steering, and a choice of four-speed all-synchromesh or automatic transmissions, it was a lot easier on the hands than its prototype. This front chassis view gives the game away—the Excalibur is longer and wider than Stuttgart's masterpiece, bumpers were uncommon on SS models and were never of integral type, and the shrouding around the "dumb irons" is a cover-up for independent front suspension.

(*Below*) An Excalibur SS in the metal, though actually a 1976 four-seater phaeton, is not significantly different in appearance from its 1969 counterpart. From this angle, the wide-rim wheels are not very obvious, but—as always—the bumpers are too heavy to be authentic 1929. The accessory trunk with its canvas covering was a favourite extra of the Classic Era. Nonetheless, the writer has been deceived by an approaching Excalibur in the Californian dusk—until the unmistakeable beat of a well-muffled American V-8 told the truth.

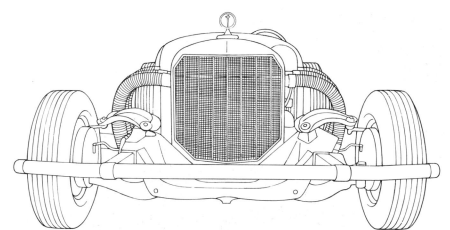

American kit-cars were more an extension of the sport of hot-rodding. "Fancy foreign" models were coming into fashion, but they were expensive, especially in California where extra freight had to be added to the impost of duty. An Austin-Healey catalogued at $2,985 probably cost $3,400 on the road, and dealer-service was none too reliable. So why not build yourself a sports car which looks the part, by taking an old Ford V-8 chassis, shortening it, and fitting a glass-fibre roadster body which does not rust, like the all-steel confections of the Old World? Such a proprietary body could cost anything from $395 to $800. Thus a skilled mechanic could, with the aid of some judicious "hopping up", duplicate at least some of the foreign import's qualities for less than half its price, and still have access to mechanical spares at junkyard prices.

From mere "drop on" body kits—at peak, Californian backyard industry was offering replacement coachwork for Volkswagen, Austin-Healey, and MG as well as for native denizens of the local wrecking yard—a firm would progress to chassis design. Bocar, a major operation, built space-frames and trailing-link suspensions to take proprietary components. Woodill, whose interests ran more to touring machinery, combined their own cruciform-braced chassis and glass-fibre bodies with old-type Ford springing units. Fibersport of Illinois used Crosley engines and chassis, but threw in a Morris gearbox as preferable to Crosley's three-speeder. Kellison would sell a frame, or blueprints for the handyman who wanted to make his own, and their bodies came in various stages of completion from rough shells at $380 up to completely equipped items ready to go on a chassis at around the $600 mark.

The British kit-car business, likewise, operated at several levels. Dellow offered "remanufactured" cars in their early days, these being based on the chassis and registration documents of a near-scrap Ford Ten. Buckler's kits were designed to fit similar remains, although they, like Falcon of Epping, sold their own space-frames. Rochdale pursued the Lotus principle of a monocoque coupé shell—often with four seats to the Elite's two. Other concerns specialized in streamlined glass-fibre bodies which dropped straight onto Ford, or pre-war Austin 7, chassis. As these also dropped straight onto the car's registration documents, one had something with the authentic 1959 look, even though brakes and handling were by no means up to modern standards. The writer has fearsome memories of such a Ford Ten Special, further enlivened by a special cylinder head and multi-carburettor manifold. The quickest way to change gear was to pull hard on the bracing rod for the remote control! The performance was considerable, but the retardation offered by the 1935-type brakes was not. Some of these drop-on bodies were quite interesting: Conversion Car Bodies and Tornado Cars offered sports station wagons in glass fibre. Tornado's Sportsbrake of the early 1960s was a somewhat primitive anticipation of the Reliant Scimitar, just coming into prominence at the end of our period.

Bigger firms, however, went far beyond a mere body. They supplied chassis and suspensions as well, and would sometimes supply the engine even if they did not make it. The Elva, Fairthorpe, Ginetta, Tornado, and Turner were all serious sports cars. Lotus offered both the Elite and the Elan fully manufactured or as kits, while others with either option were the long series of TVR coupés from Blackpool with engines by MG, Coventry-Climax, or Ford, and the Welsh Gilbern. By the end of our second decade, they had progressed to sophisticated four-seater sports sedans with Ford V-6 engines and overdrive or automatic options. But the cars were still available to the home builder, right up to the introduction of the E.E.C.'s Value Added Tax with its "goods and services" clause.

Just how long the task took depended on the skill and patience of the builder—and on the manufacturer's optimism. Turner considered that their 1961 sports-car kit could be put together in 24 hours. At the other end of the scale, Savage, a Californian builder who offered only bodies, reckoned that 600 hours were par for a really good turnout.

Neither luxurious nor sporting—in concept, at any rate—were the all-wheel-drive vehicles, an important spin-off of World War II. Archetype of the whole family was the Jeep, created by Bantam (the old American Austin company) in 1940, but produced in bulk by Ford and Willys. The latter firm had it in civilian production by the end of 1945, and its manufacture continued without interruption right through our period, undisturbed by 1954's Kaiser-Willys merger or by the dropping of the Willys label in 1963. Among foreign licencees were Hotchkiss in France (Jeeps outlived private car production by a good fifteen years) and Mitsubishi in Japan.

In its basic form, the Jeep was a simple go-anywhere vehicle with a high ground clearance, minimal bodywork, and disengageable drive to the front wheels. It had synchromesh and hydraulic brakes, but no other amenities. Rear-wheel drive was recommended for normal road work, to save wear on tyres and transmission. Its main advantage, apart from off-road performance, was its use of cheap standardized components. Disadvantages were discomfort, harsh suspension, and a fearsome thirst for fuel. By 1951, several Jeep derivatives were on the market. Britain offered the Landrover, France the Delahaye VLR, and Italy the Fiat Campagnola. Japan's contenders were the Toyota Land Cruiser and the Nissan Patrol, both with six-cylinder truck engines. The Fiat and Delahaye featured all-independent springing, a step in the right direction, but the latter proved too complicated for the French Army's liking and soon vanished from the scene.

Sophistication was on the way. There had been a Jeep station wagon (initially with two-wheel drive only) as early as 1947, and this was followed by the Jeepster—available, like later wagons, with a six-cylinder engine, and endowed with sporting open four-seater bodywork. Landrovers acquired proper, if poorly soundproofed, cabs in place of full-length canvas tilts, as well as station-wagon options. A diesel Landrover was catalogued from 1958, to improve operating economy. A real breakthrough came in 1963 with the Jeep Wagoneer, a six-cylinder overhead-camshaft wagon capable of 90 mph (145 km/h) with no loss in off-road performance. Better still, it could be had with automatic and power steering.

During the 1960s, the light 4×4 increased in popularity, with entries in the U.S.A. from International Harvester, Ford, and Chevrolet. Austin's Gipsy (1958), with all-independent springing, never matched the Landrover's success, but this was hardly surprising since the latter had notched up its first half-million units in 1966. The 1970 Range Rover, a 3.5-litre V-8, would mark the final combination of luxurious road transport and cross-country ability. It offered disc brakes, permanently engaged four-wheel drive with central differential lock, and a cruising speed of 85 mph (133 km/h)—although not, curiously, power assistance for low-geared steering which required 4.4 turns from lock to lock. The Range Rover was billed as the world's first 4×4 sedan: yet it was not. Way back in 1940, the Russian GAZ 11–73, a six-cylinder sedan of mixed American origins, had been produced in four-wheel-drive (GAZ-61) form, though it had never been marketed, any more than would be the later cross-country editions of the 1946 Pobeda and subsequent Moskvitch sedans. Citroën sold few of their Saharas (1958), which were 2CVs converted to all-wheel drive by the simple expedient of cramming a second complete power pack in the boot.

A more important step forward was the Jensen FF, announced in 1965 and based on the Anglo-American CV8 sports sedan, with which it shared its main chassis, front suspension, Chrysler V-8 engine, auto-

with the firm's 1939 prestige limousine, the straight-eight Grosser. The latter needed a supercharger to extract 230 horsepower from 7.7 litres, or about 32 % less power for 20 % more capacity. Further, it could weigh as much as 7,500 lb (3,400 kg), so 105 mph (170 km/h) was hard work, especially on the ultra-heavy versions used by the Nazi hierarchy.

(*Right*) Tailor-made for heads of state and oil millionaires: the interior of a Mercedes-Benz 600 Pullman, 1966, showing the rearwards-facing jump-seats and trim worthy of a first-class carriage at the zenith of the railroad era. For this ultimate in chauffeur-driven automobiles, with 6.3-litre fuel-injected V-8 engine, power steering, automatic transmission, and air suspension, the makers used a longer-than-standard wheelbase of 3.9 m (154 in), adding up to something like 6.2 m (246 in). Weight was 2,630 kg (5,800 lb). Between 1964 and 1981, production ran to 2,677 of all types, long and short.

The fate of an illustrious specialist coachbuilder. In Germany, Hermann Spohn of Ravensburg had been famed before the war as the "house" supplier to Maybach, makers of six- and twelve-cylinder super-cars. After 1939, there were no Maybachs, and Spohn kept in business by customizing Cadillacs and the like for members of the American forces. It was also arranged that he would clothe the 1956 Gaylord Gentleman (*above*), an American specialty car with Cadillac power intended to sell for $17,500 (£6,250), though this one never got off the ground, and Spohn's relations with its sponsors were any-thing but happy. By the end of the decade the firm was out of business, and a toy maker took over the Ravensburg works. A clever touch on the Gaylord was the slide-out tray for the spare wheel in the boot.

Domestic comfort had an older and more practical aspect: if your foreign licensees aren't happy, there's always the home market. The Simca 6 (*right*) was the post-war French edition of the Fiat *topolino*, and its design had paralleled the native Italian offering since 1936. By 1951 it had the latest styling and overhead valves, but it could not stand up to competition from such modern babies as the 4CV Renault and 2CV Citroën, both four-door and four-seater sedans. Back in Italy, however, Fiat persevered with their not-quite-identical twin, the 500C, until early 1955, with sales in six seasons exceeding 375,000—good going for a pre-war design up against all-new creations by Renault and Morris, among others.

ingredients from the motorcycle industry: small two-stroke engines (which could be reversed, thus obviating the need for a separate reverse gear), positive-stop gear changes, primitive brakes, handlebar steering (on the Messerschmitt), and either three wheels or differential-less back ends (Isetta, Heinkel, Fuldamobil). Most British contenders had three wheels only to save tax, while the Japanese breed was kept alive by concessionary rates on anything with a capacity of less than 360 cc, a length of less than 3 metres, and a width not exceeding 1.5 metres. In Spain, where the streets resembled run-down motor museums and the economy still reeled from three years of civil war followed by five more of isolation, there was no car industry, but a thriving one making motorcycles. Thus the "bubbles" proliferated, though only Gabriel Voisin's Biscuter design achieved really large-scale production.

In actual fact, few of these curiosities did. Of Germany's babies, the best-sellers were Goggomobil (370,000-odd), Isetta (160,000), Lloyd (132,000), and Messerschmitt (50,500), although foreign licence production boosted Heinkel's total far beyond the domestic level of a mere 6,400. In France, the Rovin sold modestly all through the fifties, while the soapbox-like Mochet with its 125-cc engine, hand-starting, and 30-mph (50-km/h) top speed had a certain vogue among those whose alcoholic tendencies had lost them their licences: under French law it required no such paperwork. Of eight or nine British contenders, the only ones seen in quantity were the perennial (1948–65) Bond with swivelling frontal power pack, single-cylinder Villiers engine, and perilous handling—and the Reliant, an old-school three-wheeler with two driven rear wheels and an updated edition of Austin's good old 747-cc four-cylinder Seven, later replaced by an overhead-valve unit of Reliant's own design. Both these factories were still building three-wheelers in 1969, though by this time they were under the same ownership, and Bond had progressed to a four-seater sedan with a rear-mounted Hillman Imp power pack.

Rear engines were fairly general practice, though of the four-wheelers the Biscuter and the British Berkeley drove their front wheels by chain, and three Germans (Gutbrod, Kleinschnittger, and Lloyd) relied on a scaled-down DKW formula. The Messerschmitt was tandem-seated, with a cockpit canopy reminiscent of their wartime Bf 110 fighter air-craft. In its original form, it had a twist-grip clutch and foot-operated gear change, though car-type controls were later adopted. The French Reyonnah had folding front wheels to allow it to park in the hallways of apartment blocks. On Zündapp's Janus, a four-seater even shorter than a Mini, such dimensions were achieved by a rhomboid configuration with Isetta-type doors at each end, and back-to-back seating. This was too much for anyone, though amazingly it found 7,000 buyers. On the British Gordon, made by a football-pool firm, the engine lived in a protuberance at the side of the body. The Argentinian Leeds was amphibious, with an auxiliary propeller drive.

The better minicars (Galy, Heinkel, Isetta) ran to hydraulic brakes, and springing by rubber in torsion was found on several German cars—as well as on the early Japanese Mazda, which also offered such refinements as automatic transmission and a tiny four-cylinder engine. The Goggomobil was a full four-seater attaining 50 mph (80 km/h) on 300 cc. Four-stroke engines were fitted to Heinkels, Isettas, Mazdas, Rovins, and another Japanese car, the Aichi Cony. The ultimate in low comedy was surely Egon Brütsch's Mopetta (1957): 69 in (1.75 m) long, and 26 in (65 cm) wide, it resembled an aircraft drop-tank on three wheels. Power was transmitted from the 49-cc moped engine, via a chain, to the left-hand rear wheel, and fuel consumption was a bird-like 111 mpg (2.4 litres/100 km). A top speed of 22 mph (35 km/h) was depressing, and the solitary occupant felt very vulnerable, out of the sight-line of truck drivers!

Increasing affluence killed the bubble as it would kill the scooter. It offered very little and was not, relatively speaking, a bargain. In Britain, one paid £319 for a Bond, £343 for a Messerschmitt, and £430 for a Reliant in 1956—not the best of values when a full-size 1,172-cc Ford Popular sedan cost only £414. In Germany, admittedly, the whole brigade undercut the Volkswagen (DM 3,790 in basic form), but only the Goggomobil and Lloyd (DM 3,097 and 3,350 respectively) were proper four-seaters, and only the Goggomobil made it into the sixties, challenged hotly by bigger twins such as BMW's 700 and the NSU Prinz family. It is significant that in 1956 Lloyd, too, moved up to a 600-cc four-stroke twin.

In France, the 2CV Citroën was always a better bet, while in Britain

(*Above*) Sporty bubble from Germany—the 1958 Messerschmitt Tiger. It's still steered by handlebars, and the crew's tandem seats lie beneath a canopy straight off a World War II Bf110 fighter plane. But there's now an extra rear wheel, shaft drive, and hydraulic brakes, while the 493-cc two-stroke twin engine gives nearly 20 horsepower, and speeds are up in the high 70-mph range (125 km/h). The bubble's heyday is, however, nearly over—and though the Tiger was catalogued for four seasons, only some 250 were sold, by contrast with over 50,000 of the original three-wheelers.

(*Right*) While Saab and DKW stayed with two-strokes into the mid-1960s, the air-cooled Lloyd—Carl Borgward's "elasto-plast" car—discarded not only its wood-and-fabric body, but its DKW-type 293-cc two-stroke twin engine. By 1959 it had grown into this 593-cc Alexander series, still a transverse twin with front-wheel drive, but now with an overhead camshaft and a useful 25 horse-power, not to mention an all-synchromesh transmission. Perhaps unwisely, the parent Borgward Group tried to sell it in America, where local road conditions called for sustained maximum revs which the motor couldn't take. In any case, sub-utility twins could not compete against the Volkswagen, and Lloyd's sales of 176,000 Alexanders represented barely six months' production of the contemporary Beetle. The fall of Borgward in 1961 was almost predictable.

(*Right*) Product of a caravan (trailer-home) firm and designed by Laurie Bond, the British equivalent of Germany's Egon Brütsch, the Berkeley with its three-piece glass-fibre structure, motorcycle-type transmission, chain-driven front wheels, and light weight—around 800 lb (320 kg)—sold some 2,000 units between 1956 and 1960, plus an additional 2,500 three-wheeled versions better suited to Britain's fiscal climate. Most had two-stroke twin (322-cc) and vertical-three (492-cc) air-cooled engines by Excelsior, but the B95/105 series with a heavier grille featured Royal Enfield's 50-horsepower overhead-valve twin and speeds close to 100 mph (160 km/h).

(*Below*) You could make a station wagon out of almost anything, even the tiny 1961 Bond three-wheeler with its single chain-driven front wheel and alarming characteristics on full lock. This is actually the Ranger model, a van for 350-lb (150-kg) payloads. For a minicar, the Bond had a remarkably long run—1948 to 1965—during which such early crudities as mechanical starting, rear-wheel brakes only, cable-and-pulley steering, and no rear suspension at all (the tyres were supposed to cope) were eliminated. This one has a 246-cc two-stroke Villiers engine, three-wheel brakes, and partly glass-fibre bodywork: as on many such vehicles, one reversed the power unit's rotation to go backwards.

the *coup de grâce* was administered by the Mini in 1959. Finally, from 1957, there was the Fiat 500 with 479-cc air-cooled twin engine and no motorcycle attributes at all. But its non-synchromesh gearbox took some learning, and in its original form it was horribly underpowered, barely attaining 50 mph (80 km/h) and needing nearly 16 seconds to reach 30 mph (50 km/h). This took one back to the 1920s, since comparable figures for the orthodox babies of 1949–50 were 8.7 sec (Morris Minor), 9.7 sec (4CV Renault), and 9.8 sec (Fiat *topolino*). Fortunately for all concerned, the Italian engineers were quick to uprate their new miniature, and it went on to sell for fifteen years, wreaking fresh havoc in the scooter market.

This, the last of the Goggomobils, and the 600-cc NSU represented the remains of a once huge army of models in 1969—although in Japan the breed survived, with Daihatsu and Honda joining Mazda, Mitsubishi, Subaru, and Suzuki in this sector.

In Britain, the contraction of the industry and over-zealous attempts at full market coverage were major causes of a decline already noted. By 1968, too, the cumbersome Leyland combine controlled Jaguar, Rover, and Triumph, as well as former members of the British Motor Corporation. And as we have seen, the Mini, perhaps the most significant technical breakthrough of the whole twenty years, was hardly a "world car".

Here the contraction was seen at its most dramatic. If we assess a major manufacturer in terms of a potential of over 1,000 vehicles a year, Britain had fourteen such in 1951. The empires were Nuffield (MG, Morris, Wolseley, Riley), Rootes (Hillman, Humber, Sunbeam-Talbot), BSA (Daimler, Lanchester), Rolls-Royce/Bentley, Standard-Triumph, and big firms such as Austin, Ford, and Vauxhall with only a single make apiece. By the end of 1960, regroupings and abdications had brought this total down to nine, and it had fallen further to six by

the end of our period. The decline would have been even more marked but for the rise of two hitherto small makers, Lotus and Reliant, during the second decade.

What Britain always offered was variety. In 1953, buyers had the choice of 41 models in large-scale production, and 24 assorted exotics. Relative figures for France, Germany, and Italy were 16, 10, and 7 respectively in the first category—and 4, 10, and 22 in the second. Even in 1969, British industry still fielded 38 popular and 25 specialist models, way ahead of all her major rivals. And this was largely due to the incidence of two national institutions, one old and one new: the sports car and the kit-car.

Britain also clung obstinately, and with some success, to the upper-middle-class touring model of modest capacity, as typified by the Rileys and Triumphs of the 1930s, and as championed in France by Salmson until their demise in 1957. These were, of course, distinct from the volume-selling quality machines (Rover, Jaguar). Perhaps most typical of the category were the Sunbeam-Talbots and Sunbeams of 1951–66, cases of designing an American "dress-up" package into a complete car. The original 90 (1948 on) might use standardized Rootes components: the dashboard was an aesthetic and ergonomic catastrophe, and the steering-column gear-change deplorable. Traditional "sports saloon" bodywork spelt cramped accommodation for four, and even less room for their baggage. Yet stylistically the car was a success, it handled well, cruised effortlessly at 75 mph (120 km/h), and won rallies. One never thought of it as a *mélange* of Hillman and Humber bits.

The same could not be said of the Rapier (1956), which was a Minx in a party frock. Until it was given a "Talbot" grille in 1958, it looked like a Minx from the front, too. The individuality lay in the equipment one got for one's £986—more than was asked for popular 1.5-litre cars, but less than for an imported Fiat or Borgward: overdrive on the top

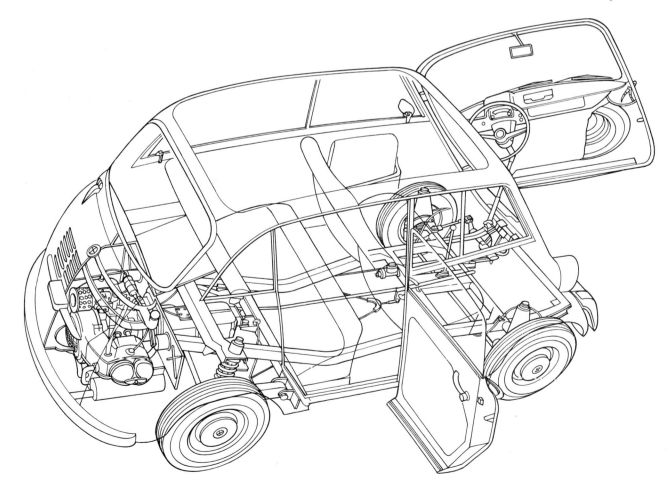

Minicars international. The Isetta, born in Italy and bred in Germany, had evolved by 1957 into this bigger four-wheeler, the BMW 600. Retained are the front-opening door with its jointed steering column (plus in-built spare wheel stowage) while the front end generally is similar. Making the car a full four-seater means adding a rear door on the right-hand side, and the underfloor-mounted rear engine is now a development of BMW's famous motorcycle-type flat-twin, giving 19.5 horsepower from 600 cc. This one was a little too controversial for anyone, and the makers fared a lot better with their conventionally styled 700 series (1959–65) which had no "bubble" affinities.

One of the better French minicars was the Vespa 400 (*above*) of 1958, made by a subsidiary of the famed Italian scooter firm. Outwardly, this neat little cabrio-limousine resembled the Fiat *topolino*—but its 400-cc engine, again a twin-cylinder two-stroke, lived at the rear with its three-speed transmission. The "bonnet" was empty, apart from a battery in a tray behind the detachable grille. By contrast, the 1951 Reyonnah (*left*), also French and tandem-seated like the Messerschmitt, was pure low comedy. It actually had four wheels, the two rear ones close-set, but the front wheels and their outriggers folded inwards for convenient storage in a hallway. Engines were available with 175 or 200 cc, and the cockpit canopy tilted sideways *à la* Messerschmitt.

two ratios, part-leather trim, a full set of instruments with circular black dials, key-starting (as yet uncommon in Britain), two-speed wipers, pile carpeting, and twin reversing lamps.

MG's Y-type (1948–53) and the original Z Magnette (1953–58) pursued the same theme, while others in this class—though bigger all round—were the Armstrong Siddeley, the early 3-litre Alvis, the classical RM Rileys (current until 1954), the razor-edge Triumph Renown (which also disappeared around this time), and the old-school beam-axle AC sedans. ACs, Rileys, and MGs had a sporting flavour: the Triumph had not. Yet even the homely and pedestrian Humbers and Wolseleys retained some shreds of character until 1957, although thereafter the latter breed, at any rate, faded into a painful and badge-engineered decadence.

The tragi-comedy of badge-engineering has already been discussed, but throughout our period Britain also produced countless successful sports models. Scarcely a year passed without some exciting new development.

In 1951, the choice lay between the ageless Morgan, the even more archaic HRG with its beam axles and mechanical brakes, the TD-type MG, the American-engined Allards, the Jowett Jupiter, the 2.5-litre sports Lea-Francis, and the Jaguar XK120 with its twin-overhead-camshaft six-cylinder engine and 120-mph (190-km/h) top speed. Just coming into production, though more of a supercar than a straightforward sporting machine, was the first of the DB2 Aston Martins.

1952 saw the Austin-Healey with its big and lazy four-cylinder engine. In 1953 its great rival, the Triumph TR2, went into production along with a roadster edition of the 2.3-litre Sunbeam-Talbot, the Alpine. 1954's star offering came from AC, whose Ace featured all-independent springing and open bodywork in the Ferrari idiom. MG went modern with the aerodynamic A in time for the 1955 Motor Show. 1957 Triumphs and Jaguars acquired disc brakes, and Lotus applied glass-fibre unitary construction to their Elite coupé—not quite a first, but very nearly one. In 1958 came a successor to the early MG Midgets, Austin-Healey's Sprite. It was available with MG badging in 1961, when we also saw the first Jaguar E-type: a monocoque with independent rear suspension.

Thereafter things moved fast. In 1962 the big Triumph was restyled, and it, too, would be given independent rear springing in 1964. Then AC put an American Ford V-8 into their Ace to produce the ferocious Cobra, the Triumph range had a small sports model in the shape of the all-independently sprung Spitfire, MG came up with the unitary B family, and Lotus' backbone-framed Elan roadster set new standards in handling. All this added up to three safe American best-sellers—Jaguar, MG, and Triumph—to see the British motor industry into the seventies. It was not until 1973, and the advent of Fiat's mid-engined X1/9, that Americans would wake up to the truth: the Classic British sports car was hopelessly outmoded. Not that this stopped them buying it. The MG-B retained a dedicated following to the end in 1980.

Italy, as we have seen, was becoming the world's stylist. She had always been the purveyor of driver's cars *par excellence*, and she still was. The Italian car had unmistakable characteristics. Gear ratios were governed by the mountainous nature of the homeland, and sometimes appeared odd to outsiders. The early acceptance of five-speed boxes—Ferrari were using these at the beginning of our period, and Fiat from 1952—tended, however, to eliminate the almost traditional gap between first and second. Italians liked a long-arm driving position. Noise

221

(*Top left*) Update of a traditional British theme: the small, semi-luxury sporting sedan. In 1952 form, the Sunbeam-Talbot 90 (it was a Sunbeam in most export markets) used a straightforward 2.3-litre overhead-valve four-cylinder engine descended directly from the 1933 Humber Twelve, as well as four speeds with synchromesh, coil-spring independent front suspension, and an unmistakable British shape refined to the extent of recessed headlamps and a curved single-panel screen. A robust chassis and a dependable 85 mph (136 km/h) were offset by a cramped interior, a horrible steering-column gearshift, and inadequate luggage accommodation—but a 90 won the 1955 Monte Carlo Rally.

(*Bottom left*) If one chose a single car to typify the Italian image of the 1950s and 1960s, this would be it: street-legal rather than designed for street use, the Ferrari 250GTO of 1962. The "O" stands for *omologato* (homologated for GT racing) and the type number, as almost always, signifies the capacity of an individual cylinder. In the case of a V-12, this adds up to just under 3 litres. As yet, Ferrari are content with one overhead cam-shaft per block and semi-elliptic rear springs. But with its six dual-choke Weber carburettors, the GTO offers 295–300 bhp at 7,400 rpm. Later examples have five-speed gear-boxes, yet only 39 were made. By the early 1980s, collectors were paying $85,000 (£42,000-plus) for good specimens.

(*Top right*) The Dyna-Panhard with its overhead-valve flat-twin engine driving the front wheels, and with liberal use of light alloys, had been one of the sensations of the 1946 Paris Salon. Even more sensational had been 1954's all-alloy sedan propelling six people at 120 km/h (75 mph) on only 850 cc. But by 1965 the car was too rough and crude, and Citroën—Panhard's owners—had dropped the sedans, leaving only a pair of sports coupés with all-disc brakes and peculiar styling. This 24BT was a full four-seater, but sales were falling and the last Panhards were delivered during 1967.

(*Bottom right*) If there's no choice, the customers take what they can get, which in the late 1960s meant, for Czechoslovak citizens, the Skoda 1000MB family: the front-engined Octavia was on its way out, and the big V-8 Tatra was for official use only. Thus, this roomy if cumbersome rear-engined 1-litre sedan with its swing-axle rear end accounted for over two and a quarter million sales between 1964 and 1977. The design changed little during the period (this right-hand-drive car dates from the mid-1970s), it was tough, and export pricing was always competitive. In 1969 the four-door Skoda cost only £30 more than a Mini in Britain, and was fractionally cheaper in Switzerland than a basic VW Beetle 1200.

levels were often inacceptable by the standards of other lands and, in a country of low rainfall, rustproofing was not taken seriously. Automatics were unpopular: even in 1970, the only Italian cars listed with such transmissions were the Maseratis and Fiat's new luxury V-6, a Mercedes-Benz competitor. Italian cars were an acquired taste, but fun if one became accustomed to them.

The industry was limited by an impoverished home market. New car registrations would not pass the 100,000 level before 1953, and even in 1956 there was only one vehicle for every 36 inhabitants. Fiat alone were physically capable of fulfilling the entire domestic requirement, and in the early 1950s they still enjoyed some 90 % of what sales there were. Lancia's potential was in the region of 5,000 units a year, and a 1,750-cc Aurelia sedan, at 1,830,000 lire (£1,075 or $3,000), was very expensive alongside the 975,000 lire asked for a Fiat *Millecento*, the universal family car.

And if France offered little domestic competition, in Italy there was none at all. In the lower echelons, it was Fiat or nothing. In the upper-middle-class sector, of course, Lancia competed against the state-owned Alfa Romeo company, moving towards mass production with a new line of unitary designs. The effect of this would eventually be to force Lancia into the arms of Fiat, a state of affairs accentuated by taxes based on cylinder capacity. In 1958, the class over 2 litres—which meant Lancia's Flaminia and a trickle of Maseratis and Ferraris—accounted for only 0.5 % of all new registrations, and even the phenomenal economic growth of 1960–64 had little effect. A 4 % share looked encouraging on paper, but most of the extra went to Fiat, on the strength of their bigger six-cylinder sedans. In any case, sales in this sector seldom exceeded 2,000 a year, so the beneficiaries of the new affluence were Fiat, and the losers the scooter manufacturers whose clientele moved up to Fiat 500s.

As for the super-cars, they represented a *succès d'estime* rather than a major economic factor. The writer who asserted that one saw more Ferraris in Sydney than in Milan was certainly exaggerating, but there were precious few of them anywhere, especially in our first decade. Up to 1960, the total production of roadgoing cars cannot have exceeded 850 units, while Maserati probably made less than 500—even if their six-cylinder GT3500, announced in 1958, accounted for 2,000 cars before it was dropped in 1964. In this latter year the 655 new Ferraris, 390 Isos, and 310 Maseratis were overwhelmed by 583,000 Fiats, 56,000 Alfa Romeos, 32,000 Autobianchis made by a once-independent Fiat

associate, 30,000 Lancias, and 20,370 assorted BMC designs built by Innocenti in Milan.

The industrial growth rate in 1960 reached a staggering 20.3 %, which meant plenty of foreign exchange, not to mention a flood of VWs, Opels, Simcas, and the like to leaven the somewhat dull diet of the everyday Italian motorist. Fiat's market share plummeted to 65 %. But the Italian car remained as uncompromisingly Italian as ever.

France had still to resolve her economic problems in 1951, and the draconian rationalization of 1946, aimed at conserving steel, was only a prelude to the wholesale weed-out of weaker brethren within the industry. Of the smaller manufacturers, only Panhard, Rosengart, and Talbot were alive in 1955—the last two barely so. As we have seen, Ford disposed of their French interests to Simca, and two years later Citroën took control of Panhard. The appeal of the latter's all-aluminium front-wheel-drive flat-twins was sufficient to keep them in production, but only so long as demand lasted. There would be no all-new Panhard.

The specialists were doomed. Delahaye-Delage, Hotchkiss, Salmson, Talbot, and even Bugatti were still quoted in 1951, but their home sales were sabotaged by a tax watershed that descended above 15CV, or approximately 2.9 litres. The Salmson sat on the safe shore, and so, of course, did the Citroën Six: the *grandes routières* did not. The straight-eight Bugatti was assessed at 17CV, the Hotchkiss at 20, and the magnificent Talbot Lago Grand Sport (the most powerful sports car of the 1940s) at a punitive 26. Thus they could scarcely sell at home, while small runs and uncompetitive prices pushed export prices to unacceptable limits. There was no cash for new models to challenge Jaguar and Mercedes-Benz. Hotchkiss as well as Salmson had a stake in the "safe" 13CV class—but what hope had a 1933 design against that more ageless ancient, the 11CV Citroën, still modern in concept if not in appearance, and selling for half the money? They tried hard: from 1950 they also listed the 2-litre Grégoire, with its flat-four engine driving the front wheels of an advanced unitary structure, but they only managed to produce 260 such cars in three years.

Talbot hung on even longer, introducing a new 2.5-litre sports coupé in 1955. They even contrived to buy V-8 engines from BMW, but the U.S. list price of $6,995 was way above Jaguar's, and it was all over by 1958. Hotchkiss and Delahaye had merged, to abdicate into truck manufacture, which left the Chrysler-engined Facel Vega as the sole upholder of a once-great tradition. And where Hotchkiss' front-wheel drive and Delahaye's Jeep derivatives had failed through complexity and lack

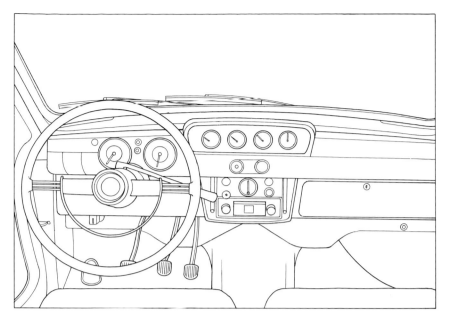

Britain still made small, semi-luxury sporting sedans, though these were in decline. A very successful one—over 7,000 sold in 1956–57 alone—was the Sunbeam Rapier. Much of its sheet metal and all the base mechanics were Hillman Minx. So is this dashboard pressing (*above*), but a good disguise is lent by the combination of large and small gauges. From 1958 onwards, too, Rootes would dispense with the unpleasing column shift. The interior was traditional British—and who worried about half-plastic seats when he got nearly 145 km/h (90 mph) from 1.4 litres, plus six forward ratios (overdrive was standard on top and third), all for a little over £1,000 ($2,800)?

Britain remained the home of the small specialist maker, building something "different" from assorted proprietary mechanical elements. The Paramount (*below*) went through three sponsors during an interrupted 100-car run from 1950 to 1956. It was another case of the semi-sporting four-seater that nobody really wanted, but the car was quite pleasing in its final form, if somewhat heavy. The grille, originally aping the Sunbeam-Talbot, had assumed a BMW style by 1953. The very ordinary engine, with 1,508 cc and four cylinders, untuned and giving a modest 47 horsepower, came from the Ford Consul—as did the three-speed gearbox, although mercifully with floor instead of column shift. Interesting were the wing-mounted fuel tanks, holding 63 litres (15 gallons) for a range up to 640 km (400 miles).

of finance, Facel were to commit suicide with an attempt at an all-French 1.6-litre sports car.

But while the Old Guard faded out, never to return, the rump of mass producers bounced back successfully. France actually benefited from the restrictive practices of her rulers. Not only were the foreigners shut out until 1960, but domestic makers were gently discouraged from internal competition. If we take the 1954–56 period as typical, we find that farmer's hack, the 2CV Citroën, at the bottom of the ladder. One step up, Renault had it all to themselves with the established 4CV and (from 1956) the 845-cc Dauphine. In the 8CV category, there was no real overlap between the Simca Aronde and the roomier Peugeot 203, while Peugeot's 403 (1955) was an altogether bigger sedan which filled a hole between the 203 and the 2-litre contenders—the aged Citroën *traction*, Renault's Frégate, and the Simca-Ford V-8. For the prestige market, there was the Citroën Six, until the new Déesses started to reach the public in the summer of 1956.

Prosperity, of course, bred competition, but not until the industry could afford it. In 1961, Renault challenged the *deux chevaux* with an in-line four, also front-wheel-driven and also with utility bodywork. Citroën's bizarrely styled Ami and the rear-engined Simca 1000 took on the entrenched small Renaults from 1961, too. Buyers of sedans with 1,100–1,200 cc had a choice, by 1968, between front-wheel drive from Peugeot or Simca, and the rear-engined Renault 10. Simca was now "marking" Peugeot in the 8/10CV class, while the sector over 1.5 litres resolved into a battle between Peugeot and Renault, or the *système* Panhard versus front-wheel drive. The big D-series Citroëns continued to represent prestige, but if one mistrusted things hydropneumatic, there were always imported Mercedes-Benz and Jaguars—at a price. Of nearly two million French cars produced in 1969, all but 2,673 were the work of the big four—Renault, Peugeot, Citroën, and Simca.

Rationalization bred enormous runs. Citroën's *traction* lasted twenty-three years, and their D-series another eighteen. Both their Ami and Simca's less successful rear-engined 1000 ran for seventeen years, the original 4CV Renault for fifteen, and the excellent mid-sixties 16 for fourteen. In 1982, the *deux chevaux* was thirty-four years old and still going strong, while the Renault 4 was comfortably over its majority. There were few mistakes: against the Renault Dauphine's strange handling and rust-proneness must be set a sales record of more than two million. Their Frégate might be a case of belated Vanguarditis, but at peak it was good for around 35,000 a year. As for styling, the French were not interested in periodic facelifts for the sake of change. The Vanguard enjoyed three different shapes in sixteen years—the Frégate (and for that matter, most of its compatriots) looked much the same at the end as at the beginning.

Odder, perhaps, was the reversal of tradition that took place in France. We owe the traditional engineering of the automobile to Panhard, while the combination of shaft drive and a direct top gear is usually attributed to Louis Renault. Yet from 1952 Renault became addicted to gearboxes with all-indirect ratios, and Panhard were among the first to throw their own layout overboard. After the stagnation of the thirties, France seemed determined to dispense with the old shibboleths of a front engine and rear drive: Citroën had finally quit in 1938, and Panhard followed suit once the war was over. Renault had their rear-engined 4CV at the 1946 Paris Salon, and from 1961 they would divide their allegiance between this layout and front-wheel drive. Simca explored a rear engine in 1960, and front-wheel drive, on Fiat lines, seven years later. The conservative house of Peugeot, by contrast, waited until 1966 to take the plunge, though thereafter they would reserve the *système* Panhard for their biggest cars.

If there was a classically French type, it was, as always, the *commer-*

Less usual Swedes. Seldom seen in any guise other than the regular two-door sedan was the long-lived Volvo PV444 family. This one (*top left*) dates from 1953 and carries rare cabriolet coachwork by Valbo. As yet, this tough rally-winner of the future was little known outside its homeland, and specification was virtually unchanged from the prototype's 1944 *début*: a 44-horsepower 1.4-litre three-bearing pushrod engine, three-speed transmission, and coil-spring rear suspension. The 1800 coupé (*opposite, top*), by contrast, was a volume-production type of which some 39,000 were delivered between 1961 and 1972. Frua did the styling, and early examples (the first 6,000) were put together by Jensen in England. It was powered by a 1,778-cc five-bearing four with two SU carburettors rated at 100 horsepower. The four-speed all-synchromesh transmission could be had with or without overdrive, and the front disc brakes were servo-assisted. Top speed was 106 mph (170 km/h), but people bought Volvos because of the engine's astonishing durability. The seven-figure odometers fitted from the mid-1960s were no idle boast.

Swedish sales drives mean making cars that will cover a goodly proportion of home-market requirements, and earn some foreign exchange at the same time. The 120-series Volvo Amazon (*bottom left*) and Saab 95 station wagon (*opposite, centre*) from the early 1960s have nothing in common save their nationality and, not only on home ground, their ability to win rallies. On the Volvo, a front-mounted 1,583-cc four-cylinder pushrod engine drives the rear wheels via a four-speed all-synchromesh gearbox, and proportions are wholly European though there's still a hint of 1955 Chrysler in the styling. On the Saab, a longitudinal three-cylinder two-stroke engine of recognizable DKW ancestry drives the front wheels via a three-speed transmission, but four forward speeds are on the way. If the Swedish factories aren't yet in the really big production league, runs are long: four-door members of this Volvo family (there were wagons and two-door sedans as well) accounted for 234,208 units between 1956 and 1967, while the two-stroke Saab's eighteen-year career came to an end that same season. Not that the base chassis/body structure was finished: Saab merely inserted a four-stroke 1.5-litre German Ford V-4 engine and went on making this 95 (and the parallel 96 two-door sedan) until January, 1980. Styling evolution was so gradual that people were not aware that the final 95/96 series was not at all similar to the original 92 of 1949–50, with its limited window area, restricted rearward vision, tiny grille, and half-skirts to all four wheels, disastrous in a Swedish winter and not destined to last very long. There was also a world of difference between a 764-cc two-stroke twin and the 65-horsepower Ford unit, although curiously the 96 (but not later Saabs) retained a column gearshift to the end.

Practical transportation for long Russian winters: two of the three basic models a private citizen of the U.S.S.R. could buy in 1968—the third was the little rear-engined V-4 Zaporozhetz. The Moskvitch 408 (*bottom left*) has lost its outward Opel affinities down the years, but its high ground clearance shows to advantage in this snow shot—and the car had acquired the quad headlamps, if not the front disc brakes, of the Degenerate West. Old-fashioned features are column shift and no synchromesh on bottom, though there are four forward speeds. On the credit side, the customer was well prepared for trouble, with an adjustable radiator blind, a huge tool kit, a starting handle, and towing hooks at each end as a last resort. The 408 had a 1,357-cc pushrod four-cylinder engine, but already a more powerful overhead-camshaft unit was on its way in the 412 series. From an earlier generation and already due for replacement was the Volga M22 station wagon (*bottom right*), a 1961 derivative of a model first seen in 1955. Looks are 1946 American, and one feels it could well be the car Willys would have launched if they hadn't been fully occupied with Jeeps in the immediate post-war era. Unitary construction features instead of Detroit's usual separate-chassis techniques, but the rest is only too familiar: 2.4-litre four-cylinder overhead-valve engine, three-speed transmission, column shift, independent coils at the front, and semi-elliptics at the back. This one also sits a safe 7.5 in (19 cm) off the ground, and it weighs in at a solid 3,263 lb (1,480 kg). Its replacement, the M24 visible in 1969, will have an early-1960s Detroit shape, an extra forward gear, and a brake servo, but otherwise Soviet motorists receive the mixture as before.

ciale, or dual-purpose sedan. We have already traced its career when exploring the saga of the station wagon. Suffice it to say here that France produced the two best examples of our period: the 2CV Citroën, of course, and the five-door Renault 16, earliest and best of the hatchback generation and, incidentally, one of the few "wagons" which handled exactly like a sedan.

In the Communist countries, private cars had a low priority, being divided between vehicles made for official use and cut-price exports. One has only to compare motoring in the two Germanies to see the difference. In 1963 the Democratic Republic had one car to every 50 inhabitants, as against one to every 7.2 in the West. Ten years later, the respective ratios were 1:10 and 1:3.7, with over fourteen times as many cars circulating in the *Bundesrepublik*.

Engineering and styling alike were utilitarian. The cars were designed to cope with bad roads and a total lack of garage service in the Western sense. Hence the high clearances—a 1965 Moskvitch stood 1.5 in (3.8 cm) further off the ground than a contemporary Ford Cortina—and the voluminous tool-kits. Volgas and Moskvitches offered a collection of thirty pieces where a jack and a wheelbrace were fast becoming the norm in the West, and any tools whatever were "optional at extra cost" in the U.S.A. Model changes were few and far between. In Czechoslovakia, four models saw Skoda through from 1950 to 1970, and of these the first three (the 1100, 1200, and 440) were all variations on the same basic pre-war theme of a Fiat-like overhead-valve four-cylinder engine at the front of a backbone chassis. In the U.S.S.R., cars were

graduated inexorably by rank. Basic transport was represented by the Moskvitch, now far removed from its Opel prototype, and actually with an overhead-camshaft engine by 1968. In the 2/2.5-litre class came the Pobeda and its successor, the Volga. At the top of the tree came the big limousines (ZIS, ZIM, ZIL, Chaika), old-fashioned American in appearance, and reflecting assorted Packard and Pontiac influences. None of them could be bought by Soviet citizens, though a few ZIMs were sold in Sweden and Finland. From 1960, the range was rounded out by a true small car, the 887-cc Zaporozhetz, not unlike a Fiat 600, and with a rear-mounted air-cooled V-4 engine.

East German productions reflected the heritage of the Saxon factories. The big prestige cars (EMW, Sachsenring) were direct descendants of the pre-war 326 BMW, while everything else was DKW-derived, although the Eastern IFA F9 with its three-cylinder engine got into production three years ahead of its Western counterpart. Even these went through with minimal change: new, simple transverse-twins in 1948, 1955, and 1958, and three types of three-cylinder, those of 1950, 1956, and 1966.

Coachwork variations were a needless luxury, though Skoda's backbone frame permitted some convertibles, and in East Germany the late-1950s Wartburg range ran to a sports coupé and even to a seldom-seen roadster. Station wagons were, however, generally available. Engineering was unsophisticated, except in Czechoslovakia with her long tradition of a self-sufficient automobile industry, capable of making anything had the "brake" been released. But even in 1969 there were no

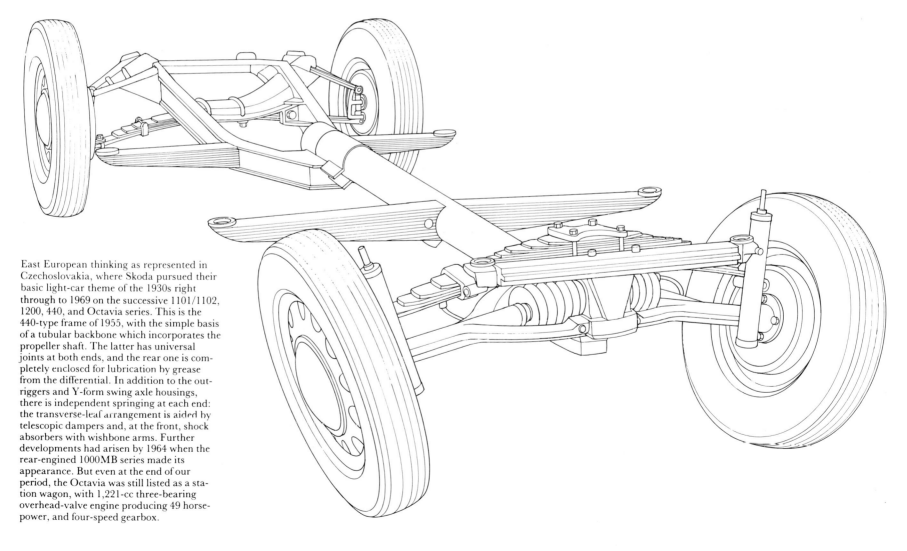

East European thinking as represented in Czechoslovakia, where Skoda pursued their basic light-car theme of the 1930s right through to 1969 on the successive 1101/1102, 1200, 440, and Octavia series. This is the 440-type frame of 1955, with the simple basis of a tubular backbone which incorporates the propeller shaft. The latter has universal joints at both ends, and the rear one is completely enclosed for lubrication by grease from the differential. In addition to the outriggers and Y-form swing axle housings, there is independent springing at each end: the transverse-leaf arrangement is aided by telescopic dampers and, at the front, shock absorbers with wishbone arms. Further developments had arisen by 1964 when the rear-engined 1000MB series made its appearance. But even at the end of our period, the Octavia was still listed as a station wagon, with 1,221-cc three-bearing overhead-valve engine producing 49 horsepower, and four-speed gearbox.

automatics, except on the big Russian limousines. Disc brakes, likewise, were confined to these, and to the latest Fiat derivatives from Russian and Polish factories. All synchromesh gearboxes were recent.

As for the concept of "putting all the works up one end", only the rear-engined Zaporozhetz could count as a recent recruit. The big, executive Czech Tatra descended directly from a line going back to 1934, and although Skoda's 1000MB was launched as late as 1964, the company had been experimenting with rear engines during the thirties. The East German cars—and the Syrena from Poland—had front-wheel drive because of their DKW ancestry. Handling mattered little, since cars were not intended to be driven for pleasure. The Skoda was skittish in conventional form, and verged on the perilous when the engine was shifted aft.

In Holland, the ingenious little DAF revived the same national-car concept that had bred the Volvo in Sweden and the Holden in Australia. Ease of driving, mechanical simplicity, and a form of transmission best suited to flat country: these resulted in a belt-driven 600-cc twin which was a true stepless automatic.

In Sweden, the transformation from a major importer to a significant exporter and manufacturer was a slow process, and it took quite a while for Volvo even to edge VW out of first place in the national best-seller league. In some ways, Sweden was the antithesis of pre-war Czechoslovakia: the Czechs, entrenched behind the toughest protectionary tariffs in Europe, sought to become self-sufficient, and the result was too many models—eighteen from six manufacturers at the time of the Nazi occupation in 1939. These ranged from utility two-strokes (the good old DKW theme again) up to seven-seater limousines, all on an annual production potential of 12,000 units.

The Swedish approach was the opposite. Saab covered the small sector, and Volvo the medium-sized models. Inevitably, there would have to be room for foreign imports, and in 1962 the Scania-Vabis truck firm, VW's concessionaires, were bringing in some 40,000 Beetles a year. Sweden imported nearly 200,000 cars in 1965, and was still taking over 150,000 a year in the early seventies, despite some range-widening by her two native manufacturers. In fact, the big move was away from "national cars" to models that would be acceptable in export markets.

First, there had to be a breakaway from the American idiom. When the first Volvos were built in 1927, the American car with its big, lazy engine and tough suspension was ideal for Swedish roads, and Volvo copied it without any deviation until 1944. Wartime fuel shortages changed all this, as did the growing bulk of the American prototype. In their first post-war design, the PV444, Volvo achieved an admirable compromise—American styling and an American-type three-speed gearbox, allied to compact proportions and a 28-mpg (10.1-litres/100 km) thirst. And while Volvo scaled American ideas down to reasonable proportions, Saab set out to achieve a better DKW, with the perfect aerodynamic shape to be expected of an experienced aircraft manufacturer. It was also as small as the home market would take: 30% of the country's population might be concentrated in her three biggest cities, but in long snowy winters the "bubble" had no future.

Whether the efficient-looking windscreen wipers were meant for occasional rain or frequent sandstorms is not clear, but one useful element of the interior—apart from its floor-mounted gearshift for four forward speeds—was a conspicuous handgrip on the front passenger's side, which may also have inspired nostalgia about more traditional means of transport.

The Middle East was no exception to the comforting, if not always comfortable, fact that light pickup vehicles on car chassis were common in the ranges of manufacturers in "emergent" countries. Here is the Egyptian Ramses of 1966, whose line included a two-door sedan and a convertible. From the front one might suspect Fiat origins, and indeed Fiat did have a branch factory at Helwan. Seen from the rear, however, the boot reveals a transverse overhead-camshaft vertical-twin engine, and this stamps it as an Arabic-speaking cousin of the NSU Prinz family from Germany. With 36 horsepower and 600 cc, top speed was 120 km/h (75 mph) and, when cruising, fuel consumption was a commendable 6.6 litres/100 km (42 mpg)—although the latter, misprinted as 606 in the English part of the sales catalogue, might be enough to frighten away any foreigner! Hydraulic brakes, rack-and-pinion steering, independent suspension with coil springs, and unitary construction were further features of a car weighing just 680 kg (1,500 lb).

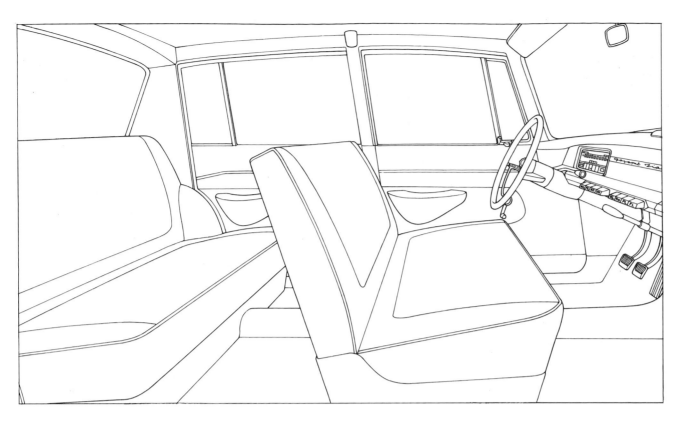

By the early sixties, Japan was catching up with the rest of the world—and the 1961 Toyota Tiara, for all its Simca-like grille, has marked affinities with the widely exported Corona family of the late 1960s. It isn't obviously a case of outmoded styling and, compared with such contemporary efforts as Italy's Fiat 1300/1500 and the British F-type Vauxhall Victor, it is almost beautiful. A lot could be done with two-tone interior trim, too (*left*), although seat facings were not always leather in such a car, as drivers discovered after long runs in hot weather! The contrasting colours of the facia and door cappings made a welcome change from the

TIARA

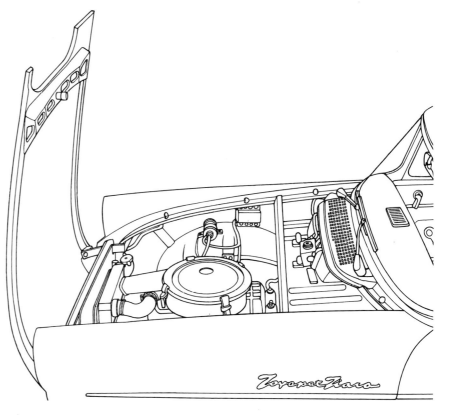

1940s idiom of black with brown leather (British) or dark tones with mud-shade cloth (the Continental equivalent). The elongators have had a go at this scene, from one of the first Japanese brochures in a European language: the actual interior length was 1.67 m (66 in). One may, however, expect no surprises from the engineering standpoint, and none are there. Under the forward-hinged hood (*right*) lies a 1,453-cc 65-horsepower overhead-valve pushrod four-cylinder engine of almost square dimensions, transmitting its output to a hypoid rear axle via a three-speed synchromesh gearbox. Three speeds with the typically 1950s column shift, to be sure, were an "old-fashioned" theme also found at the time on European Fords, Opels, and Vauxhalls. Suspension arrangements are likewise orthodox (*below*): a ball-joint and wishbone set-up, *à l'Américaine*, at the front (*upper*), and semi-elliptics with auxiliary coils and an anti-roll bar at the rear (*lower*). A separate chassis was retained, brakes were hydraulic, and there was a station wagon in the range. Quoted maximum speed was 135 km/h (84 mph), though the 40 mpg (7 litres/100 km) as an estimate of fuel consumption was almost certainly on the optimistic side.

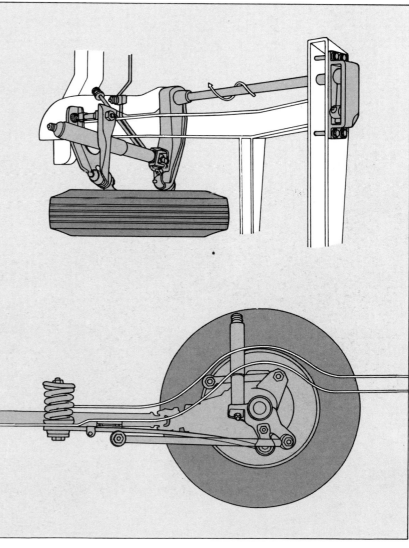

231

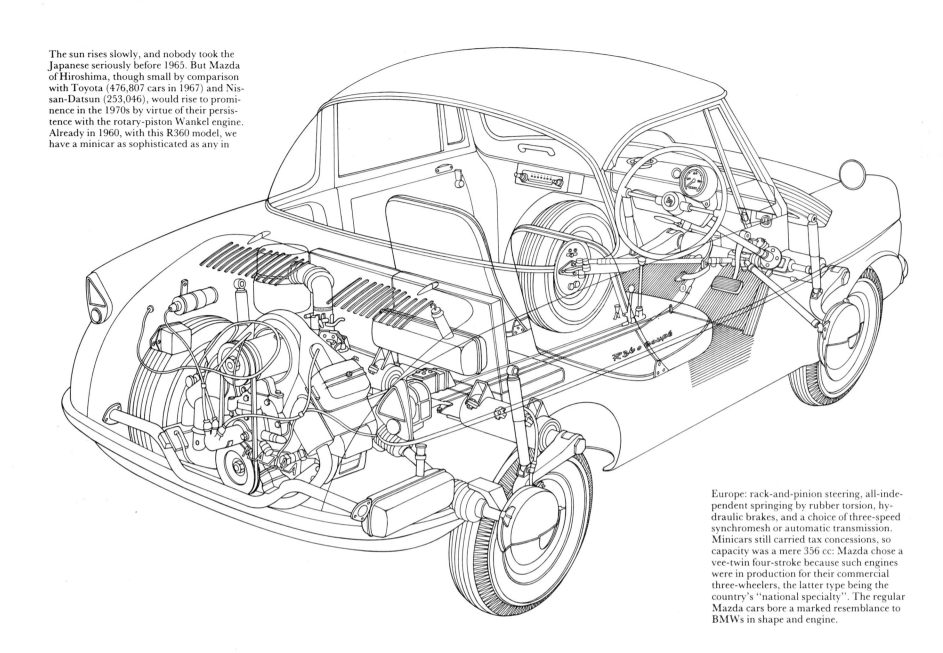

The sun rises slowly, and nobody took the Japanese seriously before 1965. But Mazda of Hiroshima, though small by comparison with Toyota (476,807 cars in 1967) and Nissan-Datsun (253,046), would rise to prominence in the 1970s by virtue of their persistence with the rotary-piston Wankel engine. Already in 1960, with this R360 model, we have a minicar as sophisticated as any in

Europe: rack-and-pinion steering, all-independent springing by rubber torsion, hydraulic brakes, and a choice of three-speed synchromesh or automatic transmission. Minicars still carried tax concessions, so capacity was a mere 356 cc: Mazda chose a vee-twin four-stroke because such engines were in production for their commercial three-wheelers, the latter type being the country's "national specialty". The regular Mazda cars bore a marked resemblance to BMWs in shape and engine.

From South America, little of any technical interest emerged, the majority of cars being licence-produced versions of European or American designs. Brazil's list was headed by Volkswagen, the American big three, and Alfa Romeo. In Argentina, Detroit's opponents were Citroën, Fiat, Peugeot, and Renault, the British Motor Corporation's local outlet having faded by 1967. Also a recent casualty in both countries was the once-ubiquitous DKW, sold as a Vemag in Brazil. There were two Argentine strains, the Wartburg-like Graciela made in a state-owned plant at Cordoba, and the West German Auto Union 1000 from Santa Fé. Native designs were few and far between, although in Argentina the Autoar firm had made a few cars with Willys and Fiat engines, and IKA's Torino (1966) was a fine coupé with a 3.8-litre overhead-camshaft six-cylinder engine. Brazilian originals included the VW-based Puma sports coupé and the curious range of the combined Ford-Willys interests. Of these, the Galaxie was obsolescent Detroit, and the Rural-Willys our old friend the Jeep Station Wagon. The Itamaraty, however, derived directly from the Aero-Willys sedan, production of which had ceased in the U.S.A. during 1955. The brand-new Corcel could best be described as a Renault 12 with Ford styling overtones, the result of the former Willys-Overland concern's link with Renault.

But even if the end-product was often a curious international cocktail, there was quite a lot of it, whereas there had been nothing in 1950, and only modest truck production ten years later. Brazilian private-car production shot up from 142,877 in 1966 to well over a quarter of a million in 1969. Argentina, less stable and in the grip of galloping inflation, delivered 153,665 new cars that year.

Austria's sole contributions were the Denzel—a species of local Porsche forced out of business by competition from its better-known German rival—and the Fiat derivatives of Steyr-Puch. Belgium had nothing to offer, and sundry Danish bids to make a national car had fizzled out by 1955. From 1959, Egypt was building twin-cylinder NSUs under the Ramses name, while an assortment of Morrises (Hindustan), Fiats (Premier), and Standards (Triumph) came from Indian factories. All were obsolete even then, the Hindusthan being a slightly modified 1954 Morris Oxford.

Australia, by contrast, went from strength to strength. She had to, initially at any rate, since successive administrations pursued a maddeningly ambivalent attitude towards imports, and all the time her automobile population was steadily increasing. In 1956, the industry employed 80,000 people, and even tyres were being produced locally.

The 1956 FE-series Holden, first major redesign for the *marque*, was created from scratch in Australia.

The Holden remained a national car throughout our period. The theme was simplified, compact American, a return to the principles of Model-A and the 1929 Chevrolet Six, and it stayed that way. A 9.5-in (24.2-cm) ground clearance and simple electrics distinguished it from others of its ilk. By 1956, production was in excess of 70,000 cars a year, and the first quarter million had been delivered. The half million came up in 1957, while the breed's share of the national market climbed from 23 % in 1951 to 45 % in 1960.

From 1957, GM's Holden would be challenged, first by Chrysler, and then by Ford. The British Motor Corporation was also producing its own Australian line. Standard-Triumph and VW, too, were assembling in the Commonwealth, and together these six firms had cornered 91 % of the market. But with Japanese imports edging up to the 60,000 mark, things were bound to change. Japan was too near, and within a decade the British would have been squeezed out. Australian Motor Industries would be building Toyotas instead of Triumphs, and at the bottom of the Holden range Isuzu would replace near-Vauxhalls.

Nobody could have predicted any of this in 1951, or even 1959. *Chacun à sa commerce d'exportation* most emphatically did not apply to Japan: she had none. In 1950, she registered 42,588 private cars—almost exactly as many as in a rural British county, Somerset, at that time. Her three car makers were turning out antiquated machinery of less than a litre's capacity, with side-valve engines. She had no steelworks capable of making wide sheet, no modern machine tools, and no foreign currency with which to buy them. All bodies had to be hand-formed, and some very awkward shapes resulted.

She also suffered from a complex network of Automobile Control Laws, with strict rules governing the construction of every class of vehicle. A 50 % sales tax was bad enough, but taxes also doubled on cars of over 1,500 cc and, in any case, narrow and tortuous roads dictated compact proportions. The pre-war 722-cc Datsun measured only 123 in (3.12 m) long and 47 in (1.2 m) wide, dimensions which resulted in a full four-seater comparable in size to Fiat's *topolino*, only far less sophisticated. Brakes were mechanical, there was no synchromesh, and the transverse-leaf front springing was pure Austin Seven.

Even in 1955, Japanese cars were most unimpressive. A customer had the choice of two essentially pre-war designs, the 860-cc Datsun or the 903-cc Ohta, giving 24/25 horsepower from old-fashioned flathead engines, and capable of a leisured 45 mph (64 km/h) thanks to abysmal gearing—top was 6.5:1, as on some of the nastiest pint-sized sixes of the 1930s. Hydraulic brakes had arrived, but not independent front suspension. In the 1.5-litre class, a little more sophistication was apparent, but not much. Overhead valves were used by Toyota and Prince alike, although only the latter had other than beam axles at both ends, and three forward speeds sufficed. The Toyota's wrap-round rear window looked curiously anachronistic.

A national Japanese type did exist, but it was merely a light commercial three-wheeler with motorcycle-type engine and controls, a strange creature which accounted for 43,802 units in 1951, and reached its zenith in 1960 with over 278,000 such vehicles sold. Although several important car makers, notably Daihatsu and Mazda, were heavily involved in this sector, only Daihatsu sought to adapt the theme to private-car use, on their short-lived Bee (1954) with rear-mounted 540-cc vee-twin engine. Other Japanese minicars followed European ideas.

After 1955, Japan caught up. Overhead valves, independent front suspension, and tubeless tyres made their appearance, while Mazda offered an automatic transmission, and Datsun's first serious sports car—the S211—featured rather ugly glass-fibre coachwork. Bigger engines were on their way, with a 1.9-litre 80-hp four in Prince's Gloria. While Toyota and Nissan/Datsun dominated the scene, Prince always challenged strongly, as did a flood of assorted minicars—Mazda, Mitsubishi, Mikasa, Subaru, and Suzuki. In addition, Hino built 4CV Renaults under licence alongside their heavy trucks, and another truckmaker, Isuzu, produced a local version of the Hillman Minx. There were 2-litre cars from Nissan, Toyota, and Isuzu in 1962, and thereafter Japan never looked back. The industry's first million year was 1967. It had broken two million the following season, and ten million cars would pour out of Japanese factories in 1971.

With an eye on world markets, the manufacturers tended to push their minicars into the background, though such creatures were still listed in 1966 by Aichi, Daihatsu, Mazda, Mitsubishi, Subaru, and Suzuki, while Toyota offered an 800-cc twin-cylinder sedan and Honda

A contrast from Brazil, the Puma, was conceived in this form in 1967, though a later car is shown here. If it looks different from other local products as by Willys-Overland, this is due to the inspiration of designer Gennaro Malzoni, who created its glass-fibre shape. Underneath, the mechanics are what one can buy locally: Volkswagen flat-fours of 1,500 or 1,600 cc. The latter version in twin-carburettor guise offered 90 horsepower, so the Puma (described as "an extension of your body") had a potential of 180 km/h (110 mph). Production was, however, modest—207 cars in 1970, or almost exactly a thousandth of the local output of stock VWs. Making the international influence even clearer, Puma had a European importer in Zürich and a catalogue written in French but printed in Holland.

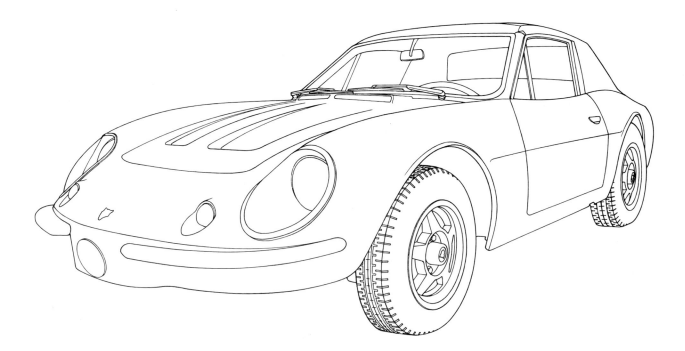

their astonishing little S600 sports car, soon to be enlarged to 797 cc. Isuzu, Nissan, and Prince had diesel-powered sedans ready to move in on taxicab business, the bigger Nissans and Isuzus could be had with front disc brakes, and the option list for Mitsubishi's six-cylinder Debonair included reclining seats and air conditioning. Also visible were independently sprung rear ends, and rack-and-pinion steering. Nissan, Prince, Toyota, and Mazda all used overhead-camshaft engines in some models, and Toyota had an automatic transmission as well. 1967 would see the first Japanese Wankel-engine car, Mazda's Cosmo coupé. The Japan Auto Trade Federation's Handbook referred proudly to the new international outlook, and the nation's escape from a "requirement for swift acceleration capacity from low speed, and a large capacity in slope climbing". Rear engines were found only in minicars and in Hino's small Renault-based Contessa. As for front-wheel drive, it was signally absent before the advent of the Honda minicars in 1968, though it had been seen briefly ten years ago on the little Mikasa roadster.

Most fascinating of all, the industrial background resembled the whole series of European-style mergers run through a movie projector at high speed. Ohta was absorbed by the Tokyu Kurogane truck firm, Aichi and Prince came under Nissan control before fading away in 1967, and Daihatsu and Hino became Toyota subsidiaries. Soon, too, the Japanese would be drawn into the international picture, with liaisons between Chrysler and Mitsubishi, General Motors and Isuzu, and Ford and Mazda. In 1981, a deal between British Leyland and Honda would lead to a race of almost wholly Japanese Triumphs.

Even in 1969, the sun had risen, though it had yet to scorch the car makers of the West.

(*Above*) "Australia's own car" still pursued the same theme in 1963 as it had in 1948, and successfully: over a quarter of a million EH-series Holdens were sold in three seasons. As yet the Holden had few challengers. The locally built Ford Falcon was only just getting into its stride, Chrysler were not big enough to exploit the Valiant's success to the full, and as for the Japanese, they were still selling less than 35,000 cars a year in the Commonwealth. The dog's-leg windscreen remains as a legacy of the fifties and, while buyers can specify automatic as well as three-on-the-column, General Motors—unlike Chrysler—have yet to offer a locally produced V-8. There is, however, a choice of two over-square-dimensioned seven-bearing overhead-valve in-line sixes, giving either 100 horsepower from 2.4 litres or 115 from 3, the latter sufficing for 100 mph (160 km/h). The Holden's soft suspension offered an excellent ride on the rough stuff at the price of unpredictable high-speed handling.

(*Opposite*) Oriental versatility in the late 1960s, the 1966 Toyota Corona 1600 sedan (*top*) and the 1967–68 Honda S800 roadster (*bottom*). On the one hand, a family car with not a single heretical feature—on the other, a sports car which should have been a warning to British makers, but wasn't. The Toyota was first seen in Europe with 1.5 litres and 74 bhp, and as yet all-drum brakes featured. In this guise it exceeded 85 mph (135 km/h) and turned in 25–30 mpg (9–10 litres/100 km). The Honda, by contrast, had a tiny jewel of a 791-cc twin overhead-camshaft four-cylinder engine, delivering its 70 horsepower at an astronomical 8,000 rpm, with four carburettors fed by electric pump, disc front brakes, and chain final drive to the rear wheels. All a little too complicated, though Honda actually sold over 1,500 in Britain, where the opposition was at its strongest. Their real success would, however, come in 1968 with the N1300, first of the company's full-size front-wheel-drive sedans. Toyota were already going places. Vehicle production multiplied eightfold between 1959 and 1967, and in the latter season they accounted for 41% of Japan's car exports and 24% of domestic sales. Toyotas were also being turned out by eight foreign assembly plants.

234

BIBLIOGRAPHY

A book of this nature is inevitably a distillation of other men's flowers, and I have probably consulted as many as four hundred books over the past fifteen months. There is still, however, a tendency of authors to concentrate on personalities, cars, and countries rather than on a given period, and readers wishing to broaden their knowledge about this era of "the apogee of the motor car" will usually have to look through what happened before and after it as well.

This certainly goes for John Day's *Bosch Book of the Motor Car* (Collins, London, 1975), which explains the whole corpus of technical development in simple language and lucid diagrams, and was constantly on hand to reassure me that I had omitted no item of significance. But when it comes to the complete product, nothing has yet been published to improve on Graham Robson's *The Post-War Touring Car* (Haynes, Yeovil, 1978): though it may lay its principal stress on sporting machinery, the author is a technical writer of considerable historical knowledge. My own *The Motor Car 1946–56* (Batsford, London, 1978) illustrates the point that if you want a reference book you have to write it yourself—it covers a wider canvas of types than Robson, but stops less than halfway through our period, and one pays for the comprehensiveness with some lack of detail. In the realm of publicity, there is still no better guide than Frostick and Havinden's *Advertising and the Motor Car* (Lund Humphries, London, 1970), with its witty commentary and splendid illustrations, which extend far beyond the classic landmarks of the game.

One approaches purely national histories with some caution and, in any case, my own linguistic abilities (and perhaps the reader's) limit their usefulness. It is also easy to be overwhelmed by the comprehensiveness of market coverage after about 1955, and thus to become too specialized. For Britain, I have once again drawn heavily on David Culshaw's *Motor Guide to Makes and Models* (Temple Press, London, 1959), which takes the story up to 1956. It has stood the test of time admirably, as has Doug Nye's *British Cars of the Sixties* (Nelson, London, 1970), without which no student can hope to survive the badge-engineering jungles of B.M.C. and Rootes. In a narrower field, Peter Filby's *Specialist Sports Cars* (David & Charles, Newton Abbot, 1974) sorts out the wares of the myriad small makers in these islands, the realm of glass-fibre and do-it-yourself kits.

When it comes to "Detroit iron", I cannot overemphasize my debt to Richard Langworth and his *Encyclopaedia of American Cars 1940–70* (Beekman Press, New York, 1980), a sage commentary on the trans-Atlantic industry, and backed with precious tables of power-train options and production statistics, a sure way of finding out who offered what first. I must also put in a kind word for the Crestline series of one-make pictorial histories which, at the time of going to press, already covered all Ford and Chrysler products, and has since completed a survey of General Motors' American products as well. The limitations of the theme mean that the commentary is often superficial, and the books come expensive outside their homeland, but as quick-reference works they are hard to beat.

My guide to Spain has been, as ever, Joaquim Ciuro Gabarro's *Historia del Automovil en España* (CEAC, Barcelona, 1970), an encyclopaedic guide to a little-known industry. Pedr Davis' *Australians on the Road* (Rigby, Adelaide, 1979) arrived in time, too, to bring me up to date on the Commonwealth automobile scene, on which little of a general nature has appeared since the mid-fifties. Once again, those German *Autotypenbücher* (I still maintain there's no one-word translation of the term!) helped sort out what happened in the two Republics after World War II—the two vital ones, both published by Motorbuch Verlag of Stuttgart and from the pen of Werner Oswald, being *Deutsche Autos 1945–75* and *Kraftfahrzeuge der DDR*. If their commentary sometimes lacks detail, the sheer concentration of data makes up for this. Another invaluable German work from the same publisher is H.P. Rosellen's *Deutsche Kleinwagen*, the best guide to the bubble-car era yet published, although the author has not so far turned his scholarship to the minicars of other lands. A fortunate discovery has been a set of the yearbooks of the Japan Auto Trade Federation for a number of seasons during the period: these are printed in English, and not only explain the complex ranges, but also give statistics for the emergent period of Japanese industry that are not otherwise easy to obtain.

One hesitates to recommend international yearbooks—there are so many of them, and their scope is limited in relation to their price. I must, however, confess that I have drawn heavily on two still current, *World Cars* (with us since 1962, and in English) and the *Katalognummern* of *Automobil Revue* of Berne (issued to coincide with every Geneva salon, but printed in German and French only).

I still rate John McLellan's *Bodies Beautiful* (David & Charles, Newton Abbot, 1975) as the best quick guide to the history of styling. There is fascinating pictorial coverage with a shrewd commentary, on the greatest of the Italian stylists, in the two works authored by Michael Frostick and published by Dalton Watson of London—*Pininfarina: Master Coachbuilder* and *Pininfarina: Architect of Cars*.

As to one-make histories, their name is legion, and the recent tendency to concentrate on individual models rather than makes may force the reader to choose between a book-buying spree and staying away from this fascinating sector. Space does not permit me to mention at least sixty works which I have consulted in quest of the odd item, but the following are exceptional either for their sheer excellence, the importance of the subject, or the way in which they extend period coverage:

Daniels, Jeffrey. *British Leyland, The Truth about the Cars* (Osprey, London, 1980)

Filby, Peter. *Amazing Mini* (Gentry, London, 1981)

Hendry, Maurice D. *Cadillac: The Complete History* (Automobile Quarterly, New York, 1979)

Kimes, Beverly Rae. *Buick: A Complete History* (Automobile Quarterly, New York, 1981)

Langworth, Richard M. *Kaiser-Frazer: The Last Onslaught on Detroit* (Automobile Quarterly, New York, 1975)

Langworth, Richard M. *Tiger, Alpine, Rapier: Sporting Cars from the Rootes Group* (Osprey, London, 1982)

Langworth, Richard M. and Robson, Graham. *Triumph Cars* (Motor Racing Publications, London, 1979)

McComb, F. Wilson. *M.G. by McComb* (Osprey, London, 1978)

Whyte, Andrew. *Jaguar: The Story of a Great British Marque* (Patrick Stephens, Cambridge, 1980)

Finally, of course, no student of any period of automobile history should be without G.N. Georgano's *Complete Encyclopaedia of Motor Cars* (Ebury Press, London), at the time of writing into its third edition since 1968. With such a vast canvas to cover, there is little room for detail, but no historian worth his salt would dream of printing anything without checking through this work to make sure he has left out no matter of essence. And here I should add my personal gratitude to Nick Georgano for granting me full access to the whole project's research files, which include the extra depth unavailable to the general reader.

INDEX

Page numbers in italics indicate illustrations.